Study Guide

for use with

Principles of Corporate Finance

Sixth Edition

Richard Brealey
Bank of England
and
London Business School

Stewart Myers
Massachusetts Institute of Technology

Prepared by
V. Sivarama Krishnan
Cameron University

 Irwin
McGraw-Hill

Boston   Burr Ridge, IL   Dubuque, IA   Madison, WI   New York   San Francisco   St. Louis
Bangkok   Bogotá   Caracas   Lisbon   London   Madrid
Mexico City   Milan   New Delhi   Seoul   Singapore   Sydney   Taipei   Toronto

McGraw-Hill Higher Education

A Division of The McGraw-Hill Companies

1 2 3 4 5 6 7 8 9 0 CUS/CUS 9 0 9 8 7 6 5 4 3 2 1 0 9

ISBN 0-07-234658-2

http://www.mhhe.com

Contents

Preface

This Study Guide to *Principles of Corporate Finance* (the text) by Brealey and Myers is designed to help you learn the principles and practice of finance quickly and as easily. The Guide has been prepared as an aid to students and will enable you get the best of out of the text, your finance course work, and this Guide itself. While each student will find her or his own approach and technique to learn from and use this guide, there are at least three ways in which it can help you.

- **As a read-ahead guide to the text and class-work:** The Study Guide can be used as a read-ahead and preparatory guide before you read and work with each chapter of the text. The Guide takes you quickly through the different sections described in the text and can prepare you for the rigors of the detailed discussions found in the text. Each chapter in the Guide sets the scene for the corresponding chapter in the text and explains the concepts and theories contained in the chapter. The Guide explains how each chapter relates to the other chapters in the text.

- **As a study tool and an aid:** The Guide is designed to work with the text and provides you with a number of practice exercises of different types with detailed answers to the exercises given.

- *As an aid to post-class review and for exams:* **The** Guide summarizes the main points of each chapter in a simple and easily understood language. The exercises and the lists of terms will again come in handy when you are preparing for exams.

THE STRUCTURE OF THE GUIDE

Each chapter of the Study Guide refers to the corresponding chapter of the text and includes the following sections:

INTRODUCTION: The introduction at the beginning of each chapter tells you what the chapter is all about. It sets the scene for the chapter by relating it to the other chapters.

KEY CONCEPTS IN THE CHAPTER: This section contains clear and succinct explanations of the concepts and ideas discussed in the corresponding chapter of the text. The term *concept* is used very broadly and includes ideas, theories, models or a particular perspective used by Professors Brealey and Myers. The section parallels the main descriptive part of the corresponding chapter in the text. This section will be very useful in following the theoretical concepts and ideas discussed in the text. You will find it easier to follow the text if you read this part before you read the text. Then, come back and read the section again to fully digest the concepts and theories.

WORKED EXAMPLES: Nearly all the chapters include a number of worked examples (exceptions are Chapters 1, 34 and 35). These examples mirror problems you find in the text and problems you are likely to face in exams (and in corporate finance practice, too). The exercises are complete and explain the rationale or models used. Where appropriate, problems are solved through alternate approaches. Chapter 3 includes a sub-section explaining the use of a business calculator to solve time value of money problems. For those who have not used business calculators before, this part should be of help.

SUMMARY:
The summary is a brief overview of what each chapter covered.

LIST OF TERMS: Each chapter includes a list of new terms, which you encounter in the text. Many of these terms are used in the fill-in-questions. You might want to check this section as soon as you read the chapter to see if you can understand the term and its usage. The text has a glossary of all the terms at the back. A complete alphabetical with reference to the chapter numbers is given at the end of the Guide. The list of terms can be a very useful tool for exams and quizzes.

EXERCISES: The exercises take three forms. A set of fill-in questions includes the new terms you find in each chapter. By completing these questions, you can have a personalized chapter-by-chapter glossary of your own. The second set of exercises consists of problems. These are similar to the types of problems used as worked examples. The third set of exercises is a list of essay questions. The answering these questions require critical thinking, review and analysis of the concepts you learned in each chapter and will be good practice for exams.

ANSWERS: We provide answers to all the exercises other than the essay questions. Complete solutions are given unless a similar problem has been solved earlier in the same chapter. It would be fun to attempt the problems first, before checking the solutions. Again, these are great practice for exams and tests.

Well, I can go on and include tips, suggestions and other great ways to use this guide. But, I am sure that you have seen and heard them all and you can design your own best approach. I am concluding with one simple advice. Finance is useful because it has great practical value. As you study the different chapters of this Guide and the text, try to put yourself in the position of a manager faced with the issue or problem you are contemplating. See if you can help that manager, because soon you would be that manager! Good luck and have FUN.

V. Sivarama Krishnan
July 1999

1

Finance and the Financial Manager

INTRODUCTION

This chapter, like the customary introductory chapter in most textbooks, gives a brief introduction to the topics covered by the book and provides an overview of the book. The chapter is organized in six sections and covers the following topics succinctly.

- Organizational forms for business and the advantages and disadvantages of the corporate form
- The role and the organizational position of the financial manager
- Separation of ownership and management
- Financial markets and financial institutions
- Overview of the book

KEY CONCEPTS IN THE CHAPTER

Corporate and Other Forms of Business Organization: Common organizational forms for businesses include the s*ole proprietorship* – the typical form for a small business owned and managed by a single individual; the *partnerships*, and *corporations*. As the business grows and becomes larger, they tend to be organized as corporations with a large number of stockholders. Most businesses evolve from smaller *privately held* corporations to large *public* corporations. The corporate form enjoys the advantages of limited liability for the owners (stockholders) and the ability to attract large amounts of capital. Professional managers are hired to manage today's typical corporations. This separation of ownership and management gives the firm permanence. Corporations have distinct legal identity and are governed by the *articles of incorporation*. Corporations enjoy considerable flexibility of operation.

The disadvantages of the corporate form include costly legal and accounting set-up and double taxation of earnings.

Financial Manager's Role: Corporations use different *real assets* to run their business and finance the acquisition of these assets partly by raising finances through issue of *financial securities,* which are in the *financial markets* (figure 1.1). The financial manager's primary role is deciding which assets to invest in and how to finance them. Thus the two types of decisions the financial manager is called upon to make are *investing decisions (capital budgeting)* and *financing decisions*. Corporate finance is primarily concerned with these decisions.

1

Most firms will have other managers in charge of marketing, production, and other functions who work with the financial manager(s) in managing a corporation's operations. Today corporations operate in a global market place with offices and factories located in many countries. Financial markets are also global and companies often raise financing from investors located in many different countries.

Throughout the book, the term financial manager is used in a generic sense meaning anyone who deals with investment and/or financing decisions for a business. Except in very small businesses, the role is typically split into separate positions with the *treasurer* dealing with cash management, raising capital and dealing with investors and financial institutions; and the *controller* entrusted with responsibility for managing the firm's internal accounting, preparation of financial statements, and tax obligations. While small firms typically have a treasurer as the only financial manager, larger firms will have a controller also. As the firm gets larger, the organization of the financial management function becomes more complex and a *chief financial officer (CFO)* oversees the treasurer and the controller with additional responsibility for financial policy and corporate planning. The CFO is part of the top management team for the firm and often is a member of the board of directors. Important financial decisions are often referred to the board of directors and are subject to their approval.

Separation of Ownership and Management: Large corporations have hundreds of thousands of shareholders and it will be impossible to have the "owners" manage the business directly. Thus separation of ownership and management becomes a necessity allowing continuity in management un-affected by changes in ownership. It also paves the way for hiring of professional managers to manage the business. The disadvantage of this separation of ownership and management is that it causes potential *principal-agent problems*. The managers are the agents of the stockholders, who are the principals. The managers may not always act in the best interest of the stockholders. Agency costs are the costs incurred when managers do not act in the interests of the stockholders and their actions need to be monitored. Obviously, owner-managers do not incur any agency costs, as there are no conflicts of interest. Other principal-agent situations in corporate finance include the relationships between the senior managers and the junior managers and that between the lenders and stockholders. The value of a company can be seen as a pie with a number of different claimants such as stockholders, lenders, employees, and even the government. The different claimants are connected by a web of explicit and implicit contracts. To the extent that the interests of the different claimants differ, conflicts and potential agency problems arise. The principal-agent problem would be easier to solve but for the fact that the parties involved have different information about the value of the business. In other words, agency problems are complicated by *information asymmetry*. Financial managers need to recognize the information asymmetry involved before attempting solutions to the agency problems. The problems of agency costs and information asymmetry receive detailed coverage in later chapters.

Financial Markets and Institutions: Corporations issue stocks and bonds to raise funds for their operations. These are known as *primary issues* and the market in which these issues are sold is known as the primary market. The bonds and stocks later trade in *secondary transactions* which do not affect the company's cash position or the balance sheet. The daily transactions in the New York Stock Exchange are examples of secondary transactions. Financial markets include physical exchanges such as the New York or Frankfurt Stock Exchanges or network of dealers operating through the electronic media. Examples of the latter kind include the over-the-counter exchange and the inter-bank foreign exchange market.

Financial institutions such as banks and insurance companies are also important sources of financing for businesses. These institutions are known as financial intermediaries and they enable flow of capital from the people and institutions, which have savings to the businesses and individuals who need financing. Examples of financial intermediaries include banks, savings and loan companies, mutual funds, and insurance companies. The intermediaries repackage the cash flows they receive from their investments into a form that serves the need of their customers such as depositors, insurance policy holders and investors. Financial institutions provide *payment mechanism* for the economy and offer *risk pooling,* loans and deposits, and other services to their customers. They are essential to well-functioning market economies.

Overview of the Textbook: The next 34 chapters of the book cover topics, which can be broadly classified into three groups: investment decisions, financing decisions, and decisions where investment and financing interact in such a way that they cannot be separated. The table below provides a summary listing of the different sections, chapters, and topics covered in the book.

Sections	Part	Chapters	Topics
Introduction	1	1	Finance and financial managers
The investment decision		2-6	How to value assets
	2	7-9	Risk
	3	10-12	Managing the investment process
Financing decision	4	13-15	Corporate financing and market efficiency
	5	16-19	Dividend policy and debt policy
	6	20-22	Options and their applications
	7	23-25	Valuing different kinds of debt
	8	26-27	Risk management
Financial planning	9	28-29	Financial analysis, financial planning, and strategy
Short-term financial management		30-32	Managing short-term assets and liabilities
Mergers and governance	10	33-34	Mergers and corporate governance
Conclusion	11	35	What do we know and do not know about finance

CHAPTER SUMMARY

This chapter provides an introduction to the topic of corporate finance and the role of the financial manager. The chapter discusses the corporate form of ownership. Large corporations are typically organized as public corporations and are usually owned by thousands of stockholders. Corporations enjoy distinct identity, the stockholders have limited liability, and the owners are not associated with managing the company. The separation of ownership and management enables businesses to hire professional managers to run the business and allows the business to operate independent of changes in ownership.

The financial manager plays an important role in the management of the company and is concerned with decisions relating to investment and financing. Depending on the size of the company, the finance function may be organized in different ways. Small companies have a treasurer while larger firms may have a treasurer and a controller. While the treasurer is in charge of cash management and obtaining finances for the business, the controller's job is to see that money is used efficiently and well. Very large corporations have a chief financial officer, who oversees the treasurer and the controller and is part of the senior management team of the company.

Shareholders would want the managers to maximize their wealth by maximizing the value of the company's stock. Managers might be interested in objectives other than stockholders' interests. This conflict is one of the several different types of agency problems affecting the management of large corporations. Other principal-agent problems include the stockholder-bondholder conflict. The agency problems are complicated by the fact that the agents often have better information than the principals do.

LIST OF TERMS

Agency problem	Investment
Agent	Limited liability
Bond	Partnership
Capital budgeting	Principals
Chief financial officer	Real asset
Controller	Share
Corporation	Securities
Financial assets	Sole proprietorship
Financial market	Stock
Financing	Tangible asset
Intangible asset	Treasurer

EXERCISES

Fill-in Questions

1. Most large businesses are organized as _____.

2. The financial manager is concerned with _____ and _____ decisions.

3. A _____ is responsible for managing cash and raising finances for the business.

4. The _____ oversees the treasurer and the _____ and is part of the senior management team.

5. A company's _____ include machinery, buildings, and patents.

6. Many accounting firms are organized as _____.

7. A one-person business is organized as a _____.

8. Trademarks, patents, and technical expertise are examples of _____assets.

9. Stocks and bonds are examples of _____ assets.

10. Shareholders of a corporation have _____.

11. Debt securities issued by corporations are called _____.

12. Purchasing new machinery for expanding production capacity is _____.

13. Managers are _____ of shareholders, who are the _____.

14. _____ is the process of investment decision making.

15. _____are complicated by the information asymmetry between managers and stockholders.

16. A _____ confers part ownership of a corporation.

17. Corporations issue _____ in capital markets to raise money.

Problems

1. Identify the investment and financing decisions from the following list:
   a. Buying new machinery
   b. Issuing bonds
   c. Acquiring a company
   d. Borrowing from the local bank
   e. Receiving credit from a supplier
   f. Buying new computers to replace the old machines affected by the year 2000 problem
   g. Building a new warehouse

2. Separate the real assets from the financial assets:
   a. Shares of IBM
   b. Patents for a new process to manufacture microprocessors
   c. Roads
   d. Brand names
   e. Treasury bonds
   f. An IOU from Bill Gates

Essay Questions

1. Why are most large businesses organized as corporations?

2. "Separation of ownership and management is necessary and desirable." Discuss.

3. "Agency problems will not exist if there was no information asymmetry." Discuss.

4. Describe the differences between each of the following:
   a. A tangible asset and intangible asset
   b. Investment and financing
   c. The treasurer and the controller
   d. A corporation and a partnership

ANSWERS TO EXERCISES

Fill-in Questions

1. Corporations
2. Investment, financing
3. Treasurer
4. Chief financial officer, controller
5. Real assets
6. Partnerships
10. Limited liability
11. Bonds
12. Investment
13. Agents, principals
14. Capital budgeting
15. Agency problems

7. Sole proprietorship
8. Intangible
9. Financial

16. Share
17. Securities

Problems

1. a. Investment
   d. Financing
   g. Investment

   b. Financing
   e. Financing

   c. Investment
   f. Investment

2. a. Financial assets
   d. Real assets

   b. Real assets
   e. Financial assets

   c. Real assets
   f. Financial assets

2
Present Value and the Opportunity Cost of Capital

INTRODUCTION

This chapter introduces the three basic and related concepts that form the very foundation of modern day finance: *present value* (PV), *net present value* (NPV) and *opportunity cost*. Present value gives the value of cash flows generated by an investment and NPV gives the effective net benefit from an investment after subtracting its costs. Opportunity cost represents the rate of return on investments of comparable risk. Application of these concepts enables you to value different kinds of assets, especially those which are not commonly traded in well-functioning markets. The chapter also presents the economic theory behind the concepts.

KEY CONCEPTS IN THE CHAPTER

Present Value: One dollar of cash received next year is worth less than one dollar received today. If you have one dollar today and you can invest it at an interest rate of r, this investment will be worth $1(1+r)$ next year. Therefore, how much is $1 to be received next year worth today? This value is its *present value* and you can see that it will be $1/(1+r)$. PV of any cash flow (C_1) received next year, will then be $C_1/(1+r)$ or $C_1 \times [1/(1+r)]$[1]. Thus, present value of any future cash flow is its current equivalent. The process of computing PV of future cash flows is called *discounting* and the rate of interest or return used in computing the PV is called the *discount rate*.

Opportunity Cost: What rate should be used to discount a future cash flow generated by an asset? This rate is the *opportunity cost of capital* and determined as the rate of return expected to be received from alternate investments forgone. The rate should reflect the investment's risk. In simple terms, it is the rate of return on investments of comparable risk. One typically looks to the capital market to identify an investment of comparable risk. We deal with explicit models for measurement of risk and estimation of rates of returns in later chapters. The terms discount rate, opportunity cost, and hurdle rate are often used synonymously.

---

[1] This process can be extended to future cash flows beyond next year. Chapter 3 deals with the mechanics of computing the PV for cash flows received at different points in time.

Net Present Value: NPV of an asset or investment is the present value of its cash flows less the cost of acquiring the asset. Smart investors will only acquire assets that have positive NPVs and will attempt to maximize the NPV of their investments. Presence of well functioning capital markets enable us to extend this rule to the managers of corporations which have a number of shareholders with different consumption preferences. The *rate of return* received from an investment is the profit divided by the cost of the investment. Positive NPV investments will have rates of return higher than the opportunity cost. This gives an alternate investment decision rule. Good investments are those that have rates of return higher than the opportunity cost. This opportunity cost can be inferred from the capital market and is based on its risk characteristics of the investment.

Separation of Ownership and Management: Section 2-2 explains the theoretical foundation for the NPV rule for investment decisions and the role of capital markets in enabling the individuals to satisfy their individual consumption preferences. As long as the capital market is perfectly competitive (see assumptions listed on page 22), managers of corporations can use the universal rule of choosing only investments that have positive NPVs. This will maximize the stockholders' wealth and this wealth can be traded in the capital market freely. Individual investors can choose their patterns of consumption preferences. Thus, corporate investment decisions can be separated from individual stockholders' preferences for consumption, allowing a clear separation of ownership and management. This is a necessary condition for the operation of large capitalist economies.

Shareholders and the Role of Managers: Shareholders own the corporation and would like to maximize their wealth. Individual shareholders will have different preferences with respect to consumption and saving. However, managers need not worry about individual stockholders' preferences as long as the capital market is competitive. Managers should act to maximize the stockholders' wealth. They can do this by investing only in positive NPV projects. Profit maximization is not a satisfactory goal as the definition or timing of profits can be vague and ambiguous. Profit by itself also does not capture the risk involved in the investment. Assuming that firms operate in competitive markets, a manager maximizing stockholders' wealth also maximizes the society's wealth; the increased wealth comes from value created by the business.

What makes managers act in the interest of stockholders and not in their own narrow self interests? Three major factors cause the managers, by and large, to be efficient and act in the best interests of shareholders. These are: i) managers are monitored by different specialists such as board of directors and investment bankers, ii) poorly performing managers are likely to lose their jobs when the companies run by them get taken over, and iii) compensation packages for managers typically include incentives based on stock performance.

The Capital Market and its Role: The existence of the capital market enables efficient exchange of capital between lenders and borrowers. Lenders save and postpone consumption and borrowers can consume now based on expected future income[2]. Existence of a well-

---

[2] It is important to note that both lenders and borrowers can be individuals, corporations, and governments

10

functioning capital market enables us to separate the individual stockholders consumption preferences from the corporate management decisions. The capital market is considered perfectly competitive if the following assumptions are satisfied:

- No individual can influence prices
- Free access to market, cost-free trading, and free availability of information
- No distorting taxes

With perfectly competitive markets, separation of owners' individual interests from the corporation's investment decisions is complete. While the perfect market assumptions may appear to be too good to be true, it is generally accepted that markets satisfy these assumptions to a very high degree of approximation.

Explanation of Formulas and Mathematical Expressions

Notations: C_0 = Investment (or Cost of) in the project = Cash flow at time 0
C_1 = Cash flow at time 1
r = Discount rate or opportunity cost of capital

Formulas: $PV = [1/(1+r)] \times C_1$ = Discount factor x Cash flow
Discount Factor = $1/(1+r)$
$NPV = C_0 + [1/(1+r)] \times C_1$
Rate of return = Profit/Investment

Investment Decision Rules:
i) Accept positive NPV investments
ii) Accept investments with rates of return higher than the opportunity cost or hurdle rate

Points to keep in mind:
i) C_0 will usually be negative
ii) Discount factor will be < 1
iii) Discount rate should be a function of the risk of the cash flow
iv) Higher the discount rate, lower the discount factor and lower the PV

WORKED EXAMPLE

Jill Bates, a software engineer has the opportunity to invest in two projects. Details are given in the table below.

(city, state, and national). Also, borrowing as described in this chapter is generic and we will see in later chapters that there are different forms of exchange of capital.

1. Calculate the rate of return on each investment.
2. If the opportunity cost or the hurdle rate for the projects is 15 percent, calculate the NPV for the projects.
3. Calculate the NPV if the opportunity cost is 25 percent.
4. Do you think it is correct to discount the two project cash flows with the same hurdle rate? Why or why not?
5. How would you determine the right hurdle rate or opportunity cost for each project?
6. Ms. Bates does not have all the money needed to buy the resources needed for the projects. Does that change her decision on the projects?

Project	Description	Investment	Payback
A	Developing a simple software package for a local bank.	$12,000	$14,400
B	Developing a complex software package for an "E-Commerce" company. The payment for the project will be received in the form of stocks in the company.	$12,000	$20,000

SOLUTION

1. Rate of Return on Project A   = ($14,400 - $12,000)/$12,000   = 20 percent
   Rate of Return on Project B   = ($20,000 - $12,000)/$12,000   = 66.7 percent

2. NPV of project A = -$12,000 + ($14,400/1.15) = $521.74
   NPV of project B = -$12,000 + ($20,000/1.15) = $5,391.30

3. NPV of project A = -$12,000 + ($14,400/1.25) = - $480
   NPV of project B = -$12,000 + ($20,000/1.25) = $4,000

4. The two projects appear to have very different risks; project B is more risky and will have a higher hurdle rate.

5. Look at the rates of return on stocks of companies in similar businesses or with comparable risks.

6. Ms. Bates should be able to raise the money needed to invest in the project through the capital market.

CHAPTER SUMMARY

The chapter introduces the key concepts relating to valuation of corporate assets. Corporate assets are typically not traded in markets, unlike real estate or used cars, and therefore need to be valued using present values of cash flows generated by the assets. Present value of an asset is a function of the cash flow produced by the asset and the riskiness of the cash flow. The chapter also introduces two equivalent rules for investment decisions - the NPV and the rate of return rules. The chapter explains the role of capital market and presents the theoretical basis for the NPV rule. The capital market also forms the basis for the widely practiced separation of ownership from the management of corporations. This allows managers to focus on maximizing the corporation's value without worrying about individual stockholders' consumption preferences.

LIST OF TERMS

Capital market
Discount factor
Discount rate
Hurdle rate
Net present value

Opportunity cost
Present value
Rate of return
Separation of ownership and management

EXERCISES

Fill-in-Questions

1. Present value of a cash flow to be received one year from now will _____ when the discount rate increases.

2. Discount factor will generally be _____ than one.

3. If the discount rate is 12 percent, the discount factor for a cash flow received one year from now will be _____.

4. The NPV rule for investment requires managers to invest only in projects that have _____ NPV.

5. Managers should invest in projects with rates of return _____ than the opportunity cost of capital.

6. A future cash flow is multiplied by the _____ to give its present value.

7. The _____ of an asset is the difference between the PV of its cash flows and its cost.

8. Financial managers will benefit the stockholders if they _____ the individual stockholders consumption preferences and focus only on the NPV of the projects on hand.

9. The expected return from comparable investments in the securities markets gives the _____ for the project.

10. Opportunity cost of capital for a project is _____ on alternate investments of comparable risk.

11. Higher risk projects will have _____ opportunity cost of capital.

12. We need a theory of valuation for corporate assets because they _____ traded in well-functioning markets.

Problems

1. You can buy a 1-year T-bill for $955 now. The bill will pay $1,000 one year from now. What is your rate of return on this investment?

2. Neon Danders, a professional football player will be paid $15,000,000 by his NFL franchise. He will be paid $5,000,000 now and $10,000,000 1 year from now. Using a discount rate of 12 percent, calculate the PV of Danders' pay.

3. Calculate the discount factors for the following discount rates: (a) 20 percent, (b) 30 percent, and (c) 100 percent.

4. May Belline is planning to buy an old apartment building and modernize it into a new condo complex of 6 condominiums. She can buy the building for $400,000 and the cost of modernizing is estimated to be $350,000. The project will be completed in one year and each condominium is expected to sell for $200,000. Calculate: (a) the expected rate of return on the project, (b) PV of the cash flows from the sale of the condos, and (c) the NPV of the project. Assume the opportunity cost for the project to be 20 percent.

5. John Miser has $20,000 to invest. He is considering two projects. Project A requires an investment of $10,000 and will pay $11,000 after one year. Project B also requires $10,000 but will pay only $10,700 after one year. What should Mr. Miser do if his opportunity cost of capital is: (a) 6 percent, (b) 9 percent, or (c) 12 percent.

6. One ounce of gold sells for $290 now. You can also sell a contract to sell gold one year from now at $308 per ounce. (a) If you buy gold now and also sell the contract for future sale of gold (with cash flow to come one year from now) at the above prices, what will be your expected rate of return? (b) If the rate of return on safe 1-year bonds is 5 percent, what is the likely cost of storing gold for one year?

7. Imagine an economy in which there are just three individuals: A, B, and C. Each has money to invest and a number of possible investment projects, each of which would require $1,000. A has $2,000 to invest and two projects with returns of 11 percent and one project with a return of 7 percent. B has $1,000 to invest and has projects yielding 11 percent and 7 percent. C has $1,000 to invest and projects offering 15 percent and 12 percent returns. (a) What projects will be undertaken if there is no lending or borrowing? (b) If they do borrow from and lend to each other, what projects will be undertaken and what will the interest rates be?

8. ABC Corp. has opportunities to invest in three projects with potential payoffs next year linked to the state of the economy. Each project requires an investment of $3 million. The payoffs for different states of the economy are given below:

Project	State of the Economy and Project Payoffs			Hurdle Rate
	Recession	Normal	Boom	
A	$2 million	$4 million	$6 million	20 percent
B	$3 million	$3.5 million	$4 million	10 percent
C	$1.5 million	$4 million	$6.5 million	35 percent

Calculate the expected cash flows next year, the rate of return, and the NPV for each project. Which project(s) should be accepted by the company?

9. a. Calculate the NPV and rate of return for each of the following investments. Assume that the opportunity cost of capital to be 15 percent for all the investments.

Project	Initial Cash Flow	Cash Flow in Year 1
A	-$6,000	$12,000
B	-$8,000	$12,000
C	-$16,000	$24,000
D	-$21,000	$30,000

b. It is learned that all four projects require the use of a team of engineers who are very busy and will be available to work on only one of the four projects. In other words, you can choose only one of the four projects. Which one will you choose?

Essay Questions

1. "Corporate managers will generally act in the interests of their stockholders." Discuss.

2. Explain why corporate managers need not be concerned with the stockholders' individual consumption preferences, even though they are managing the firm on behalf of the stockholders.

3. Explain the NPV and rate of return rules for investment decisions.

4. "Many of our stockholders are retired and cannot afford to lose any of the value of their savings; therefore, we demand a higher return on our investments than do many other companies." Discuss.

5. Explain how the existence of capital market benefits consumers and businesses.

ANSWERS TO EXERCISES

Fill-in Questions

1. Decrease
2. Less
3. $1/1.12 = 0.893$
4. Positive
5. Greater
6. Discount factor
7. NPV
8. Ignore
9. Opportunity cost
10. Rate of return
11. Higher
12. Are not

Problems

1. $(\$1,000-\$955)/\$955 = 4.71$ percent

2. $\$5,000,000 + $ PV of $\$10,000,000$ received 1 year from now $=$
   $\$5,000,000 + \$10,000,000/1.12 = \$13,928,571.14$

3. (a) $1/1.2 = 0.833$ (b) $1/1.3 = 0.769$ (c) $1/2 = 0.5$

4. (a) Rate of return = Profit/Cost; Cost = $\$750,000$;
   Profit = $\$1,200,000 - \$750,000 = \$450,000$
   Rate of return $= \$450,000/\$750,000 = 60$ percent

   (b) PV of cash flows = $\$1,200,000/1.20 = \$1,000,000$

   (c) NPV = $\$1,000,000 - \$750,000 = \$250,000$

5. Calculate the NPVs at each cost of capital for both projects.
   a. NPV of project A at 6%   = ($11,000/1.06) - $10,000 = $377.36
      NPV of project B at 6%   = ($10,700/1.06) - $10,000 = $94.34
      Accept both projects.

   b. NPV of project A at 9%   = ($11,000/1.09) - $10,000 = $91.74
      NPV of project B at 9%   = ($10,700/1.09) - $10,000 = -$183.49
      Accept A, reject B.

   c. NPV of project A at 12%   = ($11,000/1.12) - $10,000 = -$178.57
      NPV of project B at 12%   = ($10,700/1.12) - $10,000 = -$446.43
      Reject both projects.

6. a. Expected rate of return = ($308 - $290)/$290 = 6.21 percent

   b. To get 5 percent return on the gold transaction, the sale price should be
      $290 x 1.05 = $304.50; therefore the likely storage costs will be $308 - $304.50 = $3.50

7. a. In the absence of lending and borrowing, A will undertake the two projects with 11
      percent return, B will undertake the project with 11 percent return and C will undertake the
      15 percent project.

   b. C will borrow from either A or B to undertake the 12 percent project in addition to the 15
      percent project. One of the 11 percent projects will be dropped. The rate of interest will
      be 11 percent.

8. Project A: Expected cash flow next year = ($2 m + $4 m + $6 m)/3 = $4 m
               PV of cash flow = $4 m/1.20 = $3.333;   NPV = $0.333 m

   Project B: Expected cash flow next year = ($3 m + $3.5 m + $4 m)/3 = $3.5 m
               PV of cash flow = $3.5 m/1.10 = $3.182;   NPV = $0.182 m

   Project C: Expected cash flow next year = ($1.5 m + $4 m + $6.5 m)/3 = $4 m
               PV of cash flow = $4 m/1.35 = $2.963;   NPV = -$0.037 m

   Accept projects A and B. Reject C.

9. a. Project A:
      NPV = $12,000/1.15 - $6,000 = $4,434.78,
      Rate of return = ($12,000-$6,000)/$6,000 = 100 percent

      Project B:
      NPV = $12,000/1.15 - $8,000 = $2,434.78,
      Rate of return = ($12,000-$8,000)/$8,000 = 50 percent

17

Project C:
NPV = $24,000/1.15 - $16,000 = $4,869.57
Rate of return = ($24,000-$16,000)/$16,000 = 50 percent

Project D:
NPV = $30,000/1.15 - $21,000 = $5,086.96
Rate of return = ($30,000-$21,000)/$21,000 = 42.9 percent

All four projects are good investments.

b. Since only one of the four projects can be chosen, the right decision will be to choose the project with the highest NPV. Choose Project D. This is an example where the NPV rule and the rate of return rule give different decisions.

3

How to Calculate Present Values

INTRODUCTION

This chapter describes the technique for calculating present values. The lessons learned in Chapter 2 form the foundation on which we can build up expertise on calculating present values. We start with the cash flow one year from now and extend the basic approach to the computation of present value of any stream of cash flows. It is very useful to learn short cuts to calculate the present values of three special types of cash-flow streams, which occur often in real life finance problems. These are:

- Perpetuity: a fixed payment each year forever
- Cash flows growing at a constant rate: payments increasing at a constant rate each year forever
- Annuity: a fixed payment each year for a limited number of years

The chapter also explains the difference between compound interest and simple interest and the effect of different compounding intervals.

Present value calculations can be done in several ways: using the basic formulas, using the tables given in the text provided, or using business calculators. We provide solutions using both the tables and a popular business calculator (the BA II Plus).

KEY CONCEPTS IN THE CHAPTER

Present Value of a Stream of Cash Flows: We learned in the last chapter that the present value (PV) of a cash flow received one year from now is:

$PV = C/(1+r)$; where C is the cash flow and r is the discount rate.
$PV = DF_1 \times C$, where DF_1 is known as the discount factor and $= 1/(1+r)$

We can extend this to calculate the PV of any future cash flow.

PV of C_2 received two years from now is $\qquad = C_2/(1+r)^2 = DF_2 \times C_2$
PV of a cash flow received t years from now $\quad = C_t/(1+r)^t = DFt \times C_t$;
where $DF_t = 1/(1+r)^t$.

For a stream of cash flows C_1, C_2,... C_t received at 1, 2,...t years from now, the present value is the sum of present values of the individual cash flows.

$$PV = \frac{C_1}{(1+r)} + \frac{C_2}{(1+r)^2} + \ldots\ldots + \frac{C_t}{(1+r)^t} = DF_1 x C_1 + DF_2 x C_2 + \ldots + DF_t x C_t$$

Appendix 1 in the text gives values of the discount factors for different rates of return. The general formula for the present value of a stream of cash flows, known as the discounted cash flow formula, is given below:

$$PV = \sum_{t=1}^{n} \frac{C_t}{(1+r)^t}$$

All time value of money (TVM) problems use this basic relationship. Here is an example of a present value problem. Mary just signed up with a women's professional basketball team and has been offered a contract which pays her $3 million next year, $4 million the year after and $5 million in three years. If the discount rate is 12 percent, what is the present value of the total payments to Mary?

Present value = $3/1.12 + 4/(1.12)^2 + 5/(1.12)^3 = 2.6786 + 3.1888 + 3.5589 = \$9.4263$ million

Alternately we can use the discount factors given in Appendix 1.

Year	Cash flow	Discount factor (12%)	Present value
1	$3 million	0.893	3x0.893 = 2.679
2	$4 million	0.797	4x0.797 = 3.188
3	$5 million	0.712	5x0.712 = 3.560
Total			$9.427 million

The steps involved in this approach to computing present values of a stream of cash flows are:

1. Write the column showing cash flows in each year.
2. Write next to it the discount factors (from Appendix Table 1).
3. Multiply across.
4. Add to get the total present value.

We can use a business calculator to directly calculate the present values. This is shown in the worked examples given later in this chapter.

Future Value: $1 invested at an annual rate of r will grow to $1(1 + r) at the end of 1 year. This is the future of $1 when compounded at a rate of r for 1 year. If the amount is invested for 2 years the future value will be $1(1 + r)^2$. In general, future values can be expressed as:

FV = PV $(1+r)^t$ = FVF x PV; where FVF is the future value factor = $(1+r)^t$ and is given in Appendix 2.

20

Example: I have $121,000 invested in mutual funds as part of my pension plan. How much will this amount accumulate in 15 years if the mutual funds earn an annual return of 12 percent?

Future value = $121,000 $(1.12)^{15}$ = 121,000 x 5.474 = $662,354
(5.474 is the future value factor for 12 percent and 15 years given in Appendix 2)

Special Streams of Cash Flows: There are three special types of cash flow streams commonly encountered in business and everyday life. Short-cuts are available to compute the present values (and future values) of these special cases. The special cases are discussed next.

Perpetuity: We defined perpetuity as a stream of cash flows with fixed payments each year with payments coming forever. Imagine you have $5,000 invested in a bank account and the bank promises to pay you $250 every year as long as you have the money with the bank. The rate of return on this investment is $250/$5,000 = 5%. This can go on forever if you keep the deposit with the bank. Thus, the rate of return on a perpetuity = payment/present value. Or,

$$r = C/PV; PV = C/r$$

Thus, it follows that the present value of a stream of equal payments received each year forever will be simply the payment divided by the rate of return.

Alternately, you might prefer to remember that the annual payment is just the principal value times the interest rate ($250 = $5,000 x 0.05, or C = PV x r). Now you can rearrange the expression to get PV = C/r.

Example: Early Lawson wants to endow a Chair in the Computer Science Department at Main State University. The University suggests an endowment with an annual income of $75,000. If the endowment investments can earn 8 percent annually, how much should Mr. Lawson donate now?

Donation = Annual Payment/Rate of return = $75,000/0.08 = $937,500

Cash flows growing at a constant rate: The present value of a stream of cash flows growing at a constant rate, g, is given by the following formula:

$PV = C_1/(r-g)$, where C_1 is the cash flow to be received one year from now. The formula works as long as r is greater than g.

Example: Main State University (refer to the previous example) suggests that the endowment income should be annually adjusted for expected salary growth of 5 percent. How much should the initial endowment be if the first year's income is $75,000 and the estimated rate of return on the investments is 8 percent?

Donation = $75,000/(0.08-0.05) = $2,500,000

Annuity: Annuities are "truncated" perpetuities. Thus the present value of an annuity for 15 years is the difference in the present values of a perpetuity now (first payment at the end of this year) and the present value of another perpetuity with first payment at the end of 15 years. You can generalize this approach and get the present value for a t-year annuity as PV (perpetuity A) – PV (Perpetuity B), where the payments for A starts next year and payments for B starts at the end of t years.

$$PV(PerpetuityA) = \frac{C}{r}$$

$$PV(PerpetuityB) = \frac{C}{r} x \frac{1}{(1+r)^t}$$

PV(Annuity for t years) = PV(Perpetuity A) – PV(Perpetuity B)

$$= C(\frac{1}{r} - \frac{1}{(1+r)^t})$$
$$= C(\text{Annuity Factor}).$$

The values of the annuity factors for a range of r and t are given in Appendix 3. This annuity assumes that payments will come at the end of each year and is called *ordinary annuity*. A stream of cash flows with payments at the beginning of each year is called an *annuity due*. Since the payments for the annuity due begins one year earlier, the present value of the annuity due will be higher than the present value of an ordinary annuity by a factor of (1+r) or PV (Annuity due) = PV (Ordinary annuity) x (1+r). Typical examples of annuities include mortgage loans and car loans. Please note that these loans are usually structured as monthly annuities.

Example: Jane Doe bought a car for $21,000 and financed 90 percent of the purchase price with a loan at an annual interest of 6 percent. Ms. Doe will repay the loan with 48 monthly payments starting next month. What is her monthly payment?

> PV = C x (Annuity factor), where C is the monthly payment and PV in this case will be the loan amount. C = Loan amount/Annuity factor
> The loan amount = $21,000 x 0.9 = $18,900
> Annuity factor = $[(1/r) - (1/r)(1+r)^t]$; r = monthly interest rate = 6/12 = 0.5%
> Annuity factor = $(1/0.005) - [1/(0.005 x 1.005^{48})]$ = 42.580
> Payment = $18,900/42.580 = $443.87

Simple Interest, Compound Interest, and Present Values: When interest is computed only on the original principal, year after year, the interest is said to accrue as simple interest. When the interest computed for each year (or period, where interest is credited other than on an annual basis) is added to the original principal and earns interest in subsequent periods, you are getting compound interest. A deposit of $100 earning simple interest of 10 percent annually earns only $100 x 0.10 x 5 = $50. If the deposit is earning compound interest, you will earn $100 x 1.10^5 - $100 = $61.10. The difference gets larger and larger as the number of periods increase. For example, $100 deposited at 10 percent annually accumulates to $300 on simple interest, but becomes $672.70. It is obvious that deposits earning compound interest will earn significantly more compared to those earning only simple interest.

Most finance problems involve compound interest and unless otherwise stated, it is reasonable to assume compound interest.

<u>Compounding intervals:</u> Computation of interest requires specifying the frequency of accounting for interest. A 12 percent annual rate of interest can mean different things depending on how frequently the interest is credited (or debited) to the account. If the interest is credited semi-annually, you have compounding twice a year. This gives you an effective interest rate of $(1 + r/2)^2 - 1$. In general, compounding m times a year gives $(1 + r/m)^m$ after 1 year. As m approaches infinity, $(1 + r/m)^m$ approaches $(2.718)^r$, which is e^r. This is called continuous compounding. \$1 invested at a continuously compounded rate of r grows to $\$e^r$ in 1 year and to $\$e^{rt}$ in t years. Appendix Table 4 gives values of e^{rt}.

Nominal and Real Interest Rates: Nominal interest rates and cash flows measure what happens in ordinary dollar units, while real rates and cash flows measure what happens in units of purchasing power. The relationship between real and nominal cash flows are given by the equation:

Real cash flow = Nominal cash flow/(1+inflation rate)

The relationship between nominal interest rate and real interest rate are given by the following equation:

$$1+r_{nominal} = (1+r_{real})(1+\text{inflation rate})$$

For example, if the nominal interest rate is 7 percent and inflation rate is 2 percent, the real rate is $(1.07/1.02) - 1 = 4.9\%$.

Bonds: Bonds are debt instruments issued by corporations and governments. They usually carry regular interest payments, called coupons, and have a stated term or maturity. When you invest in a bond, you receive yearly (or more commonly, half-yearly) coupon payments. At the end of the term of the bond, you will receive the principal or face value of the bond. If we know the required rate of return for the investment in the bond, we can calculate the present value of these payments. The price of the bond should equal the total present value of all the coupon payments and the face value payment. For example, if a 10 percent return is required on a 3-year 6 percent coupon bond with a face value of \$1000, the price will equal:

$$PV = 60/1.10 + 60/1.10^2 + 1060/1.10^3 = \$900.53$$

Conversely, if we know the price, we can compute the return earned on the bond investment. This return is the yield to maturity for the bond or the internal rate of return (discussed in Chapter 10) for the investment in the bond. Most bonds have semi-annual coupons and the yield and price calculations will have to be adjusted for this fact.

Summary of Formulas and Mathematical Expressions

Formulas: $PV = (1/(1+r)^t) \times C_t$ = Discount factor x Cash flow
Discount Factor = $1/(1+r)^t$

Present value of a stream of cash flows:

$$PV = \sum_{t=1}^{n} \frac{C_t}{(1+r)^t}$$

PV of special types of cash flows:

PV of a perpetuity   = C/r
PV of an annuity   = C[(1/r) – (1/r(1+r)^t)]
                      = C[Annuity Factor]
Annuity factor   = [(1/r) – (1/r(1+r)^t)]
PV of a growing perpetuity = C_1/(r-g)

Relationship between nominal and real interest rates: $1+r_{nominal}$ = $(1+r_{real})$(1+inflation rate)
This expression approximates to: $r_{nominal}$ = r_{real} + inflation rate

Using a Business Calculator: Business calculators have become a common tool of the business student and are very useful for solving all types of present value problems. While the details of operations differ for the different models, all business calculators share common features, which enable you to solve for the different parameters in typical TVM problems. In this guide, we provide calculator solutions (using Texas Instruments' BA II Plus model) in addition to solutions using formulas or the present value tables given in the text.

Most business calculators are designed to solve TVM problems in one of two formats:
i) the annuity and a single future value format and ii) net present value of uneven cash flows format. The annuity format allows you to calculate any one of five parameters given the other four. The parameters are: present value (PV), future value (FV), payment (PMT), the number of years (periods), and the rate of return or interest rate (I). The NPV format allows direct calculation of NPV or the internal rate of return (IRR) for any stream of cash flows.

Example: What is the present value of $1,600 invested for 5 years in an account earning 6 percent annually?

Solution: PV = $1,600, FV = Solve, PMT = 0, N = 5, I = 6; Answer: FV = -$2,141.16.

The calculator shows the answer as a negative number to indicate that the direction of cash flow will be the opposite of the initial flow; i.e. you deposit $1,600 now and you receive $2,141.16 five years later. In order to avoid any confusion, from now on, we will follow the convention of using positive numbers for cash inflows and negative numbers for outflows.

Example: What is the annual payment which will repay a 3 year, $21,000 loan at an interest rate of 9 percent? Assume equal payments.

Solution: This is an annuity problem.
PV = $21,000, FV = 0, N=3, I = 9; PMT = Solve = -$8,296.15

Example: You have $72,000 in a mutual fund earning an average of 15 percent annual return. What will be the accumulated value of your account at the end of 12 years?

Solution: PV = -$72,000, PMT = 0, N= 12, I = 15, FV = Solve = +$385,218

Example: You have $72,000 in a mutual fund earning 15 percent annual return. How many years will it take to accumulate $500,000?

Solution: PV = -$72,000, FV = +500,000, PMT = 0, I = 15, N = Solve = 13.87 years.

24

Example: You have $72,000 in a mutual fund. If you want to accumulate $500,000 in 12 years, what annual rate of return should you earn?

Solution: PV = -$72,000, FV = +500,000, PMT = 0, N = 12, I = solve = 17.53 %

WORKED EXAMPLES

Problem 1: Chien Chen invests $2,500 in a mutual fund where it is expected to earn a return of 12 percent. How much will Chen have in the account at the end of 4 years?

Solution using the appendix tables: FV factor from Table 2 for 12 percent, 4 years = 1.574; FV at the end of 4 years = 1.574 x $2,500 = $3935.00

Using calculator: PV = -$2,500, PMT = 0, N = 4, I = 12, FV = solve = +$3,933.80
Note: The difference between the two solutions is because of the rounded value for FV factor in the table. The calculator solution is more accurate.

Problem 2: Jane Doe wants to create an endowment income of $12,000 a year for her alma mater, but proposes that the first payment not be made until 3 years' time. If she can earn a return of 6 percent on her investments, how much should she invest now?

Solution using the appendix tables: The present value of the perpetuity will be $12,000/0.06 = $200,000. This amount has to be invested by the end of 2 years so that the first payment of $12,000 will be received at the end of 3 years. PV of this today = PV factor for 6 percent for 2 years x $200,000 = 0.890 x $200,000 = $178,000.

Solution using calculator: FV = +$200,000, PMT = 0, N = 2, I = 6, PV = solve = $177,999.29

Problem 3: Mary Corelli borrows $125,000 to buy her home. The loan carries an annual interest of 9 percent and requires 180 equal monthly payments. Calculate the monthly payment. What will be the balance on the loan when she has made 90 payments?

Solution using calculator: PV = Loan amount = +$125,000; FV=0, N=180, I = 9/12 = 0.75
PMT = Solve = -$1,267.83

To calculate the outstanding balance after 90 payments, calculate the PV for 90 payments (180-90). FV = 0, PMT = -$1,267.83, N = 90, I = 0.75, PV = Solve = $82,757.11. (This problem cannot be solved using the appendix tables as the table does include values for the range of interest rate and number of periods needed for the problem. You can calculate the annuity factor for the interest rate of 0.75 percent and 180 periods or 90 periods using the formula: Annuity factor = $[(1/r) - (1/r(1+r)^t)]$. The value for 180 periods = 98.593, Payment = $125,000/98.593 = $1,267.84. The factor for 90 periods = 65.275, Loan balance = 65.275x$1,267.84 = $82,758.26)

Problem 4: What is the price of a 10-year, 10 percent coupon bond with a $1,000 face value if investors require a 12 percent return? What is its yield to maturity if its price is $1,100? Assume annual coupon payments.

25

Solution using calculator: PMT = Coupon payment = $100, FV = Face value = $1,000, N = 10, I = 12, PV = Price = Solve = $887.

Yield to maturity for a price of $1,100: PV = -$1,100, FV = +$1,000, PMT = +$100, N = 10, I = Yield to maturity = solve = 8.48 %

Using Appendix Tables:
Price of the bond = Coupon payment x annuity factor + Face value x PV factor

Annuity factor for 10 years, 12 % interest rate = 5.650, PV factor = 0.322
Price of the bond = 5.650 x $100 + 0.322 x $1,000 = $887
To find the yield to maturity, you have to find the price at different interest rates and by trial and error get the value closest to $1,100. Price at 9 % = 6.418 x $100 + 0.422 x $1,000 = $1,063.80. Price at 8 % = 6.710 x $100 + 0.463 x $1,000 = $1,134. The yield to maturity will be about 11.5%.

CHAPTER SUMMARY

This chapter completes what was started in chapter 2 and describes the technique calculation of present values of different streams of cash flows. Shortcuts or formulas are developed for special streams of cash flows such as perpetuity, annuity and growing perpetuity. These have wide applications in finance. The chapter also discusses simple and compound interest and compounding frequencies. The present value technique is applied to valuation of bonds. Present value computations are made easier by the tables that give the values for the discount, future value or annuity factors for a range of returns and periods. The text has the following appendices:

Table 1.	Present value of $1 (discount factors)
Table 2.	Future value of $1 (future value factors)
Table 3.	Present value of an annuity $1 at the end of each year for t years)
Table 4.	Future values with continuous compounding
Table 5.	Present value of an annuity received as a continuous stream.

LIST OF TERMS

Annuity	Internal rate of return
Compound interest	Nominal interest rate
Continuously compounded rate of interest	Perpetuity
Coupon rate	Real interest rate
Discounted-cash-flow (DCF) formula	Simple interest
Discount rate	Yield to maturity
Face value	

EXERCISES

Fill-in Questions

1. _____ interest is calculated on initial investment only, without reinvestment of interest.

2. The formula for present value is also called the _____ formula.

3. The present value of a future cash flow is calculated by discounting it at the appropriate _____.

4. _____ interest is calculated on the accumulated amount of the investment, with interest reinvested.

5. A constant stream of cash flows for a limited number of years coming at regular intervals is called a (an) _____.

6. A constant stream of cash flows that go on forever is called a _____.

7. The interest rate, which is the stated rate in loan and other transactions, is the _____ interest rate.

8. Nominal interest rate less the rate of inflation is the approximate _____ interest rate.

9. The amount of money repaid at the maturity of a bond is the _____.

10. Most bonds usually pay regular interest payments called the _____.

11. The principal amount owed on a bond is repaid on its _____.

12. The rate of return on a bond investment when it is held to maturity is called its _____.

Problems

1. Here are some investments earning different interest rates and invested for different periods. Calculate the accumulated values at the investment period for each one.

   a. $1,000 invested for 4 years at 8 percent interest.
   b. $1,000 invested for 8 years at 9 percent.
   c. $250 invested for 5 years at 7 percent
   d. $250 invested for 10 years at 7 percent.
   e. $800 invested for 5 years at an annual rate of 12 percent.
   f. $800 invested for 5 years at an interest rate of 3 percent every quarter.
   g. $800 invested for 5 years at an interest rate of 1 percent every month.

2. How long will it take $1,000 to double when it is invested at (a) 3 percent, (b) 5 percent, (c) 10 percent, (d) 12 percent, or (e) 15 percent?

3. How much should I be prepared to pay for (a) $2,000 in 10 years' time at an interest rate of 10 percent and (b) $2,000 in 5 years' time at an interest rate of 21 percent?

4. An investment of $10,000 will produce income of $2,500 a year for 5 years. Calculate its NPV if the discount rate is 9 percent.

5. An investment costing $4,000 will produce cash flows of $1,500 in year 1, $1,200 in year 2, and $2,000 in year 3. Calculate its net present value at (a) 0 percent, (b) 6 percent, and (c) 12 percent.

6. Mary Jane has already saved $10,000 in a mutual fund account and expects to save an additional $9,000 for each of the next 2 years. She expects to pay $12,000 each at the end of 2 years and 3 years for her son's college education. How much can she afford to spend now on a vacation if she expects to earn (a) 7 percent and (b) 10 percent?

7. I will receive from my late uncle's estate $40 in 1 year's time and annually thereafter in perpetuity. What is the value of this perpetuity at an interest rate of (a) 8 percent and (b) 10 percent?

8. How much is the previous perpetuity worth if it begins in 5 years' time instead of 1?

9. I now discover that my uncle's will provides that I receive $40 in 1 year's time and that this amount is to be increased annually at a rate of 6 percent. What is the present value of this growing stream of income at an interest rate of (a) 8 percent and (b) 10 percent?

10. Bollywood Inc. is expected to pay a dividend of $4 next year. The dividends are expected to grow at a constant rate of 8 percent. If the shareholders require a return of 12 percent, what will be the likely price of the stock?

11. Reenbee Construction is expected to pay a dividend of $2 next year. The company's shareholders require a return of 14 percent. If the current share price is $40, what rate of dividend growth must they be expecting?

12. I took a car loan of $20,000 from my bank. The loan carries an annual interest rate of 12 percent and has to be repaid in 30 equal monthly payments. Calculate the monthly payment.

13. I am saving for the deposit to buy a house. I have just invested $1,000 and I expect to save a further $1,000 at the end of each of the next six years. If I invest my savings at 12 percent interest, how much will I have after 6 years?

14. A store offers the following credit terms on a color television set "slashed" to a price of only $320: only $20 down and 18 monthly payments of $20. (a) Is this an attractive proposition if I can borrow at 1 percent per month? (b) What monthly interest rate is being charged? (c) What annual rate is being charged?

15. How much does $1,000 grow to at continuously compounded interest when invested for (a) 9 years at 6 percent and (b) 6 years at 9 percent?

16. I can get a nominal interest rate of 4 percent on my money market account. If the expected inflation rate is 2 percent, what is the real interest rate I am getting?

17. Jane wants to save for her 3-year-old daughter's college education. She believes she has 15 years to accumulate the needed $65,000. What is the annual amount she needs to invest in a mutual fund that would give her an annual return of 12 percent?

18. What annually compounded rate is equivalent to an interest rate of 12 percent compounded: (a) semi-annually, (b) quarterly, (c) monthly, (d) weekly (or 52 times a year), (e) daily (365 times a year), and (f) continuously?

19. Value a bond which pays 8 percent coupon, has a face value of $1,000, 10 years till maturity, and the investors require a rate of return of 10 percent. Assume annual coupon payments.

20. If the above bond is selling at a price of $1,070, what is the yield to maturity?

21. An U.S. Treasury bond of 12 years maturity and 9 percent coupon is quoted with a yield to maturity of 8 percent. (a) Calculate its correct price, given that it makes semi-annual coupon payments and the quoted yield is semi-annually compounded. (b) Calculate the (incorrect) price that would have been obtained by assuming annual payments and compounding.

ANSWERS TO EXERCISES

Fill-in Questions

1. Simple
2. Discounted-cash-flow
3. Discount rate
4. Compound
5. Annuity
6. Perpetuity

7. Nominal
8. Real
9. Face value
10. Coupon rate
11. Maturity date
12. Yield to maturity, internal rate of return.

Problems

1.

	Calculator solutions					Using Appendix Table 1 factors	
	N	I	PV	PMT	FV = Solve	FV Factors	Solution
a	4 years	8 percent	-1000	0	1360.49	1.360	$1360
b	8 years	9 percent	-1000	0	1992.56	1.993	$1993
c	5 years	7 percent	-250	0	350.64	1.403	$350.75
d	10 years	7 percent	-250	0	491.79	1.967	$$491.75
e	5 years	12 percent	-800	0	1409.87	1.762	$1409.60
f	20 quarters	3 percent	-800	0	1444.89	1.806	$1444.80
g	60 months	1 percent	-800	0	1453.36	1.817	$1453.60

2. Using the calculator: PV = $1,000, FV = -$2,000, PMT = 0, (a) I = 3, N = solve = 23.45 years; (b) I = 5, N = solve = 14.21 years; (c) I = 10, N = solve = 7.27 years; (d) I = 12, N = solve = 6.12 years; and (e) I = 15, N = solve = 4.96 years. You can get the approximate answers using Table 1 and looking for the number of years for which the FV factor is close to 2 for each interest rate.

3. a. PV = $2,000, N= 10, I = 10, PMT = 0, FV = solve = -$5,187.48. Alternately, using the FV factor from appendix Table 1: factor for 10 years, 10 percent = 2.594, FV = $2,000 x 2.594 = $5,188
    b. PV = 2,000, N= 5, I = 21, PMT = 0, FV = solve = -$5,187.48
        Alternate solution using table 1: factor for 5 years, 21 percent = 2.594, FV = $2,000 x 2.594 = $5,188

4. You can find the present value of the cash inflows which are in the form of an annuity. Then, subtract the initial investment of $10,000.
    Using calculator: N = 5, I = 9, PMT = -$2,500, FV = 0, PV = solve = $9,724.13
    NPV = -$10,000 + $9,724.13 = -$275.87
    From Table 3, the PV factor for 5 years, p percent = 3.890, PV = $2,500 x 3.890 = $9,725
    NPV = -$10,000 + $9,725 = -$275

5. This problem can be most easily solved using the calculator's cash flow work sheet and the NPV function. Enter the cash flows as follows:
        CF_0 = -$4,000 (Initial cash flow),
        CO_1 = $1,500, FO_1 = 1 (This indicates that this cash flow occurs only once)
        CO_2 = $1,200, FO_2 = 1
        CO_3 = $2,000, FO_3 = 1
    Once the cash flow data are entered, you proceed to the NPV function work sheet by pressing the NPV key. Entering the appropriate values for I (discount rate), and going down the work sheet using the down arrow key, you can compute the NPVs.
    (a) I = 0, NPV = $700; (b) I = 6, NPV = $162.33; and (c) I = 12, NPV = -$280.52

6. The amount she can afford to spend on her vacation is the difference between the present values of her savings and the college education costs. First calculate the present value of Mary Jane's savings for the next two years (an annuity with two payments) and add this to her current savings of $10,000.

    a. PV of the 2 year annuity; N = 2, I = 7, PMT = -$9,000, FV = 0, PV = Solve = $16,272.16
        Total PV of savings = $16,276.16 + $10,000 = $26,276.16.
        PV of education costs:
        $12,000 at the end of 2 years: N = 2, I = 7, PMT = 0, FV = -$12,000, PV = Solve = $10,481.26
        $12,000 at the end of 3 years: N = 3, I = 7, PMT = 0, FV = -$12,000, PV = Solve = $9,795.57
        Total PV of education costs = $10,481.26 + $9,795.57 = $20,276.83

30

Amount she can spend on vacation = $26,276.16 - $20,276.83 = $5,999.33

b. PV of the 2 year annuity; N = 2, I = 10, PMT = -$9,000, FV = 0, PV = Solve = $15,619.83
Total PV of savings = $15,619.83 + $10,000 = $25,619.83
PV of education costs:
$12,000 at the end of 2 years - N = 2, I = 10, PMT = 0, FV = -$12,000, PV = Solve = $9,917.36
$12,000 at the end of 3 years - N = 3, I = 10, PMT = 0, FV = -$12,000, PV = Solve = $9,015.78
Total PV of education costs = $9,917.36 + $9,015.78 = $19,497.05
Amount she can spend on vacation = $25,619.83 - $19,497.05 = $6,122.78

7. a. PV of perpetuity = C/r = $40/0.08 = $500
   b. PV of perpetuity = $40/0.10 = $400

8. Using Table 1, PV factor for 5 years, 8 percent = 0.681
Present value of the perpetuity = 0.681 x $500 = $340.50

9. a. This is a growing perpetuity. PC = C/(r-g) = $40/(0.08 - 0.06) = $2,000
   b. If r = 10 percent, PV = $40/(0.1 - 0.06) = $1,000

10. The stock can be valued as a growing perpetuity. Price = $4/(0.12 - 0.08) = $100

11. Price = Dividend/(r-g) = $40, Dividend = $2, r = 0.14
Solving for g, g = 0.14 - $2/40 = 9 percent

12. Calculator solution: N = 30, I = 1, PV = $20,000, FV = 0, PMT = solve = -$774.96. You can also do this using the Appendix Table 3 interpreting the 12 percent annual interest rate as 1 percent/month and finding the factor for 30 "years". Annuity PV factor from Table 3 for 30 periods and 1 percent = 25.81. Payment = $20,000/25.81 = $774.89

13. See this as a six year annuity plus an initial $1,000. Using the table you can calculate the PV of the annuity plus the initial $1,000. Then calculate the FV of this amount for six years.
Factor from Table 3 for six years, 12 percent = 4.111, PV of annuity = $1,000 x 4.111 = $4,111
PV of total amount available = $4,111 + $1,000 = $5,111
FV factor from Table 2 for 6 years and 12 percent = 1.974
FV in six years = $5,111 x 1.974 = $10,089.11
Calculator solution: N = 6, I = 12, PV = -$1,000, PMT = -$1,000, FV = solve = $10,089.01

14. a. You are taking a loan of $320-$20 = $300. If your interest rate is 1 percent per month, your payment will be $300 divided by the annuity factor for 18 periods, 1 percent (Table 3). Annuity factor for 18 periods, 1 percent = 16.40; Monthly payment = $300/16.40 = $18.29. Since you are required to pay more than this amount, this is not an attractive proposition.

   b. For payment of $20/month, the annuity factor has to be = $300/$20 = 15. This is very close to the factor for 18 periods and 2 percent (14.99). So the effective interest being charged is 2 percent/month. Effective annual rate = $(1.02)^{12} - 1 = 26.82$ percent.

15. a. and b. The answer for both parts are the same because the product of interest rate (r) and number of years (t) is the same and the future value factor for continuous compounding is given by the formula e^{rt}. The value for the factor from Table 4 = 1.716, FV = $1,000 x 1.716 = $1,716

16. The approximate real interest rate = 4 – 2 = 2 percent.
    The exact real rate = (1.04/1.02) – 1 = 0.0196 = 1.96 percent

17. This can be solved easily with the calculator as follows:
    N = 15, I = 12, PV = 0, FV = $65,000, PMT = solve = -$1,743.58
    Alternately, you can use the Appendix tables to solve this problem in 2 steps. First calculate the PV of $65,000 needed in 15 years. Then find the annual payments that will give you this PV.
    PV factor for 15 years, 12 percent (Table 1) = 0.183
    PV of $65,000 needed in 15 years = $65,000 x 0.183 = $11,895
    Annuity Factor from Table 3 for 15 years and 12 percent = 6.811
    Annual investments required = $11,895/6.811 = $1,746.44

18. The equivalent annually compounded rate or the effective annual rate (EAR) is given by the formula $(1+i/m)^m - 1$, where i is the nominal annual rate or the annual percentage rate (APR) and m is the frequency of compounding. The EAR for the different compounding frequencies is:

    (a) m = 2, EAR = 12.36%; (b) m = 4, EAR = 12.5509%; (c) m = 12, EAR = 12.6825%; (d) m = 52, EAR = 12.7341%; (e) m = 365, EAR = 12.7475%; and (f) EAR = $e^{0.12}$ = 12.7497%.

19. Calculator solution: N = 10, I = 10, PMT = $80, FV = $1,000, PV = solve = -$877.11
    Using Tables: Value = Coupon Payments x Annuity factor + Face value x PV factor
             = $80 x 6.145 + $1,000 x 0.386 = $877.60

20. Calculator solution: N = 10, PV = -$1,070, PMT = $80, FV = $1,000, I = YTM = 7 percent.
    Using the factors from Tables 1 and 3, you can, by trial and error, get the same result.

21. (a) Calculator solution: N = 2x15=30, I = 4, PMT = $45, FV = $1,000,
    PV = solve = -$1,086.46;
  (b) Incorrect price: N = 15, I = 8, PMT = $90, FV = $1,000, PV = solve = -$1,085.59

Using the Appendix tables: (a) Price = $45 x 17.29 + 1,000 x 0.308 = $1,086.05
                           (b) Price = $90 x 8.559 + $1,000 x 0.315 = $1,085.31

4

The Value of Common Stocks

INTRODUCTION

This chapter applies the lessons learned from the last two chapters to valuing stocks and other assets. The chapter begins with a description of market activities related to stock trading and follows this with an explanation of stock valuation. Unlike bonds, stocks do not have specified cash flows; however, the value of a share can be seen as the present value of the dividends paid by the stock. This principle of stock valuation, with some modifications, can be applied to valuing businesses in general. The value of any asset is the present value of the free cash flows or cash flows generated by the asset. The discount rate for computation of the present value should be the required rate of return demanded by the investors for investing in the asset.

The chapter describes three equivalent ways of looking at the value of a stock: i) as the present value of future dividends, ii) as the present value of free cash flow, and iii) as present value of current earnings plus the present value of growth opportunities. The current market price of a stock can also be used to estimate the market capitalization rate on the stock. This rate is of practical application in setting rates for regulated utilities and other industries.

KEY CONCEPTS IN THE CHAPTER

How Stocks are Traded: Corporations issue new shares in the primary market which is essentially a distribution network of investment bankers and brokerage firms, who sell these initial issues to individual investors, mutual funds, and other buyers. Once issued, the stocks trade in the secondary markets. Well-known secondary markets include the New York Stock Exchange (NYSE), the "over-the-counter market" which is a network of dealers displaying prices through the National Association of Security Dealers' Automated Quotation system (NASDAQ). The Wall Street Journal and other newspapers publish price, dividend, P/E ratio, and other information on stock market transactions.

Valuation of Common Stocks: The value of a share can be derived by evaluating the cash flows generated by the investment. If the stock is expected to pay a dividend of DIV_1 at the end of the year and the expected price of the stock at the end of the year is P_1, then for an investor requiring a return of r, the price of a stock today is:

$$P_0 = \frac{DIV_1}{(1+r)}$$

This can be extended to future years, so that the price next year can be written as:

$$P_1 = \frac{DIV_2}{(1+r)}$$

Substituting this into the previous equation for P_0 gives:

$$P_0 = \frac{DIV_1}{(1+r)} + \frac{DIV_2}{(1+r)^2}$$

You can substitute the value for P_2 in terms of D_3 and P_3 and so on. This gives you the value of P_0 as the present value of dividends expected to be paid on that stock.

$$P_0 = \sum_{t=1}^{\infty} \frac{DIV_t}{(1+r)^t}$$

The value of a firm will be the present value of all future dividends paid on its current outstanding stock. Future dividends on new stocks issued in later years should not be included.

Estimation of Market Capitalization Rate: The expected return, r, is often called the *market capitalization rate*. All securities in the same risk class are priced to offer the same expected return. If one stock offered a higher return, everyone would rush to buy it, pushing its price up and the expected return down. We can use the valuation of a growing perpetuity learned in Chapter 3 to value a stock for which the dividend is expected to grow at a constant rate. If the expected dividend growth rate is g, then

$$P_0 = DIV_1 /(r-g); \text{ this formula requires that } r > g.$$

For such a stock, the market capitalization rate r is given by:

$$r = \frac{D_1}{P_0} + g$$

This is a useful formula to estimate the capitalization rate or the required rate of return on a company's stock. This is the *cost of equity* for the company. Care has to be taken to see that the estimated growth rate is realistic and closely approximates the market perception of the stock. Regulators use this to estimate the fair rate of return on gas and electric utilities. For companies which have a regular pay out of dividends and reinvestment of remaining earnings, the growth rate can be approximated as: g = return on equity x plow back ratio, where the plow back (or retention) ratio is the fraction of earnings reinvested in the business.

Some cautionary notes on the estimation of the capitalization rate are in order. As estimates for a

36

single stock may be unreliable, it is better to look at the average of estimates for a number of companies. Remember that the estimated growth rate should reflect long-term average growth rate rather that the current high or low rate.

The Relationship Between Price and Earnings: The valuation model derived earlier shows the relationship between dividends and stock price. Investors often classify stocks as *growth* or *income* stocks depending on the relative growth of earnings and the earnings-price ratio. A growth stock typically has low earnings price ratio and provides most of the return to investors in the form of capital gains. It is important to note that growth, per se, does not add value; only growth opportunities which have positive net present value are valuable and worth pursuing. Depending on the type of growth opportunities, we consider three cases.

a. Zero growth case: In this case, all earnings will be distributed as dividends, therefore $DIV_1 = EPS_1$, where EPS_1 is the earnings per share. $r = DIV_1 /P_0 = EPS_1 /P_0$ or the expected return equals dividend yield and earnings price ratio. This is the only case where the earnings price ratio equals the capitalization rate.

b. Growth rate is positive but the projects have zero NPV: Part of the earnings are reinvested and $(EPS_1 /P_0) > (DIV_1 /P_0)$. The investors exchange reduction in current dividends for gain in long-term dividends; however, the return earned is exactly equal to the opportunity cost of capital and there is no gain in value. Again, $EPS_1 /P_0 = r$.

c. A company with positive NPV growth opportunities: In this case, the company's growth adds value and the price of the stock is increased by the investment in the growth opportunities. A dollar of current dividend is traded off for more than one dollar equivalent in future dividends. This growth adds to the value of the company. The relationship among the stock price, earnings and the present value of growth opportunities (PVGO) can be expressed by the following equations:

$$P_0 = \frac{EPS_1}{r} + PVGO$$

$$\frac{EPS_1}{P_0} = r(1 - \frac{PVGO}{P_0})$$

The earnings price ratio will be less than the capitalization rate if the PVGO is positive. The larger the PVGO as a percentage of the stock price, the more the earnings price ratio will understate the capitalization rate. PVGO is rarely negative as firms are not required to invest in projects with negative NPVs. Typically, the growth stocks will have a higher percentage of their value represented by PVGO and will thus have low earnings price ratios.

Price-earnings (P/E) ratios are the inverse of earnings price ratios and are published along with stock price quotations in the newspaper. They are based on the most recent earnings announcements rather than next year's earnings. Stocks of companies with high PVGO will show high P/E ratios. This implies higher expected future earnings. Of course, stocks whose current earnings are low may also show high P/E ratios. It should be remembered that high P/E ratios do not mean low cost of capital. It should also be remembered that earnings numbers are influenced by the company's choice of accounting procedures and are unlikely to reflect the amount of money, which could be paid out without affecting its capital value. The P/E ratio can therefore be very misleading, even for comparisons of similar companies.

Valuation of a Business Using Discounted Cash Flow: Valuing a business is similar to valuing a stock. Instead of looking at dividends, one has to look at the *free cash flow* produced by the business. The free cash flow is the cash flow that can be withdrawn from the business each year after meeting all its investment needs. Growing firms typically invest more than the depreciation amount and might even exceed their earnings. During these years their free cash flow will be negative. When the investment needs are less than their earnings, the business generates free cash flow, which is similar to dividends. The value of the business will be the present value of the free cash flows generated by the business. The procedure includes estimating free cash flows to a time *horizon* when the cash flows follow a steady growth or constant growth pattern. The steps involved in valuation of a business are given below:

1. Estimate free cash flow. Cash flow may be negative in early years of rapid growth.

2. Choose the horizon date. Free cash flows are estimated to the horizon date from which point the cash flows form a simple growth pattern, so that one of the short-cut valuation formulas can be applied.

3. Estimate the horizon value. This may be very sensitive to the assumptions and will have to be cross checked with other criteria or benchmarks such as P/E ratios, market to book ratios of other similar companies, and the year when PVGO becomes zero.

WORKED EXAMPLES

1. Estimation of PVGO: ABM Inc. is expected to earn $12 per share next year. The company is expected to distribute dividends of $6 and reinvest the remaining earnings on projects with an average ROE of 24 percent. Its capitalization rate is estimated to be 18 percent. Calculate the stock price, the P/E ratio, and the PVGO. What percentage of the stock price is represented by the PVGO?

Dividends next year = DIV_1 = $6
Plowback ratio = ($12-$6)/$12 = 0.50
Growth rate = Plow back ratio x ROE = 0.50 x 0.24 = 0.12
Price = $6/(0.18-0.12) = $100
P/E ratio = $100/$12 = 8.33
PVGO = P − (EPS_1/r) = $100 − ($12/0.18) = $33.33
This is 33.33 percent of the value of the stock.

38

An alternate way of estimating the PVGO is to look at the investment made in the first year and its NPV. The $6 invested in the first year earns $6 x 0.24 = $1.44 in perpetuity. PV of this cash flow is $1.44/0.18 = $8, NPV = $8-$6 = $2. Each year the company is making similar investments which are growing at 12 percent. Thus, the PVGO is a growing perpetuity = $2/(0.18-0.12) = $33.33.

2. Dracula and Frankenstein (DF) is an established movie producer that specializes in horror movies. The projected earnings and cash flow for the company are given below. Steven Lucas wants to buy the business and requires a rate of return of 20 percent on his investment. Estimate the value of the business.

Dollars million

Years	1	2	3	4	5	6
Assets	50	75	100	125	140	151.2
Earnings	12	18	24	30	33.6	36.29
Net Investment	25	25	25	15	11.2	12.10
Free cash flow	-13	-7	-1	15	22.4	24.19
Earnings growth from previous period (%)		50	33.3	25	12	8

The cash flows start growing at a constant rate of 8 percent from the end of 5 years. At this stage, the business is reinvesting one-third of each year's earnings and is earning a ROE of 24 percent. Therefore, the growth rate = 24 x 1/3 = 8 percent. We can choose 5 years as the horizon. The value of the business at this point is that of a growing perpetuity growing at 8 percent. Horizon Value = Value at the end of five years = 22.4/(0.20-0.07) = $172.31 million

Value of the business = Present value of free cash flows

$$PV(FreeCashflows) = \frac{-13}{1.2} + \frac{-7}{(1.2)^2} + \frac{-1}{(1.2)^3} + \frac{15}{(1.2)^4} + \frac{22.4 + 172.31}{(1.2)^5} = \$69.21 million$$

CHAPTER SUMMARY

This chapter applies the principles of discounted cash flow to valuing stocks and businesses. The cash flows generated by a stock are the dividends and therefore the value of a stock will be the present value of all future dividends paid by it. This does not imply that the return on a stock investment is only in the form of dividends. The value of stock held for one year is the present value of the dividends expected to be received and the expected price at the end of the year. Thus, the return received on a stock investment is the dividend yield and the expected capital gain from the price appreciation. Extending this logic for longer periods will lead to the result that the current price is the present value of all future dividends.

Using the simplifying assumption of constant dividend growth, current price of a stock can be derived as the value of a growing perpetuity: $P_0 = D_1/(r-g)$. The assumption of constant growth should be seen as an approximation rather than an exact condition. The formula also gives one a simple approach to estimating market capitalization rate or cost of equity capital from current market price of the stock: $r = (D_1/P_0) + g$.

The stock valuation model can be used to derive the relationship between earnings, growth opportunities, and current stock price. The current price of a stock is the sum of the present value of the current earnings in perpetuity and the present value of growth opportunities or PVGO. This relationship also leads to the result that the earnings price ratio will understate the capitalization rate for companies with significant growth opportunities.

The approach used to value stocks is extended to value businesses. In general, the value of a business will be the present value of the free cash flows generated by the business. Free cash flows are similar to dividends and are the earnings less net investments needed to be made in the business to generate the earnings.

LIST OF TERMS

Cost of equity capital	Payout ratio
Dividend yield	Plowback ratio (Retention ratio)
Free cash flow	Price-earnings ratio (P/E ratio)
Growth stock	Primary market
Income stock	Return on equity (ROE)
Market capitalization rate	Secondary market

EXERCISES

Fill-in Questions

1. New York Stock Exchange is an example of a _____.

2. The market capitalization rate for a firm's common stock is also known as its _____.

3. The _____ is the return that investors require from investment in a stock or bond.

4. Annual dividend per share/share price = _____.

5. The proportion of earnings retained in the business is called _____.

6. New issues of stocks are issued through the _____, which is a network of investment bankers and brokerage firms.

7. The proportion of earnings paid out as dividends is called _____.

8. A firm with significant opportunities to invest in positive net present value projects will have a high _____ ratio.

9. Stocks, which give a high proportion of their return in the form of dividends, are usually called _____.

10. Stocks, which are expected to have high price appreciation, are known as _____.

11. The cash generated by a company net of its investment needs is the _____.

12. The ratio of the net profit earned by a company to the book value of stockholders' equity is _____.

Problems

1. JBH Inc. is expected to pay dividends of $2, $3, and $5 for the next three years. Thereafter, the dividends are expected to grow at a constant rate of 8 percent. If the required rate of return is 16 percent, what will be the current stock price? What will be the stock price next year and at the end of three years?

2. M Corp. is expected to pay a dividend of $6 a share next year. The dividends are expected to grow at the rate of 6 percent annually. If the current stock price is $60, what is the implied market capitalization rate?

3. You forecast that ITT will pay a dividend of $2.40 next year and that dividends will grow at a rate of 9 percent a year. What price would you expect to see for ITT stock if the market capitalization rate is 15 percent?

4. If the price of ITT is $30, what market capitalization rate is implied by your forecasts of problem 3?

5. Great Leaps Corp. stock is currently selling at $45. Next year's earnings are expected to be $3. Assuming that the current level of earnings can be maintained without any new investment, calculate the PVGO if the investors require a return of: (a) 10 percent (b) 15 percent.

6. Jack Corp. retains 60 percent of its earnings and invests them at an average return on equity (ROE) of 15 percent. Jill Inc. retains only 30 percent of its earnings but invests them at an average ROE of 25 percent. Which company has the higher P/E ratio?

7. Bear Corp. shares are expected to pay a dividend of $4 next year. The dividends are expected to decrease (because the company's sales are declining on account of an industry wide decline) at the rate of 15 percent annually. If the market capitalization rate is 15 percent, what will be the current stock price?

8. The current earnings of M & M Corp. are $5 a share, and it has just paid an annual dividend of $2. The company is expected to continue to retain 60 percent of its earnings for the next 3 years and that both earnings and dividends will grow at 20 percent a year over that period. From year 4 on, the payout ratio is expected to increase to 70 percent and the growth rate to fall to 10 percent. If the capitalization rate for this stock is 15 percent, calculate (a) its price, (b) its price-earnings ratio, and (c) the present value of its growth opportunities.

9. Big Bull Corp. is expected to pay dividends of $3, $5, and $7 for the next three years. Thereafter, the dividend is expected to grow at the rate 8 percent. If the market capitalization rate is 16 percent, calculate the current stock price and the stock price for each of the next three years.

10. Calculate the dividend yield and capital gains for each of the next three years for the Big Bull Corp. of problem 9.

11. Mac & Burgers Corp. has the following estimated earnings and net investments.

Dollar millions

Years	1	2	3	4	5	6
Assets	24.00	40.00	52.00	60.00	68.00	73.44
Earnings	4.80	8.00	10.40	10.80	10.88	11.75
Investments	16	12.00	8.00	8.00	5.44	5.88

The company will continue a payout ratio of 50 percent beyond year 6 and earn 16 percent on the assets. If the market capitalization rate is 15 percent, estimate the value of the business as the present value of free cash flows.

12. What is the horizon value at the end of year 5? If the industry values for mature companies similar to Mac & Burgers in year 5 are: P/E ratio = 16 and Market-to-book ratio = 1.5. Compare alternate valuation methods to the horizon value estimated using the constant growth model.

Essay Questions

1. "High P/E ratios imply high growth." Discuss.

2. What is the relationship between earnings price ratio and market capitalization rate?

3. A company's earnings figure represents money, which in principle may be distributed to shareholders. Explain why the stock price represents the present value of dividends rather than earnings.

4. Some companies have a policy of retaining all earnings and never paying a dividend. Does this invalidate the principle that the stock price equals the present value of future dividends? Discuss.

ANSWERS TO EXERCISES

Fill-in Questions

1. Secondary market
2. Cost of equity
3. Market capitalization rate
4. Dividend yield
5. Plowback (retention) ratio
6. Primary market

7. Payout ratio
8. P/E ratio
9. Income stocks
10. Growth stocks
11. Free cash flow
12. Return on equity

Problems

1. $P_0 = DIV_1/(1+r) + DIV_2/(1+r)^2 + DIV_3/(1+r)^3 + P_3/(1+r)^3$;
   where $P_3 = DIV_4/(r-g) = 5 \times 1.08/(0.16 - 0.08) = \$67.50$;
   $P_0 = (2/1.16) + (3/1.16^2) + (5 + 67.5)/1.16^3 = 50.40$; $P_1 = (3/1.16) + (5 + 67.5)/1.16^2 = \$56.47$

2. $r = DIV_1/P + g = \$6/\$60 + 0.06 = 0.16 = 16\%$

3. $P_0 = DIV_1/(r-g) = \$2.4/(0.15 - 0.09) = \$40$

4. $r = DIV_1/P + g = \$2.40/\$30 + 0.09 = 0.17 = 17\%$

5. (a) PVGO = P – EPS_1/r = \$45 - \$3/0.10 = \$15; (b) PVGO = \$45 - \$3/0.15 = \$25

6. $P_0 = EPS_0 (1+g)$ (payout)/(r-g); g = ROE x plowback; PE ratio = (1+g) (payout)/(r-g)
   For Jack Corp., P/E ratio = 1.09 x 0.4/(r - 0.09).
   For Jill Inc., P/E ratio = 1.075 x 0.7/(r - 0.075).
   P/E ratios for Jack Corp. and Jill Inc. are shown for different values of r:

r	10%	12%	14%
Jack Corp.	43.6	14.5	8.72
Jill Inc.	30.1	16.72	11.58

   We can solve for the value of r at which the P/E will be same for both companies. The value turns out to be 11.06% and the P/E is 20.8.

7. $P_0 = \$4/[0.15-(-0.15)] = \$13.33$

43

8. $DIV_0 = \$2$, $DIV_1 = \$2 \times 1.2 = \$2.40$, $DIV_2 = \$2.40 \times 1.2 = \$2.88$, $DIV_3 = \$2.88 \times 1.2 = 3.46$
   $EPS_4 = \$5 \times 1.2^3 \times 1.1 = \$9.50$, $DIV_4 = \$9.50 \times 0.7 = \$6.65$, $P_3 = \$6.65/(0.15 - 0.1) = \$133$
   $P_0 = (2.4/1.15) + (\$2.88/1.15^3) + [(\$6.65 + \$133)/1.15^3] = \$96.09$, $P/E = \$96.09/2 = \$48.05$
   $PVGO = \$96.09 - (EPS_1/r) = \$96.09 - (\$6/0.15) = \$56.09$

9. $DIV_4 = \$7 \times 1.08 = \$7.56$, $P_3 = \$7.56/(0.16 - 0.08) = \$94.50$,
   $P_0 = \$3/1.16 + (\$5/1.16^2) + [(\$7 + \$94.50)/1.16^3] = \$71.33$,
   $P_1 = \$5/1.16 + (\$101.5/1.16^2) = \$79.74$, $P_2 = \$101.5/1.16 = \$87.50$

10. Dividend yield for year $1 = \$3/71.33 = 4.21\%$, Capital gains $= (P_2 - P_1)/P_1 = 11.79\%$
    Dividend yield for year $2 = \$5/79.74 = 6.27\%$, Capital gains $= 9.73\%$. From year 3 onwards, the dividend yield will be 8% and the capital gains will also be 8%. The capital gains for a stock with constant growth dividends will always be the growth rate in dividends.

11. The earnings, investments, and free cash flows (in \$ millions) for the first 5 years are given in the table below. From year six, the free cash flows are growing at 8 percent. We can calculate the horizon value at the end of year 5 and then discount all cash flows and the horizon value to the present at the market capitalization rate of 15 percent.

Years	1	2	3	4	5
Earnings	4.80	8.00	10.40	10.80	10.88
Investments	16.00	12.00	8.00	8.00	5.44
Free cash flow	-11.20	-4.00	2.40	2.80	5.44

Value of cash flows from year 6 onwards = Free cash flow$_6$/(r-g) = (5.44x1.08)/(0.15-0.08)
$$= 5.88/0.07 = \$84 \text{ million}$$
Value of the business = PV(Free cash flows)

$$= \frac{-11.20}{1.15} + \frac{-4}{(1.15)^2} + \frac{2.40}{(1.15)^3} + \frac{2.80}{(1.15)^4} + \frac{5.44 + 84}{(1.15)^5}$$

$$= \$34.88 \text{ million}$$

12. Horizon value using free cash flow approach = \$84 million
    Horizon value using the PE ratio = 16 x \$5.44 = \$87.04 million.
    Using market-to-book = 1.5 x 68 = \$102 million

5

Why Net Present Value Leads to Better Investment Decisions than Other Criteria

INTRODUCTION

Chapters 2 and 3 introduced the concept of the net present value (NPV) and its use for making investment or capital budgeting decisions. This chapter starts with a review of the NPV approach to investment decision making and then presents three other widely used measures. These are:

- the payback period,
- the book rate of return, and
- the internal rate of return (IRR).

The chapter describes these methods and their major drawbacks. The measures are inferior to the NPV and should not, with the qualified exception of the IRR, normally be relied upon to provide sound corporate investment decisions. The IRR can provide correct and sound decisions if used properly. The primary reason why a chapter is devoted to these measures is that these are commonly used in corporate practice and are often popular. Hence, you should understand the methods and the pitfalls in their use.

The chapter also describes how to take capital budgeting decisions when one is faced with the so-called capital rationing problem. This introduces a fourth method called the profitability index. More complex constraints can be dealt with using a technique called linear programming.

KEY CONCEPTS IN THE CHAPTER

NPV Basics: The first section gives a review of the net present value method. The NPV represents the value added to the business by the project or the investment. It represents the increase in the market value of the stockholders' wealth. Thus, accepting a project with a positive NPV will make the stockholders better off by the amount of its NPV. The NPV is the theoretically correct method to use in most situations. Other measures are inferior because they often give decisions different from those given by following the NPV rule. They will not serve the best interests of the stockholders.

Here is a review of the steps involved in calculating NPV, the decision rule for using NPV, and the advantages of NPV. This is followed by similar discussion of each of the other measures.

<u>Calculating NPV:</u>

Forecast the incremental cash flows generated by the project. Determine the appropriate discount rate, which should be the opportunity cost of capital. Calculate the sum of the present values (PV) of all the cash flows generated by the investment.

NPV = PV of cash inflows - initial investment.

<u>Decision rule and interpretation:</u>

Accept projects with NPV greater than zero. For mutually exclusive projects, accept the project with the highest NPV, if the NPV is positive. The NPV represents the value added to the stockholders' wealth by the project. The discount rate should reflect the opportunity cost of capital or what the stockholders can expect to earn on other investments of equivalent risk.

<u>Advantages:</u>

The NPV approach correctly accounts for the time value of money and adjusts for the project's risk by using the opportunity cost of capital as the discount rate. Thus, it clearly measures the increase in market value or wealth created by the project. The NPV of a project is not affected by "packaging" it with another project. In other words, NPV(A+B) = NPV(A) + NPV(B). The NPV is the only measure that provides the theoretically correct measure of a project's value.

Payback Period: The payback period is simply the time taken by the project to return your initial investment. The measure is very popular and is widely used; it is also a flawed and unreliable measure.

<u>Calculation:</u>

The cash flows from each year are added to find out the point in time at which the cumulative cash flows equal the initial investment.

<u>Decision rule and interpretation:</u>

Accept projects with payback less than some specified period. E.g. Accept projects with payback of 4 years or less. Payback represents the number of years required for the original cash investment to be returned, but the time value of money is ignored. Therefore, it will be misleading to think that all cash flows after payback represent profit.

<u>Advantages and disadvantages:</u>

It is simple to calculate and easy to comprehend. However, payback period has very limited economic meaning because it ignores the time value of money and the cash flows after the payback period. It can be inconsistent and the ranking of projects may be changed by packaging with other projects.

Discounted payback is a modified version of the payback measure and uses the discounted cash flows to compute payback. This is an improvement over the traditional payback in that the time value of money is recognized. A project, which has a measurable discounted payback, will have a positive NPV. However, the other disadvantages of payback still apply. It is also not simple anymore.

Book Rate of Return (BRR): This is a rate of return measure based on accounting earnings and is defined as the ratio of book income to book assets.

Decision rule and interpretation:
Accept projects with returns greater than the average return on the book value of the firm, or some external yardstick. Book rate of return depends on the accounting rules followed by the company and not on the cash flows generated by the project. This is extremely unlikely to maximize the stockholders wealth.

Advantages and disadvantages:
Accounting earnings are reported by firms to the stockholders and the book return measure fits in with the reported earnings and the accounting procedures used by firms. However, the measure suffers from the serious drawback that it does not measure the cash flows or economic profitability of the project. It does not consider the time value of money and gives too much weight to distant earnings. The measure depends on the choice of depreciation method and on other accounting conventions. BRR can give inconsistent ranking of projects and rankings may be altered by packaging. There is very little relationship between the book return and the IRR. Chapter 12 discusses some of the problems of using book returns.

Internal (or Discounted-Cash-Flow) Rate of Return (IRR): IRR is defined as the discount rate at which the NPV equals zero.

Calculation:
It is calculated by trial and error. Follow the steps for calculating the NPV and calculate the NPV for several discount rates. Start with a low discount rate and then calculate the NPV at progressively higher rates till the NPV calculated has a negative value. In general, the NPV will decrease as the discount rate is increased. Plot the NPVs (y-axis) against the discount rate (x-axis). The IRR is that discount rate at which the line crosses the X-axis (NPV=0).

Decision rule and Interpretation:
Accept projects that have an IRR greater than the opportunity cost of capital. IRR is often interpreted as the effective rate of return for the investment made in the project. Strictly, this interpretation is true only for a one-period project.

Advantages and Disadvantages:
Used properly, the IRR will give the same result as the NPV for independent projects and for projects with normal cash flows.[1] As long as the cost of capital is less than the IRR, the NPV for the project will be positive. IRR can rank projects incorrectly, and the rankings

_____

1 Normal projects are projects with initial investment (negative cash flows) followed by a number of positive cash flows.

47

may be changed by the packaging of the projects. For mutually exclusive projects, IRR can give incorrect decisions and should not be used to rank projects. If one must use IRR for mutually exclusive projects, it should be done by calculating the IRR on the differences between their cash flows.

IRR can also be misleading in cases where the project cash flow patterns are reverses of the normal project. These projects give cash inflows first, followed by outflows. Thus, it is like borrowing and in such cases, the IRR decision rule should be reversed. The project should be accepted only if the IRR is *less than* the hurdle rate.

Another problem with IRR is that for projects whose cash flows change sign more than once there will have more than one IRR. In such cases, it may not be obvious whether a high IRR is good or bad. One will need to look into the "NPV profile" (the NPV-discount rate graph) to identify the discount rate range for which the NPV is positive. *Modified IRR* is an improvement over the IRR and is used to overcome the problem of multiple IRRs. The cash flows that change signs during the project's life are discounted using the opportunity cost of capital and added to the cash flows of other years. This removes the multiple changes of sign. IRR does not allow different discount rates to be used for different time periods', i.e., no account can be taken of the term structure of interest rates.

Capital Rationing and Profitability Index: Occasionally, companies face resource constraint or capital rationing. The amount available for investment is limited so that all positive NPV projects cannot be accepted. In such cases, stockholder wealth is maximized by taking up projects with the highest NPV per dollar of initial investment. This approach is facilitated by the *profitability index* (PI) measure. Profitability index is defined as: NPV/Investment. The decision rule for profitability index is to accept all projects with a PI greater than zero. This rule is equivalent to the NPV rule. The modified rule applied in the case of capital rationing is to accept projects with the highest profitability index first, followed by the one with next highest, and so on till the investment dollars are exhausted. This rule will maximize the NPV and stockholder wealth. If the resource constraint is on some other resources, the profitability index needs to be modified to measure the NPV per unit of the resource that is rationed. When more than one resource is rationed, a more complicated (linear programming) analysis is needed. The profitability index cannot cope with mutually exclusive projects or where one project is contingent on another.

Capital constraints are often self-imposed to force divisions to focus on priorities and to weed out projects that stem from over-optimism. Such cases are termed *soft rationing*. The more serious case of capital rationing is when a firm cannot raise capital to finance all its positive NPV projects. This implies capital market imperfections and is termed *hard rationing*. The use of NPV and PI is still justified in such cases as long as the firm's stockholders have opportunities to invest in capital markets in projects comparable to the ones taken up by the firm.

NPV and Other Criteria: The NPV is superior to other criteria because: i) it is the only measure which considers the time value of money, properly adjusting for the opportunity cost of capital,

48

ii) gives consistent measures of the project's value (i.e. not affected by packaging with other projects), and iii) it clearly measures the value added to the stockholders' wealth. However, the other three criteria for the evaluation of projects are found to be popular in corporate practice. If you have to use them, make sure you use them in the best possible way and understand the limitations of them. For example, always compare mutually exclusive projects on the basis of the difference between their cash flows. Remember that it is the cash flows that determine the value of a project. Inadequate forecast of the cash flows can be far more disastrous than using the wrong appraisal technique. Cash flow forecasts are difficult to make and can be expensive. It does not make sense to waste the forecasts by using an inferior method of evaluation.

WORKED EXAMPLE

Bar Breweries is considering an expansion project with an estimated investment of $1,500,000. The equipment will be depreciated to zero salvage value on a straight-line basis over 5 years. The expansion will produce incremental operating revenue of $400,000 annually for 5 years. The company's opportunity cost of capital is 12 percent. Ignore taxes. Calculate: (a) payback period, (b) book rate of return, (c) NPV, (d) IRR, and (e) profitability index.

SOLUTION

First calculate the annual earnings and cash flows:
    Operating revenues   = $400,000
    Less depreciation   = $300,000
    Book Income   = $100,000
    Cash flow   = $400,000

a. Payback = $1,500,000/$400,000 = 3.75 years

b. Average book income = $100,000,
    Average book value of investment = ($1,500,000+0)/2 = $750,000
    Book rate of return = $100,000/$750,000 = 13.33%

c. NPV calculation:

	Amount	Discount factor	Present value
Year 0 Initial investment	-$1,500,000	1	-$1,500,00
Years 1 through 5 Cash flow	$400,000	3.605	$1,442,000
Net Present Value			-$58,000

d. IRR is calculated by trial and error. Calculate the NPV at different discount rates:
    NPV at 10 percent = $400,000(discount factor for 10%, 5 years) - $1,500,000
                    = $400,000 x 3.791 - $1,500,000 = $16,400
    NPV at 11 percent = $400,000 x 3.696 - $1,500,000 = -$21,600

49

IRR lies between 10 percent and 11 percent.
IRR = 10 +[16,400/(16,400+21,600)] = 10.43%
Note: You can obtain the solution directly by using the calculator.
PV = -$1,500,000, FV = 0, PMT = $400,000, N = 5, I = IRR = solve = 10.42%

e. Profitability Index = NPV/Investment = -$58,000/$1,500,000 = -0.04

SUMMARY

This chapter provides a comparison between the different criteria used to evaluate projects. The chapter begins with a review of the NPV, which has already been introduced in the earlier chapters. This is followed by a detailed discussion of three commonly used, but inferior, criteria for evaluation of capital budgeting projects. The payback period is simply the number of years required to recoup the project's initial investment. Aside from its simplicity, there is not much to be said for the payback; it ignores the time value of money, ignores all cash flows after the payback period, and leads to inconsistent ranking of projects. The book rate of return is an accounting measure and suffers from all the weaknesses inherent in accounting earnings being subject to the relatively arbitrary nature of accounting assumptions. The book return does not use cash flows in its computation. Again, the measure can lead to poor decisions.

The internal rate of return or IRR is based on discounted cash flows and can give correct decisions for independent projects. The decision rule is to accept projects with an IRR greater than the cost of capital. Any project that satisfies this rule will have a positive NPV. However, the measure should not be used for selection of the best among mutually exclusive projects. A modified approach is needed to get the correct decision using IRR when selecting among mutually exclusive projects. The approach involves calculating the IRR for the differences in cash flows of the two mutually exclusive projects. NPV is superior to the above as it gives the correct decision and is a direct measure of the value added to the stockholders' wealth.

The only exception to the superiority of NPV is when the firm is constrained by capital rationing. This implies that the firm cannot finance all positive NPV projects and should therefore choose projects that give the highest NPV for each dollar of investment. The profitability index that is defined as the ratio of NPV to the investment amount is used to achieve this selection.

LIST OF TERMS

Book rate of return
Capital rationing
Discounted-cash-flow rate of return
Discounted payback
Internal rate of return

Linear programming
Mutually exclusive projects
Payback period
Profitability index

EXERCISES
Fill-in Questions

1. The _____ is the time it takes an investment to repay its initial investment.

2. The _____ is the time beyond which cash flows could disappear and still leave the project with a positive net present value.

3. The _____ is defined as the book income/book investment.

4. The _____ is the discount rate for which the NPV equals zero.

5. _____ is needed to deal with capital rationing or resource constraint problem spread over more than one year.

6. _____ are competing projects among which only one can be selected.

7. The NPV of the project divided by the investment is called _____.

8. _____ is another name for the IRR.

9. _____ exists when a firm is constrained by limited availability of funds to invest.

Multiple Choice Questions
Choose from among the five criteria to which the statement applies. Net present value (NPV), payback (P), book rate of return (BRR), internal rate of return (IRR), or profitability index (PI):

	NPV	P	BRR	IRR	PI	None
1. Could be misleading if the project cash flow patterns are reversed.						
2. Affected by the depreciation method used.						
3. Puts too much weight on distant cash flows.						
4. May have several values.						
5. Gives the same accept-reject decisions as NPV on single projects.						
6. Works well for single period capital rationing.						
7. Ignores cash flows beyond some point.						
8. Can use multiple discount rates.						
9. Gives consistent rankings even if the projects are packaged together differently.						
10. Gives the same decisions as the NPV for independent projects.						

Problems

1. Black and Company is considering an investment in a new plant which will entail an immediate capital expenditure of $4,000,000. The plant is to be depreciated on a straight-line basis over 10 years to zero salvage value. Operating income (before depreciation and taxes) is expected to be $800,000 per year over the 10-year life of the plant. The opportunity cost of capital is 14 percent. Calculate (a) the book rate of return, (b) the payback and discounted payback periods, (c) NPV, (d) IRR, and (e) the profitability index. There are no taxes.

2. Mary Lee owns a computer reselling business and is expanding her business. The estimated investment for the expansion project is $85,000 and it is expected to produce cash flows after taxes of $25,000 for each of the next 6 years. An alternate proposal involves an investment of $32,000 and after-tax cash flows of $10,000 for each of the next 6 years. The opportunity cost of capital is 13 percent. Calculate (a) payback, (b) book rate of return, (c) IRR, and (d) NPV and advise Mary.

3. Refer to problem 2. Is there an opportunity cost of capital that would make Mary indifferent between the two projects?

4. For each of the following projects, calculate the IRR, NPV, and the profitability index. Assume the cost of capital to be 10 percent. Rank the projects using each criterion.

Projects	Cash flow in $ (1,000)			
	Year 0	Year 1	Year 2	Year 3
Project A	-100			145
Project B	-100	115		
Project C	-100	230	-120	
Project D	-45	20	20	20

5. An investment of $100 will produce a level stream of cash flows for T years. Find what level of cash flows will give an IRR of: (a) 12 percent and (b) 14 percent for T = 6 years and T = 10 years.

6. Plymouth and Company is considering the following mutually exclusive investments. Calculate the payback, IRR, and the NPV for the two projects. Assume a cost of capital of 13 percent. Which project would you choose? Why do the ranking by the different methods differ?

Projects	Project cash flows – ($1,000s)			
	Year 0	Year 1	Year 2	Year 3
Project A	-400	220	310	0
Project B	-400	130	190	260

7. Ruckhouser Corp. has an opportunity cost of capital of 10 percent and the following projects. Assuming theses to be independent projects, select the best project(s) for the company. Explain why all the projects will not be selected.

Projects	Cash flow in $ (1,000)				
	Year 0	Year 1	Year 2	Year 3	IRR -%
Project A	-112	40	50	60	15
Project B	45	60	-70	-70	16
Project C	-100	-26	80	80	11
Project D	146	-70	-60	-50	12
Project E	-100	450	-550	175	29

8. Refer to question 7. How would your decision change if the projects were not independent projects?

9. Fingerhaus Inc. is considering a project with an investment of $300,000. The project is expected to generate annual cash flows of $85,000 in the first two years and $100,000 from years 3 to 7. At the end of year 8, the company will have to incur a cash flow of $250,00 to clean up the plant facility. Calculate the NPV and IRR for the project. Assume a cost of capital of 12 percent.

10. M & M Corp. has existing operations that will generate cash flows of $150,000 in year 1 and $200,000 in year 2. If the company makes an investment of $40,000 now, it can expect to receive $230,000 in year 1 and $180,000 in year 2. M & M's cost of capital is 12 percent. Calculate the NPV and IRR of the project. Why is the IRR a poor measure of the project's profitability in this case?

11. Please refer to problem 10 above. M & M Corp. finds that the investment needed for the project is $50,000 instead of $40,000. Evaluate the project.

12. Mickey Minn Corp. is considering the following projects. The company is facing resource constraints and can invest only $800,000 this year. Advice the company.

Projects	Investment ($1,000s)	NPV ($1,000s)	IRR (%)
A	100	8	13.9
B	400	43	14.4
C	300	25	16.0
D	200	23	14.1
E	200	21	16.1
F	200	19	15.7

Essay Questions

1. IRR should never be used to evaluate mutually exclusive projects. Discuss.

2. Why is NPV superior to the other measures of project profitability?

3. IRR, used properly, will give correct decisions. Discuss.

4. How can the problem of capital rationing be handled? Discuss the role and limitations of profitability index as the criterion to be used for projects under capital rationing.

5. Why is the measures payback and book rate of return used in capital budgeting?

ANSWERS TO EXERCISES

Fill-in Questions

1. Payback period
2. Discounted payback
3. Book rate of return
4. Internal rate of return
5. Linear programming

6. Mutually exclusive projects
7. Profitability index
8. Discounted-cash-flow rate of return
9. Capital rationing

Multiple Choice Questions

1. IRR
2. None
3. BRR
4. IRR
5. IRR

6. PI
7. P
8. NPV
9. NPV
10. IRR

Problems

1. (a) Operating revenues   = $800,000
   Less depreciation   = $400,000
   Book Income   = $400,000
   Cash flow   = $800,000

   Average book income = $400,000
   Average book value of investment = ($4,000,000+0)/2 = $2,000,000
   Book rate of return = $400,000/$2,000,000 = 20 %

(b) Payback period = $4,000,000/$800,000 = 5 years
   Discounted payback is the number of years needed to get the PV of the cash flows to equal

54

the initial investment.
Using the calculator: PV = -\$4,000,000, PMT =\$800,000, FV = 0,
I = 14%, N = solve = Discounted payback = 9.2 years.

  (c) NPV: Present value of cash flows = \$800,000 x 5.216 = \$4,172,800
NPV = \$4,172,800 - \$4,000,000 = \$172,800
Alternately, using the calculator you can find the present value of the cash flows to equal
\$4,172,892. NPV = \$172,892
(N = 10, I = 14, FV = 0, PMT = \$800,000, PV = solve = \$4,172,892)

  (d) IRR can be directly obtained by using the calculator:
PV = -\$4,000,000, PMT = \$800,000, FV = 0, N = 10, I = solve =
IRR = 15.1%

2. Proposal 1: Payback = \$85,000/\$25,000 = 3.4 years
Book income = \$25,000 – Depreciation = \$25,000 – (\$85,000/6) = \$10,833
Book rate of return = \$10,833/\$42,500 = 25.5%
IRR = 19.1% (PV = -\$85,000,FV = 0, PMT = \$25,000, N = 6, I = IRR)
NPV = present value of cash flows - \$85,000 = \$99,939 - \$85,000 = \$14,939
(PMT = \$25,000, FV =0, N = 6, I = 13, PV = solve = \$99,939)

Proposal 2: Payback = \$32,000/\$10,000 = 3.2 years
Book rate of return = \$4,667/\$16,000 = 29.2%
IRR = 21.6 %
NPV = \$7,975

Mary should choose proposal 1 as it has a higher NPV. IRR, BRR, or the payback should not
be used to choose among mutually exclusive projects.

3. The cost of capital at which the two projects will produce the same NPV can be found by
calculating the IRR of the difference in cash flows between the two projects. Proposal 1
requires an additional investment of \$53,000 and generates extra cash flows of \$22,000 for six
years. The IRR for this set of cash flows is 17.6 % (PV = -53,000, PMT = 15,000, N = 6, I =
IRR). This also means that for any cost of capital below 17.6%, proposal 1 will have a higher
NPV.

4. Project A:
IRR = 13.2% (PV = -100, FV = 145, PMT = 0, N = 3, I = IRR)
NPV = \$8,940 (PV of \$145 received 3 years from now is \$108.94)
Profitability index = 8.94/100 = 0.0894

Project B:
IRR = 15%; NPV = \$4,545; Profitability index = 0.0455

Project C:
IRR = -20% and 50%. The project has two IRRs because of the pattern of cash flows (two sign changes).
NPV = -100 + 230/1.1 – 120/1.21 = 9.917 = $9,917
Profitability index = 0.0992

Project D:
IRR = 15.9%; NPV = $4,737; Profitability index = 4.737/45 = 0.1053

Ranking of projects:

IRR:	1. C	2. D	3. B	4. A (also C)
NPV:	1. C	2. A	3. D	4. B
PI:	1. D	2. C	3. A	4. B

5. (a) Using the Appendix table 3, the annuity factor for 12% and six years is 4.111. Cash flow = $100/4.111 = $24.32. The factor for 10 years is 5.650. The cash flow = $100/5.650 = $17.70.

(b) Using the calculator: PV = -100, FV = 0, I = 14%, N =6 years, PMT = solve = $25.72. For 10 years, N = 10, PMT = $19.17

6. Payback for A = 1 + 180/310 = 1.58 years.
Payback for B = 2 + 80/260 = 2.31
NPV for A = $37,466; NPV for B = $44,035
IRR for A = 19.7%; IRR for B = 18.7%

Based on NPV, the company should choose project B. Payback and IRR rank project A better because of the difference in cash flow patterns. Project A has more of its cash flow in the earlier years.

7. The NPVs for the projects are as follows:

Project A = $10,765
Project B = -$10,898
Project C = $2,585
Project D = -$4,789
Project E = -$13,974

Only projects A and C have positive NPVs. The others are really "borrowing" projects and should not be selected as the cost of borrowing (IRR) is higher than the opportunity cost of capital.

8. If the projects were mutually exclusive, one would select project A as it has the highest NPV.

9. Using the calculator:
   $CF_0 = -300{,}000$, $CO_1 = 85{,}000$, $FO_1 = 2$, $CO_2 = 100{,}000$, $FO_2 = 5$
   $CO_3 = -250{,}000$, $FO_3 = 1$, IRR = solve = 16.6%; NPV: $I = 12%$,
   NPV = 30,054

10. Incremental cash flows are: $CF_0 = -40{,}000$, $CO_1 = 80{,}000$,
    $CO_2 = -30{,}000$; NPV: $I = 12$, NPV = \$7,512; IRR = 50 %

11. With an increase of \$10,000 in the initial investment, the project's NPV will become
    negative.   NPV = -\$2,488; IRR = 0.

12. The profitability index and ranking based on PI for the different projects are:

Project	PI	Ranking
Project A	0.080	6
Project B	0.108	2
Project C	0.083	5
Project D	0.115	1
Project E	0.105	3
Project F	0.095	4

    Projects D, B, and E should be selected to invest the \$800,000.

6

Making Investment Decisions with the Net Present Value Rule

INTRODUCTION

This chapter discusses the details and nuts and bolts issues of making investment decisions and applying the NPV rule in practice. Specifically, the chapter focuses on two tasks faced in capital budgeting. The first problem faced by anyone making investment decisions is to determine which items should be included in the cash flow analysis. The answer, of course, is to include all the cash flows relevant or incremental to the project. The chapter describes the items to be included and also excluded.

The second problem in the application of the NPV rule to investment decision making relates to the fact that most investment decisions interact with or affect other activities or decisions of the firm. These project interactions have to be carefully sorted out and included in the project analysis and decision. This often requires modifying the NPV rule to consider annual costs or benefits from the project under consideration. A typical example might involve alternative proposals, with different project lives, for the replacement of existing machinery. The proper evaluation in this case will be to compare the alternatives in terms of the equivalent annual costs rather than the total costs for each alternative. This technique finds extensive application in a number of different situations.

KEY CONCEPTS IN THE CHAPTER

Focus on Cash Flow: Capital budgeting decisions should be based on analysis of cash flows and not accounting earnings. It is important to understand that accounting earnings can differ from cash flows because of the set of rules followed by accountants in classifying income and expenditures. Care has to be taken to ensure that cash flows are counted at the point of time they are received or paid out. This might require more than simple manipulation of accounting numbers.

Incremental, After-tax Cash Flow: Project evaluation should be based on after-tax cash flows caused by or incidental to the project. All the cash flows that are created by the project or are changed by the acceptance of the project should be considered. The following are some useful pointers in identifying the relevant cash flows:

Incremental, not average: It is easy to confuse between the average cost and incremental cost. What is relevant to the project analysis is the portion of the cost (or revenue) that will change because of the project. Expenses incurred regardless of what happens to the project should not be considered, as they are not affected by the project.

All incidental effects: All cash flows flowing out of the decision on the project should be included in the project analysis. If the project causes a sales increase in another division's business or an increase in administrative expenses, these should be included in project evaluation.

Working capital changes: Changes in working capital (accounts receivable plus inventory minus accounts payable) needs caused by the project are part of the cash flows that should be included. It is easy to ignore these and one has to be careful to account for the changes in inventory, receivables, and accounts payables. The investment in working capital is usually recovered at the end of the project.

Sunk costs: Sunk costs are costs already incurred or will be incurred anyway regardless of what happens to the project. These should be ignored as they are not affected by the project decision.

Opportunity costs: Opportunity costs of all resources, including managers and other personnel, should be included even if there may not be an explicit cash flow relating to that item. When a project uses a resource already owned by the company, the resource is taken off alternate use. Thus, the execution of the project precludes alternate use of the resource and the project should be charged for the use of the resource.

Allocated overheads: Accounting rules followed by companies often included allocated charges for use of services. These are often based on the company's historic costs and experiences and do not bear any direct relationship to the project's actual usage of services or other resources. Thus allocated overheads should be ignored and be counted only to the extent they are actual incremental costs.

Financing charges: Interest payments and other financing charges are normally not included in project cash flows. Throughout this chapter, we assume that the project is financed through all equity funds. This enables us to separate investment financing decisions. The effect of financing mix will be built into project evaluation in later chapters through appropriate adjustments to the cost of capital.

Depreciation: Depreciation is not a cash flow but has cash flow consequences because it is a deductible expense for tax purposes. Most corporations keep two sets of books – one for reporting earnings to stockholders and another for tax returns filed with the Internal Revenue Service (IRS). Our tax laws permit accelerated depreciation for most assets used in business. These are based on notional lives assigned to classes of assets. Table 6.4 in the text gives the depreciation schedules for different classes of assets. The effect of depreciation is to provide a reduction in taxes or *tax shield* equal to the dollar amount of depreciation multiplied by the marginal tax rate of the company.

NPV in Other Currencies: The general principles of finance you learn in this book have universal relevance and applicability. Thus, while an American company will compute its cash flows and NPVs in US dollars, a Japanese firm will do the same using the same principles we discuss in this and other chapters, but in the Japanese yen. A German company will have its cash flows in the *Euro[1]*, the new common European currency. Some details will differ, though. For example, nominal interest rates, inflation rates, and the opportunity cost of capital may be different from country to country. The tax rates and depreciation rules are decided by the local governments in each country and can be substantially different.

Consistent Treatment of Inflation: Inflation affects both the project cash flows and the opportunity cost of capital used to discount the cash flow. One has to be careful to treat inflation effects consistently and correctly. The opportunity cost of capital estimated from current market costs are *nominal* costs with inflation effects already built into them. Thus, it is easiest to discount *nominal* (money) cash flows at a *nominal* discount rate. Some companies prefer to project cash flows in *real* terms and discount them at a real rate of interest. The relationship between nominal rates, real rates, and inflation is given by the equation:

$$1 + r_{nomial} = (1 + r_{real})(1 + \text{inflation rate}).$$

It is important to be consistent in the treatment of inflation. Either discount nominal cash flows with a nominal rate or discount real cash flows with a real rate; do not mix them.

Project Interactions*:* Most investment decisions involve more than one choice or affect other activities of the business. At the least you can always decide to invest or not to invest, invest now or invest a year from now. Other choices might involve replacing old machinery which still has some useful life left, or choosing between machines with different project lives. Often when one investment proposal is accepted, it means that other alternative proposals must be rejected. These are all choices that are mutually exclusive. While the NPV rule is still useful, it is essential to take a sufficiently broad view of net present value and to remember that the goal is to maximize the present value of the whole company.

One useful measure of a project's effective cost or benefit is the equivalent annual cost (EAC) or benefit. The EAC is particularly useful for deciding among similar facilities (such as machines) with different lives and for deciding on when an existing facility should be replaced. Some typical cases of project interactions and approaches to deal with them are discussed below.

Optimal timing of investment: The fact that a project has a positive NPV does not mean that it is best undertaken now. It may be even more valuable if undertaken at a later date. The optimal choice of timing is the one that maximizes the NPV. Imagine you have some 5 year vintage

---

1 The Euro has become the common unit of account for eleven European countries from January 1999. It will be another three years before you start exchanging actual Euro notes and coins. During this period, each country will have its currency locked into a fixed exchange rate with the Euro.

whiskey for which you can get $1,000 now or $2,000 if you sell it five years from now. If the present value of $2,000 received 5 years from now is higher than $1,000, it makes sense to wait. It is quite likely that you will get even more than $2,000 if you sell six years later or seven years later. The optimal choice will be the one that gives the highest present value.

Projects with different lives: The basic NPV rule will not provide correct decisions in the evaluation of mutually exclusive projects with different lives. The NPV rule does not take into account the value of a likely replacement project. We can convert the projects costs or benefits into annual equivalents and choose the better alternative. Converting the present value (or NPV) into equivalent annual costs is easy; you simply divide the present value by the appropriate annuity factor.

The replacement decision: The capital cost of a new machine can be restated in terms of the equivalent annual cost (EAC). Its optimal life is the one that minimizes its EAC. We can decide whether to replace an existing machine by comparing its cost for the next year (including the loss of salvage value over the year) against the EAC of the new machine.

EAC is simple to compute and use in a world of certainty. Inflation can be factored in or do the analysis in real terms. Other important considerations, such as technological changes or other uncertainties, could complicate the problem.

The cost of excess capacity: Currently available excess capacity of any resource (plant, computers, or a warehouse) may not be free as increased utilization of the resource (such as a computer) may bring forward the date of future replacement of the facility. It is, therefore, essential to consider the cost (an opportunity cost, really) of the use of this excess capacity and factor that into the project's cash flows.

Fluctuating load factors: A large plant may have positive NPV but is justified only if the NPV is higher than another size plant which might be able to do the job well enough. In other words, you have to consider different sizes of investment and choose the size which has the highest (positive) NPV. A new project may affect the value of other investments, sometimes we must work out detailed scenarios to unravel these effects.

WORKED EXAMPLES

1. Macaroni and Pizza Inc. is considering a new project which requires an investment of $4 million. The project is expected to generate sales revenue of $1 million in the first year, $2 million in the second year and $3 million for years 3, 4, and 5. The cost of goods sold is expected to be 75 percent of sales revenue. Other costs are expected to be 7 percent of sales in the first year and 5 percent of sales thereafter. The project will need working capital investment of $200,000 in the first year and an additional $100,000 in the second year. The investment in plant ($4 million) will be depreciated using the MACRS schedule for the 5 year class. If the company's opportunity cost of capital is 10 percent, calculate the NPV for the project. Assume that the plant will operate for 6 years, and at the end of 6 years, the plant

can be sold for a salvage value of $300,000. The tax rate for the company is 36 percent.

SOLUTION

Cash flows ($1000s)

Years	0	1	2	3	4	5	6
1. Investment and salvage	-2,000						192[1]
2. Sales		1,000	2,000	3,000	3,000	3,000	3,000
3. Cost of goods sold		750	1,500	2,250	2,250	2,250	2,250
4. Other costs		70	100	150	150	150	150
5. Depreciation		400	640	384	230	230	116
6. Pre-tax profit [2-3-4-5]		-220	-240	216	370	370	484
7. Tax at 36% of 6		-79	-86	78	133	133	174
8. Profit after tax [6-7]		-141	-154	138	237	237	310
9. Operating cash flow [8+5]		259	486	522	467	467	426
10. Change in working capital		-200	-100				300
11. Total cash flows [1+9+10]	-2,000	59	386	522	467	467	918
12. Present value at 10%	-2,000	54	319	392	319	290	518
13. Net present value	-2,000+54+319+392+319+290+518 = -108						

Notes: 1. Salvage value $300,000 less tax of $108,000 = $192,000

2. Sugar & Honey Cakes is considering replacing their oven with a new one. They have received two offers. Oven A has an initial cost of $34,000, annual operating costs of $6,000, and an operating life of 4 years. Oven B has an initial cost of $24,000, annual operating costs of $8,000, and operating life of 3 years. Which oven is the better choice? Assume an opportunity cost of capital of 12 percent.

SOLUTION

Present value of costs for oven A = $34,000 + $6,000 x 3.037 = $52,222
Equivalent annual cost = $52,222/3.037 = $17,195
Present value of costs for oven B = $24,000 + $8,000 x 2.402 = $43,216
Equivalent annual cost = $43,216/2.402 = $17,992
A is the better choice as it has lower EAC.
(3.037 and 2.402 are the annuity factors for 4 years and 3 years for discount rate of 12 percent.)

3. Joe Vino inherited a cellar of wines from his aunt. The local wine dealer offered Joe $70,000 for all the entire collection. A sommelier (wine expert) friend of Joe suggested that if he kept the wines for another five years he could sell them for $150,000. If Joe's opportunity cost is 14 percent, what is the best course of action for Joe?

SOLUTION

Present value of \$150,000 received 5 years from now = $\$150,000/1.14^5 = \$77,905$
Joe will be better off waiting 5 years.

SUMMARY

This chapter describes the application of the NPV rule to actual project evaluation. The focus is on two key problems faced by anyone engaged in capital budgeting decisions: i) what to discount and ii) how to deal with project interactions. Project evaluation should use incremental after-tax cash flows. Specifically, the evaluator should consider all cash flows incidental to and caused by the project. Care has to be taken to ensure that items like working capital increases are considered and sunk costs are ignored.

Treatment of inflation in project evaluation should be consistent and avoid confusion between real and nominal cash flows. If nominal cash flows are used, they should be discounted with a nominal cost of capital. By the same token, real cash flows should be discounted by a real cost of capital.

Project interactions can be of several different types. Some typical cases include: optimal timing of investment, project with unequal lives, replacement decision for old machinery with useful life, cost of excess capacity, and fluctuating load factors. For optimal timing, one has to look at the choice which will maximize the NPV. Some of the other problems can be evaluated using the technique of EAC. It is also necessary, in the case of excess capacity, to explicitly recognize the opportunity cost of using the capacity, the cost being early replacement of the resource being used. Evaluation of projects with fluctuating load factors should include explicit consideration of alternatives with different capacities and choosing the one with the highest NPV. The essential point to note in the evaluation of all mutually exclusive projects is the definition of alternative projects available and possible. Also, remember that most projects have interactions that will result in mutually exclusive choices.

LIST OF TERMS

Accelerated depreciation
Equivalent annual cost
Net working capital
Nominal interest rate
Opportunity costs
Real interest rate

Recovery period class
Straight-line depreciation
Sunk costs
Tax depreciation
Tax shield

64

EXERCISES

Fill-in Questions

1. Costs that occurred in the past and are irrecoverable are called _____.

2. The cost of a resource for its best alternate use is its _____.

3. Current assets minus current liabilities equal _____.

4. An interest rate adjusted for inflation, so that it represents an increase in purchasing power, is called the _____ rate.

5. The stated interest rates in most transactions have no adjustment for inflation and is the _____ rate.

6. Under_____, the amount of depreciation is the same each year.

7. _____ is the general term for any depreciation method that provides larger deductions in the early years of the asset's life.

8. To work out the after-tax cash flows from an investment, we need to know what_____ is allowed, rather than how it is depreciated for accounting purposes.

9. The tax depreciation allowed for a particular asset depends on which_____it belongs to.

10. The tax depreciation amount multiplied by the tax rate is called the depreciation _____.

11. The _____of equipment is the constant annual charge which, over the life of the equipment, has the same present-value cost as the equipment.

Problems

1. Gates Hardware Inc. (GHI) is considering an investment of $5 million in plant and machinery. This is expected to produce sales of $2 million in year 1, $4 million in year 2, and $6 million in year 3. Subsequent sales will increase at the expected inflation rate of 10 percent. The plant is expected to be scrapped after 6 years with a salvage value of $1 million. It is depreciated for tax purposes on a straight-line basis of $1 million per year. Operating costs are expected to be 70 percent of the sales. Working capital requirements are negligible. GHI pays tax at 35 percent. Calculate the expected cash flows in each year and the NPV of the investment when the required rate of return is 16 percent.

2. Repeat the calculation of problem 1, doing the analysis in *real* instead of nominal terms.

Discount at the approximate real rate of 5.45 percent.

3. How does your analysis of problem 1 change if the new plant qualifies for tax depreciation under the 5-year recovery period class?

4. Garfield Corp. is evaluating an investment project which will cost $40 million and generate taxable revenues of $11 million per year for 7 years. There will be no salvage value at the end of this period. Garfield is currently unsure whether the investment will belong to the 3-year, 5-year, or 7-year recovery period class. Calculate the NPV of the project for each of these three possibilities. Garfield's tax rate is 35 percent and its required return is 15 percent.

5. An investment of $200,000 in a computer is expected to reduce costs by $40,000 a year in perpetuity. However, the prices of computers are predicted to fall at 10 percent a year for the next 5 years. When should the computer be purchased if the cost of capital is 13 percent?

6. The Bluebird Company must choose between machines A and B, which perform exactly the same operations but have different lives of 2 and 3 years, respectively. Machine A costs $30,000 initially and has annual costs of $5,000. Machine B has an initial cost of $40,000 and annual costs of $7,000. If Bluebird's cost of capital is 10 percent, which machine should it choose.

7. A machine costs $100,000. At the end of the first year, $5,000 must be spent on maintenance. Each year, the cost of maintenance rises by 15 percent. How long should the machine be kept before it is scrapped if the opportunity cost of capital is 10 percent? (Assume the machine has a zero salvage value.)

8. XYZ Company is considering whether to replace an existing machine or to spend money on overhauling it. The replacement machine would cost $18,000 and would require maintenance of $1,500 at the end of every year. At the end of 10 years, it would have a scrap value of $2,000 and would not be maintained. The existing machine requires increasing amounts of maintenance each year, and its salvage value is falling as shown below:

Year	Maintenance Cost	Salvage Value
0	$2,000	$2,500
1	$3,000	$2,000
2	$4,000	$1,500
3	$5,000	$1,000
4	$5,000	0

If XYZ faces an opportunity cost of capital of 15 percent, when should it replace the machine?

9. The acceptance of a particular capital budgeting proposal will mean that a new computer costing $200,000 will be purchased in 1 year's time instead of in 3 years' time. This also implies that an extra computer programmer costing $30,000 a year must be hired in year 1 instead of year 3. Work out the present-value cost of these two items when the opportunity cost of capital is 14 percent.

10. Bayerhouser Timber has vast tracts of timber land. One tract in the northwest region has timber ready for harvest and at current market prices will fetch a net revenue of $12 million. If the company waited for 1 year, 2 years, 3 years, and 4 years, the values would be $15 million, $17 million, $18 million, and $19 million respectively. What is the optimal harvesting point for the company if the cost of capital is 15 percent?

11. How will your answer change if you are told that the above estimates for the timber values are real dollars and not nominal dollars and the cost of capital is nominal value with an inflation component of 5 percent?

12. Redo problem 3 in the worked examples by assuming a cost of capital of 16 percent.

Essay Questions

1. Project evaluation should consider only incremental after-tax cash flows. What are incremental, after-tax cash flows?

2. Depreciation is not a cash flow and therefore should not be considered in project evaluation. Discuss.

3. "We always allocate a proportion of company overhead to a new project in relation to its payroll requirements. After all, in the long run, there's no difference between average and marginal cost." Discuss.

4. Describe how to work out the economic life of a piece of machinery and how to decide when to replace an existing machine which performs the same function.

ANSWERS TO EXERCISES

Fill-in Questions

1. Sunk costs
2. Opportunity cost
3. Net working capital
4. Real interest
5. Nominal interest
6. Straight line depreciation
7. Accelerated depreciation
8. Tax depreciation
9. Recovery period class
10. Tax shield
11. Equivalent annual cost

Problems

1. The cash flows and the present values are given in the table below.

Cash flows ($1000s)

Years	0	1	2	3	4	5	6
1. Investment and salvage	-5,000						650[1]
2. Sales		2,000	4,000	6,000	6,600	7,260	7,986
3. Cost of goods sold		1,400	2,800	4,200	4,620	5,082	5,590
4. Depreciation		1,000	1,000	1,000	1,000	1,000	0
5. Pre-tax profit [2-3-4]		-400	200	800	980	1,178	2,396
6. Tax at 35% of 5		-140	70	280	343	412	839
7. Profit after tax [5-6]		-260	130	520	637	766	1,557
8. Operating cash flow [7+4]		740	1,130	1,520	1,637	1,766	1,557
9. Total cash flows [1+8]	-5,000	740	1,130	1,520	1,637	1,766	2,207
10. Present value at 16%	-5,000	638	840	974	904	841	906
11. Net present value	-5,000+638+840+974+841+906 = 103						

Notes: 1. Salvage value $1,000,000 less tax of $35,000 = $650,000

2. The real cash flows and the present values are given in the table below.

Cash flows ($1000s)

Years	0	1	2	3	4	5	6
1.Nomianl cash flows (same as in problem 1)	-5,000	740	1,130	1,520	1,637	1,766	2,207
2. Real cash flows[1]	-5,000	673	934	1,142	1,118	1,097	1,246
3. Present value at 5.45%	-5,000	638	840	974	904	841	906
4. Net present value	-5,000+638+840+974+841+906 = 103						

Notes: 1. The real cash flows are calculated by the following formula = $C_t/1.1^t$

3. See the table below.

Cash flows ($1000s)

Years	0	1	2	3	4	5	6
1. Investment and salvage	-5,000						650[1]
2. Sales		2,000	4,000	6,000	6,600	7,260	7,986
3. Cost of goods sold		1,400	2,800	4,200	4,620	5,082	5,590
4. Depreciation		1,000	1,600	960	576	576	288
5. Pre-tax profit [2-3-4]		-400	-400	840	1,404	1,602	2,108
6. Tax at 35% of 5		-140	-140	294	491	561	738
7. Profit after tax [5-6]		-260	-260	546	913	1,041	1,370
8. Operating cash flow [7+4]		740	1,340	1,506	1,489	1,617	1,658
9. Total cash flows [1+8]	-5,000	740	1,340	1,506	1,489	1,617	2,308
10. Present value at 16%	-5,000	638	996	965	822	770	947
11. Net present value	-5,000+638+996+965+822+770+947 = 138						

4. The tables below give the cash flows and the NPV for the 3 different scenarios.

Cash flows ($1000s)

	3- Year class	5 year class	7 year class
Investment	-40,000	-40,000	-40,000
PV of depreciation tax shield	10,719	9,662	8,778
Net revenues	29,747	29,747	29,747
Net present value	466	-591	-1,475

5. The NPV of purchasing the computer after t years is $(-200{,}000 \times 0.90^t + 40{,}000/0.13)/1.13^2$. This expression takes its maximum value of $114,098 (over integer t) for t = 2 years.

6. Present value of costs for A = $38,678, EAC = $22,286
   Present value of costs for B = $57,408, EAC = $23,085
   A is cheaper.

7. The maintenance cost at the end of year 1 is $5,000, year 2 is $5,000 x 1.15 = $5,750, and so on. You can calculate the PV of the maintenance costs and the initial investment of $100,000 and convert them into EACs for 5 years, 10 years, and so on. The lowest EAC is for 12 years as shown in the table below.

Years kept	PV of cost	Annuity factor	EAC (PV/Ann. Factor)
5	119,459	3.791	$31,512
10	149,192	6.145	$24,279
11	155,974	6.495	$24,014
12	163,063	6.814	$23,931
13	170,475	7.103	$24,000

8. The present value of total costs of the new machine is $24,663. This converts to an EAC of $4914.20. The costs of each year's operation of the old machine (adjusted to the end of each year) are given below.

Years	Cost of operation	How calculated
1	$3,175	(2000+2500)x1.15-2000
2	$4,250	(3000+2000)x1.15-1500
3	$5,325	(4000+1500)x1.15-1000
4	$6,900	(5000+1000)x1.15

The old machine should be replaced after 2 years.

9. Present-value cost of change in computer timing = $40,444. Present-value cost of extra programmer = $49,400.

10. The table below gives the present values of harvesting at different years.

Years	0	1	2	3	4
Net revenue	12,000	15,000	17,000	18,000	19,000
Present value at 15 %	12,000	13,040	12,854	11,835	10,863

The optimal timing will be to harvest at the end of year 1.

11. The real values will have to be discounted at the real rate of (1.15/1.05) - 1 = 9.5%. The table below gives the present values of harvesting at the end of different years.

Dollars in 1000s

Years	0	1	2	3	4
Net revenue	12,000	15,000	17,000	18,000	19,000
Present value at 9.5%	12,000	13,699	14,178	13,710	13,216

The optimal harvesting will be at the end of 2 years.

12. Present value of $150,000 received 5 years from now = $150,000/1.16^5 = $71,417
   Joe will be better off waiting 5 years.

7

Introduction to Risk, Return, and the Opportunity Cost of Capital

INTRODUCTION

Most investors generally dislike uncertainty or risk and agree that a safe dollar is worth more than a risky one. Investors will have to be persuaded to take higher risk by offering higher returns. This chapter is the first of the three chapters, which deal with the risk and return trade-off, and its implications to incorporate finance and the opportunity cost of capital for investments. The chapter deals with risk as faced by individual investors holding portfolios of securities. Later chapters will connect this to the opportunity cost of capital for corporations.

Chapter 7 starts with a detailed description of the historic performance of different securities in the U. S. capital markets. This lesson is used to provide basic benchmarks for risk and return. The chapter also describes how we can measure the risk of securities and the role of diversification in reducing risk. The statistical measures of variance and standard deviation are used to measure the risk of individual securities and portfolios. Individual stocks are more risky than portfolios. As the number of the stocks in a portfolio increases, the risk of the portfolio is reduced. The reduction in risk however levels off once the number of stocks in the portfolio reaches a certain number. Thus, there is a certain level of risk that you can never diversify away. This undiversifiable risk stems from economy-wide perils that affect all businesses; it is called market risk. The risk a security adds to a well-diversified portfolio depends on its market risk. This risk is called beta and finds extensive applications in later chapters.

Statistics: This chapter uses some basic statistical concepts and will be easy to follow if you already know some elementary statistics. The text gives all the necessary definitions, but you may want to refresh your memory from a statistics textbook. It will help if you are familiar with the terms such as variance, standard deviation, and covariance, and normal distribution.

KEY CONCEPTS IN THE CHAPTER

A Historic Lesson in Risk and Return: The chapter begins with a description of the performance of five different classes of securities over the 72-year period from 1926. The five portfolios are: the U. S. treasury bills, the long-term U. S. government bonds, long-term corporate bonds, common stocks of large companies represented by the Standard & Poor's 500 (popularly known as the S&P 500), and a portfolio of small firm common stocks. The five portfolios represent different risk classes. The treasury bills are considered risk-less and the benchmark for the safest investment possible. On the other extreme the portfolio of small-company stocks has provided the highest historic returns, but has also carried the highest level of risk. The S&P 500 portfolio is considered representative of the stock market as a whole. The portfolio, while comprising only 500 stocks of over 8,000 shares in the market, accounts for more than seventy percent of the market value. The historic returns for the Treasury bill portfolio have averaged 3.8 percent in nominal terms compared to the S&P 500 portfolio return of 13 percent and the small-firm portfolio's return of 17.7 percent. These historic averages are often used to estimate required rates of returns or opportunity cost of capital.

Use of historic returns: Historic data are often used for valuation or cost of capital estimation. Two types of average measures are calculated from the historic data: the arithmetic average and the geometric mean. The arithmetic average will be higher than the geometric mean and is the appropriate yardstick to use for valuation or cost of capital estimation.

Interest rates change frequently, and the expected return on the market will change with them. However, the risk premium on the market (the difference between the market return and the return on the risk-free investment (t-bill) is fairly stable. Therefore, when we wish to estimate today's expected return on the market portfolio, we should take today's treasury-bill yield and add to it the normal risk premium (the long-term average) equities have earned above treasury bills. As an example, the current t-bill yield is about 4.5 percent. The long-term average risk premium is 9.2 percent. Therefore, the expected market return can be estimated as $4.5 + 9.2 = 13.7$ percent.

Risk: The idea of risk is a familiar one and implies uncertain outcomes. It also means that there are a number of possible outcomes and some of the outcomes are not desirable. The return from an investment in a stock or a portfolio of common stocks cannot be predicted with any accuracy. It is risky. The use of statistics helps us to analyze this type of risk in a precise way. The spread of past returns gives a good indication of the range of uncertainty about future returns. Hence, the need for the history lesson above. The spread, or the uncertainty of outcomes, is measured by the standard deviation or the variance.

The standard deviation of the annual returns on the Standard & Poor's Composite Index over the 72 year period analyzed in the Brealey and Myers text is 20.3 percent compared to only 3.2 percent for the portfolios of treasury bills. The higher risk of the stock portfolio explains its high return, which is 9.2 percent over that of the t-bills.

Diversification and Risk: Diversification is an important concept with powerful implications. When stocks are combined into portfolios, it is observed that the risk of the portfolio decreases as the number of stocks in the portfolio increases. The risk in a diversified portfolio is lower than for a single security because the returns of different stocks do not move perfectly together. Statistically, individual stock returns are less than perfectly correlated. When we hold many stocks, the risks, which are unique to each one, tend to cancel, as they are largely unconnected. Some risks, though, stem from uncertainty about factors, which affect the whole of the market. This market risk cannot be eliminated by diversification and must be borne by investors, and investors can expect to earn a higher return for bearing it.

72

Calculation of Portfolio Returns and Risk Measures: The chapter describes how the expected return and standard deviation of a portfolio may be calculated from the characteristics of the individual stocks. It also describes how we can calculate the risk that a particular stock adds to an incompletely diversified portfolio. The section on formulas and computations describe the methods. If these seem too complicated to you, the chapter also gives the following useful rule of thumb to the benefits of diversification. The variance of a portfolio consisting of equal holdings of N stocks is equal to:

Average covariance + (1/N) (average variance – average covariance)

The average variance of annual returns on individual stocks is about 1,500, and the average covariance between pairs of stocks is about 400. As N becomes larger, 1/N becomes very small and the significance of the individual variances becomes less and less. Thus, the variance of the portfolio returns gets closer to the average covariance of 400. The standard deviation of the returns from a portfolio is simply the square root of their variance, and would approach 20 percent.

Beta: The contribution each security makes to the risk of a well-diversified portfolio depends on the security's covariance with other securities in the portfolio. This will depend on how sensitive it is to the changes in the market portfolio. Beta measures this sensitivity. The average stock return will tend to move up and down nearly in tandem with the market. It will move up 5 percent when the market moves up 5 percent. Of course, sometimes it will go up (or down) more or less than the market. However, on average, it moves one for one with the market. This means that its beta is 1. A stock that is more sensitive to market movements might tend to move twice as far (10 percent) in response to a market rise of 5 percent. Conversely, it would tend to fall 10 percent if the market fell 5 percent. This stock is twice as sensitive as the average, and its beta is 2.

The beta of a portfolio is the weighted average of the betas of the stocks included in it. In other words, if a portfolio consists of 30 percent of stocks with betas of 1.5 and 70 percent of stocks with betas of 0.8, the beta of the portfolio is (0.3 x 1.5) + (0.7 x 0.8) = 1.01. When a portfolio is well diversified, the amount of unique risk it contains is negligible. In this case, the standard deviation of the portfolio will be its beta multiplied by the standard deviation of the return on the market portfolio. This makes beta an important number. Beta measures how much a stock contributes to the risk of a well-diversified portfolio.

Diversification and Value Additivity: Diversification is good for individual investors. Since it would be relatively easy for investors to diversify directly by holding a variety of stocks, they have no reason to pay more for the stocks of companies, which are already diversified. This has implications for corporate attempts at diversification for the purpose of risk reduction. The implication is that the value of a project does not depend on how its returns mesh with the returns from other activities of the company, which undertakes it. If the capital market establishes a value

73

PV (A) for asset A and PV (B) for asset B, the market value of a firm that holds only these two assets is:

$$PV (AB) = PV (A) + PV (B)$$

This is known as the value-additivity principle.

Explanation of Formulas and Mathematical Expressions: The chapter describes a number of formulas for calculating expected returns, standard deviations, variances, and betas of securities and portfolios.

Expected return of portfolios: The expected return of a portfolio of stocks is the weighted average of the expected returns on the individual stocks. Expected portfolio return, r_p, i.e. given by:

$$r_p = x_1 r_1 + x_2 r_2 + \ldots\ldots + x_n r_n$$

where x_1 = proportion of portfolio in stock 1, r_1 = expected return on stock 1, etc.
Example: Stocks A, B and C have returns of 12 percent, 16 percent, and 11 percent respectively. What is the expected return of a portfolio which includes 40 percent of its value invested in A, 40 percent in B, and 20 percent in C?

$$\text{Expected return} = (0.4 \times 12) + (0.4 \times 16) + (0.2 \times 11) = 13.4 \%$$

Portfolio variance: Portfolio variance is not the simple weighted average of the individual standard deviations (unless they are perfectly correlated). The portfolio variance is a function of the individual variances of the different stocks and the covariance of all the pairs of stocks in the portfolio.

$$
\begin{aligned}
\text{Portfolio variance } &= x_1^2 \sigma_1^2 + x_1 x_2 \sigma_{12} + \cdots + x_1 x_N \sigma_{1N} \\
&+ x_1 x_2 \sigma_{12} + x_2^2 \sigma_2^2 + \cdots + x_2 x_N \sigma_{2N} \\
&+ \cdots + \cdots + \cdots \\
&+ x_N x_2 \sigma_{N1} + x_N x_2 \sigma_{N2} + \cdots + x_N^2 \sigma_N^2
\end{aligned}
$$

where, σ_1^2 = variance of stock 1 (σ_1 is its standard deviation)
σ_{12} = covariance between stock 1 and stock 2, = $\sigma_1 \sigma_2 \rho_{12}$, where ρ_{12} is the correlation between stock 1 and stock 2.

If there are N equal-size holdings (i.e. $x_i = 1/N$),
portfolio variance = $(1/N)^2 [N \times \text{average variance} + (N^2 - N) \times \text{average covariance}]$
$= \text{average covariance} + (1/N) \times (\text{average variance - covariance})$

A security's contribution to portfolio risk: From the top row of the portfolio variance calculation:

Stock l's contribution to risk = $x_1(x_1\sigma_1^2 + x_2\sigma_{12} + \cdots + x_N\sigma_{1N})$
Proportionate contribution to risk = $x_1\sigma_{1P}/\sigma_P^2$
where σ_{1P} is its covariance with the portfolio and σ_P^2 is the variance of the portfolio.

Here σ_{1P}/σ_P^2 is the sensitivity of stock 1 to changes in portfolio value.
Since σ_{1M}/σ_M^2 = beta, beta measures a stock's contribution to the risk of the market portfolio.

The effect of individual stocks on portfolio risk: The risk of a well-diversified portfolio depends on the market risk of the securities included in the portfolio. Beta (β) measures the market risk of a stock as its sensitivity to market movements. Stocks with betas greater than one are usually more sensitive (than the average stock) to market movements. Stocks with betas less than one are less sensitive to market movements. The beta of a portfolio is the weighted average of the beta of the securities included in it. That is,

$$\beta_P = x_1\beta_1 + x_2\beta_2 + \cdots + x_N\beta_N$$

The standard deviation of a well-diversified portfolio is its beta times the standard deviation of the market portfolio. A diversified portfolio of high-beta stocks is therefore more risky than a diversified portfolio of low-beta stocks. Beta is important because it measures how much a stock contributes to the risk of a well-diversified portfolio.

WORKED EXAMPLES

1. The Treasury bill rate is 3.5 percent. The market risk premium (the difference between the return on the market portfolio and that on Treasury Bills) has historically been about 9.2 percent, and the standard deviation of annual market returns has been about 20 percent. Flybynight Funds offer you a mutual fund with an expected annual return of 21 percent with a standard deviation of 20 percent.

SOLUTION

The market portfolio offers an expected return of 12.7 percent (3.5 + 9.2) with a standard deviation of 20 percent. The prospective investment seems to offer a greater expected reward with less risk and therefore looks attractive! However, you might want to check out the antecedents of the company.

2. Calculate the standard deviation and expected return for the portfolio given below, and work out how each stock contributes to the portfolio's risk.

Stock	Percentage held	Expected return	Standard deviation	Correlation among stocks		
				Stock 1	Stock 2	Stock 3
Stock 1	40	15	18	1	0.1	0.4
Stock 2	30	16	24	0.1	1	0.5
Stock 3	30	20	36	0.4	0.5	1

SOLUTION

To work out the standard deviation of a portfolio, we need to first calculate the covariance between stocks.

Covariance $\sigma_{ij} = \sigma_i \sigma_j \rho_{ij}$

Given below is a table of all the covariances. All values are rounded off to whole numbers.

Stocks	Stock 1	Stock 2	Stock 3
Stock 1	18x18x1 = 324	18x24x0.1 = 43	18x36x0.4 = 259
Stock 2	24x18x0.1 = 43	24x24x1 = 576	24x36x0.5 = 432
Stock 3	36x18x0.4 = 259	36x24x0.5 = 432	36x36x1 = 1296

Notice that this table is symmetric about the diagonal (that is, $\sigma_{12} = \sigma_{21}, \sigma_{13} = \sigma_{31}$, etc.). To get the portfolio covariance, each covariance (σ_{ij}) is multiplied by the percentages held in each of the stocks ($x_i x_j$). The table below gives the values for covariance multiplied by the corresponding $x_i x_j$.

Stocks	Stock 1	Stock 2	Stock 3
Stock 1	0.4x0.4x324 = 51.8	0.4x0.3x43 = 5.2	0.4x0.3x259 = 31.1
Stock 2	0.3x0.4x43 = 5.2	0.3x0.3x576 = 51.8	0.3x0.3x432 = 38.9
Stock 3	0.3x0.4x259 = 31.1	0.3x0.3x432 = 38.9	0.3x0.3x1296 = 116.6

The portfolio variance is the sum of the values all the cells.

Portfolio variance = 51.8 + 51.8 + 116.6 + 2(5.2 + 31.1 + 38.9) = 370.6

Portfolio standard deviation = $\sqrt{370.6}$ = 19.25 %

Portfolio return = (0.4 x 15) + (0.3 x 16) + (0.3 x 20) = 16.8 %

The sum of each row in the variance calculation shows how much each stock contributes to the total variance.

Contribution by stock 1 = σ_{1P}/σ_P^2 = (51.8 + 5.2 + 31.1)/370.9 = 0.24
Contribution by stock 2 = σ_{2P}/σ_P^2 = (5.2 + 52.1 + 38.9)/370.9 = 0.26
Contribution by stock 3 = σ_{3P}/σ_P^2 = (31.1 + 38.9 + 116.6)/370.9 = 0.50

To get the sensitivity of each stock to changes in the portfolio value or beta of the stock with respect to this portfolio, we need to divide the proportionate contribution by the percentage of each stock in the portfolio.

$$\beta_1 = 0.24/0.4 = 0.6, \ \beta_2 = 0.26/0.3 = 0.87, \ \beta_1 = 0.50/0.3 = 1.67$$
(Note that these are betas with respect to this portfolio and not the market.)

3. Bulldog Fund has three stocks in its portfolio. The percentage of each stock held and the beta for each stock are: Stock A – 35%, beta = 1.2; Stock B – 45%, beta = 0.9, Stock C – 20%, beta = 1.8. Calculate the portfolio beta.

SOLUTION

Portfolio beta = (0.35 x 1.2) + (0.45 x 0.9) + (0.2 x 1.8) = 1.19

SUMMARY

This chapter provides the first formal introduction to risk and the measurement of risk. The chapter starts with a succinct description of the history of the U. S. capital market from 1926. This history lesson is a useful way to understand the risk-return trade off faced by an investor in the capital market. The market performance provides useful benchmarks of risk and return with the U. S. Treasury bills as the risk-free investment and the market portfolio of common stocks as the risky investment with significantly higher expected return. Later chapters use these benchmarks for modeling the risk and expected return of an investment.

The chapter also introduces you to the effects of diversification. Shareholders can, and do, reduce their risk very significantly by diversification. The risk that matters to them is, therefore, the market risk that each security adds to a diversified portfolio. This leads to the risk measure, beta, which is the sensitivity of a security's return to the return on the market portfolio. It is the beta of a security, that determines how much risk that security contributes to a diversified portfolio. Later chapters will revisit beta and it will be a very useful tool in estimating the opportunity cost of capital for investment projects.

The value of diversification does not imply that corporations can create shareholder value by diversifying their business assets. The value of a project depends only on its cash flows and its market risk and not on how well its returns relate to the other activities of the company. This implies value additivity: the value of project A and the value of project B combined is simply the sum of value of A and the value of B.

LIST OF TERMS

Beta (β)
Correlation
Covariance
Diversification
Expected market return (r_m)
Expected return
Market portfolio
Market return

Market risk
Market risk premium (r_m - r_f)
Risk-free rate of return (r_f)
Standard deviation (σ)
Unique risk
Value additivity
Variability
Variance (σ^2)

EXERCISES

Fill-in Questions

1. Combining stocks into a portfolio provides an investor _____ and risk reduction.

2. The difference between the risk free rate and the _____ is called the _____.

3. Standard & Poor's Composite Index is often regarded as the_____.

4. Diversification cannot eliminate all risk because all stocks are subject to _____.

5. The average annual _____ between 1926 and 1997 was 13 percent.

6. Diversification reduces _____.

7. The principle of _____ means that PV(AB) = PV(A) + PV(B).

8. The _____ of the market as a whole is one.

9. The _____ of the S&P 500 portfolio has averaged about 20 percent over the 72-year period of 1926 to 1997.

10. Projects, which have the same risk as the market portfolio, can be evaluated by a discount rate equal to the _____ plus the normal risk premium for the market portfolio.

11. The contribution a stock makes to the portfolio risk is measured by its _____.

12. _____ is the square of standard deviation.

13. The covariance between two stocks is the product of their standard deviations and the _____ coefficient between them.

14. The variability of a well-diversified portfolio depends almost entirely on the average _____ between individual stocks.

Problems

1. S. T. Poor & Company is considering investing in a project which has risk similar to the market risk. The current risk free rate as measured by the rate on treasury bills is 4.5% and the average for the last three years was 5.2 percent. The return on the S&P 500 portfolio for the last three years were 22 percent, 32 percent, and 35 percent. Suggest an appropriate discount rate for the project.

2. Stock A has an expected return of 16 percent and standard deviation of 28 percent. Stock B has an expected return of 21 percent and standard deviation of 36 percent. Calculate the expected return and standard deviation of a portfolio which is invested equally in the two stocks if the correlation coefficient between the stock returns is: (a) 1, (b) 0.5, and (c) –0.5.

3. Refer to the problem 2 above. If the correlation coefficients of stock returns of A and B to the market portfolio were 0.7 and 0.3 respectively and the standard deviation of market returns is 14 percent, what will be the betas for A and B?

4. A portfolio of stocks has risks similar to a portfolio consisting of 40 percent of Treasury bills and 60 percent of Standard & Poor's index. The Treasury bill rate is 5 percent, and you expect a normal risk premium of 9 percent on Standard & Poor's index. What return would you expect from the portfolio of stocks?

5. Refer to problem 4. What will be the beta of the portfolio?

6. Your investment will give a return of either -10 or +30 percent. (a) Calculate the expected return and the standard deviation of return if these outcomes are equally likely. (b) Calculate them if there is a 0.6 probability of the -10 percent return and a 0.4 probability of the +30 percent return.

7. A portfolio consists of the three stocks with betas of 0.8, 1.4, and 1.6. If the portfolio is equally invested in each stock, what is the portfolio beta?

8. The diagram below shows the effect of diversification. Label the diagram with appropriate words for the different letters.

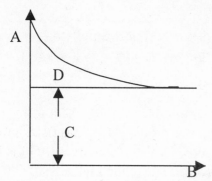

9. Details of the stocks held in a portfolio are given below.

Stocks	Beta	Expected return	Percentage held
Stock A	1.1	14	25
Stock B	0.8	10	18
Stock C	1.4	17	23
Stock D	1.5	19	34

Calculate the expected return and the beta of this portfolio.

10. Calculate the betas of the following stocks if the standard deviation of the market returns is 14 percent.

Stocks	Standard deviation	Correlation coefficient with the market portfolio
Stock P	18%	0.7
Stock Q	24%	0.3
Stock R	38%	0.5
Stock S	42%	0.2

11. The average variance of the annual returns from a typical stock is about 1,500, and its average covariance with other stocks is about 400. Work out what this implies for the standard deviation of returns from: (a) a fully diversified portfolio, (b) a portfolio of 64 stocks, (c) a portfolio of 16 stocks, (d) a portfolio of 4 stocks. Assume equal-size holdings of each stock.

12. You hold a portfolio of 16 Stocks, each of which has a variance of 1,500 and a covariance of 400 with the other stocks. One stock comprises 25 percent of your portfolio, and the other stocks are held in equal amounts of 5 percent each. (a) What is the standard deviation of your portfolio? (b) How many stocks held in equal amounts would give approximately the same standard deviation?

Essay Questions

1. Corporate diversification is good for the stockholders as it reduces the risk of the firm. Discuss.

2. Why is it that diversification cannot eliminate all the risk?

3. Describe what is meant by the beta of a stock. Why is a stock's beta more important than its standard deviation?

4. Is it possible for a company's stocks to have a high standard deviation but a low beta? What kind of industries will this stock belong to?

5. Stockholders of publicly quoted companies do not benefit from corporate diversification since they can diversify for themselves. Discuss under what conditions (if any) this principle extends to the case of a privately held company which is 100 percent owned by a single individual.

ANSWERS TO EXERCISES

Fill-in Questions

1. Diversification
2. Expected market return, market risk premium
3. Market portfolio
4. Market risk
5. Market return
6. Unique risk
7. Value additivity

8. Beta
9. Standard deviation
10. Risk free rate
11. Beta
12. Variance
13. Correlation
14. Covariance

Problems

1. Discount rate = risk-free rate + risk premium
   = 4.5 percent + 9.2 percent
   = 13.7 percent

2. Expected return = (0.5 x 16) + (0.5 x 21) = 18.5 percent

   a. Variance of the portfolio = $0.5 \times 0.5 \times 28^2 + 2 \times 0.5 \times 0.5 \times 28 \times 36 \times 1 + 0.5 \times 0.5 \times 36^2$
      = 1024, standard deviation = 32 [Since the correlation coefficient is 1, the standard deviation will be the weighted average of the standard deviations of the two stocks.
   b. Variance = 772, Standard deviation = 27.8 percent.
   c. Variance = 268, Standard deviation = 16.4 percent.

3. $\beta_A = (28/14) \times 0.7 = 1.4$, $\beta_B = (36/14) \times 0.3 = 0.8$

4. expected return = $(0.4 \times 5) + 0.6 \times (5+9) = 10.4$ percent

5. Beta of the portfolio = $(0.4 \times 0) + (0.6 \times 1) = 0.6$ (The T-bill being risk-free will have beta of zero.)

6. a. Expected return = 10 percent, Standard deviation = 20 percent.
    b. Expected return = 6 percent, Standard deviation = 19.6 percent.

7. Portfolio beta = $(0.8 + 1.4 + 1.6)/3 = 1.27$

8. A = Portfolio standard deviation, B = Number of stocks, C = Market risk, D = Unique risk

9. Expected return = $(0.25 \times 14) + (0.18 \times 10) + (0.23 \times 17) + (0.34 \times 19) = 15.67$ percent
    Portfolio beta = $(0.25 \times 1.1) + (0.18 \times 0.8) + (0.23 \times 1.4) + (0.34 \times 1.5) = 1.25$

10. $\beta_P = (18/14) \times 0.7 = 0.9$, $\beta_Q = 0.51$, $\beta_R = 1.36$, $\beta_S = 0.6$

11. Portfolio variance = Average covariance + $(1/N)$ (Average variance – Average covariance).
    For fully diversified portfolio, N is very large and Portfolio variance = Average covariance.
    For others substitute the value of $N = 64$, 16, and 4 to get the answers.
    a. Standard deviation = Square root of $400 = 20$ percent;   b. 20.43 percent;
    c. 21.65 percent; d. 25.98

12. a. Variance = 510, Standard deviation = 22.58 percent.
    b. Variance = $400 + (1/N)(1500-400) = 510$, Solving for N, $N = 10$

8

Risk and Return

INTRODUCTION

Chapter 7 introduced risk and risk measurement. The chapter also showed us how diversification enables an investor to reduce risk, but that there is a limit to risk reduction. Only risk unique to individual securities can be diversified away; the risk that a security bears as part of the overall economic system remains in the portfolio. This risk was termed market risk. This chapter builds on the lessons of chapter 7 and presents formal models linking risk and expected return. The chapter begins with a discussion on portfolio theory pioneered by Harry Markowitz. This theory formed the basis for the most popular and widely used model of risk-return relationship: the Capital Asset Pricing Model or CAPM. The CAPM has some empirical evidence to support the basic conclusions derived from the model. Recently, it has been challenged by other theories that purport to rely on assumptions less restrictive than the ones used by CAPM. The chapter presents three alternate theories to CAPM. While CAPM is far from perfect, it remains the most widely accepted model, primarily because of its relative simplicity and ease of application.

KEY CONCEPTS IN THE CHAPTER

Portfolio Theory: Stock market returns of individual stocks covering relatively short periods closely approximate the normal distribution. This enables one to describe the entire distribution of the returns in terms of two parameters- the mean and standard deviation. Individual investors are assumed to be risk-averse, meaning that they would like to be compensated for bearing more risk. This also means that they like higher returns and lower risk. The standard deviation of returns measures risk.

The portfolio theory gives the basic principles of selecting the optimal portfolio in terms of risk and return. We learned in the last chapter that when two stocks are combined into a portfolio, the risk (standard deviation of the portfolio) is less than the average of the two individual standard deviations. Of course, when combining securities into a portfolio, an infinite number of combinations are possible. But investors would choose only those which are *efficient portfolios*. Portfolios are considered efficient if, for a given standard deviation, they give the highest return, or for a given return they have the lowest standard deviation. Investors need only consider efficient portfolios, for all other portfolios give them a poor deal.

Investors have more than two stocks to choose and we can extend the idea of efficient portfolio to the universe of available securities. All the efficient portfolios can be identified and depending on one's own risk-return preference, an investor can choose the best portfolio of his liking. The technique of *quadratic programming* can be used to choose the efficient portfolio of one's preference. If one were to graph the set of all efficient portfolios selected from all the stocks available it will look like the curve shown in Figure 1. Every investor will only choose a portfolio on this curve. Any choice not on the efficient set will be dominated by a portfolio on the efficient set. The curve BC represents all the available efficient portfolios.

Figure 1

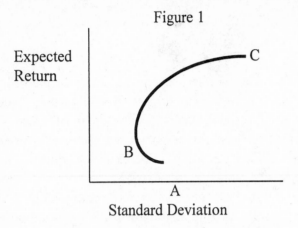

Investors' choices can be expanded by introducing the possibility of lending or borrowing at the risk-free rate. This will allow the investors to combine investing in the stock portfolios given by the efficient set with lending or borrowing (borrowing can be seen as negative lending). The possibilities are shown in Figure 2.

Figure 2

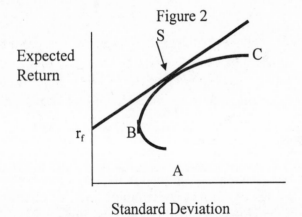

The figure shows that investors can choose along the line starting from the risk-free rate to the portfolio S. If the investor chooses to invest all her money in risk-free lending, she will have the risk-free rate at zero standard deviation. Any point between r_f and S will have part of the money invested in the stock portfolio S and the remaining lent at the risk-free rate. Any investor is free to choose points to the right of S. This would mean that the investor is borrowing money at the risk free rate and investing that along with his own money in portfolio S. You can clearly see that regardless of where the investor wants to be, the stock portfolio will be the same, namely the portfolio S. In other words, S is the best of all the efficient portfolios and every investor will be invested in this portfolio. This will also mean that every stock will be held as part of this portfolio.

An investor's job can be separated into two parts: first, to choose the best (risky) portfolio of stocks S and, second, to combine it with the right amount of lending or borrowing to adjust to the preferred level of risk. This is known as the separation theorem: the job of selecting individual stocks in one's portfolio can be independently of one's risk preference. In a competitive market, there is no reason to concentrate portfolios in particular stocks, and we can identify S as the market portfolio. Everyone holds S. Risk preference only decides what fraction of one's investment goes to S.

Capital Asset Pricing Model: Capital Asset Pricing Model (CAPM) is an extension of what we saw in Figure 2. Investing in risky assets such as the market portfolio, S, should carry a premium compared to the risk-free rate. Otherwise, investors will not take the risk. The market portfolio is the basic benchmark of risk in the CAPM. The risk premium on the market portfolio, measured as the difference between the market return and the risk-free rate is called the market risk premium. The beta for the market portfolio is 1. The CAPM postulates a linear relationship between risk and return as shown in Figure 3. Figure 3 shows the *security market line* (SML).

Figure 3

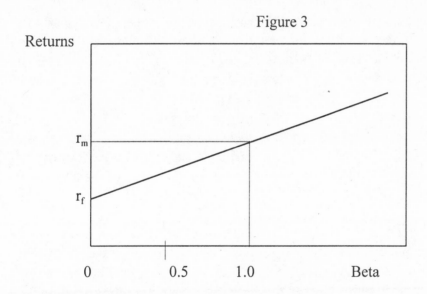

The risk of each stock is measured by its beta and the risk premium varies in direct proportion to beta. All stocks will lie along the SML and the expected return on a stock can be calculated by adding the risk premium to the risk-free rate.

Expected risk premium = $r - r_f = \beta(r_m - r_f)$

A key implication of the CAPM is that it is the risk of a stock that matters in its contribution to portfolio risk. This is what is measured by beta and it depends on the stock's sensitivity to changes in the value of the market portfolio.

Validity of CAPM: Over the years, a lot of research has been done to test the validity of CAPM.

Remember, however, the CAPM is a theory about expected returns. We can only measure actual returns. This makes it difficult to test the theory as it is conceived. Another problem in testing CAPM is that the market portfolio should include all assets, not just stocks traded in stock exchanges. In practice, most of the tests use stock market indexes such as the S & P 500 as proxies for the market portfolio.

One of the best known tests of the CAPM's validity involved analyzing portfolio returns over the period 1931 to 1991. The study, conducted by Fischer Black, grouped all New York Stock Exchange stocks into 10 portfolios selected according to the ranking of the betas of their stocks. Every year these portfolios were readjusted, using monthly data from the previous 5 years, so that portfolio 1 always contained the 10 percent of stocks with the lowest betas, portfolio 9 the next 10 percent, up to portfolio 10 with the highest beta stocks. The performance of these portfolios was assessed over the 60-year period. The results showed a strong positive relationship between beta and returns and thus broad support for the CAPM. However, it was found that the security market line was flatter than the theory predicted and it was above the risk-free rate.

In recent years, the relationship between beta and the risk premium has been particularly flat. It has been argued that some of these results could be attributed to sampling errors (the realized average returns are not the same as the previously expected ones). There is also evidence that suggests that beta is not the only factor that affects expected returns. Firms, which are small, and ones, which have low market-to-book ratios, seem to provide higher average returns irrespective of their betas. It is difficult to judge the economic significance of these results. The small-firm effect is found to be less in more recent studies. It is also possible that some of the results which cast doubts on the validity of the CAPM can be produced by statistical strategies (known as "data mining"). The supporters of the CAPM believe that the broad conclusions of the theory are valid.

Consumption CAPM: The consumption CAPM is an alternate theory to the CAPM. The CAPM assumes that investors are concerned with their wealth and uncertainty about the same. The consumption CAPM holds that risk and expected return should be related to changes in investors' aggregate consumption rather than their wealth. Investors' wealth is not directly relevant to the stock returns. One need not worry about defining the market portfolio. However, you have to estimate aggregate consumption and its changes. Empirically, it is observed that estimated aggregate consumption changes rather gradually through time. This does not give a good explanation of past average rates of return. In short, the model has not caught on and its practical appeal seems limited.

Arbitrage Pricing Theory: The arbitrage pricing theory (APT) was the first serious challenger to CAPM. It does not involve many of the restrictive assumptions of CAPM. It postulates that each stock's return depends on several pervasive macroeconomic factors and the risk premium depends on the factor weights. The general model can be written as:

$$\text{Return} = a + b_1(\text{factor 1}) + b_2(\text{factor 2}) + \cdots$$

Alternately, the risk premium: $r - r_f = b_1(premium_1) + b_2(premium_2) + \cdots$

The APT is general and has appealing features. The market portfolio has a role in the model and thus we need not be concerned with measuring the same. The model is general and is dependent on the absence of arbitrage opportunities. The model does not specify either the number of factors or identity of these factors. The major problem is that there is little agreement on what the factors are. There have been many empirical attempts at identifying the factors. These have been met with limited success. The APT is still a long way from replacing the CAPM as the primary theory for risk-return relationship.

The Three-Factor Model: Eugene Fama and Kenneth French incorporate the small-firm effect and the book-to-market ratio effect seen in empirical studies into a formal risk-return relationship model. The model can be represented as:

$$r - r_f = b_{market}(r_{1market-factor}) + b_{size}(r_{size\ factor}) + b_{market-to-book}(r_{market-to-book})$$

The model is a practical extension of CAPM.

WORKED EXAMPLES

1. Mr. Hernandez wants to invest $10,000. He has a choice of a risky portfolio, M, of stocks with an expected return of 15 percent and a standard deviation of 18 percent. He can also lend and borrow at the risk-free rate of 6 percent. Show how he can construct a portfolio with standard deviations of (a) 9 percent, (b) 27 percent, and (c) 36 percent. Calculate the expected return for each of these portfolios.

SOLUTION

Since the standard deviation of lending or borrowing at the risk free rate is zero, the portfolio standard deviation is the fraction invested in M multiplied by its standard deviation. Thus if he invests half of his money ($5,000) in M, the portfolio standard deviation will be: 0.5 x 18 = 9 percent. If he borrows $5,000 and invests $15,000 ($10,000 of his own plus the borrowed $5,000) in M, the standard deviation of his investment portfolio will be 1.5 x 18 = 27 percent. Similarly, to get a portfolio with standard deviation of 36 percent, he will have to borrow $10,000 and invest $20,000 in M. The expected return for each portfolio will be:

a. (0.5 x 6) + (0.5 x 15) = 10.5%
b. (1.5 x 15) – (0.5 x 6) = 19.5
c. (2 x 15) – (1 x 6) = 24%

2. The Treasury bill rate is 5 percent and the market portfolio return is expected to be 13 percent.
    a. What is the market risk premium?

b. What is required rate of return on an investment which has a beta of 1.6?

c. If the expected return on Joy Wish Corp. stock is 17 percent, what is its beta?

d. If an investment with a beta of 1.8 were expected to give a return of 19 percent, would you accept it?

SOLUTION

a. Market risk premium = 13 – 5 = 8%

b. Required rate of return for an investment of beta of 1.6 = 5 + 1.6(13 - 5) = 17.8%

c. Return = $5 + \beta(8) = 17$, $\beta = \dfrac{17-5}{8} = 1.5$

d. Required rate of return = 5 + 1.8(8) = 19.4 %. The investment return is less than the required rate of return. Hence, its NPV will be negative.

3. ABC Corp. wishes to use the Fama-French 3-factor model to estimate its cost of equity capital. The company has estimated the following factor sensitivities and factor risk premiums:

Factors	Factor Sensitivity	Factor risk premium
Market factor	1.5	5.2 percent
Size factor	-0.4	3.2
Book-to-market factor	0.2	5.4

If the risk free rate is 6 percent, estimate the cost of equity capital for the firm.

SOLUTION

Risk premium = $1.5x5.2 – 0.4x3.2 + 0.2x5.4 = 7.60$ percent
Cost of equity capital = $6 + 7.6 = 13.60$ percent.

SUMMARY

The chapter describes the basic principles of portfolio selection and the theories of which provide formal models of the linkage between risk and return. Risk averse investors choose portfolios based on risk and return. It makes sense to choose only efficient portfolios--portfolios which provide the highest return for a given level of risk. In presence of the possibility of risk-free lending and borrowing, investors will end up choosing the one portfolio that, in combination with risk-free lending/borrowing, gives the best choices regardless of one's own risk preferences. This forms the basis for the widely accepted theory, Capital Asset Pricing Model. The CAPM uses the market portfolio as the basic benchmark for risky investments and the risk of any stock or investment is measured relative to the market portfolio. The risk measure is beta and it reflects the stock's sensitivity to changes in the value of the market portfolio. The risk-return relationship is captured by the security market line and the risk premium on any stock is proportional to its beta.

The CAPM theory finds some empirical support, though recently questions have been raised about the strict validity of the security market line. Alternate theories of risk-return relationship include the consumption CAPM, the arbitrage pricing theory, and the three-factor model. Each of these theories has intellectual appeal and might someday prove to be a replacement to the CAPM; however for the present the CAPM still rules. The primary attraction of the CAPM is its relative simplicity and ease of practical application. The CAPM should be seen as an approximate and partial explanation of the risk-return trade off faced by the investor. We will find many applications of the CAPM in the later chapters.

LIST OF TERMS

Arbitrage pricing theory
Capital Asset Pricing Model
Consumption beta
Consumption CAPM
Efficient portfolios
Expected risk premium

Market risk premium
Normal distribution
Quadratic programming
Security market line
Three-factor model

EXERCISES

Fill-in Questions

1. The _____ uses less restrictive assumptions than the CAPM does and postulates that returns are dependent on pervasive macroeconomic factors.

2. The distribution of stock returns when considered over fairly short periods, closely follow _____.

3. A(n) _____ is a portfolio that gives the highest expected return for a given standard deviation or the lowest standard deviation for a given return.

4. Fama and French proposed the _____.

5. Optimal portfolio selection can be done using the_____ technique.

6. The _____ relates the risk premium to the sensitivity of the investment to changes in consumption, and this sensitivity measure is called the _____.

7. The _____ relates the risk premium to sensitivity of the asset's returns to changes in the value of the market portfolio.

8. The expected return on a stock investment, according to CAPM, equals the risk free rate plus
_____.

9. The difference between the expected market return and the risk-free rate is _____.

10. According to the CAPM, the expected returns from all investments must plot along the
_____.

Problems

1. Pick the better investment from each of the following pairs of portfolios.
   a. Portfolio A: expected return 14 percent, variance 400.
      Portfolio B: expected return 13 percent, variance 441.
   b. Portfolio J: expected return 20 percent, variance 529.
      Portfolio K: expected return 20 percent, variance 400.
   c. Portfolio R: expected return 8 percent, variance 225.
      Portfolio S: expected return 9 percent, variance 225.
   d. Portfolio X: expected return 12 percent, variance 380.
      Portfolio Y: expected return 15 percent, variance 460.

2. Calculate the expected return for the following portfolios:
   a. beta = 1.2
   b. beta = 1.8
   c. beta = 0.5
   d. beta = 0
   Assume the risk free rate to be 6 percent and the expected market risk premium to equal 15 percent.

3. Your broker is urging you to invest in one of three portfolios on which the returns are expected to be as follows: portfolio A, 12 percent; portfolio B, 16 percent; portfolio C, 20 percent. You believe these estimates, but you also have sufficient data to calculate the betas of the portfolios with confidence. You find the betas are 0.5 for A, 1.1 for B, and 2.0 for C. Which portfolio is best and why? (Hint: See if you can duplicate portfolio B by some combination of A and C.)

4. Stock J has a beta of 1.2 and an expected return of 15.6 percent, and stock K has a beta of 0.8 and an expected return of 12.4 percent. What must be (a) the expected return on the market and (b) the risk-free rate of return, to be consistent with the capital asset pricing model?

5. Stock A has an expected return of 14 percent and a beta of 1.1. Stock B has an expected return of 18. The risk free rate is 5.2 percent. Assume that stock A is correctly priced (i.e. it is on the security market line). If stock B has a beta of 1.4, is it correctly priced?

6. An alternate form of the CAPM is written as: $r = \alpha + \beta r_m$. Write a general expression for

α and find the value for α for each of the following cases: (a) beta = 1, (b) beta = 2, and (c) beta = 0. What is the value of beta if α = zero?

7. The return on a proposed investment is expected to be 24 percent. The standard deviation is estimated at 24 percent. The risk free rate is 6 percent. Assume the expected market risk premium to be 9 percent. Assume that the standard deviation of market returns to be 15 percent. If the project correlates fairly highly with the economy, comment on the attractiveness of the project.

8. You are told that MM Inc. stock has a beta of 1.3. Estimate its cost of equity capital.

9. A three factor APT model has the following factors and risk premiums:

Factors	Risk premiums
Change in GNP	4 %
Change in dollar exchange rates	-2
Change in energy prices	-1

Calculate the expected rates of return on the following stocks, assuming the risk-free rate to be 5.5 percent.
   a. Company A: $b_1 = 0.5$, $b_2 = -1.5$, $b_3 = 0.3$
   b. Company B: $b_1 = 1.2$, $b_2 = 0$, $b_3 = -0.5$
   c. Company C: $b_1 = 2$, $b_2 = 0.5$, $b_3 = -2$

10. Use the information on factor risk premiums from the worked example three-factor model problem to calculate the required rate of return on the following stocks with factor sensitivities to market, size, and book-to-market as follows:
   a. Factor sensitivities: 1.2, 2, and 0
   b. Factor sensitivities: 1.5, 0.3, and 1
   c. Factor sensitivities: 0.5, 0, and 1.5

11. Can a security have a negative expected rate of return and still considered to be correctly priced? What will be its beta?

Essay Questions

1. Explain the basic principles of portfolio theory. What is an efficient portfolio?

2. Explain the separation theorem and how it leads to all investors choosing the same portfolio of common stocks.

3. Compare and contrast the CAPM, consumption CAPM, and the APT.

4. The CAPM can be considered a special case of the APT. Discuss.

ANSWERS TO EXERCISES

Fill-in Questions

1. Arbitrage pricing theory
2. Normal distribution
3. Efficient portfolio
4. The three-factor model
5. Quadratic programming

6. Consumption CAPM, consumption beta
7. Capital asset pricing model
8. Risk premium
9. Market risk premium
10. Security market line

Problems

1. The efficient portfolios are:
   a. Portfolio A - higher return, lower variance
   b. Portfolio K - same return, lower variance
   c. Portfolio S - higher return, same variance
   d. Cannot decide between the two without knowing the investor's risk preference

2. The expected returns can be calculated by the formula: $r = r_f + \beta(r_m - r_f)$
   a. $r = 6 + 1.2(9) = 16.8\%$
   b. $r = 22.2\%$
   c. $r = 10.5\%$
   d. $r = 6\%$

3. A portfolio containing 60 percent A and 40 percent C will have the same beta as that of B but has lower return (15.2 %) than that of B. Thus, B is a better choice.

4. $r_f + 1.2(r_m - r_f) = 16$, $r_f + 0.8(r_m - r_f) = 12.4$ Solving for r_f and r_m, gives you: $r_f = 6$ percent, $r_m = 14$ percent.

5. Stock A return $= 5.2 + 1.1(r_m - 5.2) = 14$, $r_m = 13.2$ percent.
   Expected return for B, as per CAPM $= 5.2 + 1.4(13.2 - 5.2) = 16.4$ percent.
   This is lower than the expected return given. Stock B will not be on the SML.

6. $\alpha = (1 - \beta)r_f$
   a. If $\beta = 1$, $\alpha = 0$.
   b. If $\beta = 2$, $\alpha = -r_f$
   c. If $\beta = 0$, $\alpha = r_f$
   If $\alpha = 0$, $\beta = 1$

7. Beta for the project $= \dfrac{\rho_{mp}\sigma_p}{\sigma_m}$, where ρ_{mp} is the correlation coefficient for the project returns with the market returns and σ_p and σ_m the standard deviation of the project returns and the market returns respectively. If the correlation coefficient is positive 1 (the highest possible

value), the beta for the project will be = 24/15 = 1.6. Substituting the values in the CAPM formula for required rate of return, you get required return = 6 + 1.6(9) = 20.4 percent. The project's return is higher than this and it appears to be a good project.

8. Based on historic market risk premium of about 9.2 percent, the risk premium for this stock will be 1.3x9.2 = 12 percent. Add this to the current risk-free rate to get an estimate of the cost of equity capital.

9. The returns for the different stocks are:
   a. r = 5.5 + 0.5(4) - 1.5(-2) + 0.3 (-1) = 10.2 %
   b. r = 5.5 + 1.2(4) + 0 -0.5(-1) = 10.8 %
   c. r = 5.5 + 2.0(4) + 0.5(-2) -2(-1) = 14.5 %

10. The returns are:
   a. r = 6 + 1.2(5.2) + 2(3.2) + 0 = 18.64 %
   b. r = 6 + 1.5(5.2) + 0.3(3.2) + 1(5.4) = 20.16 %
   c. r = 6 + 0.5(5.2) + 0 + 1.5(5.4) = 16.70%

9

Capital Budgeting and Risk

INTRODUCTION

One of the most common and important applications of the CAPM involves estimation of the company cost of capital and required return for projects. Chapter 9 describes this application in detail. It is important to remember that the required rate of return on a project is a function of the risk of the project and does not depend on whom or which company undertakes it. The risk of the project, which is relevant, is, of course, its market risk or beta and not the total risk. A company's stock beta and its cost of capital reflect the nature of all its assets as well as the financial leverage or the debt it carries in its balance sheet. Using the company cost of capital as the discount rate for all its new projects would be a serious error. Nevertheless, we may still want to know what return is expected from the securities of a company. From this, we can work out what return is required from projects whose risks are similar to those of the company's existing business. Riskier projects should have a higher hurdle rate and safer projects a lower cutoff rate.

The chapter also discusses estimation of betas for companies using market information and the relationship between beta, financial leverage, and operating leverage. We can estimate the beta of a stock by comparing the stock's returns over time against the market returns. However, individual company beta estimates tend to be unstable and it is often better to calculate the beta for the industry group to which the company belongs.

Other related topics covered in the chapter include the risk and betas for foreign projects and the common, but often erroneous, practice of using arbitrary risk premiums (fudge factors) to adjust for projects considered risky. The concept of certainty equivalent, an alternate approach to adjust for the risk of cash flows, is also explained in this chapter.

Most of the discussions on risk-adjusted returns in the chapter use the CAPM as the theoretical risk-return model. The basic principles covered apply to alternate models like the APT or the three-factor model as well.

KEY CONCEPTS IN THE CHAPTER

Project Risk, Required Rate of Return, and Cost of Capital: We have already learned that diversified investors require returns on their investment based on the market risk or non-diversifiable risk of their investments. The required rate of return on a project should thus be a function of only its market risk or beta. It should not make any difference as to which company undertakes the project. This follows directly from the CAPM and the value additivity principle. Thus, the discount rate used to evaluate a project should be estimated using the project's beta.

Cost of capital for a company is the required rate of return demanded by the investors on the securities issued by the company. In practice, this is the weighted average of the return on the company's securities, typically debt and equity. Companies estimate their cost of capital using market data and use this company cost of capital as the discount rate for evaluating new projects. Typically the estimated beta is used to compute the cost of equity capital using the CAPM formula: $r = r_f + \beta(rm - r_f)$. This cost of equity is appropriate and correct only if the project under consideration is exactly like the existing operations of the company, which is unlikely to be the case for any company with more than one type of business. Please remember that required rate of return demanded by investors depends on the use to which the capital is put.

This does not mean that company cost of capital estimates have no practical value. In fact, they are extremely useful in estimating market's assessment of the required rate of return on the typical mix of the company's assets. Thus, for any project, which is of comparable risk, the company cost of capital might be a very good measure. For projects, which have higher risk, a higher discount rate will need to be used and projects, which have lower risk, should be evaluated with lower rate of return.

Estimating Beta for a Project: The required rate of return for a project depends on its systematic risk and is measured by its beta. The problem of choosing a suitable discount rate for a project therefore amounts to working out what sort of beta it has. We cannot do this directly because individual investment projects are not traded in the New York Stock Exchange. The best approximation is obtained by estimating the betas of companies, which are in the same business as the project. If one can estimate the betas for a number of companies in an industry and then estimate an average beta for the industry, this will be a reliable estimate for the industry represented by the companies.

The beta of a company's stock measures how its price responds to market movements and is estimated by plotting returns on the stock against returns on the market index. Monthly returns are commonly used and the slope of the fitted line through the scatter of points is the beta of the stock. The line is often referred to as the *characteristic line* for the stock. One can also use published betas produced by a number of brokerage and advisory services. Standard and Poor and Merrill Lynch, among others, publish information on betas. It is important to note that estimates of individual company betas are highly unstable and it is better to use industry betas with any adjustment for financial leverage as discussed later. A beta, calculated for an industry group, would generally provide a more accurate measure of the beta of a project than that of the estimate for a single company.

The typical information published with beta include the following:

- Beta: the regression-analysis estimate of beta
- Alpha: the intercept of the fitted regression line
- R^2: the proportion of the variance of price changes explained by market movements
- Residual standard deviation: the standard deviation of the unique risk of the stock

96

- Standard errors of beta and alpha: measures of the probable accuracy of these estimates
- Adjusted beta: the earlier estimate adjusted to take account of the effect of estimation errors.

The R^2 gives the percentage of the variance of the stock returns explained by the market return or a measure of its market risk. A stock with an R^2 of 35 percent has 65 percent unique risk. Thirty five percent of its risk is market risk.

Beta and Financial Leverage: The beta of a project in a strict sense should reflect its business risk. The typical beta measured using stock returns reflect not only the business risk, but also the effect of any financial leverage or borrowing of the company. When a company borrows money it increases the risk of the stockholders. Thus, other things equal, financial leverage increases the risk of the company and the beta of a stock with leverage will be higher than the pure asset beta. We can derive the effect of leverage on beta using the relationship:

$$\text{Value of assets} = \text{value of equity} + \text{value of debt}$$

with all the values measured in market values. The beta of a portfolio is the weighted average of the individual security betas. Consider the company's assets as financed by a portfolio of liabilities or sources of funds, i.e. partly by equity and partly by debt. Therefore, the beta of the assets should equal the beta of the weighted average of the betas of the liabilities.

$$\beta_{assets} = \beta_{equity} x \frac{equity}{V} + \beta_{debt} x \frac{debt}{V}$$

where V = equity + debt

The beta of debt is often very close to zero. Therefore, we can rewrite the relationship as:

$$\beta_{assets} = \beta_{equity} x \frac{equity}{V}$$

$$\beta_{equity} = \beta_{assets} x \frac{V}{equity}$$

These equations can be used to calculate the beta of assets from the market-estimated beta of a leveraged company stock.

Example: ABC Corp. stock has a beta of 1.3. The company has a debt/assets ratio of 30 percent. Assuming the debt beta to be zero,

$$\beta_{assets} = 1.3 x 0.7 = 0.91$$

What will happen if the company reduces its debt to 20 percent of assets? Again, we can use the relationship above to figure out the beta for the stock.

$$\beta_{equity} = \beta_{assets} \, x \, \frac{V}{equity}$$

$$\beta_{equity} = 0.91 x \frac{1}{(1-0.2)} = 1.14$$

The impact of leverage on beta and the cost of capital presented in this chapter ignores the effect of taxes. We will deal with that in Chapter 19.

Betas and Discount Rates for International Projects: The conventional wisdom on overseas investments is that they are generally riskier than investments in one's own country. This perception is based on the general feeling that things get more uncertain when one leaves one's home country. However, this ignores the fact that the risk that matters should be the non-diversifiable risk that is measured by beta and that beta is a function of not only the standard deviation of the project's cash flows but also the correlation of the project's cash flows to the domestic market returns. While the standard deviation for foreign projects can be higher than their domestic counterparts, it is also generally true that the correlation of such projects are a lot less than a comparable domestic project will have to the domestic market return. Thus, it does not automatically follow that foreign projects will have higher betas and should be evaluated at higher discount rates. One should analyze both the standard deviation and the correlation of the project to domestic market returns. This will apply to a foreign company undertaking a project in the U.S. as well.

Cost of Capital Across Countries: It is a mistake to compare interest rates and costs of capital across countries without adjusting for the differences in inflation. The nominal interest rates across countries will differ because of the differences in inflation. Thus, the fact that interest rates in Japan are 3 percentage points lower does not mean that it is cheaper to borrow in Japan and Japanese companies enjoy a lower cost of capital advantage. One has to compare the real interest rates before making any judgement. Of course, it is possible that the savings and therefore, the supply of loanable funds could be different and relatively large in one country relative to the demand for loans. In such a case, the country could have a lower real rate. This line of argument assumes that capital does not easily flow across borders; an assumption not too realistic in an increasingly global economy.

Arbitrary Discount Rates: Corporate managers often face the task of setting discount rates for projects which are different from the typical project handled by them. These projects may be considered riskier than normal and are often evaluated with an arbitrary and higher discount rate than normal. The higher discount rate may be assigned to cover for an imprecise cash flow estimate and/or for the perceived higher uncertainty surrounding the project. One needs to think through the nature of the risk involved and distinguish between systematic and unique risk. The question is not simply what makes an asset's future earnings uncertain. What matters is the extent to which abnormally low earnings are likely to coincide with low earnings in the economy as a whole. It is also better to sort out the cash flow estimation problems by correcting the estimates rather than add an arbitrary risk premium for a vaguely defined risk. High discount rates heavily penalize projects with cash flows in later years of the project's life.

Cyclicality, Operating Leverage, and Beta: High standard deviation of earnings does not necessarily mean high beta. What matters are the earnings variability and its relationship to the market returns. Cyclical firms, whose earnings are strongly dependent on the state of the business cycle, tend to have high betas. Variability of earnings can be due to unique risk. A strong relationship between a firm's earnings and aggregate earnings means high market risk. The *accounting beta* or the *cash-flow beta* can be used to measure this. These betas are estimated using the accounting earnings or cash flows instead of security returns.

Beta is also a function of the operating cost structure. Other things equal, higher fixed costs will mean higher beta. The high level of fixed cost produces a leverage effect which makes profits particularly vulnerable: a small percentage change in revenues will produce a much larger percentage change in profits. Companies with high fixed costs (often called high *operating leverage*) tend to have high betas. The relationship can be expressed as follows:

$$\beta_{asset} = \beta_{revenue} \left\{ 1 + \frac{PV(fixed \, cost)}{Pv(asset)} \right\}$$

Certainty-Equivalent Cash Flows: The standard approach for calculating present value of a stream of uncertain cash flows is to discount the cash flows using a *risk-adjusted rate* derived from the CAPM or some other risk-return model. That is:

$$NPV = \sum_{t=0}^{n} \frac{C_t}{(1+r)^t}$$

where $r = r_f + \beta(r_m - r_f)$. This procedure would be inappropriate for a project whose beta is expected to vary through time. In such cases, it is better to use the certainty equivalent cash flows (CEQ) which are cash flows fully adjusted for the risk involved so that they can be discounted using the risk-free rate. Thus, the NPV can be written as:

$$NPV = \sum_{t=0}^{n} \frac{CEQ_t}{(1+r_f)^t}$$

The certainty equivalent CEQ_t is some fraction of the expected cash flow C_t. The two methods must give the same present value, so

$$NPV = \sum_{t=0}^{n} \frac{CEQ_t}{(1+r_f)^t} = \sum_{t=0}^{n} \frac{C_t}{(1+r)^t} = \sum_{t=0}^{n} \frac{C_t}{(1+r_f)^t} x \frac{(1+r_f)^t}{(1+r)^t}$$

$$CEQ_t = a_t C_t, \text{ where } a_t = \frac{(1+r_f)^t}{(1+r)^t}$$

The certainty equivalent approach is suited for projects where cash flows have uneven risk through the life of the project, so that using one constant discount rate will lead to incorrect decisions.

WORKED EXAMPLES

1. J. B. McIntosh is interested in finding the appropriate discount rate for its new project for making blue, pink, red and yellow widgets. The average beta of a group of colored widget manufacturers is 1.4 and their average debt-equity ratio is 0.30. McIntosh plans to have a debt-equity ratio of 0.20. If the risk-free rate is 6 percent and the expected risk premium on the market portfolio is 9 percent, what is: (a) the required return for the project and (b) the required return on the shares of the company?

SOLUTION

The average beta of the shares of the other widget manufacturers is 1.4. Debt to equity ratio of 0.3 means debt/assets = 0.3/1.3 = 0.23. Equity/asset = 1 - 0.23 = 0.77. Assuming beta for debt is zero,

$$\beta_{asset} = \beta_{equity} x \frac{equity}{V} = 1.4 x 0.77 = 1.08$$

Required rate of return for the project = 6 + (1.08 x 9) = 15.72 percent
Debt/asset ratio for McIntosh = 0.2/1.20 = 0.17, Equity/asset = 1 - 0.17 = 0.83

Beta of the shares of McIntosh = $1.08 x \frac{1}{0.83} = 1.30$

Return on McIntosh shares = 6 + (1.30 x 9) = 17.7 percent

2. Jale Breaker Inc. is considering a project, which requires an investment of $100,000 now to buy the exclusive rights to a new high tech prison security system from Victor Conway. The security system is still under trial. The results of the trial will be known next year. The experts associated with the project feel that there is a 50 percent chance that the trials will be successful. If found successful, Jale Breaker Inc. will be required to invest $2,000,000 to install the system in prisons in 20 states. The project will generate a cash flow of $500,000 forever, starting from year 2. Typical prison security system companies have a beta of 1.2. The risk free rate is 6 percent and the market risk premium is 9 percent. The cost of capital for the typical project is thus estimated at 16.8 percent. Mr. Breaker, CEO of the company,

feels that the project has very high risk and therefore wants to discount the cash flows from the project using a rate of 34 percent (double the normal rate). Calculate the NPV of the project using the 34 percent discount rate. Is there a more appropriate way to evaluate the project?

SOLUTION

NPV using 34 percent discount rate = $-100,000 - \dfrac{2,000,000}{1.34} + \dfrac{500,000/0.34}{1.34} = -\$495,083$

A more appropriate approach will be to evaluate the project in steps. The cash flows from the $2,000,000 investment made next year have the same risk as other security system projects or the discount rate for this should be: $r = r_f + \beta(r_m - r_f) = 6 + (1.2 \times 9) = 16.8$ percent. The NPV of the investment of $2,000,000 will then be:

$$NPV = -2,000,000 + \dfrac{500,000}{0.168} = \$976,190$$

There is a 50 percent chance of this happening. That is, for the initial investment of $100,000, the company will get either zero (the trial fails) or $976,190 (trial succeeds). Thus, the overall project NPV for the initial investment of $100,000 is:

$$NPV = 0.5(-100,000 + \dfrac{976,190}{1.168}) = 367,890$$

SUMMARY

This chapter deals with the application of CAPM to practical capital budgeting problems. These problems include estimation of required rates of returns for projects and cost of capital. The chapter stresses the essential element of the CAPM – the risk that matters is the non-diversifiable risk. Thus, the required return on any investment should be related to this risk component and not the total risk. The chapter also points out the fact that the required rate of return on a project will depend on its market risk and not who undertakes the project. It is a mistake to use the company cost of capital to evaluate all the projects undertaken by a company. The company cost of capital reflects the mix of assets the company has and the only project to which one can apply the company cost of capital are those which are mirror images of the company's existing operations.

Estimation of a company's stock beta involves determining the relationship between the stock's returns and the market returns. This is easily accomplished by plotting the two sets of returns on a graph and calculating the slope of the fitted line. It is important to note that the estimated beta reflects the business risk of the company's assets and the financial risk of the company. Higher leverage or borrowings lead to a higher beta. The asset beta reflecting the pure business risk of the assets can be derived from the stock beta. The relationship can be used to find betas at different levels of leverage.

The common perception that international projects are riskier ignores the fact that international projects often have lower correlation to the domestic market returns than their domestic counterparts. This results in a lower beta, even though the variance of cash flows might be higher. This assumes that each country's investors have a predominantly domestic bias and their market portfolio essentially comprises their home country stocks.

The chapter also discusses the common but erroneous practice of adding fudge factors to account for perceived risks. The fudge factors are arbitrary risk premiums and in many cases reflect non-systematic risk. They are also often used for the correction of cash flow estimation problems. One should look at the factors causing the risk and try to identify the effect they will have on the project's beta. Remember that beta is a function of not only the project cash flows' variance, but also the correlation of these cash flows to market returns. Other things equal, a non-cyclical project will have a lower beta compared to a cyclical project.

The standard approach to project evaluation uses a risk-adjusted discount rate for discounting all cash flows. This assumes that the project's cumulative risk increases at a constant rate. There may be projects that have cash flows whose risk does not increase steadily. For such projects, the certainty equivalent approach might be preferable. This allows separate risk adjustment for cash flows of different periods.

LIST OF TERMS

Accounting beta	Financial leverage
Alpha	Financial risk
Business risk	Industry beta
Cash-flow beta	Operating leverage
Certainty equivalent	Project beta
Company cost of capital	Risk-adjusted rate
Cyclical	

EXERCISES

Fill-in Questions

1. The use of the _____ as a discount rate ignores differences in the risk of projects.

2. The discount rate for evaluating a capital budgeting proposal should be derived from the _____.

3. _____ measures the average rate of price appreciation on a stock in the past, when investors in the market as a whole earned nothing.

4. When a company raises debt finance, it increases the _____ borne by its shareholders.

5. The cost of capital depends on the _____ of the firm's investments.

6. Financial risk is produced by_____ leverage.

7. Companies with high fixed costs have high _____.

8. A firm whose revenues and earnings are strongly dependent on the state of the business cycle is said to be a _____firm.

9. We can measure the strength of the relationship between a firm's earnings and the aggregate earnings on real assets by estimating either its _____ beta or its _____.

10. Instead of discounting the expected value of a cash flow by its_____, we may discount its _____ at the risk-free rate.

11. The beta of a portfolio of stocks drawn from a single industry is called a(n) _____.

Problems

1. A firm is considering the following projects:

PROJECT	BETA	EXPECTED RETURN, %
A	0.7	13
B	1.4	16
C	1.8	21
D	0.9	15

The firm's cost of capital is 16 percent. The risk-free rate is 6 percent and the expected market risk premium is 9 percent.
a. Which projects will be accepted if the firm's cost of capital is used?
b. Which projects should be accepted ?

2. CBC Corp. is considering investing in two new projects. Project A is estimated to give a return of about 14%. The estimated standard deviation for the cash flows from the project is 30% and the correlation coefficient of the cash flows to market returns is 0.4. The standard deviation for the market returns is 15%. The expected market return is 14% and the risk free rate is 5%. The CEO of the company has decided that the project is not a good investment because of its "high risk" as measured by the standard deviation. The CEO does like Project

B which is expected to give a return of 20% with the same standard deviation of cash flows as Project A. The correlation coefficient for this project's cash flow with that of the market is estimated at about 0.9. Is the CEO right? Is Project B a better investment than project A? Explain your answer to the CEO.

3. Dummy Corp. stock has the following characteristics:

    Adjusted beta   1.33

    Alpha   - 0.56% per month

    a. How much would the stock tend to go up in a month in an unchanged market?
    b. How much would the stock tend to go up in a month when the market went up 10 percent?

4. MetaMarket Inc. stocks have a total market value of $50 million and debt of $30 million. The current Treasury bill rate is 6 percent, and the expected market risk premium is 9 percent. A plot of the returns on the stock against the market returns shows a scatter of points through which a line can be fitted with a slope of 45°.
    a.   What is the company's financial leverage?
    b.   What is the beta of the stock?
    c.   What is the beta of the company's assets?

5. MetaMarket Inc., of problem 4, now decides to invest $20 million in additional assets that are similar to its existing assets. It decides to finance this investment by borrowing a further $20 million of debt.
    a.   What is the beta of the additional assets?
    b.   What discount rate should be used for these additional assets?
    c.   What is the beta of the stock after the debt issue?

6. The market value of the shares of Astrofab Corp. is currently $24 million, and their beta is 1.4. Astrofab has a nominal $6 million of 8 percent coupon debentures outstanding which mature in 7 years. These debentures have a beta of 0.1, and they currently yield 10 percent. What is the beta of Astrofab's assets?

7. Other things being equal, which company (from each of the following pairs) do you think should be using the higher discount rate in its capital budgeting?
    a.   (i) A steel company, (ii) a brewing company
    b.   (i) a manufacturer of recreational vehicles, (ii) a mining company
    c.   (i) a company with high operating leverage, (ii) a company with high financial leverage
    d.   (i) a manufacturer of office equipment, (ii) an electric utility company.

8. A project is expected to generate net cash flows of $1,000 in each of years 1 and 2. Its beta will be 1.5 throughout its life. The risk-free interest rate is 6 percent, and the expected return on the market is 15 percent. Calculate:
    a.   the present value of the cash flows

b. the certainty equivalents of the cash flows

c. the ratios of the certainty equivalents to the expected cash flow (that is, a_1 and a_2).

9. NFL Inc. is expanding its business in Europe. It is evaluating projects in 3 countries with details as follows:

Country	Project standard deviation	Correlation of project returns to US market returns
Country A	36 percent	0.4
Country B	28 percent	0.6
Country C	42 percent	0.2
Country D	22 percent	0.8
US project	18 percent	0.9

The standard deviation of U.S. market returns is 14 percent. Calculate the beta for evaluation of the projects in each country.

Essay Questions

1. Write a short memorandum describing how you will set discount rates for projects with different risks.

2. Your company uses the DCF rate of return to appraise new investment projects in the following way:

   a. Projects with paybacks less than 3 years are accepted if their DCF rate of return exceeds 12 percent.

   b. Projects with paybacks longer than 3 years are accepted if their DCF rate of return exceeds 16 percent.

   Discuss the advantages and disadvantages of this rule.

3. Describe how you would calculate the cost of capital of a company using the CAPM.

4. Explain why foreign projects need not necessarily have a higher discount rate than their domestic counterparts.

5. Explain the difference between the use of risk-adjusted discount rates and certainty-equivalent cash flows. Give an example of a situation where you think the certainty-equivalent method is preferable.

ANSWER TO EXERCISES

Fill-in Questions

1. Company cost of capital   7. Operating leverage

2. Project beta
3. Alpha
4. Financial risk
5. Business risk
6. Financial

8. Cyclical
9. Accounting, cash-flow beta
10. Risk-adjusted rate, certainty equivalent
11. Industry beta

Problems

1. a. Only B and C will be accepted. A and D will be rejected.

   b. The company should use risk-adjusted rates based on project betas. The risk-adjusted rates based betas for the different projects are: A = 12.3 percent, B = 18.6 percent, C = 22.2 percent, and D = 14.1 percent. B and C have returns less than their required rates of return; so they should be rejected. A and D have returns higher than the required rates and should be accepted.

2. Beta for Project A = $\dfrac{0.4 x 30}{15} = 0.8$; Beta for Project B = $\dfrac{0.9 x 30}{15} = 1.8$

   Based on the betas, the required rates of returns for the projects will be 12.2 percent and 21.2 percent. This shows that project A gives a return higher than its required rate of return, while project B does not clear its hurdle rate.

3. a. -0.56 percent. b. r = $-0.56 + 1.33 x 10 = 12.74$ percent

4. a. The financial leverage = debt/assets = $\dfrac{30}{30+50} = 0.375$; b. Beta = 1; c. You can calculate

   the beta of assets using the relationship: $\beta_{asset} = \beta_{equity} x \dfrac{equity}{V} = 1 x (1 - 0.375) = 0.63$

   (assumes beta of debt = 0)

5. a. Beta = 0.63. b. Discount rate = 6 + (0.63 x 9) = 11.67 percent. c. beta = $0.63 x \dfrac{100}{50} = 1.26$

6. Value of debt: market price per bond x 6000 bonds = $902.63 x 6,000 = $5.42 million
   Value of equity: $24 million
   Total market value of firm = value of debt + value of equity
   $$= 5.42 + \$24.00$$
   $$= \$29.42 \text{ million}$$

   $$\beta_{assets} = \beta_{debt} x \dfrac{debt}{V} + \beta_{equity} x \dfrac{equity}{V} = 0.1 x 0.18 + 1.4 x 0.82 = 1.16$$

7. a. i; b. i; c. i; d. i

8. a. Using $r = 6 + 1.5(15-6) = 19.5$ percent, PV = \$1,537.09
    b. Certainty - equivalent cash flows are \$887 and \$786.80.
    c. $a_1 = 1.06/1.195 = 0.9016$ and $a_2 = (1.06/1.195)^2$.

9. The betas for the different country projects are: A = 1.03; B = 1.2; C = 0.6; D = 1.26; Beta for the U.S. project = 1.16

10

A Project Is Not a Black Box

INTRODUCTION

So far we learned the basic tools and techniques needed to evaluate projects. In particular, chapters 2 to 6 showed us how to calculate net present values and how to use them to make capital budgeting decisions. Chapters 7 to 9 explained how the risk of a project affects the discount rate that should be used to evaluate it. However, investment decisions require a lot more than the knowledge of tools and techniques. There are a number of practical issues to be considered. A manager should be able to understand what is going on inside a project. Detailed project analysis enables the manager to understand the vulnerabilities, strengths and weaknesses of a project. Chapters 10, 11, and 12 deal with these issues. The chapters address specific questions such as how to analyze capital investment projects, how to ensure that cash-flow forecasts are realistic, and how to organize and control capital expenditures.

The title: "A Project Is Not a Black Box," clearly brings out the central theme of the chapter. A black box is something that you accept without questioning what is inside. The financial manager should not simply accept a set of cash-flow forecasts, choose a discount rate, and crank out a net present value. She or he must understand the internal workings of the project and think about where those cash flows came from and what can go wrong with them. Chapter 10 describes five commonly used techniques of project analysis which can help the financial manager to understand the project's structural strengths and weaknesses, its dependence on one or more key inputs, and interrelationships the project might have with future decisions. The techniques described are: *sensitivity analysis, scenario analysis, break-even analysis, the Monte Carlo simulation*, and *decision trees*.

KEY CONCEPTS IN THE CHAPTER

Sensitivity Analysis: Of all the techniques described in this chapter, sensitivity analysis is perhaps the most useful and important one. It is simple to apply and understand and can be particularly effective in identifying the need for additional information. Sensitivity analysis captures the effect of key inputs or variables on the project, one variable at a time. It answers questions such as: what happens to the NPV of the project if the cost of goods sold turns out to be at its pessimistic worst?

The NPV of a project is arrived at by combining a number of different forecasts to estimate the after-tax cash flows and then discounting these cash flows. The forecasts include the size of the total market for the product, the company's share of that total market, the price of the product, etc. All the numbers which go into the analysis are best estimates and we cannot be sure what the actual outcome will be for any of these variables. Sensitivity analysis identifies the difference it makes if any of these forecasts turns out to be wrong. The method for accomplishing this is to identify the key variables that determine the success of the project, such as sales volume, fixed cost, unit variable cost, and selling price. By taking one variable at a time and replacing its expected value with both an optimistic and a pessimistic estimate, cash flows, and NPVs are recalculated. In this way financial managers can identify those variables which affect NPV most. Additional information or research to reduce the uncertainty of those variables, as well as other, overlooked factors, may then be in order.

The results of the sensitivity analysis is typically set out in tables such as the one below which represents part of Table 10-2 of the Brealey and Myers text.

NET PRESENT VALUE (Billions of yen)			
Variable	Pessimistic	Expected	Optimistic
Market size	1.1	3.4	5.7
Market share	-10.4	3.4	17.3
Unit price	-4.2	3.4	5.0
Unit variable cost	-15.0	3.4	11.1
Fixed cost	0.4	3.4	6.5

The table clearly shows that the impact of variations in the unit variable cost or the market share is far more significant than the impact of variations in the total market size or of the project's fixed costs. The manager can now consider actions that might reduce or eliminate the uncertainty with respect to these key components. For example, it may be worth investing in a market survey which will reduce the uncertainty about market share. A survey which indicates poor prospects for the company would allow the project to be abandoned before any major expenditure is incurred. Alternately, expenditure on a different advertising campaign might bolster market share and improve the prospects for the project. Thus, sensitivity analysis alerts the management the importance of keeping a sharp eye on what happens to components key to the success of the project. In the above example, it is alerted to the crucial nature of its variable costs and market share. Steps could be taken to remove uncertainty with respect to key material inputs. These could include hedging in commodity futures markets, negotiating long-term supplier contracts, or commission an additional design study on material efficiency.

The strength of sensitivity analysis lies in its ability to highlight key variable and key assumptions, to expose inconsistencies, and to identify where additional information is worthwhile.

Sensitivity analysis is limited in its scope, however, because of the subjectivity of the optimistic and pessimistic forecasts and because it ignores interrelationships among variables.

Scenario Analysis: Scenario analysis can be seen as the logical extension of sensitivity analysis. Altering the variables one at a time, as is done for sensitivity analysis, ignores the fact that the variables are usually interrelated. One way around this problem is to look at how the project would fare under a number of different plausible scenarios of the future. Forecasts are made for all variables so as to be consistent with a particular view of the world. In the text, for example, the forecasters are asked to consider the effects of an immediate 20 percent rise in the price of oil, and the NPV of the project is recalculated on the resulting assumptions.

Scenario analysis can be very useful to evaluate the project's exposure to a combination of changes in key variables. The manager can specify the scenarios he would like to have the project analyzed under.

Break-even Analysis: Break-even analysis calculates the sales level that will give zero NPV for the project. Knowing the break-even level, one can assess the chances of the project's success. For the textbook example used above, the assumptions of the base case were of an NPV of 3.4 billion yen from sales of 100,000 units. The sensitivity analysis showed that subtracting 10,000 units of sales (by reducing the total market size by 10 percent) reduced the NPV by 2.3 billion yen (from 3.4 billion yen to 1.1 billion yen). To reduce the NPV from 3.4 billion to zero would therefore take a reduction in sales of $(3.4/2.3) \times 10,000 = 15,000$ units. The break-even level of sales must be $100,000 - 15,000 = 85,000$ units.

Many companies (and textbooks) use the break-even level computed on a rather different basis, known as the accounting break-even level. This is the level of sales that gives a zero accounting profit. In the example above, accounting profits are made when sales exceed 60,000 units. This level of sales would be very unsatisfactory. Zero accounting profit is really a big loss as it indicates a failure to earn any return on capital, and that represents a loss equal to the opportunity cost of capital. For the example above, our sensitivity analysis tells us that if we expect sales at this level, the NPV of the project would be negative (3.4 billion - [2.3 billion x (40,000/10,000)] = -5.8 billion yen).

Break-even analysis enables managers to analyze the impact of *operating leverage* on the project's NPV. A project with high fixed costs will have a NPV which is more exposed to the level of sales. At higher sales levels, the project would do very well, but if the sales levels happen to be lower than expected, the project would fare worse than one with lower operating leverage. This technique can be useful to evaluate alternate production technologies that have different fixed-variable cost mix.

Monte Carlo Simulation: Monte Carlo simulation (or simulation, for short) may be regarded as the ultimate extension of the idea of scenario analysis. In scenario analysis, we look at a small number of specially chosen scenarios. In simulation, the analysis is extended to include a very large number of possible combinations of changes in key variables. Simulation analysis uses complex computer programs to generate possible values for all key inputs to the project. The project analyst specifies probability distributions for all these variables and the computer generates random values for the key variables and the project is simulated. The process is repeated a number of times to produce a distribution of project cash flows. From this distribution of cash flows, you can generate a distribution of IRRs. This provides you with a picture of the variability of the project's returns. All interrelationships among the variables can be taken into account in the simulation model.

Simulation involves three stages:

- Establish equations to model the cash flows of the project. These must reflect any interdependencies among variables.
- Specify the probabilities of forecast errors of different magnitudes for each variable
- Sample outcomes. The computer samples from the distribution of forecast errors, calculates the cash flows, and records them. This is repeated a large number of times until an accurate picture of the distribution of possible outcomes has been built up.

As with all models, Monte Carlo simulation has its good and bad points. On the positive side, simulation forces explicit specification of interdependencies. It can be used also to explore possible modifications to a project.

On the negative side, simulation can be time-consuming and expensive. Realism means complexity; building the model may have to be delegated, and this can diminish its credibility to the decision maker. It may replace one "black box" with another.

Beyond these points a common misuse of simulation arises when it is used to obtain distributions of "NPVs," which are calculated by discounting at the risk-free rate. The object is to avoid prejudging the risk of the project, which is reflected in the spread of the distribution. This practice, however, is highly erroneous and misleading because:

- "NPVs" calculated in this way have no real meaning and no longer represent market values of the project.
- The distribution does not give the information that would be needed to work out the market value of the project.
- The method ignores the investor's ability to diversify.
- It offends the value-additivity principle.

The distribution of IRRs might be more useful and gives a picture of the variability of the project's returns.

Decision Trees: Decision trees are very useful to analyze a sequence of different possible uncertain events and decisions through time. It can be a highly useful and effective way of analyzing decisions that are interdependent over time. Decision trees can show linkages among decisions spread over different periods and dependent on possible and uncertain future outcomes. While the basic technique is simple, the trees can get complicated very quickly.

To draw a decision tree, branches from points marked with squares are used to denote different possible decisions. Branches from points marked with circles denote different possible outcomes (with their probabilities often indicated in brackets) and the decisions and outcomes are linked in

112

the logical sequence. Present values are calculated starting from the end the most distant branches first. "Roll back" to the immediate decision by accepting the best decision at each of the later stages. (See problem 2 of our worked examples.)

Decision trees are valuable because they display the links between decisions over different time periods. Moreover, they force implicit assumptions to be expressed. In particular, they enable us to analyze such things as the option to expand, and the option to abandon a failing project. Usefulness of decision trees is limited, however, because they become unmanageably complex very quickly. They also fail to tell us how to adjust our discount rates to reflect the differences in risk among alternatives. Decision trees can identify options to abandon or bail out of an unsuccessful project. The *abandonment value* arising from the ability to cut your losses when things do not go well can add significantly to the project's NPV.

WORKED EXAMPLES

1. The following forecasts have been prepared for a new investment of $20 million with an 8-year life:

	PESSIMISTIC	EXPECTED	OITIMISTIC
Market size	60,000	90,000	140,000
Market share, %	25	30	35
Unit price	$750	$800	$875
Unit variable cost	$500	$400	$350
Fixed cost, millions	$7	$4	$3.5

Use straight-line depreciation, assume a tax rate of 35 percent, and an opportunity cost of capital of 14 percent. Calculate the NPV of this project and conduct a sensitivity analysis. What are the principal uncertainties of the project?

SOLUTION

The first step is to calculate the annual cash flows from the project for the base case (the expected values). These may be calculated as shown:

DESCRIPTION	HOW CALCULATED	VALUE ($ in millions)
1. Revenues	90,000 x 0.30 x $800	21.600
2. Variable cost	90,000 x 0.30 x $400	10.800
3. Fixed cost	$4,000,000	4.000
4. Depreciation	$20,000,000/8	2.500
5. Pretax profit	Item 1 - (items 2 + 3 + 4)	4.300
6. Tax	Item 5 x 0.35	1.505
7. Net profit	Item 5 – item 6	2.795
8. Net cash flow	1tem 7 + item 4	5.295

This level of cash flow occurs for each of the 8 years of the project. The present value of an 8-year, $1 annuity is 4.639 at 14 percent. The NPV of the project is therefore given by:

$$NPV = \$5,295,000 \times 4.639 - \$20,000,000 = \$4,563,505$$

Now that the base case has been completed, the next step is to alter the forecasts one at a time to their optimistic and pessimistic values. The easiest way to do this is to work out how much each change affects the net cash flow and then use the annuity factor as before to work out the NPV. For example, the optimistic value of the market size increases the pretax revenues by 50,000 x 0.30 x ($800 - $400) = $6 million; so it increases the (after-tax) net cash flow by $6 million x 0.65 = 3.90 million, to $9.195 million. The NPV now becomes

$$NPV = \$9,195,000 \times 4.639 - \$20,000,000 = \$22,655,605$$

The following table shows the net cash flows and NPVs corresponding to the pessimistic and optimistic forecasts for each variable.

	Net Cash Flow ($m)		NPV ($m)	
	Pessimistic	Optimistic	Pessimistic	Optimistic
Market size	2.96	9.20	-6.29	22.66
Market share, %	4.13	6.47	-0.86	9.99
Unit price	4.42	6.61	0.49	10.67
Unit variable cost	3.54	6.17	-3.58	8.63
Fixed cost	3.35	5.62	-4.48	6.07

The table clearly shows that the most crucial variable is the total market size. Both the fixed and variable costs also need watching, while market share and unit price seems less likely to cause serious problems.

2. Jill-in-the-Box is evaluating a possible investment in a new plant costing $2,000. By the end of a year, it will know whether cash flows will be $300 a year in perpetuity or only $140 a year in perpetuity. In either case, the first cash flow will not occur until year 2. Alternately, the company would be able to sell their plant in year 1 for $1,800 if the demand is low and for $2,000 if the demand is high. There is a 65 percent chance that the project will turn out well and a 35 percent chance it will turn out badly. The opportunity cost of funds is 10 percent. What should the company do?

SOLUTION

The problem can best be analyzed by the decision tree shown below. If things go well, the cash flows of $300 in perpetuity starting in year 2 will be worth $300/0.1 = $3,000 in year 1. If things go badly, the cash flows will be worth $140/0.1 = 1,400 in year 1. To analyze the decision tree, we work backwards from the most distant branches of the tree. At the decision branch points, marked with squares, we make decisions. At the uncertainty ones, marked with circles, we calculate expected values. So, if things go well (high demand), we will decide to continue with

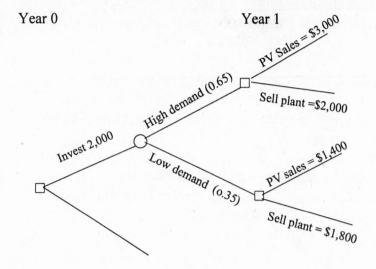

Year 0   Year 1

Invest 2,000

High demand (0.65)

PV Sales = $3,000

Sell plant =$2,000

Low demand (0.35)

PV sales = $1,400

Sell plant = $1,800

the plant at a value of $3,000 in year 1. However, if things go badly (low demand), we will prefer to sell it for $1,800 rather than wait for cash flows worth only $1,400. We can now take the expected value at the uncertainty branch point by weighting each possible outcome by its probability.

Expected value in year 1 = $3,000 x 0.65 + $1,800 x 0.35 = $2,580
Net present value of the investment = $2,580/1.1 - $2,000 = $345.45

The project is worth pursuing.

CHAPTER SUMMARY

Investment decision making involves a lot more than simply cranking out cash flow estimates, discounted cash flows, and NPVs based on these estimates. Investments are always fraught with uncertainties and a project can be vulnerable to a number of factors external and beyond the manager's control. Project analysis enables the manager to identify the project's vulnerabilities and the major threats faced by the project. The chapter describes three approaches to identifying these vulnerabilities and threats – sensitivity analysis, scenario analysis, and the Monte Carlo simulation. Sensitivity analysis is the simplest of these and evaluates the impact on the project's NPV caused by changes in key variables, one variable at a time. This type of analysis enables the manager to identify variables crucial to the project's financial health. The manager might find it prudent to spend resources on getting additional information to reduce the uncertainties related to these crucial variables. An extension of sensitivity analysis is the scenario approach where the impact on the project's NPV under different scenarios, where more than one variable might change, is examined. One can look at all possible combinations of variables and get a complete distribution of possible cash flows from the project by using the Monte Carlo simulation approach. This approach uses a complete model of the project and assigned distribution for the variables to obtain random values for all the variables and simulates many runs of the project.

Simulation can be very useful in understanding the risk and complexities of the project. It forces the project analyst to raise questions that otherwise might not be asked. The process has its limits, though, and can easily be abused. Simulation produces a vast array of data and, in some cases, manager could conceivably get lost in the process.

Very few projects are simple, one time "accept or reject" cases. Projects often involve linkages of decisions over time and can include options to expand, abandon, or otherwise modify the project. Decision tree analysis is ideally suited to evaluate these cases, where one is faced with a sequence of possible decisions.

It is important to remember that none of the techniques discussed in this chapter replaces the NPV analysis; they only facilitate better decision making by enabling more accurate computation of the NPV. These techniques help the manager understand the project better and learn what could go wrong with the project.

LIST OF TERMS

Abandonment value
Break-even analysis
Decision tree
Monte Carlo simulation

Probability
Project analysis
Scenario
Sensitivity analysis

EXERCISES

Fill-in-Questions

1. Sensitivity analysis, simulation, and decision trees are three different forms of _____.

2. _____ shows the effect of changes in key variables such as sales, costs, etc., on the value of an investment project.

3. The analysis of a project under different _____ gives us a way to do a kind of sensitivity analysis that takes the interrelationships among variables into account.

4. _____ identifies the level of sales for which the project gives zero NPV.

5. _____ uses a complete model of the project and distribution of all key variables to simulate thousands of project runs and produces a complete distribution of project cash flows.

6. Sequential decisions can be analyzed by constructing a(n)_____.

7. One of the difficulties of using a decision tree or simulation is that it becomes necessary to specify the _____ of different future outcomes.

8. The problem of whether to terminate a project before the end of its normal economic life is called the _____ problem.

Problems

1. Deep Drillers Inc. is evaluating a project to produce a high tech deep-sea oil exploration device. The investment required is $80 million for a plant with a capacity of 15,000 units a year. Sales are expected to average 80 percent of capacity. The plant is expected to operate for 5 years. The device will be sold for a price of $12,000 per unit. The variable cost is $7,000 and fixed costs, excluding depreciation, are $25 million per year. Use straight-line depreciation and a tax rate of 36 percent. The required rate of return is 12 percent.

   a. Calculate the NPV of the project
   b. Do a sensitivity analysis for the following pessimistic and optimistic assumptions:
      Pessimistic: Sales – 15 percent lower, Unit price – 10 percent lower, Fixed costs – 10 percent higher.
      Optimistic: Sales – 15 percent higher, Unit price – 10 percent higher, Fixed costs – 10 percent lower.

2. Colorful Creams Cosmetics Corporation (CCCC) is considering an investment of $500,000 in a new plant for producing fluorescent disco makeup. The plant, which has an expected life of 4 years, has a maximum capacity of 700,000 units per year, and sales are expected to be 85 percent of this in each of the 4 successive years of production. Fixed costs are $200,000 per year and variable costs are $1.20 per unit produced. The product will be sold at a unit price of $2. The plant will be depreciated straight-line over 4 years, and it is expected to have a zero salvage value. The required rate of return on the project is 15 percent and the corporation tax rate is 35 percent.

   a. Calculate the NPV of this project under the assumptions given above.
   b. Calculate how sensitive the NPV of the project is to variation in the level of sales, the unit price, the unit variable coot, and the level of fixed costs.
   c. CCCC is uncertain how to price its new product. What price would give a zero NPV?

3. In the investment project of problem 2, calculate what level of sales would give break-even in terms of (a) zero NPV and (b) zero accounting profit.

117

4. In problem 2, CCCC estimated that the annual sales would be 595,000 units, but there is some chance that the sales level will be inadequate to justify the capital expenditure. By commissioning a market survey, CCCC can hope to reduce this risk. CCCC's marketing department has some experience with such surveys. They estimate that there is a 20 percent chance that the survey will change the forecast sales to 500,000 or less, in which case the project would not be worth undertaking. If this does not occur (the remaining 80 percent of the time), they would expect the sales forecast to be revised upward to 640,000 units. What is the maximum amount that CCCC should be prepared to pay for a survey of this kind?

5. CCCC has another investment project with the following characteristics:
   Cost of investment: $800,000
   Expected sales volume: 21,000 units per year for 7 years
   Unit price: $150
   Unit variable cost: $120
   Annual fixed costs: $400,000
   Life of investment: 7 years (zero salvage value)
   Tax rate: 35 percent
   Required rate of return: 17 percent

   Calculate the NPV of this investment and perform a sensitivity analysis (use straight-line depreciation).

6. Analyze the project of problem 2 under the following two scenarios:

	Pessimistic scenario	Optimistic scenario
Sales volume	Expected value -20%	Expected value +10%
Unit price	Expected value -10%	Expected value +20%
Variable cost	Expected value +10%	Expected value -5%
Fixed cost	Expected value +10%	Expected value -5%

7. In problem 4, the first year of operation would give CCCC the same information as their market survey. After that year, if things go badly (with expected sales of 415,000 units), they can abandon the project to obtain a salvage value of $400,000 (less $8,500 tax) by selling the plant to another company. What value does the market survey have in the light of this option to abandon the project after it has been started?

Essay Questions

1. Describe the technique of sensitivity analysis as applied to the appraisal of capital investment projects. What reservations do you have about its usefulness?

2. Describe how to calculate the break-even point for a capital investment project. Why is it misleading to calculate the break-even point in terms of accounting profit?

3. Work out and describe in detail how you would produce and use a Monte Carlo simulation model to represent the purely financial aspects of pursuing an MBA degree in one of the top ten schools. Assume you will be in a business related career for the next 15 years. Some of the things to keep in mind include: the investment in time and money, possible benefits of the MBA, and the pitfalls (things which could go wrong). Make sure to build appropriate interrelationships between variables into the model where necessary.

4. "What possible use to us," said the Ancient and Venerable Comptroller, "is a technique that pulls numbers out of a hat and adds them? Sure! There are risks in this business, but we expect our managers to know what they're doing: if they don't, then they're out. It's all a matter of judgement, and there's nothing random about that." Is this a valid criticism of Monte Carlo simulation? How would you respond to this argument?

5. A decision must be made whether to launch a new product immediately or subject it to further market research or abandon the idea altogether. Your boss has heard that decision trees can help with this kind of problem. Write a report on how a decision tree might be used in this situation. Describe what sort of information you would need to apply this in practice and how it would be used.

6. "Simulation and decision trees are better than NPV for analyzing complex projects with expansion or abandonment options." Discuss.

ANSWERS TO EXERCISES

Fill-in Questions

1. Project analysis
2. Sensitivity analysis
3. Scenarios
4. Break-even

5. Monte Carlo simulation
6. Decision tree
7. Probabilities
8. Abandonment value

Problems

1. a. The following table derives the cash flows and NPV for the base case:

Item	Year 0	Years 1 to 5 ($1000)
Investment	-80,000	
Revenue		144,000
Variable cost		84,000
Fixed cost		25,000
Depreciation		16,000
Pre-tax profit		19,000
Tax @ 36 percent		6,840
Net profit		12,160
Net cash flow		28,160
NPV @ 12 percent		21,510

b. The sensitivity analysis is presented in the table below: ($1,000)

Sensitivity to change of	Effect on annual cash flow	Effect on NPV
Pessimistic:		
15 percent lower sales	-5,760	-20,764
10 percent lower price	-9,216	-33,222
10 % Higher fixed cost	-1,600	-5,768
Optimistic		
15 percent lower sales	5,760	20,764
10 percent lower price	9,216	33,222
10 % Higher fixed cost	1,600	5,768

2. a. The following table derives the cash flows and NPV for the base case and for the pessimistic and optimistic scenarios of problem 6. (All cash flows in $1000s)

Item	Year 0	Years 1 to 4 Expected	Pessimistic	Optimistic
Investment	-500			
Revenue		1190.0	856.8	1570.8
Variable cost		714.0	628.3	746.1
Fixed cost		200.0	220.0	190.0
Depreciation		125.0	125.0	125.0
Pretax profit		151.0	-116.5	509.7
Tax		52.9	-40.8	178.4
Net Profit		98.1	-75.7	331.3
Net cash flow		223.1	49.3	456.3
NPV at 15 percent		137.1	-359.4	802.7

120

b. The next table shows how given changes in sales, variable cost, unit price, and fixed cost affect the net cash flows and the NPV. The final column also shows the levels that give break-even points (i.e., zero NPV):

Sensitivity to change of:	Effect on cash flow	Effect on NPV	Break-even level
100,000 sales (units)	52.00	148.46	502,660
10-cent variable cost	-38.68	-110.42	$1.32
10-cent unit price	38.68	110.42	$1.88
$10,000 fixed cost	6.50	-18.56	$273,875

c. The final column indicates that a price of $1.88 gives a zero NPV.

3. a. The final column of the previous table also shows that the level of sales required for the break-even point in terms of zero NPV is 502,660 units per year.

   b. The base case gave a pretax profit of $151,000 at sales of 595,000. Each unit reduction in sales reduces pretax profits by $0.80, so sales will have to fall by 151,000/0.80 = 188,750 to eliminate profits entirely. That is, break-even sales are 406,250.

4. Without the extra information, the value of the project is its usual NPV of $137,100. With the information, there is a 20 percent chance of a zero NPV and an 80 percent chance of $203,900 (=$137,100 + 148,460 x 45/100). The new NPV is equal to $163,120 (= $203,900 x 0.80) less the cost of the information. The information must be worth $26,020 (= $163,120 - $137,100).

5.

Item	Year 0	Years 1 to 7 (Cash flows in $1,000)		
		Expected	Pessimistic	Optimistic
Investment	-800			
Revenue		3150.0	2268.0	4158.0
Variable cost		2520.0	2217.6	2633.4
Fixed cost		400.0	440.0	380.0
Depreciation		114.3	114.3	114.3
Profit before tax		115.7	-503.9	1030.3
Tax		40.	-176.4	360.6
Profit after tax		75.	-327.5	669.7
Cash flow		189.5	-213.2	784.0
NPV at 17 percent		-56.	-1636.2	2274.8

The sensitivity analysis looks as follows:

Sensitivity to change of	Effect on cash flow	Effect on NPV	Break-even level
1000 unit sales	19.50	76.48	21,740
$1 variable cost	-13.65	-53.54	$118.9
$1 unit price	13.65	53.54	$151.1
$10,000 fixed cost	6.50	-25.49	$377,700

6. See the answer to problem 2.

7. Without the abandonment option, we found in problem 4 that the project had an NPV of $163,120 less the cost of the survey, or $137,100 without the survey. This gave the survey a value of $26,020.

 With the abandonment option, there is now a 20 percent chance of abandoning at an NPV of -$46,913. This is calculated as follows: the expected first year sales of 415,000 will give a cash flow of $129.55, and there will be $400,000 less $8,500 tax from selling the plant. This makes an expected $521,050/1.15 - $500,000 = -$46,910. There is also an 80 percent chance of $203,900. Combining the two figures, we find that the abandonment option increases the NPV of the project to $153,740 (= -$46,910 x 0.2 + $203,900 x 0.8). This reduces the value of the survey information to $16,640 (= $153,740 - $137,100).

11

Where Positive Net Present Values Come From

INTRODUCTION

This chapter is short but gives some basic lessons in the economics of competition. Modern market economies have intense competition in nearly all industries. Very few firms can expect to earn economic profits or have positive NPV investments unless they have a sustainable comparative advantage in the business they are engaged in. No matter how much we know about the theory of making capital budgeting decisions, we will end up making bad decisions if our forecasts of cash flows turn out badly. This chapter shows you how you can ensure that these forecasts are as good as possible.

The first section of the chapter describes how some difficult forecasting problems may be avoided by making use of available market information. The second section focuses on the market in which the firm operates. Firms do not get positive NPV projects without there being some reason for it. A positive NPV can arise only if the firm has some comparative advantage or what the business strategists call competitive advantage. It is important to understand just the nature of such an advantage. What is it that enables the firm and not some other company to exploit the opportunity provided by the project? If you can answer this question satisfactorily, you probably have understood the project and the source of the positive NPV.

These ideas are elaborated using a small case study (Marvin Enterprises). Your company can expect a positive NPV from a project if it has competitive advantage in one or more aspects of the project. However, it is good to remember that other firms are not going to be idle and will whittle away your competitive advantage over time. In other words, competitive advantage is never permanent, so it is reasonable to expect that the source of the positive NPV will disappear over time. You want to keep this in mind when you prepare your cash flow estimates.

KEY CONCEPTS IN THE CHAPTER

Economic Rents: Economic rents are profits in excess of cost of capital. Companies can extract economic rents from its customers if they have an edge over the competition. In competitive markets, all that a firm can expect to get is a fair price covering all its costs. Competition will drive the price down to the point where the price will equal the cost of producing the product or service (cost includes the cost of capital). Whenever you have a positive NPV project, remember that the positive NPV is simply the present value of future economic rents. Look for the source of the economic rent. Economic rent may exist in the short-term when the industry is not in long-run equilibrium. Over the long-term, a company can expect to have economic rents only if it has some kind of monopoly or market power. You should be able to identify the source. Remember the following three points:

- When an industry is in a long-run competitive equilibrium, all assets earn just their opportunity cost of capital, their NPVs are zero, and economic rents are zero.

- Firms can earn temporary (or permanent) economic rents if there is temporary dis-equilibrium, or if they have some degree of monopoly or market power.

- Never accept that a project has a positive NPV unless you understand why your firm has a competitive advantage in doing it. The U.S. chemical producer's initial price spread assumptions for polygone provide an excellent example of this principle.

Market Values as Source of Price Information: Market prices provide extremely useful information about the value of commodities. Since investments in commodities do not provide annual dividends, today's price of a commodity is the present value of the future price of the same. A gold mine can look to the current gold price for the present value of future sales of gold because this is consistent with the equilibrium expected return to investors in gold. You can use market prices to reduce the chance of forecasting errors swamping the genuine information. Information that is not generally known can be analyzed separately and added to (or subtracted from) the market value.

For example, a department store investment involves at least two distinct bets: one on real estate prices and another on whether the real estate is best suited to running a department store. It is helpful to imagine the business as divided into two parts: a real estate subsidiary that buys the building and rents it out and a retailing one that rents and operates it. This forces you to consider whether the department store is the best current use for the real estate, and whether it is likely to remain so. It would be foolish to make a lousy department store investment because of optimism about real estate prices. Instead, it would be better to buy the real estate and rent it out, though a real estate company would have more expertise in this area. Conversely, it would be silly to be deterred from going ahead with a profitable department store because of pessimism about real estate prices. Instead, it is better to sell the real estate and then rent it back for the department store.

Technology, Competition, and Economic Rents: *Marvin Enterprises* is an extended and useful illustration of what happens in an industry when a firm has a technological break-through and is poised to exploit it. While the example is fictitious, the problems it poses are very real and have many parallels in today's world.

The example is about a company that has developed a new technology, but there are other firms hot on its heels and its relative advantage is expected to last for only 5 years. After 5 years, new investments will come in and drive the price of the product (gargle blasters) down to its equilibrium level. The company will therefore earn abnormally high profits (economic rents) only over the first 5 years.

The main argument of the case runs as follows: The price of a product depends on the total amount of it produced. Producers compete with each other and will expand their capacity until the new investment has a zero net present value. From this, it follows that any single producer can expect to find positive NPV projects only if he or she has some kind of relative advantage over the competition. Such advantages certainly exist: a company may have built up a good reputation for its brand name in the marketplace. You can see that these advantages are hard-won and must be protected tenaciously.

The case raises two other important issues. The first is the effect of Marvin Enterprises' new investment on its existing business. Its proposed expansion is sufficiently large to affect the price of the product it is selling. Marvin must worry about the loss of revenue on its existing operations and include this in its calculation of the NPV of the new project. In more extreme situations, this could lead to the company's wishing to suppress its new technology completely.

Second, the less efficient producers play an extremely important role. As the capacity of the industry is increased, the price of the product falls, and it becomes increasingly difficult for these producers to stay in business. If the price falls far enough, some producers may withdraw from the market, and other marginal producers may be on the point of doing so. In this situation, the price of the product will be at the point where it just pays the least efficient remaining producer to stay in business. The size of the economic rent obtained by a more efficient producer will simply reflect the difference between their costs (including the opportunity cost of the capital employed).

Beware of the misleading argument that a fully depreciated plant is cheaper to run than an otherwise identical un-depreciated one. This argument is often made, but it is falsely based on interpreting accounting income as if it were cash flow. Remember, only cash flows matter, not accounting numbers. Since, in this example, there are no taxes; there is absolutely no difference between cash flows of a depreciated plant and those of an un-depreciated one.

Here is a summary of the key points made in the discussion of the Marvin Enterprises case:

- Anticipated and prolonged economic rents are uncommon.
- High economic rents usually attract competitors; try to estimate the timing and extent of new entry.
- Identify your firm's competitive advantages, and try to capitalize on them.
- Successive generations of technology will tend to reduce the value of earlier generation assets. A growth industry has no mercy on laggards.
- The NPV of a project may be reduced by the impact it has on the firm's existing business. This can provide an incentive to slow down the speed of innovation.
- A *marginal producer* is one who will quit if the price goes any lower, i.e., for whom price equals manufacturing cost plus opportunity cost of not selling out. The economic rent to a more efficient producer is simply the difference between its costs and those of a marginal producer.

- A higher salvage value increased economic rents. The book value of the old plant was irrelevant.

WORKED EXAMPLE

The Red Robbo Rubber Company is considering a new investment in a fully automated tire plant. Its existing plant produces 1 million tires a year. It cost $80 million 5 years ago, and it could be scrapped for $30 million at any time. The production costs per tire of the old and new plants can be broken down as follows:

	Old Plant	New Plant
Raw Materials and energy	$15	$17
Labor	10	3
Other direct costs	5	5
Total direct costs	$30	$25

The new plant will be able to produce 500,000 tires a year, and it will cost $35 million. The current price of tires is $38 each. Red Robbo's new investment is not expected to affect this, but the price may fall when other companies complete their modernization programs in 2 years' time. Red Robbo's cost of capital is 10 percent, and there are no corporate taxes.

a. What is the NPV of the new plant?
b. When will the old plant be scrapped, and what is its value today?
c. The costs of raw materials and energy suddenly double. The price of tires changes to $50. What are the answers to (a) and (b) now?

SOLUTION

a. The capital outlay required on the new plant is $70 per annual tire capacity. The break-even price to give a zero NPV is therefore (10 percent x $70) +$25 (direct costs) = $32. This is the price that we should expect to see in 2years' time. With the price now at $38, Red Robbo can expect economic rents of $6 per tire per year for 2 years. The NPV of the new plant is therefore:

$$500,000x\left(\frac{\$6}{1.1}+\frac{\$6}{1.1^2}\right)=\$5,206,611$$

b. The old plant should be scrapped when it can no longer earn the opportunity cost of its salvage value, that is, 10 percent x $30 million, or $3 on each tire produced. It will be scrapped when the price falls below $33, that is, in 2 years' time. Meanwhile, it will produce cash flows of $8 million for 2 years. Its value today is therefore:

$$\frac{\$8,000,000}{1.1}+\frac{\$8,000,000+\$30,000,00}{1.1^2}=\$38,677,686$$

c. The change in energy and materials costs modifies the direct costs to $45 and $42 for the old and new plants, respectively. This increases the breakeven price on the new plant to $49, just $1 below the current price of $50. The economic rent is now only $1 per tire produced (for 2 years), so the NPV of the new plant is:

$$500,000 \times [(\$1/1.1) + (\$1/1.1^2)] = \$867,769$$

The old plant will now be scrapped only if the price of tires falls below $45 + $3 = $48. It is now sensible for manufacturers to build only sufficient new plants to push the price down to $49. The old plant is no longer expected to be scrapped but will earn $5 per tire for 2 years and $4 per tire after that. In year 2, it will be worth 4/0.1 = $40 million; so today it is worth:

$$\frac{\$5,000,000}{1.1} + \frac{\$5,000,000 + \$40,000,000}{1.1^2} = \$41,735,537$$

CHAPTER SUMMARY

Project evaluations can show positive NPVs either because the cash flow projections are too good (and wrong) or the project is really good and the company can extract economic rents on account of its competitive advantage over its rivals. Managers should ensure that when they accept positive NPV projects, they belong to the latter group. The biggest practical difficulty in applying the NPV criterion is in establishing reliable cash-flow forecasts. The chapter illustrates the most important dangers and difficulties in forecasting cash flows, and it provides advice on how best to combat them. Although it is hard to provide rules which would cover all situations, it is common sense to look for the source of the positive NPV. Throughout, the key idea is that you can expect a positive NPV only if you have some kind of relative advantage.

Market prices provide very useful information on the value of many assets and commodities. Unless you have reason to believe that you know better than the market, you would be well advised to accept the markets values. This applies to real estate or gold or oil, any of the well-traded assets or commodities. If you think an asset is worth more in your possession than its market value, you should be able to explain why.

Technological breakthroughs give companies tremendous advantage and significant economic rents. However, this advantage does not last forever; competitors catch up soon. This economic rent will be a direct function of the cost difference between the technology leader and the surviving marginal producer. Marginal producers will survive as long as the price in the market is above their cost.

LIST OF TERMS

Comparative advantage

Competitive advantage
Economic Rent
Marginal producer

EXERCISES

Fill-in Questions

1. A firm needs to have some _____ over its rivals in the same business in order to economic profits.

2. _____ is another term used to denote comparative advantage.

3. A _____ is a producer who will cease production if there is any fall in the price at which the product is sold.

4. _____ is the term used to describe profits which are in excess of the cost of capital.

Problems

1. Which of the following are true and which are false?

    a. A monopoly can obtain permanent economic rents unless it is regulated in some way.
    b. The average forecasting error for the cash flow of a project is zero.
    c. New capacity decisions must take account of the effect on sunk costs, such as investments in existing plants.
    d. No firm can earn economic rents if it has to buy inputs at a price that reflects their value to the firm.
    e. Marginal producers have assets with zero market value.
    f. Fully depreciated assets always have a present value of zero.
    g. Stock prices reflect the value of growth opportunities only after the firm has announced its plans to invest in new capacity.

2. Goldilocks Mining Company is considering opening a second gold mine. This mine will cost $15 million to develop, and it will produce 30,000 ounces of refined gold a year for 5 years at a cost of $220 an ounce. The current gold price is $280 an ounce, and the opportunity cost of funds is 10 percent.

    a. What is the NPV of this project if you assume that the gold price will grow at 5 percent per year?
    b. What is the NPV if you assume that the gold price is expected to grow at the cost of funds?

3. Universal Communicators, Inc., makes intergalactic message capsules that sell at $6 million each and cost $4 million each to manufacture. The existing plant produces 2,000 capsules per year, which represents a significant part of the total market. They are considering investing in a new plant that will increase capacity by 500 additional units. When the increased volume of production hits the market, the market price of message capsules is expected to fall to $5.5 million. Universal is currently negotiating contracts for the construction of its new plant, which will reduce production costs to $3 million. The cost of capital for this project is 10 percent.

   a. What is the maximum price that Universal should be prepared to pay for its new plant, assuming that it can expect to retain a monopoly of the more efficient production technology indefinitely?
   b. What would the plant be worth to another company that did not already produce message capsules?

4. The manufacture and sale of Bubby Tubbies is highly competitive. The industry is composed of three firms with the following capacities and manufacturing costs:

Firms	Sales (million units)	Unit cost
A	8	8
B	6	9
C	4	10
Total	18	

The demand curve for Bubby Tubbies is given by:

Price (in dollars) = $24 - 0.5 x (quantity in millions)

The industry opportunity cost of capital is 10 percent, and new plant costs $70 per unit of capacity. All the plants have indefinitely long lives but could be scrapped at salvage values of $30 per unit of capacity. Firm C discovers a way of reducing unit-manufacturing costs to $7, keeping capital costs unchanged. It manages to secure monopoly rights to the technique for an extremely long period, and it decides to challenge firm A's market leadership by immediately adding 5 million units of the new capacity.

   a. What is the present value of firm C's existing plant after the new capacity is added?
   b. What is the maximum addition to capacity before it is worthwhile to scrap firm C's original plant?
   c. What is the NPV of firm C's new investment project?
   d. Can firm C make any profitable investment without first disposing of its old plant?

5. Bay Corp. and Valley Inc. have identical plants that can each manufacture 100,000 chips a year, at a unit cost of $6. These plants could be scrapped at any time with a scrap value of $1.5 million. Bay Corp. plant has been fully depreciated for tax purposes, whereas Valley Inc. plant has been depreciated only to a book value of $1 million and will give rise to annual $500,000 depreciation allowances for the next 2 years. Since both companies pay tax at 50 percent, Bay Corp. would realize only a net of $750,000 from scrapping its plant immediately; while Valley Inc. would realize $1.25 million net. At what prices for chips will each company find it economical to cease production immediately and scrap its plant? (Assume the opportunity cost of capital is 10 percent.)

6. The market for shipping crude oil can be represented in terms of a number of types of tanker serving a number of different routes. One very simplified representation is given below. It shows, in millions, the available tonnage of each class of tanker, the total tonnage required on each route, and the operating costs of each tanker on each route.

| TANKER TYPE | TONNAGE | ANNUAL OPERATING COSTS (PER TON) | | |
		ROUTE 1	ROUTE 2	ROUTE 3
VLCC	500	$ 30	$ 34	Too large
MLCC	400	35	37	$ 38
Other	300	40	40	40
Tonnage required		300	500	250

All tankers are available for charter in a competitive market, and the price mechanism will allocate them to routes so as to minimize the total costs of transporting crude. All tankers have a useful life of 15 years and can be sold for scrap at any time for $150 per ton. Assume the cost of capital is 10 percent.

a. What type or types of tanker will be used on each route?
b. What will be the annual rental (per ton) for chartering each type of tanker?
c. What will be the market price per ton) for purchasing each type of tanker?
d. What could happen to the usage and the prices of each type of tanker if the tonnage of VLCCs increased to 700?
e. What would happen if (with no increase in the tonnage of VLCCs) an environmental lobby succeeded in banning VLCCs from 50 percent of the required tonnage of route 1?

Essay Questions

1. Describe the different kinds of biases in forecasts that can affect capital budgeting decisions. Give some guidelines for minimizing their effects.

2. Discuss the relationship among competitive advantage, economic rent, and positive NPV projects.

3. Explain clearly why a company may have an economic incentive to suppress an improvement in technology.

4. Explain clearly what is meant by the statement, "The level of economic rents is determined by the costs of the marginal producer."

5. In the Marvin Enterprises example, users of the earlier and more expensive technologies were prepared to continue to produce even at prices that gave negative profits after depreciation. Explain what factors determine their willingness to do so.

6. Describe an industry that has experienced the type of situation and decisions described in Marvin Enterprises. What are the most important similarities and differences between your example and the imaginary gargle blaster industry?

7. Discuss whether a company can still have an incentive to suppress an improvement in technology if all its shareholders hold the market portfolio.

ANSWERS TO EXERCISES

Fill-in Questions

1. Comparative advantage
2. Competitive advantage
3. Marginal producer
4. Economic rent

Problems

1. a. True
    b. False
    c. True
    d. True
    e. False
    f. False
    g. False

2. a. For each ounce of gold mined per year, the present value of the gross revenue stream is:

    280 x (annuity factor: t = 5, r = 1.1/1.05 = 4.76%; 4.358) = $1,220
    PV of costs = $220 x (annuity factor: t = 5, r = 10%; 3.791) = $834
    NPV = -15,000,000 + 30,000 [1,220 - 834] = -$3,420,000

    b. NPV = -15,000,000 + 30,000 [(5 x 400) - ($834)] = $19,980,000

3. a. Universal will gain net revenues of $2.5 million on each of its 500 new units a year, and it will lose $500,000 on each of its existing 2,000 units of output. This gives an incremental cash flow of:

    (500 x $2,500,000) - (2,000 x $500,000) = $250,000,000

At a 10 percent discount rate, the present value is $250 million, and this is the maximum price Universal should be prepared to pay.

b. Another company would not stand to lose revenues on the existing plant. The new plant would be worth $1.25 billion to such a company.

4. a. The extra capacity will drive the price down to $12.50 [$24 – (0.5 x 23)], but it is best to scrap C's old plant at any price below $13 [$10 + ($30 x 0.1)]. The existing plant is therefore worth only its salvage value of $120 million (4 x $30).

b. 4 million units, because at a price of $13 the unit will have to be scrapped. A total capacity of 22 million units will cause the price to fall to $13 = $24 – (0.5 x 22).

c. Assuming the equilibrium price is $13, the NPV of firm C's project is given as

$$NPV = [5,000,000 \text{ x } (\$6/0.1 - \$70)] - [\$4,000,000 \text{ x } (\$5/0.1 - \$30)]$$
$$= -\$50,000,000 - \$80,000,000$$
$$= -\$130,000,000$$

If firm C scraps all its old plant and the price goes to $14.50, the NPV is still negative (-$55 million).

d. It is not possible. When the price is $15, each unit of investment has a NPV of -$70 +$8/0.1 = $10, but unless the old investment has been scrapped, we also reduce the present value of the old plant by

$$4 \text{ x } \$0.5/0.1 = \$20$$

5. The incremental cash flows from Bay Corp. decision to maintain production are as follows:

	YEAR 0	YEAR 1
Net revenues after tax		0.5 x (P - 6) x 0.1
Proceeds on disposal	-0.75	0.75

Where P is the unit price in dollars and the cash flows are expressed in millions of dollars. These cash flows will have a positive NPV if the price is greater than $7.50.

Similarly, the incremental cash flows from company Z's decision to maintain production are:

	YEAR 0	YEAR 1
Net revenues after tax		0.5 x (P - 6) x 0.1
Depreciation tax shield		0.25

Proceeds on disposal   -1.25   1.00

These cash flows will have a positive NPV if the price is greater than $8.50.

6. a. We can figure out from the structure of operating costs that the total costs of transporting crude are minimized when the demands of each route are satisfied as follows:

> Route 1: 300 VLCC
> Route 2: 200 VLCC, 300 MLCC
> Route 3: 100 MLCC, 150 other

    b. Since 150 "other" tankers are in use and the remaining 150 are idle, this category of tanker represents a marginal producer, and its rent must equal the opportunity cost of salvage. Since the cost of capital is 10 percent and the salvage value is $150 per ton, the rental must be $15 per ton.

        MLCCs and "other" tankers are both used on route 3, but the MLCCs are cheaper to operate by $2 per ton. They can therefore command a $2-higher rental of $17 per ton.

        VLCCs and MLCCs are both used on route 2, with a $3 cost advantage to the VLCCs. This gives them a $3 rental advantage, and the VLCC rental is $20 per ton.

    c. Capitalizing the rentals of $20, $17, and $15, we find that the market prices of the VLCC, MLCC, and "other" tankers are $200, $170, and $150.

    d. Route 2: 400 VLCC, 100 MLCC; route 3: 250 MLCC. All "other" would be scrapped, MLCC would drop to salvage value of $150 per ton, and VLCC to $180 per ton.

    e. Compared with (a), 150 route 1 VLCCs would switch with 150 route 2 MLCCs. There is no change in tanker prices. Price for shipping oil on route 1 increases by $5 per ton.

12

Making Sure Managers Maximize NPV

INTRODUCTION

This chapter describes the organization of the capital budgeting process. The chapter also discusses the agency problems involved in investment decision making at different levels of management and possible steps needed to ensure that the managers make optimal investment decisions in the best interests of the shareholders. The measurement problems encountered when using the commonly used accounting measure of profitability are analyzed. Alternate concepts of residual income and economic value added are presented.

KEY CONCEPTS IN THE CHAPTER

Capital Budgeting Process: Capital budgeting process typically involves the following four stages.

i) <u>Preparation of capital budget</u> - This is a broad list of projects to be taken up during the year. The list has summary details and is typically generated through a *bottom-up* process with different departments, plants, or divisions coming up with their list of proposed projects.

ii) <u>Project authorization</u> - This step involves formal vetting of the projects by the top management through appropriate analyses and screening. The step ensures that the projects included reflect the firm's strategic direction. Before expenditure on individual projects is committed through *appropriation requests,* project details are prepared and analyses using NPV or other measures of project acceptability are conducted. Typically, managers are delegated authority to approve expenditures up to set ceilings with the projects requiring large investment requiring approval at the highest level or the board of directors.

iii) <u>Implementation and control</u> - Project details are monitored during construction with appropriate information feed back to top management for control and necessary corrective actions. Project cost, time schedule, and any change in key inputs or factors affecting the project viability are among the elements monitored regularly.

iv) <u>Post-audit</u> - Firms do post-audits of completed projects shortly after the project is completed. This enables the management to identify the errors and omissions with respect to project details. The step is part of a continuous learning process for everyone involved in project management and enables the firm to avoid the errors in the future.

It is important to note that there are important and often sizable investments made by firms, which are not part of the capital budgeting process. These include R and D, marketing campaigns, training and development expenditures, and investment in information technology. The control systems in place should take into account the existence of these and ensure that the expenses add value.

Information: Timely and accurate information is needed by top management to ensure that right decisions are taken and implemented. The structure and organization of capital budgeting framework should guard against the common pitfalls of *inconsistent assumptions* across the firm and at different levels of management, *bias* on the part of project sponsors, *accuracy and timeliness* of the information made available to the decision makers, and *conflicts of interest* for the project sponsors and decision makers. The key to ensure the flow of accurate and timely information is to ensure that the managers are rewarded appropriately and given incentives to take NPV maximizing decisions. In short, the structure of the rewards system should be such as to minimize the effect of agency problems.

Agency Problems: Investment decisions are among the most important decisions taken by corporate managers. The right decisions, properly implemented, will result in enhanced shareholder value; the wrong decisions on the other hand will lead to deterioration of shareholder wealth. The stockholders are the principals and the managers are the agents given the responsibility of running the firm on behalf of the stockholders. Corporate managers rarely own significant amounts of the firm's stock; therefore they do not necessarily share the stockholders' enthusiasm for maximizing NPV. This is the essence of the agency problems, which cause sub-optimal behavior on the part of the managers. Some examples of this behavior include - *reduced efforts* (or shirking), use of *perks, empire building* or expanding the business for its own sake, taking up *entrenching investments* which ensures the manager's position, and a tendency to avoid *risk* even when it is in the interest of the stockholder. The empire building propensity is caused by the fact that the manager's relative importance, authority, and position are a function of the size of the operation she or he commands rather than the value added by it. The reduction in value of the firm caused by the agency problems is the agency cost.

Mitigating Agency Costs: While the agency cost cannot be totally eliminated, the organization of the capital budgeting process and the rewards system for managers should be structured such that the agency cost is limited to the minimum possible. This is achieved through a mix of *monitoring* of managers' behavior and by designing the managers' rewards and incentives in a way to align the managers' interests with that of the stockholders. Monitoring is done at different levels and is delegated by the stockholders to the board of directors who monitor the top management. The top management in turn takes care of monitoring the managers at lower levels. Accounting firms who perform regular audits of companies' books of accounts and financial statements perform an important role in the overall monitoring of corporations. In general, small stockholders leave it to the larger stockholders to closely watch corporate performance on a regular basis. This might actually lead to the *free-rider problem*, where everyone assumes that someone else will do the job and nobody does it.

Monitoring has its limits and to be effective has to be used in combination with well-designed *compensation* plans for managers. The ideal compensation plans will succeed in aligning the managers interest with that of the stockholders. A fixed salary will never work, as this does not give any incentive to the manager to do the best she or he can. Part of the problem in rewarding managers is the fact that managerial inputs cannot be measured effectively, while the output depends on not only managerial input but also on external factors on which the manager has no control. In practice, more and more firms are designing managerial compensation packages such that they include a fixed component and bonuses or rewards for improved corporate performance. Rewards for the top management can be based on the overall corporate performance or price of the firm's shares. However, compensating managers at divisional and plant levels on the basis of the company's share performance is not fair and will not produce the best efforts from these managers. Here one has to use other measures of performance.

Measuring Performance: If performance based compensation plans for managers are to be effective, the measures of performance have to reflect the performance accurately. The traditional tool used in the past is the accounting *return on investment (*ROI). The ROI and accounting earnings or net income have two major advantages: i) it measures performance on absolute basis and ii) this can be used to measure performance of managers of departments and divisions. However, the accounting measures also suffer from some major drawbacks: i) it is subject to manager's control, ii) they are often biased and are subject to the type of accounting rules used, and iii) the typical accounting profit does not include any provision for the cost of funds used in the business. This means that positive earnings and earnings growth by themselves do not reflect superior performance. Accounting earnings are also biased against new investments in that they understate a project's profitability in the early years of the project and overstate the same in the later years. Any comparison of accounting earnings across firms in different industries can be very misleading (See the text for the comparison of profits for some firms in the pharmaceutical and the chemical industry; page 439). Unless firms earn more than their cost of capital, they are not adding value to the firm or its stockholders.

An alternate measure which overcomes most of the drawbacks of the accounting earnings is the residual *income* or the *economic value added* (EVA$^@$).[1] EVA measures the value added after covering the cost of capital for the investment used in the business. It equals the income earned less the cost of funds used. A similar measure is the *economic profit* (EP) used by McKinsey and Company. This is measured as the capital used in the business multiplied by the difference between the return on investment and the cost of capital. EVA explicitly recognizes the cost of capital and focuses on profits earned after meeting the cost of capital. It has become quite popular in recent years and firms use EVA to measure and reward divisional performance. While EVA is a great improvement over the accounting earnings, it retains some of the biases of the accounting profits. Thus for new projects or investments carrying long-term benefits and short-term costs, EVA will understate the value added in the early years. The problem here is that EVA, like accounting earnings, is understating real economic income. This is often because of overstatement of depreciation or inclusion of elements, which are investments rather than

---

[1]@ - This is a copyrighted term registered by the consulting firm, Stern and Stewart.

current expenses (e.g. R & D). Effective implementation of EVA as a measurement and compensation tool requires changing some of the accounting rules or adjusting for them so that EVA is an accurate reflection of the value added.

Economic Depreciation: Economic depreciation measures the real decline in the value of the asset and thus is measured by the change in the present value of cash flows generated by the asset. Unlike accounting or book depreciation, economic depreciation can be negative (i.e. the value of the asset increases).

Explanation of Formulas and Mathematical Expressions

Notations:
C_1 = Cash receipts during the period
P_0, P_1 = Price of the asset at the beginning and the end of the period
BV_0, BV_1 = Book value at the beginning and the end of the period
r = Cost of capital
ROI = Return on investment

$$\text{Rate of return} = \frac{C_1 + (P_1 - P_0)}{P_0}$$

EVA = Income earned - Cost of capital x Investment
Economic Income = Cash receipts - Economic depreciation
Economic depreciation = $P_0 - P_1$
EP = (ROI - r) Capital employed
Book income = Cash receipts - Book depreciation = $C_1 + (BV_1 - BV_0)$

$$\text{Book ROI} = \frac{C_1 + (BV_1 - BV_0)}{BV_0}$$

Points to keep in mind:
   i)   EVA = EP
   ii) Book depreciation will always be positive or zero.
   iii) Economic depreciation may be negative or the asset value may increase.

WORKED EXAMPLE

Gatsby Inc. is considering an investment of $120 million on a project with the following expected cash flows. The project generates cash flows for 5 years and will be closed down after that. The cost of capital is estimated at 15%. Assume straight-line depreciation for book income calculations.

Year	0	1	2	3	4	5
Cash flows (millions)	120	20	30	46.3	46.3	46.3

Calculate the NPV for the project and forecast the book income, the ROI, the economic income and EVA for the project.

SOLUTION

$$NPV = -120 + \frac{20}{1.15} + \frac{30}{(1.15)^2} + \frac{46.3}{(1.15)^3} + \frac{46.3}{(1.15)^4} + \frac{46.3}{1.15^5} = 0$$

Forecast of book income and ROI:

Cash flow in millions

Years	1	2	3	4	5
Cash flow	20	30	46.3	46.3	46.3
Beginning book value	120	96	72	48	24
Ending book value	96	72	48	24	0
Change in book value	-24	-24	-24	-24	-24
Book income	-4	6	22.3	22.3	22.3
Book ROI	-0.033	0.063	0.310	0.465	0.929
Book depreciation	24	24	24	24	24

Book income = cash flow + change in book value
Book ROI　　= Book Income/Beginning book value

Forecast of economic income, economic rate of return, and EVA:

Cash flow in millions

Years	1	2	3	4	5
Cash flow	20	30	46.3	46.3	46.3
Beginning present value	120	118	105.7	75.3	40.3
Ending present value	118	105.7	75.3	40.3	0
Change in value	-2	-12.3	-30.4	-35	-40.3
Economic income	18	17.7	15.9	11.3	6

Economic rate of return	0.15	0.15	0.15	0.15	0.15
Economic depreciation	2	12.3	30.4	35	40
Economic value added	0	0	0	0	0

Economic income = cash flow + change in present value
Economic return   = Economic income/Beginning present value
Economic value added = Economic income - cost of capital x beginning value

CHAPTER SUMMARY

This chapter describes the capital budgeting process, which typically includes the four stages of *budget preparation, project authorization*, procedures for *control of projects,* and *post-audits* conducted soon after project completion. Ideally, the capital budgeting process should combine bottom-up projects generation and top down strategic planning. It is to be noted that many important investments do not necessarily go through formal capital budgeting procedures. These include R & D expenditure, major marketing campaigns, and training and development expenses. The finance manager should be aware of these and proper control evaluation procedures should be in place to ensure that these projects add value.

The chapter also discusses the need and significance of accurate information and forecasts on projects which is needed by top management in order to be able make the right decisions. Some of the problems involved include bias on the part of project sponsors, inconsistent assumptions, and conflict of interests. Monitoring and designing appropriate rewards and incentives for managers are essential to ensure that managers maximize NPV.

Structuring rewards and incentives for managers require measurement of performance. The chapter analyzes the drawbacks of the widely used accounting measures of performance. The accounting earnings and ROI understate the profitability of new projects and overstate the earnings and ROI of older projects. Alternate measures based on economic income and economic depreciation are better in measuring performance. One such measure is the newly popular EVA.

LIST OF TERMS

Appropriation request
Capital budget
Economic depreciation
Economic income
Economic profit

Economic value added
Post-audit
Project authorization
Return on investment

EXERCISES

Fill-in Questions

1. The initial step in the investment process is the preparation of the list of projects proposed to be undertaken during the year called _____.

2. The accounting ROI generally _____ the profitability of new projects and _____ that of older projects.

3. Most companies require that a formal _____ be prepared before funds are released for a project.

4. Economic income is measured by the cash flow plus the change in the _____ of the assets.

5. Project sponsors generally tend to _____ the benefits of the project and _____ the costs of the project.

6. _____ of projects are usually undertaken soon after the projects are completed.

7. Senior management can be considered as the _____ of the _____.

8. Senior managers are monitored by _____.

9. Auditing firms also provide _____ of the firm's performance.

10. Managers sometimes sponsor projects which have a _____ for their skills.

Problems

1. True or False?
   a. Fixed salaries rarely provide the right incentives for managers.

   b. Accounting ROI provides an absolute measure of performance.

   c. Inflation has little effect on the ROI as it affects both the revenues and costs.

   d. All important expenditures pass through the capital budgeting process.

   e. Economic value added as usually calculated reflect the NPV of the project.

   f. Book depreciation cannot be negative.

g. Economic depreciation can be negative.

h. Changing project hurdle rates has little effect on the number of projects proposed.

2. Joe's Café is considering an expansion project which requires an investment of $200,000 and is expected to produce after-tax annual cash flows of $60,000 for each of the next five years. The cash flows beyond five years are ignored. Calculate the NPV, IRR, pay back, and the average accounting ROI for the project. Assume a cost of capital of 15 percent and straight-line depreciation.

3. A project has the following cash flows: $C_0 = -168, C_1 = 60, C_2 = 75, C_3 = 90$.
   a. Calculate the IRR.
   b. Find the accounting rate of return for each year using straight-line depreciation.
   c. Calculate the weighted average accounting rate of return using the beginning period book value discounted at the IRR as the weight for each year.

4. An asset costs $740,000 and is expected to produce a cash flow of $180,000 each year for the next 6 years. The cost of capital is 12 percent.
   a. Calculate the accounting income using straight-line depreciation.
   b. Calculate the economic income for each year.
   c. What are the cash flows required to make the economic depreciation straight-line and provide the same present value?

5. Division X of ABC Inc. has an accounting income of $145,000. The division uses assets of $800,000 and has a cost of capital of 15%. Calculate the ROI and the EVA.

6. Given below are the income and asset values for three divisions of FOB Corp. Calculate the ROI and the EVA. Between accounting income and EVA, which measures the performance of the divisions better?

	Division 1	Division 2	Division 3
Net Income	$215 million	$400 million	$125 million
Assets employed	$2,100 million	$2,600 million	$750 million
Cost of capital	14%	11%	12%

Essay Questions

1. Describe the various stages of the capital budgeting process.

2. Discuss the relative merits of using EVA and ROI for measuring the operating performance of divisions and departments.

3. Explain the importance of timely and accurate information in the capital budgeting process.

4. "It is not possible or even desirable to eliminate all agency costs. Discuss.

5. Describe some of the problems involved in managing and controlling the capital budgeting process and ensuring that managers maximize the shareholders' wealth.

6. Compare and contrast economic and book income. Do you agree with the view that accountants should not try to measure economic income?

ANSWERS TO EXERCISES

Fill-in-Questions

1. Capital budget
2. Understates, overstates
3. Appropriation request
4. Price
5. Overestimate, underestimate

6. Post-audit
7. Agents, shareholders
8. Board of directors
9. Monitoring
10. Need

Problems

1. True or False?
   a. True   b. True   c. False   d. False
   e. False   f. True   g. True   h. True

2. NPV = $1,129
   IRR = 15.24%
   Pay back period = 3.33 years

$$\text{Average accounting ROI} = \frac{Average Accounting Income}{Average Investment}$$
$$= \$20,000/\$100,000 = 20\%$$

Average accounting income = cash flow - book depreciation = $60,000 - $40,000 = $20,000

143

3. a. IRR = 15 %

b. Accounting rates of return are given in the table below:

	Year 1	Year 2	Year 3
Cash flow	60	75	90
Beginning book value	168	112	56
Depreciation	56	56	56
Book income	4	19	34
Accounting ROI (%)	2.38	16.96	60.71

c. Weighted average accounting ROI:

Year	Discounted book value	Weight	Accounting ROI	Weighted ROI
1	168/1 = 168	168/307.73 = 0.5459	2.38	1.30
2	112/1.15 = 97.39	97.39/307.73 = 0.3165	16.96	5.37
3	$56/(1.15)^2 = 42.34$	42.34/307.73 = 0.1376	60.71	8.35
Total	307.73	1.00		15. 02

The weighted average ROI is the same (except for rounding error) as the IRR.

4. a. Accounting income = cash flow - depreciation = $180,000 - ($740,000/6) = $56,667

b.

Year	0	1	2	3	4	5	6
Cash flow		180	180	180	180	180	180
Present value	740	649	547	432	304	161	0
Economic depreciation		91	102	115	128	143	161
Economic income		89	78	65	52	37	19

c. Each year the present value should decrease by (740,000/6) = $123,333. Each year's cash flow will be the depreciation amount + 12 percent of the previous year's present value. The present value and cash flows are given in the table below:

Year	Present value	Cash flow
0	$740,000	
1	$616,667	$212,133
2	$493,333	$197,333
3	$370,000	$182,533
4	$246,667	$167,733
5	$123,333	$152,933
6	0	$138,133

5. ROI $= \$145,000/\$800,000 = 18.13\%$
   EVA $= \$145,000 - 0.15 \times \$800,000 = \$25,000$

6.

	Division 1	Division 2	Division 3
Net income	$215 million	$400 million	$125 million
ROI	215/2100 = 10.24%	400/2,600 = 15.38%	125/750 = 16.67%
EVA	215 - 0.14 x 2100 = -$79 million	400 - 0.11 x 2600 = $114 million	125 - 0.12 x 750 = $35 million

The EVA is a better measure of performance as it adjusts for the capital employed and the business risk through the cost of capital. Division 1 has not earned enough income to cover its cost of capital.

13

Corporate Financing and the Six Lessons of Market Efficiency

INTRODUCTION

This chapter is the first of 15 chapters dealing with corporate financing decisions. So far, we have focused on the asset side of the balance sheet. Now the focus shifts to raising funds to finance corporate investments. While both financing and investment decisions can add or destroy value; it is much harder to find positive NPV financing decisions. Financial markets are efficient and fierce competition one encounters in these markets is likely to eliminate any possible gain. The chapter explains the concept of market efficiency in detail and reviews evidence supporting and contradicting market efficiency. The chapter concludes with the six lessons or key implications of market efficiency for the corporate finance manager.

This chapter is a very important precursor to corporate financing decisions because understanding market efficiency and its implications is key to understanding all financing decisions. While analyzing investment decisions, we have assumed away the financing question or taken the financing as given. The same approach, in reverse, is used for evaluating the financing decisions; (i.e., with the investment decisions as given, what will be the best financing decision?). The primary goal of maximizing the NPV remains the same. The main lesson in this chapter is that owing to the competitive nature of the financial markets, it will be very hard to find positive NPV financing opportunities, or simply put, there is no easy way to make money.

KEY CONCEPTS IN THE CHAPTER

NPV of Financing Decisions: When corporations raise money from the capital market through bond or stock issue, they receive funds in exchange for explicit or implied promise of future payments to the investors who buy these bonds or stocks. The NPV for a financing decision can be calculated just like it was done for the investment decisions, though the pattern of cash flows will be somewhat different, with cash inflows at the beginning and outflows in later years. The discount rate used for computing present values should reflect the normal cost of the type of financing used. In general, financing decisions differ from investment decisions in the following ways: i) financing decisions are often more complex because of the variety of financing forms used - debt, equity, long-term and short term debt, convertible debt, debt with adjustable interest rates, to name some typical forms used; ii) it is harder to find positive NPV financing decisions because of intense competition in the capital market, and iii) financing decisions can often be reversed more easily than most investment decisions. The important difference between financing and investment is that firms rarely have a competitive advantage in financing unlike in real product markets where they have often built up competitive advantage in terms of brand loyalty and reputation for quality and service. It is also true that financial markets are far less segmented than some might imagine. Capital flows freely across borders and different types of markets.

Market Efficiency: A market is considered efficient when prices in the market fully reflect information about the securities. Since new information about securities, by definition, will be random, price changes also must be random. In other words, day to day price changes cannot be predicted and will be totally random. A British statistician did find stock price changes to be random and actual price changes observed were found to be as random as the results of a serial coin tossing game with a slightly higher pay-off for heads. A direct implication of market efficiency is that it will not be easy to find positive NPV financing or investment opportunities. In other words, it will not be possible to find under-priced or overpriced securities. Economists have classified market efficiency into three forms based on the type of information that is reflected in security prices. These are briefly described below.

Weak form efficiency: The market is said to be weak form efficient if prices fully reflect all information about past prices. In other words, market prices will not follow any predictable patterns. Any forecast based on past price patterns will be useless as investment tools and will not help an investor make superior returns. Competition for profits will destroy any useful patterns or cycles.

Semi-strong form efficiency: The market is said to be semi-strong form efficient if security prices fully reflect all publicly available information such as announcement of earnings, issues of stocks or bonds, stock splits, mergers, etc. In essence, a semi-strong form efficient market will react quickly and instantaneously to new information and it will be impossible to trade on the news and make money.

Strong form efficiency: The most rigorous form of efficiency implies that security prices will fully reflect all information including that which is not publicly available. It implies that even information which is unearthed by careful and expensive research analysts and investment managers will not give you superior returns, as the prices will reflect even this information.

Semi-strong form efficiency implies weak form efficiency and strong form efficiency implies weak and semi-strong form efficiencies.

Investment Analysts and Market Efficiency: Market efficiency is the result of competition among investment analysts and portfolio managers to exploit any mis-pricing observed in the market. These analysts and portfolio managers spend enormous amounts of resources to uncover the latest and most useful information about any stock they are interested in. Typical investment analysts can be classified into one of two types: *fundamental analysts* who study the firm's business and all the factors which affect the company's earnings prospects; and *technical analysts* who study historic prices and attempt to identify specific patterns using charts and other tools. Competition among fundamental analysts will ensure that market prices reflect all

148

available information and competition among technical analysts ensures that prices reflect historic price information.

Empirical Evidence: Market efficiency is one of the most researched topics in financial economics and empirical evidence generally finds it to be efficient. Different types of tests were used to test the different forms of market efficiency. Weak form efficiency was tested by using trading rules suggested by technical analysts who claimed to have discovered patterns in price movements. It was invariably found that these trading rules did not generate superior profits. Other tests for weak form efficiency included tests for significant relationships between successive daily or weekly returns. Tests have found little serial correlation in daily or weekly returns for markets in many different countries. Tests for semi-strong form efficiency have included analyzing market reactions to earnings announcements, stock splits, accounting changes, and mergers or other significant corporate events. In general, these tests have shown that market reaction is swift and nearly instantaneous leaving very little time to make profitable trades once the news is announced. Performance of mutual fund managers and stock analysts has been used to test the strong form efficiency. If these professionals show superior performance, it can be interpreted as market inefficiency. While some fund managers appear to have shown consistently better performance, most studies have failed to find superior performance by fund managers and analysts. In general, few mutual funds do consistently better than the market averages or comparable benchmarks. When the mutual fund performance is adjusted for expenses, the returns on average are lower than comparable market benchmarks. This is fairly strong support of the efficient market hypothesis.

Evidence Against Market Efficiency: While the evidence for market efficiency is very convincing, researchers have also discovered a number of *anomalies* or *puzzles*, which seem to indicate some market inefficiencies. These anomalies include: significantly higher returns for smaller stocks, persistent patterns of higher returns for the month of January compared to other months, lower returns for Mondays compared to Fridays, and patterns indicating differing returns for different times of the trading day. Researchers have offered different explanations for these puzzles and anomalies. The small firm effect, for example, may be explained as one of three possible cases: i) higher risk premium required by investors and not fully captured by the CAPM, ii) result of the specific time period used for the study - the effect would disappear if one looked at the returns for the nineties, and iii) a possible exception to the efficient market theory.

It is important to note that few of these anomalies and puzzles have actually yielded opportunities for making money.

Relative vs. Absolute Efficiency: An implication of market efficiency is that securities are fairly priced and the prices reflect the intrinsic value of the securities. The stock market crash of October 19, 1997 - prices dropped 23 percent in a single day - raised serious doubts about the market's ability to value securities correctly. If the prices were fair the day before the crash, it is hard to argue that they remained fair the day after. While one can justify large price changes as the result of changes in expectations of earnings growth, it will be hard to argue that the market or the investors can always correctly price securities on an absolute basis. The pricing or

149

valuation is correct only in a relative sense. It is impossible to test absolute intrinsic valuation and thus absolute efficiency. We can price the stock of General Motors and be reasonably sure about its valuation, only if we assume that Ford or some other automobile manufacturer comparable to GM is priced reasonably correct. In the absence of such a benchmark for comparison, we cannot be sure of our valuation. Thus, while we are reasonably certain about the market being relatively efficient, one cannot make any claim about absolute market efficiency.

Implications of Market Anomalies: Market anomalies may lead to under-pricing or overpricing of the firm's stock. It is important to note that overpricing of your firm's stock does not mean that it is good to issue stocks and invest in negative NPV projects; you are better off in investing in the capital markets in other securities. Under-pricing of your stock precludes you from issuing stocks.

The Six Lessons of Market Efficiency: While the anomalies and puzzles raise serious questions about market efficiency, the finance manager will do well to heed some basic lessons about market behavior. These are summarized below.

Lesson 1 - Markets have no memory: This stresses weak form efficiency and clearly implies that attempts at timing the market for bond or stock issue are unlikely to result in value maximizing decisions. Historic prices and recent trends are not much help in forecasting the market trend. It is unfortunately true that many managers try to time the market by picking the best time to issue securities.

Lesson 2 - Trust market prices: It is not possible for most investors to consistently find bargains or under-priced securities in the market. Market prices reflect the collective wisdom of all the investors and analysts and therefore will be the best estimates of the value of the securities. In other words, it is unreasonable and unwise to assume that one can predict the prices better than the market itself. The Orange County story is an excellent example of how a county treasurer lost $1.7 billion betting on his ability to forecast the direction of interest rate changes.

Lesson 3 - Read the entrails: Market prices tell us a lot about the future. Security prices typically reflect what investors expect to happen in the future. For example, the difference between short-term and long-term interest indicates the expected changes in interest rates. The return offered by a company's bonds and the variability of its common stock prices are good indicators of the probability of its going bankrupt. Market reactions to corporate announcements such as mergers, acquisitions, and restructuring give managers fair indication of the valuation effect of these actions. The market reaction to Viacom's takeover bid of Paramount in 1993 is a good example of this lesson (page ...). A very good measure of the market reaction is the abnormal return, which is the net return on the stock surrounding the event after taking into account the normal or expected return. (Abnormal return = actual return - expected return, where the expected return is measured as $a + b\, r_m$).

Lesson 4 - There are no financial illusions: Investors are concerned with the firm's cash flows and are unlikely to be impressed by accounting gimmicks or other cosmetic changes which do not enhance the cash flows. Therefore, a firm cannot expect to increase its value by merely cosmetic changes such as stock splits or by manipulating the earnings reported to shareholders.

Lesson 5 - The do-it-yourself alternative: Investors will not pay others for anything that they can create or do themselves at a lower cost. An implication of this lesson is that corporate combinations pursuing diversification for risk reduction is unlikely to be valued highly in the market as investors can duplicate this strategy at lower costs by buying shares of companies in different industries.

Lesson 6 - Seen one stock, seen all: Unlike branded products, stocks do not have unique qualities; investors buy a stock if the expected return it offers is fair compensation for the risk it entails. This means that stocks, which offer similar return-risk trade off, are near perfect substitutes for each other or the demand for any given stock is highly elastic. The implication is that large blocks of a stock can be sold at close to the market price as the market is convinced that you have no private information. Scholes' study of secondary offerings confirmed that large offerings had only a very small effect on the price.

Explanation of Terms and Mathematical Expressions

NPV of financing = Present value of amount raised - Present value of all future payments

NPV of a loan (or bond issue) = Amount borrowed - PV (interest payments) - PV (principal payments)

Abnormal return = Actual return - Expected return
Expected return = $a + b\, r_m$, where a is the return on the stock when the market return is zero and b is the beta of the stock.

Abnormal return measures the extra return on a stock as a reaction to a specific announcement by the company and is used to measure the impact of an action taken by the company using the event study method.

WORKED EXAMPLE

a. Salken Inc., a Japanese machine tool manufacturer, is planning to expand its manufacturing base in the US and has been offered a special loan of $25 million by the state of Tennessee. The loan is for a term of 5 years and carries an interest of 4% to be paid annually. Salken's normal borrowing rate for 5 year borrowing is 6%. What is the value of this special loan to Salken?

b. SD Cambridge and Company, an Internet firm, is trying to decide on an issue of new shares. The company already has 6 million shares outstanding and it is authorized to issue up to an additional 2 million shares.

i.   What proportion of the firm will have to be sold in order to raise $15 million if shares can be sold: at $50 each and at $30 each?

ii. The company's shares are currently selling at $50. What is the loss to the existing shareholders if the shares are actually sold to new investors at $30?

iii. If the market is efficient, what is the likely price at which the company can sell the shares?

SOLUTION

a. The special loan offer is obviously a good one and the value of the special loan can be calculated by computing the NPV of the loan using Salken's normal borrowing rate of 6%.

   NPV = + 25 - PV (interest payments) - PV (principal) = 25 - 4.212 - 18.682 = $2.106 m

b. i) Number of shares to be issued to raise $15 m:
   @ $50/share = 15,000,000/50 = 300,000; total shares after the issue = 6,300,000
   Proportion sold to new investors = 300,000/6,300,000 = 4.76%
   @ $30/share = 15,000,000/30 = 500,000; total shares after the issue = 6,500,000
   Proportion sold to new investors = 500,000/6,500,000 = 7.69%

   ii) Value of the firm before the new issue = $50 x 6,000,000 = $300 m
       New capital raised   = $30 x 500,000 = $15 m
       Total value of the firm after issue   = $315 m
       Value per share   = $315/6.5 = $48.46/share
       Loss to existing stockholders   = 6,000,000 ($50-$48.46) = $9.24 m

   iii) If the market is efficient, the stocks could be sold at a price closer to $50 than at $30.

CHAPTER SUMMARY

This chapter covered one of the most important ideas of modern financial economics - the efficient market hypothesis. The financial markets are characterized by intense competition among investors trying to exploit all the information they have and thus causing prices to be fair and competitive. This means that all one can hope for is a fair return. It is not easy to make money in the financial markets; one can only get fair returns for the risk born. Market prices fully reflect information available about the securities. The efficiency is termed weak form, semi-strong form, or strong form depending on the type of information which is reflected in the security prices (historic prices for weak form, public information for semi-strong form, and all information for strong form). The three forms are nested; strong form efficiency implies the other two forms and semi-strong form implies weak form efficiency. Empirical evidence strongly supports weak form and semi-strong form and offers qualified support for the strong form. Researchers have discovered several anomalies and puzzles. This has led to some serious challenges to the efficient market hypothesis. Market efficiency implies fair valuation of assets; however, valuation can only be relative. There is no way we can be sure about intrinsic valuation of assets in an absolute sense. We can only be certain of market efficiency in a relative sense.

Efficient market provides six important lessons to the finance manager. A smart manager will heed these lessons, as ignoring them is unlikely to lead to value enhancing decisions.

LIST OF TERMS

Abnormal return
Efficient market
Elasticity of demand
Fundamental analysis
Random walk
Semi-strong form efficiency

Stock dividend
Stock split
Strong-form efficiency
Technical analysis
Weak form efficiency

EXERCISES

Fill-in-Questions

1. In an efficient market, security prices fully reflect _____ about the securities.

2. The three forms of market efficiency are _____, _____, and _____.

3. A strong form efficient market implies _____ also.

4. The prices of securities appear to follow a _____ in which each successive price change is independent of all previous price changes.

5. Analysts who research basic business information about the company and the industry to estimate the company's earnings and stock price are called _____ analysts.

6. _____ analysts study the history of past prices to discover patterns that they believe can be exploited to earn high returns.

7. A strong form efficient market implies that investors can only earn a _____ return on their investment.

8. If prices reflect all published information, the market satisfies the conditions for _____.

9. If prices fully reflect historic information on prices, the market is said to be _____.

153

10. The _____ of an article is the percentage change in the quantity demanded for one-percent change in its price.

11. The abnormal return on a firm's stock is the difference between its actual return and its _____ return.

12. A _____ increases the number of outstanding shares and reduces the unit price.

Problems

1. True or False?

   a. A market which is weak form efficient will also be semi-strong form efficient.

   b. A strong form efficient market will also be weak form efficient.

   c. In an efficient market, investors can only earn the risk free rate of return.

   d. The demand elasticity for stocks is fairly low.

   e. Stock splits will enhance shareholder value.

   f. If short-term interest rates were lower than long-term rates, it would be better to borrow short-term.

   g. In an efficient market investors cannot expect to earn high abnormal returns.

2. O'Reilly Ketchups is planning to invest in a new food processing plant in Ireland and the Irish government has offered them a low interest loan for $15 million. The loan has a term of 3 years and an interest rate of 3%. The cost of a comparable bank loan for O'Reilly will be 5%. What is the value of the special loan to O'Reilly?

3. Oats and Barley Inc. has 26 million shares outstanding and the stock is currently selling at $120. The company announced a 3 for 2 stock split. What will be the stock price after the split becomes effective? How many outstanding shares will there be after the split?

4. Dream.com is an Internet company and it believes that its stock is currently overvalued by the market. Its shares are selling at $60 although management believes they are worth only $40. There are currently 10 million shares outstanding, and the company plans to raise $50 million by issuing 1 million shares at $50 each. The existing shareholders can sell their rights to subscribe to this issue for $9,090,900. Assume that the existing stockholders sell their rights and all the new shares are taken up by new investors. How much will the original shareholders have gained if: (a) the shares were worth only $40 before and (b) they were

154

worth $60?

5. You can buy a 12 percent coupon, 15-year bond at $1,000 (face value). It is expected that one year from now, the bond will yield 10 percent. (a) If this forecast is correct, what will be your return on this investment? (b) What implications does this have for forecasting interest rates in terms of (i) its usefulness and (ii) its difficulty? Assume interest is paid annually.

6. The highly respected economic forecasting department of a major United States bank announces that its latest forecast predicts a significant upturn in economic activity and corporate profits starting in 2 years and lasting for 3 or 4 years. What effect on share prices do you expect this to have (a) immediately, (b) in 2 years, and (c) in 6 years?

7. Identify for which two of the following items demand is least elastic with respect to price and for which two it is most elastic: (a) steak, (b) tobacco, (c) a financial security, (d) gasoline, (e) tuxedos, and (f) shortening.

8. Happy Luck Club has a market value of $40 million. Don't Worry Inc. has a market value of $20 million. A proposed merger between them seems likely to reduce the standard deviation of their equity returns from 40 percent individually to 35 percent combined. What would you expect the market value of the combined company to be after the merger?

9. Which of the following is most likely to result in an increase in the value of a company's shares? (a) It announces that its long-awaited contract with the federal government has now been finalized, and production will begin as soon as a satisfactory specification can be agreed upon. (b) As a result of a change in its depreciation policy, the earnings figure in its newly released annual report is almost double the figure for the previous year. (c) It announces a 50 percent increase in its dividend. (d) Its main competitor announces a price cut.

10. In 1998, Daimler Benz, the German automobile manufacturer, and Chrysler Corporation agreed to merge. Each Chrysler share was to be exchanged for 0.625 shares of Daimler. Shortly after the announcement, Chrysler shares were selling for $52 and the Daimler shares were selling at $96. (The basic share is traded in German marks, but its equivalent (American Depository Receipts (ADR) was traded in the New York stock exchange.). Some saw this as an opportunity to make money with no risk and an example of market inefficiency. What do you think?

Essay Questions

1. "Financing decisions are easier to make, but it is harder to increase shareholder value through financing decisions." Discuss.

2. "There are so many anomalies and puzzles that efficient market is an exception rather than the rule." Discuss.

3. Band-Aid mutual fund has earned high annual returns for each of the last three years beating the market handily. Can this be seen as clear evidence against the strong form efficiency?

4. George Soros manages a very large hedge fund with assets over $5 billion. His fund has earned very high annual returns through sophisticated trading techniques in a variety of markets (foreign exchange, stock markets, and bond markets in many different countries). How will you respond to the argument that cases like Mr. Soros clearly show that markets are inefficient and lots of money can be made through various trading techniques?

5. "Performance of some very successful mutual funds is proof that the market is inefficient." Discuss.

ANSWERS TO EXERCISES

Fill-in Questions

1. Information
2. Weak form, semi-strong form, strong form
3. Semi-strong form and weak form
4. Random walk
5. Fundamental analysts
6. Technical

7. Fair
8. Semi-strong form
9. Weak form
10. Demand elasticity
11. Expected
12. Stock split (or stock dividend)

Problems

1. True or False
   a. False   b. True   c. False   d. False
   e. False   f. False   g. True

2. Value of the special loan to O'Reilly = NPV of the loan financing at 5 percent
   $$= +15 - PV(\text{interest payments}) - PV(\text{principal})$$
   $$= +15 - (2.7232 \times 0.45) - (0.8638 \times 15)$$
   $$= \$0.817 \text{ million}$$

3. Stock price after the split   = $120 x 2/3 = $80
   Number of shares after the split   = 26 x 3/2   = 39 million shares

4. a.   If the shares were worth $40:
       Value before issue = $40 x 10 = $400 million
       After the issue, the existing stockholders receive $9.0909 million and 10/11th of the value of the firm before the issue plus the $50 million raised by the issue.

       Value after the issue = $9.0909 + 10/11(400+50) = $418.182 million
       The existing shareholders have benefited by $18.182 million.

b. If the shares were worth $60:
Value before issue = $60 x 10 = $600 million
After the issue, the existing stockholders receive $9.0909 million and 10/11th of the value of the firm before the issue plus the $50 million raised by the issue.
Value after the issue = $9.0909 + 10/11(600+50) = $600 million

5. a. The value of the value of the bond one-year from now will rise to $1,147.33. An investor buying the bond today will receive the coupon of $120 plus $1,147.33 earning a total return of 26.73 per cent.

   b. Any one who can forecast interest rates accurately can make a lot of money. It will be extremely difficult to make accurate forecasts.

6. There will be an immediate effect on the stock price to the extent that the forecast represents an improvement for the company's prospects. There will be no effect in later years.

7. The tobacco and tuxedos will have the lowest elasticity and the financial security and shortening will have the highest.

8. The value of the combined company will be about $60 million; the market prices for each company already reflect their market risk as measured by their beta.

9. The award of the contract is likely to result in an increase in its stock price to the extent this is not already expected and reflected in the price. The other news are unlikely to cause an increase in stock price.

10. If Chrysler shares were to fully reflect the value of the impending merger, they should be selling at $96 x 0.625 = $60. Thus, it appears that they are undervalued. However, an arbitrage transaction involving buying Chrysler shares and selling Daimler shares in equivalent quantities is unlikely to be risk free. Two factors to be considered are: i) potential foreign exchange risk (Daimler shares are priced in German marks), and ii) possible breakdown in the merger talks. Thus, the market price is probably a reflection of the risks involved rather than an opportunity to make money in a risk free transaction.

14

An Overview of Corporate Financing

INTRODUCTION

This chapter provides a broad introduction to corporate financing and gives a descriptive overview of the three main generic types of securities companies issue: common stock, debt, and preferred stock. The chapter also gives you a glimpse of derivative securities such as options of various kinds. This is the first of the many chapters on long-term financing decisions. While companies finance a large part of their new investments from internally generated funds, they also use large amounts of externally raised money. Most of this external funding comes from the issuance of either debt or equity.

The simple classification of external financing sources as debt and equity takes away all the details in which these can be different. The debt securities issued by a company can differ in so many little details, with some important consequences for the firm. Even equity issues can have different classifications based on voting rights. All these have given rise to a number of technical terms used in the world of corporate finance. The chapter explains these terms and the context of the use for them. Students of finance are expected to have at least a passing familiarity with this language of investment banking. The list of the main new terms and the set of fill-in questions should prove to be very useful in learning these terms.

The first section of the chapter provides a description of the changing patterns of corporate financing in the U.S. The section also includes a very interesting comparison of the financing patterns across countries. It is important to realize that comparisons of this type have to take into account the differences in accounting rules and conventions followed in different countries. Each of the next four sections covers common stock, debt, preferred stock, and derivatives. At the end of the chapter, you will realize that there are many different manifestations of equity, debt, and even preferred stock. The later chapters will get into the rationale for the existence of the many forms of corporate securities.

KEY CONCEPTS IN THE CHAPTER

There are a few new concepts in this chapter. The chapter essentially provides a descriptive overview of corporate financing. We will give here key terms and substantive material included in the text.

Patterns of Corporate Financing: For 1997, the following summary pattern emerged for uses and sources of funds by the U.S. non-financial corporations: (all figures indicate percentages)

Uses	Percent	Sources	Percent
Capital Expenditure	83	Internally generated	85
Net working capital	17	External financing	
		Net stock issue - -14	
		Net debt issue - 29	
			15
Total	100	Total	100

The pattern during the period 1988 to 1997 was similar though year to year variations were there. For seven of the ten years, companies bought back stock or there was net negative stock issue. These large net repurchases of this decade are atypical. More commonly, you will find a small percentage of stock issue. What is also common is the high percentage of funds provided by internally generated cash. Companies have to make two basic financing decisions: what percentage of profits to be paid out as dividends (the remaining to be reinvested in business) and what mix of debt and external equity should be used to finance the deficit. These questions take you directly to dividend and debt policies and are discussed in chapters 16, 17, and 18. Overall, financing decisions can be regarded as the marketing of a package of securities with rights to the company profits and cash flows.

In general, during the last 45 years or so, companies' balance sheets have shown a marked increase in the proportion of debt to total assets (from a little over 30 percent in the fifties to over 60 percent in the nineties). At least part of the reason is that progressive inflation has increased the market values of assets relative to their book values. It is also observed that debt ratios of the nineties are similar to the ratios of the 1920s and 1930s. We will also see some other explanations discussed in later chapters. Despite this large increase, the proportion of debt in U.S. balance sheets does not seem too out of line when international comparisons are made. One has to be careful to correct for accounting differences before drawing conclusions about differences across countries. The U.S. companies are in the middle of the international pack compared.

Common Stock: Common stock represents ownership of the company and the common stockholders, as the owners of the company, have a general preemptive right to anything of value that the company may wish to distribute. The stockholders are residual claimants of everything the company has. They receive distribution of profits usually in the form of dividends. While most companies have only one form of common stock, some companies have issued stocks of different classes with different voting rights.

A company is allowed to issue shares up to the amount specified by its *authorized* share capital, which can only be increased with the permission of the shareholders. Outstanding shares are those held by investors. Shares that have been issued but subsequently repurchased by the company (and held in its treasury) are called treasury shares. They are said to be issued but not outstanding. All issued shares are entered in the company's accounts at their par value. Because

160

some states do not allow companies to sell shares below par value, par value is generally set at a low figure, which has no economic significance.

Stockholders, as owners of the company, have the ultimate control of the company. Their control over the company's affairs is manifested by their right to vote on appointments to the board of directors and on some other issues such as a merger of the company with another. Stockholders have to vote approval of major changes in the articles of incorporation of the company. Voting may be on a majority basis or on a cumulative basis. Cumulative voting makes it more likely for minority groups to obtain representation on the board. Under this system shareholders may, if they wish, allot all their votes to one candidate. For example, if six directors are to be elected, a shareholder can allocate all six votes from each share to a single candidate and does not have to choose six candidates to vote for. Where there are different classes of stocks with different voting rights, the classes with more voting rights will generally command a premium in the market. The premium will be a function of the extra benefits the stockholders can get because of their superior voting rights.

Ownership interests in businesses may be held in forms other than common stock. While common stocks are issued by corporations, comparable ownership securities for other organization forms of business are called different names such as units in *master limited partnerships* and *real estate investment trusts*.

Preferred Stock: Preferred stock is legally considered as equity but generally has only limited voting rights. Unlike common stock, though, most preferred stock is issued with a stipulated dividend and this dividend has to be paid before any dividend to common stockholders can be paid. Preferred stockholders' claims take precedence over that of the common stockholders if the company ever goes out of business. In general, only a small portion of corporate financing needs is met through the issue of preferred stock. It can be very useful means of financing in certain special situations.

There are some interesting tax implications with preferred stock dividends. Preferred stock dividends are not tax-deductible expenses for the company paying them. However, corporations receiving preferred stock dividends have to pay tax only on 30 percent of the dividends. Most of the preferred stocks is held by corporations (favorable treatment of dividend income), and most is issued by regulated utility companies (who would be made to lower their rates if they used subsidized debt instead).

Corporate Debt: There are a great variety of ways in which companies can borrow money. The common feature is that the company promises to make regular interest payments and to repay the principal amount according to an agreed schedule. The company's liability is limited, so lenders can only look to the earnings and assets of the company for their payment. Lenders cannot look beyond those assets to the shareholders for repayment. Generally, debt can be classified along the following eight dimensions:

- *Maturity*: The length of time before the debt is due to be completely repaid. Long-term debt which does not mature for more than a year is called *funded debt*. Short-term debt due in less than a year is called *unfunded debt*.
- *Provision for repayment*: Long-term loans may be repaid in a single "bullet" payment on their maturity date, or they may be repaid steadily over time. A *sinking fund* is often used to retire publicly traded bonds gradually. The borrower may also have a call provision which provides the right to repay all or part of the debt issue before maturity at some specified premium above its face value.
- *Seniority*: Debt may be junior or senior. If the company goes bankrupt, its junior (or *subordinated*) debt is not eligible to receive payment until all senior debt has been paid in full.
- *Security*: Debt may be secured by some or all of the assets of the company. A lot of corporate debt is issued as unsecured debt without explicit collateral. Secured debt has first claim, in the event of default, on the assets specified as collateral. A *mortgage* is an example of this, while long-term bonds which are unsecured are called debentures (at least in the U.S., but not in Great Britain). *Securitization* involves selling securities backed by assets to investors. The assets which are the collateral are sold to an independent trust which receives all the cash flows from the assets, which are passed on to the investors. The securities issued in this form are *asset-backed securities*. Typical assets used for securitization include credit card debt, car loans, mortgages, etc.
- *Default risk*: A bond is *investment-grade* if it qualifies for one of the top four ratings from the Moody's or Standard and Poor's rating services. Below-investment-grade debts are called *junk bonds*. Bond ratings are discussed in Chapter 23.
- *Public versus privately placed debt*: Bonds sold as a public issue are offered to anyone who wants to buy them and can be freely traded afterwards. Bonds sold in a private placement are sold directly to a small number of qualified institutional investors, and subsequently can only be resold among these investors.
- *Fixed rate or floating rate*: The interest rate may be *fixed* for the whole term of the loan when the debt is issued. Alternatively, it may be a *floating rate*, determined from time to time during the term according to an agreed formula such as "1 percent above *prime*" or "1/2 percent above *LIBOR*." Floating rate debt may be issued using a number of different benchmark interest rates.
- *Country and currency*: Although most borrowing by United States corporations is done in the United States and in United States dollars, firms may also borrow in foreign countries or in foreign currencies. When a company issues debt in a currency outside the currency's home country (e.g. yen bonds outside Japan), these are called *eurobonds*.

Leases: A contract to lease equipment is essentially an alternative form of borrowing. Leasing is considered equivalent to long-term secured debt. Chapter 25 analyzes leases.

Warrants: Warrants are often issued by companies as part of a package to sell other securities. Most commonly they are used to sell bonds. Warrants give their owner the right to purchase one share of common stock at a specified price on or before a specified future date. Thus, they are essentially call options issued by the company.

Convertible Bonds: These are bonds issued by the company that can be exchanged for (or converted to) a specified number of shares on specific future dates if the holder wishes. The holder will, of course, wish to convert if the stock price goes up well above the level when conversion makes sense. If the stock price does not go up, the holder has no obligation to convert. Essentially, a convertible bond is like a package of a bond plus a warrant. One difference is that when the convertible bondholder converts, she exchanges the bond for a certain number of shares, but pays no cash. The warrant holder has to pay cash to get his shares. Warrants and convertible bonds are covered in Chapter 22.

Derivatives: Derivatives are securities whose value depend on an underlying asset such as a commodity or market price such as interest rate or exchange rate. Corporations do not issue derivatives to raise money, but often buy them to hedge against adverse changes in external factors such as interest rates, currency values, commodity prices, etc. Four basic types of derivatives have been very popular. These are: traded options, futures contracts, forward contracts, and swaps.

Traded Options: An option gives you the right to buy (call) or sell (put) an asset without the obligation to do so. Options are traded on stocks, bonds, currencies, and many commodities.

Futures and Forwards: Futures and forward contracts allow you to buy or sell an asset at a future date for a fixed price, which is fixed when you buy the contract. Futures are standardized, exchange traded contracts. Forward contracts are custom designed and agreed to between the buyer and the seller. Banks buy and sell custom made forward contracts on currencies to corporations interested in them.

Swaps: A swap is an exchange of obligations to service different debts, for example, dollars vs. sterling or fixed rate vs. floating.

Options are covered in Chapters 20 and 21. The other derivatives are discussed in Chapter 26.

SUMMARY

This chapter provided an overview of the different types of securities issued and used by corporations. The chapter also gave a historic perspective on the changing patterns of corporate financing in the U.S. and provided international comparisons with other industrialized countries. The primary objective of the chapter is to familiarize you with the broad features of corporate securities and the terminology used in corporate finance.

Corporations use three types of securities to raise the financing they need. The simplest of these is common stock. Common stockholders are owners of the corporation and are entitled to its profits, vote on the composition of the company's board of directors, and other important matters.

Companies occasionally use preferred stock, though its use is far less common than debt and is used in special situations. Preferred stock has features of both debt and common stock – it has a fixed payment, but it is legally considered equity, and payments to preferred stockholders are not tax-deductible.

Debt is widely used by companies to meet part of their external funding needs. Debt comes in many different varieties and the chapter lists the many features taken on modern day corporate debt. Debt can be classified in terms of its maturity, repayment provisions, seniority of the debt, security, interest payment, issue procedures, and currency of the debt.

Lastly, the chapter provides a very brief introduction to derivatives. The four common derivative securities covered are – options, futures, forwards, and swaps. Corporations use these to protect against risk related to external factors.

LIST OF TERMS

Authorized share capital	Line of credit
Call	Majority voting
Commercial paper	Mortgage
Convertible bond	Outstanding shares
Cumulative voting	Par value
Debenture	Preferred stock
Derivatives	Prime rate
Eurobond	Secured
Eurodollar	Senior
Floating rate	Sinking fund
Forward	Subordinated
Funded debt	Swap
Future	Traded options
Investment grade	Treasury shares
Junk bond	Warrant
Leasing	

EXERCISES

Fill-in Questions

1. The maximum number of shares that a company can issue is known as its

    _____.

2. Shares that have already been issued and are held by investors are called
_____.

3. _____ are shares that have been repurchased by the company.

4. The _____ of a security is the value at which it is entered in the company's books.

5. _____ is the name for the voting system under which each director is voted on separately.

6. The voting system under which a stockholder may cast all of her or his votes for one candidate is known as _____.

7. Large credit-worthy companies issue _____ as the most common short-term debt security. A(n) _____ with a bank provides further flexibility to meet unexpected cash needs.

8. _____ debt is debt that matures after more than 1 year.

9. To repay its long-term loans in an orderly fashion over an extended period, a company may pay each year a sum of cash into a(n) _____ , which is then used to repurchase the bonds.

10. In the event of bankruptcy, _____ debt must be repaid before subordinated debt receives any payment.

11. _____ debt represents a junior claim which, in the event of default, is paid only after all senior creditors are satisfied.

12. In the event of default, _____ debt has first claim on specified assets.

13. A(n) _____ is secured, while a(n)_____ is a long-term bond that is unsecured.

14. The interest on a(n) _____ loan varies with the short-term interest rate.

15. Banks use the _____ as a benchmark interest rate for most of their loans.

16. A(n) _____ is a dollar that has been deposited with a bank outside the United States.

17. A(n) _____ is an issue of debt that is sold simultaneously in several countries.

18. A long-term rental agreement, known as a(n) _____ can provide an alternative to borrowing.

19. _____ stock is an equity security, which offers a fixed dividend that must be paid before any dividend can be paid on the common stock.

20. A(n) _____ option provides the right to purchase an asset at a specified price on or before a specified exercise date.

21. A(n) _____ is a long-term security issued by a company, which gives the holder the right to purchase one share of common stock at a set price on or before a set date.

22. A bond that may be converted to the company's common stock at the discretion of the holder is called a(n) _____.

23. A(n) _____ gives the holder the right to buy (or sometimes to sell) an asset at a fixed price up to a specified date.

24. A(n) _____ is like a(n) _____ contract but is generally traded on an organized exchange. Both contracts give an obligation to buy (or sell) at a fixed price at some future date.

25. An arrangement by which two companies lend to each other on different terms (for example, in different currencies) is called a(n) _____.

26. Warrants, convertibles, futures, and swaps are all examples of _____.

27. A debt security is _____ if it qualifies for one of the top four ratings from the Moody's or S&P's rating services.

28. Bonds that are not investment-grade are called _____.

Problems

1. The authorized share capital of Boom Corp. is 8 million. The equity is currently shown in the company's accounts as follows:

	Dollars
Common stock ($0.10 par value)	500,000
Additional paid-in capital	4,500,000
Retained earnings	23,000,000

Common equity	28,000,000
Treasury stock (1,000,000 shares)	4,000,000
Net common equity	24,000,000

a. How many shares are issued?
b. How many are outstanding?
c. How many more shares can be issued without the approval of the shareholders?
d. What is the share price if it is twice its book value?

2. Boom Corp. of problem 1 issues a further 1 million shares at an issue price of $4 a share. How will the equity be shown in the company's books after the issue?

3. There are nine directors to be elected, and I own a round lot of 100 shares. What is the maximum number of votes I can cast for my favorite candidate under: (a) majority voting and (b) cumulative voting?

4. The shareholders of Boom Corp. need to elect five directors. There are 4 million shares outstanding. How many shares do you need to own to ensure that you can elect at least one director (a) under majority voting and (b) under cumulative voting?

5. The Bust Card Company has the following income for the year:

Taxable income from operations	$253,000
Interest income	42,000
Dividends from preferred stock	20,000
Dividends from common stock	10,000
Total income	$325,000

It has paid interest charges amounting to $59,000 and dividends on its preferred and common stock of $35,000 and $50,000 respectively. If it pays tax at 35 percent, what is its tax bill for the year?

6. The Bust Card Company of the last problem had the following income and payments in the previous year:

Income from:
Operations	$224,000
Interest	32,000
Preferred dividends	40,000
Common dividends	40,000
	$336,000

Payments:
Interest	$44,000
Preferred dividends	$35,000
Common dividends	$45,000

How much tax should it have paid?

7. Which of the following are true and which are false?

a. If a bond is secured, the company makes regular payments of cash into a sinking fund.
b. The firm's capital expenditure requirements are usually more than covered by internally generated cash.
c. A traded option is not issued by the company whose shares can be bought or sold using it.
d. U.S. leverage ratios have risen steadily over the last 40 years.
e. Junk bonds are bonds issued by recycling companies.

Essay Questions

1. Explain how issued share capital is shown in a company's accounts, and describe what rights and privileges shareholders enjoy.

2. Describe the variety of different types of debt that a company can issue.

3. What is preferred stock, who issues it, who buys it, and why?

4. Describe the main sources and uses of companies' funds. What is meant by the financial deficit and how has its funding varied through time?

5. "It's only when a company goes to the market to raise new equity that it is forced to earn the cost of capital on its funds." Discuss.

ANSWERS TO EXERCISES

Fill-in Questions

1.	Authorized share capital	15.	Prime rate
2.	Outstanding shares	16.	Eurodollar
3.	Treasury shares	17.	Eurobond
4.	Par value	18.	Lease
5.	Majority voting	19.	Preferred
6.	Cumulative voting	20.	Call
7.	Commercial paper, line of credit	21.	Warrant
8.	Funded	22.	Convertible bond
9.	Sinking fund	23.	Traded option

10. Senior
11. Subordinated
12. Secured
13. Mortgage, debenture
14. Floating-rate

24. Future, forward
25. Swap
26. Derivatives
27. Investment-grade
28. Junk bonds

Problems

1. a. 5 million shares
    b. 4 million
    c. 3 million
    d. 2 x ($24/4) = $12

2. The books will show the equity account as follows:

	Dollars
Common stock ($0.10 par value)	600,000
Additional paid-in capital	8,400,000
Retained earnings	23,000,000
Common equity	32,000,000
Treasury stock (1,000,000 shares)	4,000,000
Net common equity	28,000,000

3. a. 100
    b. 900

4. a. More than half the outstanding shares are needed, that is, 2,000,001 shares.
    b. As long as your candidate comes out in the top of a field of six or more candidates she will get elected. This means that she needs one more than one-sixth, that is, 666,667 is sufficient.

5. The taxable income is calculated as follows:

Income from operations	$253,000
Interest income	42,000
30 percent of dividends	9,000
	$304,000
Less interest expense	59,000
	245,000

Its tax bill is 35 percent of $245,000, which is $85,750.

6. Taxable income is given by:

Income from operations	$224,000
Interest income	32,000
30 percent of dividends	<u>24,000</u>
	$280,000
Less interest expense	<u>44,000</u>
Taxable income	$236,000

Tax is 35 percent of $236,000, which is $82,600.

7. a. False
    b. False
    c. True
    d. True
    e. False

15

How Corporations Issue Securities

INTRODUCTION

This chapter describes the procedures used by companies for raising long-term funds in the capital market. It provides a wealth of institutional details and guidance to managers on decisions about long-term capital. The chapter describes the process of venture capital financing in some detail through an extension of the Marvin Enterprises you saw in Chapter 11. This chapter is structured to show the different ways in which companies raise finance in the capital markets. It starts by describing the provision of *venture capital* to young companies and then describes what happens when a company makes an *initial public offering* (IPO). The subsequent sections describe the *general cash offer* used for most public issues of debt or equity securities in the United States. Equity issues made directly to existing shareholders are called *privileged subscription issues* or *rights issues*, and these are described in Appendix A. The chapter also discusses the role of the *underwriter* and the costs of different types of issues. The chapter also covers *private placements* and their importance in financing small- and medium-sized companies.

Financial managers concerned with raising finance need to decide the method of issue, the size of the issue, the pricing of the security, the use of an underwriter, and the type of underwriting arrangement. The manager should also be concerned with the effect the issue will have on the firm's market value. All these are closely related to market efficiency. In general, it is very unlikely that financing decisions will enhance the market value of the firm as a whole. It is, however, quite possible that there may be wealth transfer between one group of security holders and another. The manager will do well to remember the lessons of market efficiency learned in Chapter 13. Here are some implications of market efficiency relevant to this chapter.

Financing Decisions and Stockholder Wealth: Financing decisions seldom affect total security holders' wealth. Furthermore, it is reasonable to assume that most financing decisions have a net present value of zero. This is because a positive NPV financing decision is one where the money raised exceeds the value of the liability created. In the highly competitive capital market, it is very unlikely that any firm could consistently fool investors in this way.

Financing Decisions and the Distribution of Wealth: Financing decisions can, however, affect the distribution of wealth between security holders. If new securities are under-priced, new holders will obtain a bargain at the expense of existing holders. This is not a problem, however, in the case of rights issues, where existing holders are given rights to subscribe in proportion to the size of their holdings. The worked example should help you to handle the kind of calculations that arise with rights issues.

The Importance of Market Prices: When a company is deciding on the issue price for new securities, the best guide to what a company can hope to obtain is the price of closely comparable securities, which are already traded.

There Are No Financial Illusions: It is the effect of financing decisions on stockholders' wealth that matters, and it is difficult to imagine that stockholders will believe one share at $20 is worth more than two shares at $10. Bear this in mind when you read about rights issues.

It is Helpful to Separate Investment and Financing Decisions: If the market believes the investment projects for which the issue proceeds are destined will provide inadequate returns, the stock price will fall. This is the result of a poor investment decision and has nothing to do with the financing operation or the issue method employed.

KEY CONCEPTS IN THE CHAPTER

Venture Capital: Equity investment in the early stages of a business is often called venture capital. Venture capital is key to the success of any growing business as the original investors and founders of the business are unlikely to have the needed capital. The investment is risky, but is rewarded by the high returns of the successful ventures. Specialist investors who are often organized as partnerships typically provide this type of financing. Wealthy individuals and financial institutions are also important players in the venture capital business. In order to monitor the progress of the business and to limit the risk of the investment, venture capital financing is provided in stages with each additional stage of funding contingent on successful completion of some set targets or milestones. *First-stage financing* generally is based on a *business plan.* The business plan describes the exact nature of the proposed business: the product, the market, the resources it will use, and the income it will generate. In obtaining an injection of equity capital, the *after-the-money valuation* is important in putting an implicit valuation on the entrepreneurs' existing equity. Successful completion of the first stage will lead to *second-stage financing* and possibly further stages before the company is ready to go public with an initial public offering.

The United States has a well-developed venture capital market. Specialist partnerships pool funds from a variety of investors and seek out fledgling companies to invest in. The nature of these investments is that for every 10 first-stage venture capital investments, only two or three may survive as successful businesses, but if one becomes very successful, it will make up for all the others.

The Initial Public Offering: The initial public offering or IPO is the first issue of shares to the general public. Generally, IPOs are done when the business has made considerable progress and is on its way to successfully establishing itself in the market. The IPO establishes a market value of the investment made by the founding entrepreneurs and the venture capitalists. A *primary offering* is one where shares are sold to raise additional cash for the company. Often a primary offering is combined with a *secondary offering* where existing shareholders (the venture capitalists and sometimes the founding entrepreneurs) sell some of their shares. An *underwriter* is used to sell the offered shares to the general investor. Underwriters are investment banks and provide a host of services related to the issue.

The first formal step of an IPO is the approval of the issue by the board and by stockholders if an increase in authorized capital is necessary. A *registration statement* is then prepared for submission to the Securities and Exchange Commission (SEC). This statement presents information about the proposed financing, the firm's history, existing business, and plans for the future. The first part of the registration statement is usually distributed as a preliminary *prospectus*, also called a *red herring*. It contains a statement printed in red ink, which draws attention to its preliminary status and that securities are not permitted to be sold until the registration becomes effective. Meanwhile, the SEC studies the documentation and requests changes to it. Finally, an amended statement is filed with the SEC. After registration, the final prospectus is issued, giving the issue price, which is fixed at this stage. A *registrar* is appointed to record any issues of stock and to prevent unauthorized issues' taking place. A *transfer agent* is also appointed to look after the transfer of the newly issued securities.

Winners curse may be a problem with some IPOs. This means that a successful bidder in an auction is likely to have overvalued the asset. Thus, investors, being unaware of other investors' valuation of the stock, can end up paying a high price. This may be the reason why IPOs are often underpriced.

Public issue can be expensive. The costs include the administrative and transaction costs as well as the cost due to underpricing of the shares. The company and its underwriters discuss and agree on the issue price. The company would, of course, like to secure the highest possible price, but too high a price and the issue will fail, leaving the underwriters in particular with a disaster on their hands. Underwriters make their profit by buying the issue from the company at a discount from the price at which they resell it to the public. There are other more hidden costs of under-pricing: on average the new investors also get a bargain when they buy new issues. A study of nearly 9,000 new issues from 1960 to 1987 indicated average under-pricing of 16 percent. Some of the recent Internet IPOs had relatively high under-pricing costs. The administrative costs include preparation of all the documentation by management, legal counsel, and accountants, besides other fees, printing and mailing costs. While these costs add up to a substantial amount, the hidden costs can be much higher.

Types of Issues: Public issue of securities can be either *general cash offers* or *rights issues*. General cash offers are made to the public and in the United States, this is the most commonly used mode for all debt and equity issues. In some other countries it is common to find rights issues (also known as *privileged subscription issues)* where the issue is offered to the existing shareholders as a right. The shareholders can sell their rights to subscribe to the issue in the market.

Companies can file a single *shelf registration* statement covering financing plans for up to 2 years into the future. This provides prior approval to issue a stated amount of securities over this period and without being tied to particular underwriters. The company is then able to issue securities gradually to the market, and it can make those decisions on short notice. Large, well-established companies often issue securities in more than one country and these are known as *International issues.*

There is considerable economy of scale in issue costs. The percentage cost is smaller for large issues than for small ones. (See Table 15-2 and Figure 15-3) We also have to consider the effects of under-pricing and price pressure. The announcement of new issues of common stock on average results in a decline in the stock price of about 3 percent (for industrial issues in the United States), which represents nearly one-third of the new money raised by the issue. This is probably an information effect: managers are more likely to issue stock when they think it is overvalued.

Dilution, Investment, and Financing: Under-pricing does not affect the value of the company. It can transfer wealth from one group of security holders to another. When people talk about *dilution*, they often mean that new issue of stocks leads to lower per share earnings and therefore lower price. Dilution can be real only if the proceeds of the issue are to be used to finance poor investment projects. However, any fall in share price which this may give rise to on the issue announcement is due solely to the poor investment decision and has nothing to do with the financing decision. Always try to avoid confusing the effects of the investment and financing decisions.

Underwriter: The marketing of a general cash offer is handled by underwriters, who also provide advice and usually *underwrite* or guarantee the issue's subscription. Their remuneration is the *spread* between the *issue price* (or *offering price*) and the price at which they buy the securities from the company. Where a new issue of common stock is unusually risky, the underwriter may handle the issue on a *best-efforts* basis (not guaranteeing to sell the entire issue) or on an *all-or-none* basis (where the deal is called off completely if the entire issue is not sold).

A syndicate of underwriters usually handles large issues. In this case, the syndicate manager keeps about 20 percent of the spread, a further 20 to 30 percent goes to pay the members of the group who buy the issue, and the remainder goes to the firms who actually sell the issue. For each public issue, a "*tombstone*" advertisement is published that lists the names of all the underwriters. Members of the underwriting syndicate are not allowed to sell securities at below the issue price, although they may be allowed to "support" the market by buying them at the market price. If the issue cannot be sold, the syndicate will be broken.

Underwriting is just like insurance. The underwriters guarantee the issue's success, promising full subscription at the issue price in return for a fee. It is worthwhile as long as the value of the guarantee is worth at least as much as the fee paid. The value of the guarantee depends on the risk of the issue failing.

Private Placements: A private placement is an alternative to public issue and has certain advantages compared to a public offering. Private placements do not involve registration and is limited to a few buyers. Transaction costs will be lower. The placement can be made very quickly. There are disadvantages too. The securities issued in this way are very illiquid and are held for long-term investment rather than resale. This is a greater disadvantage for issues of common stock than for debt issues, so private placements of common stock (called *letter stock*) are rare. Bond issues, particularly of small- and medium-sized firms, account for the bulk of private placements. They are often negotiated directly with the lender, while for larger issues an investment banker will act as agent. By 1989, the proportion of corporate debt issues made as private placements had increased to almost one-half. Since 1990, large financial institutions (known as *qualified institutional buyers*) have been allowed to trade unregistered securities among themselves, and this has provided a further boost to this market.

Rights Issue (The Privileged Subscription): Rights issue can be a very effective and inexpensive way of raising additional funding. The issue is offered to the firm's existing stockholders in proportion to their current holding in the company. The stockholders can transfer or sell their rights in the market. Rights issue effectively avoids wealth transfer between existing stockholders and new stockholders, since they are one and the same. Therefore, the actual pricing of the issue is of little consequence. If N is the number of existing shares required to receive one right (i.e. it will give you the right to buy one new share), the value of a right can be written as:

$$\text{Value of one right} = (\text{rights-on price} - \text{issue price})/(N+1)$$

The expression is derived in the worked-out example.

WORKED EXAMPLES

1. The entrepreneurs' original investment in Marvin Enterprises amounted to $100,000. First-stage financing raised $1 million and placed a $2 million after-the-money valuation on the firm. At the next stage, the enterprise was valued at $10 million.

   a. What (paper) return and increase in value had the entrepreneurs enjoyed by each of these two stages?

   b. How would your answer to the previous question change if they had agreed on a first-stage after-the-money valuation of $1.50 million instead of $2 million and a second stage valuation of $9 million?

SOLUTION

   a. The original stockholders have a paper value to their stock of $1 million at the first stage. With an additional $1 million raised, they have 50 percent of the stock. At the second stage, company value of $10 million is worth $5 million. These valuations represent 10-fold and 5-fold increases in the two stages, representing returns of 900 percent and 400 percent respectively.

b. At a $1.5 million firm valuation, the original stockholders would have a paper value to their stock of $0.5 million at the first stage. With an additional $1 million raised, they have only one-third of the company's stock, which at the second stage, company value of $9 million is worth $3 million. These valuations represent 5-fold and 6-fold increases in the two stages (returns of 400 percent and 500 percent respectively).

2. Jackrabbits Corporation is making a rights issue to raise $6 million. Just before the issue, Jackrabbits' stock price was $20, and the terms of the issue are 1 for 4 at a subscription price of $15. Calculate (a) the expected price of the stock ex-rights and (b) the value of one right. (c) Baby Rabbit owns 20,000 shares. How many rights will he have to sell to maintain the same ($400,000) investment in the company? (d) Show that in general, the value of a right is given by the formula (rights-on price - issue price)/(N + I) when the terms of the issue are 1 for N.

SOLUTION

a. After the issue is completed, all shares will be ex-rights. For every 4 shares worth $20 before the issue, there will be 5 shares worth $20 x 4 + $15 (= $95) after the issue. Each share will, therefore, be worth $95/5, so the ex-rights price is $19.

b. The value of one right is the difference between the rights-on price (the share price before the issue) and the ex-rights price. This is $1.

c. Baby Rabbit will get 5,000 rights and if he were to keep all his rights, he would end up with 25,000 shares valued at a total of 25,000 x $19 = $475,000. In order to retain his original investment, he should have $400,000/$19 = 21,053 shares. Therefore, he needs to keep only 1,053 rights and sell the remaining 3,947 rights. This will give him $3,947.

d. N shares at the rights-on price gets an additional share subscribed to at the offer price. This gives the basic equation:

$$N \times (\text{rights-on price}) + \text{issue price} = (N + 1)(\text{ex-rights price})$$

Alternatively, this can be written as:

$$[(N + 1) \times \text{rights-on price}] - (\text{rights-on price} - \text{issue price}) = (N + 1) \text{ ex-rights price}$$

$$\text{Value of a right} = \text{right-on price} - \text{ex-rights prices}$$
$$= \text{rights-on price} - \text{issue price}/(N+1)$$

SUMMARY

This chapter provided a summary description of the procedures used by corporations for raising finance through the issue of securities. Companies raise finances through a variety of ways with venture capital funding for start-up and young companies and seasoned issues for established and mature companies. The chapter highlighted some very important implications for the financial manager. These can be summarized as below:

- Larger is cheaper. This suggests that there is economy of scale in raising money and the manager can take advantage of this by avoiding small issues.

- Beware of under-pricing. Perhaps the most significant of the hidden costs of financing is under-pricing of the security. This is especially true for the IPOs. Underwriters may be tempted to go too far to reduce the fear of winners' curse make an impression on the investor.

- Winners' curse may need to be addressed in IPOs and careful design of issue procedures is needed.

- New stock issues cause lowering of stock price. This may be due to information the market might be reading into the company's actions. Managers would do well to keep the market fully informed.

- Take advantage of shelf-registration, which is particularly useful for debt issues of established, financially strong firms.

LIST OF TERMS

After-the-money valuation	Red herring
All-or-none	Registrar
Best efforts	Registration statement
Business plan	Rights issue
Dilution	Road show
First-stage financing	Seasoned stock issue
General cash offer	Secondary offering
Initial public offering	Shelf registration
Issue price	Spread
Letter stock	Tombstone
Offering price	Transfer agent
Preemptive rights	Under-pricing
Primary offering	Underwriting
Private placement	Unseasoned issue

177

Privileged subscription   Venture capital
Prospectus

EXERCISES

Fill-in Questions

1. Equity investment in young private companies is generally known as _____.

2. In order to obtain capital, the young company must first prepare a detailed _____.

3. The first injection of equity capital from the venture capital market is known as _____.

4. The proportion of the company, which the original owners will have to give up, depends on the _____ of the company.

5. The first issue of a security by a company is known as a(n) _____ or a(n) _____.

6. Before a general cash offer or a large public issue, companies often put up a _____ to familiarize the investors with the company.

7. When new shares are sold to raise additional cash for the company, it is called _____.

8. When shares of existing shareholders are offered to the public, it is called _____.

9. An issue of securities that is offered to the general public or investors is called a(n) _____.

10. An issue of securities that is offered to current stockholders is usually called a(n) _____.

11. Rights issues are also known as _____ issues.

12. For most public issues, a(n) _____ must be submitted to the Securities and Exchange Commission.

13. Information about an issue is provided in its _____, which must be sent to all purchasers and to all those who are offered securities through the mail.

14. The preliminary prospectus is called a(n) _____.

15. A(n) _____ is an advertisement, which lists the underwriters to an issue of securities.

16. A financial institution is usually appointed as _____ to record the issue and ownership of the company's securities.

17. A(n) _____ may be appointed to look after the transfer of newly issued securities.

18. The sale of a public issue is normally handled by a(n) _____, who provides financial and procedural advice and usually buys the security for less than the offering price and accepts the risk of not being able to resell it.

19. The underwriter's _____ is the difference between the price at which the underwriter buys an issue from a company and the _____ or _____.

20. Occasionally, the underwriter does not guarantee the sale of an entire issue but handles the issue on a(n) _____ basis, promising only to sell as much of the issue as possible.

21. _____ underwriting is where the entire issue is cancelled if the underwriter is unable to resell it all at the offer price.

22. _____ occurs in a general cash offer when securities are sold at an offer price which is below their market price.

23. _____ is the name given to the potential diminution of share value through the value of the firm being shared between a larger number of stockholders.

24. Stock for which there is an existing market goes by the spicy name of _____ stock.

25. The _____ right of common stockholders (to anything of value distributed by the firm) includes the right to subscribe to new offerings.

26. The _____ provides an alternative to making a public offering.

27. Privately placed common stock cannot easily be resold. It is often called _____ because the SEC requires a letter from the purchaser stating that the stock is not intended for resale.

28. _____ allows large companies to obtain prior approval for their financing plans for up to 2 years into the future.

Problems

1. DuckBills is a young company started by two brothers, Bill and Larry, with their savings amounting to $200,000. The firm received venture capital financing two years after its start-up. The venture capitalists provided first-stage financing of $2.5 million and valued the firm after-the-money at $5 million. Two years later, the firm received second-stage financing from the same venture capital company. DuckBills received $6 million and was valued at $20 million after-the-money. A year later, DuckBills was ready for its IPO and the underwriters valued the company (before the IPO) at $60 million. Calculate the returns for the brothers and the venture capital firm at each stage of financing.

2. Marvin Enterprises' first-stage financing had placed a $1 million dollar paper value on the one million shares held by the original entrepreneurs. The venture capitalists put in another $1 million and held 50 percent of the equity. A further $4 million was raised at its second-stage financing, which placed a $14 million after-the-money valuation on the company. By the time third-stage funds were needed, the enterprise was valued at $42 million.

   a. What return and increase in value had the entrepreneurs enjoyed between the first-stage and second-stage and between the first-stage and third-stage?

   b. How would your answer to the previous question change if they had agreed a second-stage after-the-money valuation of $8 million instead of $14 million, with the before-the-money third-stage valuation of $42 million unchanged?

3. ABX Corp. decides to issue the stock via a general cash offer. The board believes it can raise the $18 million the company requires by issuing shares at $36. The company has 5 million shares outstanding and the current stock price is $40. Ignoring the underwriter's spread, calculate the following:

   a. The number of new shares that ABX will have to offer.
   b. The expected price of the shares after the issue.
   c. The loss per share to existing holders.
   d. The percentage reduction in value of an existing stockholder's investment in the company
   e. The net present value of purchasing 100 shares via the general cash offer.

4. ABX is considering the alternative of a privileged subscription stock issue to raise $18 million. The terms of the issue are 1 for 10 at $36, and the corporation's current stock price is $40. Calculate the following:

   a. The market value of the corporation's equity prior to the issue.
   b. The percentage increase in market value due to the issue.
   c. The expected price of one right.
   d. The expected price of the stock ex-rights.

5. United Fasteners is issuing a 20-year bond to raise $10 million. The corporation can either:

a. Issue the bond publicly, in which case it will be sold at par and will carry a 9 percent coupon. The underwriter's spread would be 0.5 percent, and there are no other issue costs.

b. Issue the bond through a private placement, in which case it will be sold at par and carry a 9 1/8 percent coupon. The total cost of the private placement will be $20,000.

Which option should United Fasteners choose?

Essay Questions

1. Discuss the following statement: Venture capital is essential for a young, growing company, but it is also an expensive way of raising money.

2. Describe the main features of the process by which a young company might raise venture capital.

3. Discuss the following statement: Rights issue is the best way to raise new equity for an established company, as one does not have to worry about underpricing.

4. Discuss the relative merits of a public issue versus a private placement for a company wishing to raise new debt finance. What factors should be taken into account in pricing the bond issue?

5. Compare and contrast the role of the investment banker (or underwriter) in (a) general cash offers of either stock or bonds and (b) private placements of bonds

6. Describe how the costs of raising new capital depend on the type and amount of financing raised.

ANSWERS TO EXERCISES

Fill-in Questions

1. Venture capital	15. Tombstone
2. Business plan	16. Registrar
3. First-stage financing	17. Transfer agent
4. After-the-money valuation	18. Underwriter
5. Initial public offering, unseasoned issue	19. Spread; issue price; offering price
6. Road show	20. Best efforts
7. Primary offering	21. All-or-none

8. Secondary offering
9. General cash offer
10. Rights issue
11. Privileged subscription
12. Registration statement
13. Prospectus
14. Red herring

22. Under-pricing
23. Dilution
24. Seasoned
25. Preemptive
26. Private placement
27. Letter stock
28. Shelf registration

Problems

1. The brothers' initial investment of $200,000 became $2.5 million in the first stage financing providing 12.5 fold increase or 1,150 percent return. During the next phase, the $2.5 million became $7 million (half of $20 million - $6 million). This is now 35 percent of the value of the firm. The return during this phase is 180 percent. At the time of IPO, the brothers' stake is valued at $21 million ($60 million x 0.35) and the return during this phase is 200 percent. The venture capitalists' initial investment of $2.5 million became $7 million at the time of second financing providing a return of 180 percent. During the next phase their investment of $13 million became $39 million to give a return of 200 percent.

2. a. The original entrepreneurs have a paper value to their stock of $5 million at the second stage. With an additional $4 million raised at a share price of $5 per share, there were now 2.8 million shares issued and outstanding. At the third stage this has now increased to a value of $15 per share, and the paper value of the original entrepreneurs' holdings is now $15 million. These valuations represent 5-fold and 15-fold increases from stages 1 to 2 and 1 to 3, respectively (that is, returns of 400 percent and 1400 percent), and gains of $4 million and $14 million.

    b. At an $8 million second-stage after-the-money valuation, the second-stage share price would have been $2 instead of $5. To raise $4 million, it would have been necessary to sell a further 2 million shares, making 4 million shares outstanding altogether, instead of 2.8 million. The subsequent $42 million firm valuation now imputes a share value of $10.50. These valuations represent 2-fold and 10.5-fold increases to the two stages (that is, returns of 100 percent and 950 percent), with gains of $1 million and $9.5 million.

3. a. Number of new shares = $18,000,000/$36 = 500,000 shares

    b. Value of company after issue = $200,000,000 + $18,000,000 = $218,000,000
        Share price after issue $218,000,000/5,500,000 = $39.64

    c. Loss per share to existing holders = $40 - $39.64 = $0.36

    d. Percentage reduction in value = ($0.36/$40) x 100 percent = 0.90 percent

    e. NPV purchasing shares via offer = $39.64 - $36 = $3.64

182

4. a. Value of equity before issue = 5,000,000 x $40 = $200,000,000

   b. Increase in value = $18 m/$200 m x 100 percent = 9%

   c. Value of right = (rights-on price - issue price)/(N+ 1) = ($40 - $36)/11 = $0.36

   d. Ex-rights price = (rights-on price - value of right) = $40 - $0.36 = $39.64

5. a. Cost of public issue = $10,000,000 x 0.5 percent = $50,000

   b. Cost of private placement = $20,000 + additional interest cost
      Additional interest = $10,000,000 x 1/8 percent = $12,500 per year for 20 years

      If we discount these interest payments at 9 percent, i.e., the market rate for identical cash flows which are traded in the capital market, we obtain

      Total cost of private placement = $20,000 + ($12,500 x 9.129) = $134,113

   That is, shareholders will be better off if United Fasteners makes a public issue.

16

The Dividend Controversy

INTRODUCTION

This chapter addresses the issue of dividend policy. Dividend policy is among one of the most controversial issues of corporate finance. The controversy surrounds the question - do dividends increase the value of a firm? Three broad and divergent views have emerged in response to this question. The prevailing wisdom before the seminal work by Modigliani and Miller (MM) was that increased dividend payouts increase firm value. MM argued that a firm's value is decided by the success of its investments and not by how it pays dividends. A more radical view suggests that in view of the differential taxation of dividends and capital gains, dividends will reduce the firm's value as they are taxed at a higher rate. The dividend irrelevancy argument of MM assumes a world of perfect capital markets. Given the assumptions used by MM, it is very hard to dispute their claim. MM's position was a direct challenge to the traditional view, which held that high payout ratios tend to increase the value of the firm. One of the cornerstones of this position is that cash dividends today are valued more highly than cash dividends in the future because future cash dividends are more risky. While there is still debate on the issue, it appears that the traditional position has weakened considerably and there is more acceptance of the general wisdom of MM's argument.

Part of the controversy and confusion about dividends arises from the way the issue is framed. In order to decide whether dividends add value to the firm, one has to keep other variables like investment policy and debt policy constant. The dividend policy has to be isolated from capital budgeting and borrowing decisions. This would clearly imply that dividend policy trade-off is between retaining earnings for reinvestment and paying dividends and financing the investments with newly issued stocks. Keep this in mind throughout the discussions on the merits of dividends. In other words, dividend policy issue is not about paying off any excess funds the company has; but whether a company should pay out earnings as dividends when it can profitably reinvest the same.

A financial manager needs to understand the issue and trade-off involved in order to be able to make the right decisions. It is also essential that she be familiar with the terms and terminology of dividends and the current practice of corporations in establishing dividends. The chapter helps you do this with descriptive material on the mechanics of dividend payments and corporate dividend practice. The chapter also includes a description of alternative tax systems and their implications for dividends.

KEY CONCEPTS IN THE CHAPTER

Mechanics and Terminology of Dividends: Dividends have been around for a long time before the debate on whether it adds to corporate wealth started. In order to familiarize yourself with the way dividends are paid out and handled by companies, you should know terms and phrases commonly used by corporations. Here is a summary description of the mechanics and an explanation of the terms used.

<u>The mechanics:</u> The board of directors decides the amount of dividends and how they are to be paid, on the recommendation of the management of the company. Corporations in the U.S. generally pay their dividends quarterly, although any other schedule is possible. There are legal restrictions in most states on what can be paid out as dividends. Generally, dividends cannot be paid out of legal capital, usually defined as the par value of all outstanding shares. When there is no par value, the legal capital is usually defined as the receipts from the stock issue. Some exceptions to this rule may be permitted for mining companies.

The company makes an announcement of the dividend decision on the *announcement date*. The announcement gives the details of when the dividend will be paid to shareholders who are registered in the companies books.

Many companies pay regular quarterly dividends. Occasionally companies pay an extra dividend when further cash is available, or as a special dividend in circumstances unlikely to be repeated. Some companies pay dividends in the form of stocks or their products. A stock dividend affects the stock price as the number of shares increases without any change in the companies assets. Stock repurchase is another way of returning cash to the stockholders. Stock repurchases permit the investors to choose whether to receive the cash or not. It also enjoys favorable tax treatment.

Dividend reinvestment plans (DRIP) have become popular with stockholders and many companies have instituted these plans. This allows the shareholder to automatically reinvest the dividends in the company's shares often at a discount from the current market price.

<u>Terminology:</u> A number of terms are commonly used to describe the various dates and events associated with dividend payments. Here is a list:

Announcement date: This is the date on which the dividend is formally announced by the company and starts the dividend process for that specific dividend. The announcement carries details of different dates important for the payment of the announced dividend.

Ex-dividend date: This is the first day on which the stock trades without the right to receive the announced dividend. This will be a few days before the record date. A person who sells the stock before the ex-dividend date will still receive the dividend when it is paid out, even though he will not be holding the stock on that date.

186

Record date: This is the date on which the list of shareholders eligible to receive the dividend is made. This follows the ex-dividend date.

Payment date: This is the date on which checks are sent to shareholders of record. Normally, it takes about 2 weeks after the record date.

With-dividend: This denotes that shares are selling with the cash dividend attached. This will be all the trades done before the ex-dividend date.

Share repurchase: Share repurchase can be an attractive alternative to cash dividends. It is attractive for two reasons: i) it lets the stockholder choose whether to receive the cash or retain his level of ownership and ii) gains from stocks sold are treated as capital gains (assuming the stockholder has held the stock for more than one year). Companies use three different ways to repurchase stocks: open market purchase; tender offer, which is an offer to buy back a certain number of shares, often at a premium; and negotiated repurchase from individual stockholders. Open market repurchases are the most common.

Corporate Practice: A survey of corporate managers conducted by John Lintner in the mid-1950s provided very useful information on how companies decide on dividend payments. Lintner's findings are still valid. The findings can be summarized as follows:

- Firms generally set long-run *target payout ratios*. The payout ratio is a function of the company's growth prospects and earnings variability. Companies with stable earnings generally have high payouts and those that are growth companies have low payouts.

- The changes in dividends rather than the level itself is considered more important.

- Dividends follow changes in the long run, sustainable earnings flow. In other words, major changes are not made unless the managers are sure that changes in earnings are long-term and not transient. Managers also practice short-term smoothing of dividends.

- Managers are reluctant to make any major changes in dividends unless they are sure that the changes will not be reversed.

Lintner developed a simple model, which can be expressed as below:

$$DIV_1 - DIV_0 = \text{adjustment rate} \times (\text{target ratio} \times EPS_1 - DIV_0)$$

The implication of the model is that current dividends depend in part on current earnings and in part on the dividends of previous years, with more distant years being given less weight than more current years.

Information Content of Dividends and Stock Repurchases: Dividends and stock repurchases may signal important information to shareholders because they may indicate management's

187

assessment of future sustainable earnings. Dividend increases are viewed as a signal of increased future earnings. Dividend cuts signal bad news about the future. Empirical evidence supports this view.

Share repurchases are different from dividends in that they are one-time events. A company may resort to share repurchase when it has more cash than it can profitably invest. Alternately, a share repurchase may be financed by additional borrowing. In either case, the manager is clearly indicating that stockholders' money is not being retained for making unprofitable investments. Yet, another reason for share repurchase may be the manager's confidence in the future prospects of the company and feeling that the stock is currently undervalued. Empirical evidence shows that share repurchases in general are greeted positively by the investors. The positive reaction is even greater when the stock repurchase is at a significant premium to the current price.

The Dividend Controversy: The essence of the dividend controversy centers on the extent to which dividend policy affects the value of the enterprise. There is little dispute as to the relevance and importance of dividends as signals of future prospects of the company. What is to be settled is whether the dividend decisions itself contributes to a change in the value of the company. We review the three main views in this controversy.

The MM irrelevance view: MM started the whole controversy by challenging the prevailing view on dividend policy. They showed that under perfect market conditions, a firm's value is decided by its investments and not on dividends. MM's argument begins with these assumptions:

- No taxes, transactions costs, or other market imperfections.
- A fixed investment capital budgeting program.
- A financing policy in which borrowing is set.
- Remaining needed funds come from retained earnings, and extra cash is paid as dividends.
- Capital markets are efficient and transactions take place at fair prices.

Given the assumptions, it is very hard to reject MM's basic conclusion that dividend policy is irrelevant. Essentially, there are two ways of raising cash for a firm's original shareholders. They can be paid dividends or they can sell a part of their holdings in the market to receive the same amount of cash (see figure 16-1 and 16-2). In each case, the cash received is offset by a decline in the value of the old stockholders' claim on the firm. If the firm pays a dividend, each share is worth less because more shares have to be issued against the firm's assets. If the old stockholders sell some of their shares, each share is worth the same but the old stockholders have fewer shares. It follows that:

- If dividends are increased, the firm must issue more shares (because investments and borrowing are fixed).
- No one will buy the shares at less than their true value.
- The total market value of the firm is unchanged, and the sale of new shares transfers wealth between new and old shareholders.

188

- The new purchasers receive shares at a price less than that on the old shares, and it is less by the amount of the extra cash.
- In efficient capital markets, shareholders that need cash either sell shares or receive cash dividends and incur an equal drop in the value of their shares.

Thus, dividend policy is irrelevant and depends on the firm's investment and financing decisions. Note that share repurchases are the reverse of the above process: Dividend reductions are accompanied by an equivalent reduction in shares, and total wealth of shareholders is unaffected.

The MM position can be challenged using evidence of market imperfections or inefficiencies. Taxes and transaction costs, however, might drive one to the conclusion that dividends may actually decrease value (See the "leftists" view below). Other imperfections such as the existence of a special clientele who prefer high-payout stocks or dividends as purveyor of valuable information about future prospects do make a case for the relevance of dividends. We will come back to this after summarizing the other views on dividend policy.

The MM irrelevance proposition applies to share repurchases decisions also. That is, keeping investment and debt policy constant, a firm's value is unaffected by any decisions to repurchase stock. Again, this assumes away any signaling effect from share repurchases.

The Rightists: The traditional finance literature before MM has favored liberal dividends. This belief is supported by many in business and investment communities because they believe increased dividends today make shareholders better off. The main arguments made in support of dividends as against MM's irrelevance centered on: i) dividends are less risky than capital gains and ii) capital market imperfections give rise to investors who prefer high dividends for personal and institutional reasons. While these arguments appear to have some merit, deeper analysis shows them to have limited validity in refuting MM's irrelevance conclusions. While it is true that dividends are more stable than capital gains, it is also true that the risk of the cash flows of the firm is determined by the firm's investment and debt policies. The dividend payout should not have any effect. As for the clientele argument, it is conceded that there are groups of investors who like regular and high dividends and therefore high payout firms. However, the demand for high payout firms by this clientele would be fully satisfied by now and it is very hard to imagine a company can gain value by changing its payout policies.

The empirical evidence supporting the traditional view is limited and untenable. A better argument could be that investors lack complete trust in managers to spend retained earnings wisely. The dividend decision forces the managers to raise additional finances from capital markets to finance any new investment. This keeps them on a tight leash and possibly more efficient in spending.

Taxes and the Radical Left: The third, radical left position in the dividend controversy focuses primarily on the tax effects which influence the preference for cash dividends. When dividends are taxed more heavily than capital gains, paying higher dividends will actually lead to a loss in value. The firm is better off paying any excess cash through stock repurchases rather than dividends. Thus, radical left view is that dividends are bad for the stockholders as they cause avoidable taxes. Of course, this extreme view will run afoul of the IRS and therefore few managers ever declare a policy on the lines suggested by the leftists' view.

The tax law changes affect the relative advantage of capital gains over dividends. The Tax Reform Act reduced this advantage by essentially taxing both capital gains and dividends at the same rates. Last year's tax law changes bring back some of the advantages with the reduction of maximum capital gains tax rate to 20 percent on any investment held for more than one year. The maximum tax rate on dividend income is 39.6 percent.

Empirical studies give some support to the leftists' view in that investors in low marginal tax brackets appear to prefer high-payout stocks, and vice versa.

The Middle-of-the-Roaders: This position essentially holds that a company's value is not affected by its dividend policy. While conceding the effect of market imperfections on MM's theoretical arguments, this group views that the impact of market imperfections is not significant. If low or high payouts increased the value of the firm, financial managers would do so. The fact that we do not see a rush to change dividend policies one way or the other suggests that it is not terribly important. While the 1986 Tax Reform Act changed the balance between capital gains and dividends somewhat (by making taxes on dividends close to those on capital gains), the changes made last year have reversed the scale again. Since capital gains enjoy lower rates once again, it is unlikely that there will be any great increase in corporate payout ratios.

Alternative Tax Systems: The chapter includes a brief discussion of alternative tax systems employed in different countries. These can be summarized as below:

- *Classic tax system:* Dividends are taxed at both corporate and individual levels. This is the approach followed in the U.S.

- *Split-rate system:* Dividends are taxed more heavily than capital gains, but retained profits are taxed more heavily than those distributed. This is the system followed in Germany.

- *Imputation system:* Dividends are taxed at the individual level, but the corporate share of taxes is deductible from their tax bill. This approach is used in Australia.

WORKED EXAMPLES

1. Match the following dates from the left and the right columns.

(A) Friday, November 2	(a) record date
(B) Tuesday, November 13	(b) announcement date
(C) Friday, November 16	(c) ex-dividend date
(D) Tuesday, December 8	(d) payment date

SOLUTION

(A) Friday, November 2	-	(b) Announcement date
(B) Tuesday, November 13	-	(c) Ex-dividend date
(C) Friday, November 16	-	(a) Record date
(D) Tuesday, December 8	-	(d) Payment date

2. Washington Water pays $0.62 per quarter throughout 1990. Calculate the stock's dividend yield based on its recent market price of $30.00.

SOLUTION

The formula for calculating dividend yields is:

$$\text{Dividend yield} = \text{yearly cash dividends/current market price per share}$$
$$= (4 \times \$0.62)/30.00$$
$$= \$2.48/\$30.00$$
$$= 0.8267 = 8.27 \text{ percent}$$

3. If Washington Water's 1990 earnings per share were $2.80 and per share cash dividends were $2.48, what was the company's estimated dividend payout?

SOLUTION

$$\text{Payout ratio} = \text{estimated cash dividends per share/estimated earnings per share}$$
$$= \$2.48/\$2.80$$
$$= 0.8857 = 88.6 \text{ percent}$$

4. Washington Water declared a stock dividend of 15 percent and its market price was $30. Assuming nothing else changed, what would you expect the price of the shares to be after the new stock is distributed?

SOLUTION

The stock dividend, by itself, has no expected effect on the value of the shares. We conclude, then, that the aggregate value of the shares after the stock dividend must equal the aggregate value of the shares before it. Say you own 100 shares of Washington Water. The value of your holding is $3,000 (100 shares x $30 per share). After the stock dividend, you have 115 shares (100 original shares + 15 percent of 100), the total value of which is still $3,000. The value per share of the new set of shares is $26.09 (3,000/115 shares). Alternatively,

(100% + percentage stock dividend) x (price per share after stock dividend) = price per share before stock dividend

$$(100\% + 15\%)(x) = 30$$
$$(115\%)x = 30$$
$$x = 30/1.15$$
$$= 26.09$$

5. ABM Corporation's financial numbers are as follows:

Net income	$5 million
Earnings per share	$1
Number of shares outstanding	5 million
Price-earnings ratio	10

The management plans to repurchase 20 percent of the company's outstanding shares at the going market price. What effect does the stock repurchase have on the above numbers? What effect does it have on the value of the firm? Explain.

SOLUTION

The earnings per share is $1 and with a P/E of 10, the stock price will be $10. The company's market value is $50 million ($10 x 5 million). The company needs $10 million in cash to buy 1 million shares at $10 each. If it does not have the cash, it must sell assets. If it sells typical assets, its net income will shrink to $4 million. Second, the number of shares outstanding decreases to 4 million. Third, earnings per share remain at $1 ($4 million/4 million shares). And fourth, because the price-earnings ratio stays the same, the value of the shares also stays at $10 each.

Look at it this way. Prior to the repurchase, the value per share was $10, 5 million shares were outstanding, and the firm's value was $50 million. After the repurchase, the value of the shares remains at $10 each, which, when multiplied by the 4 million then outstanding, results in a total value of $40 million, which equals, not coincidentally, the value at the outset less the value of assets used to repurchase the shares. The size of the firm contracts, and no gain or loss rebounds to its shareholders.

LIST OF TERMS

Announcement date	Record date
Classic tax system	Regular cash dividend
Dividend policy	Repurchase
Ex-dividend	Special dividend

Legal capital   Stock dividend
Payment date   Target payout ratio
Payout ratio   With-dividend

EXERCISES

Fill-in Questions

1. The date on which dividend checks are actually mailed out is the _____.

2. _____ is concerned with the trade-off between retaining earnings and paying out cash and issuing new shares.

3. The _____ is the date on which the list of registered shareholders that are to receive cash dividends is made.

4. Shares bought and sold before the record date are said to be transacted _____ whereas those bought and sold after the record date are said to be transacted _____.

5. A firm's _____ consists of the par value of all its outstanding shares.

6. The date on which the company makes a formal announcement of its dividends is the _____.

7. _____ are cash dividends which a company usually expects to be able to maintain in the future; _____ are cash dividends paid irregularly and are not necessarily expected to be maintained in the future.

8. _____ are similar to stock splits in that neither makes shareholders better off.

9. The percentage ratio of cash dividends to earnings is called the _____.

10. Lintner's empirical study showed that companies tend to adjust their payout ratios towards a _____.

11. Companies sometimes buy back or _____ their own shares.

12. The United States has a(n) _____ system in which dividends are taxed at both corporate and investor levels.

Problems

1. Arrange the following dates into order of occurrence: Payment date, announcement date, ex-dividend date, and record date.

2. In June of 19XX, McDonald's Corporation split its stock 2 for 1. The cash dividend remained at $0.125 a quarter. The closing stock price on the record date was $29.875.

   a. What would you expect the price of the stock to be before the split, assuming nothing else changed?

   b. Could the adjustments in per share price and cash dividends have been accomplished by a stock dividend?

   c. If so, what size would the stock dividend have to be to accomplish this goal?

   d. What was the annual dividend yield before and after the split?

   e. What was the payout ratio, given expected annual 1989 earnings of $1.95 a share?

   f. During the past 10 years the company's payout ratio averaged about 16 percent. Are you willing to say that this particular payout contained valuable information? Why or why not?

3. On Friday, August 9, 1991, Sink, Inc. announced a quarterly dividend of 12.5 cents and a stock dividend of 10 percent payable on Monday, September 9, 1991, to shareholders of record on Friday, August 23, 1991.

   a. If the August 9 market price of $16.50 remains the same, at what price would you expect the stock to sell for after the cash and stock dividends?

   b. When would you expect the stock to go ex-dividend?

   c. Assuming that the quarterly cash dividend of 12.5 cents per share will continue after the stock dividend, what is the effective percentage increase in the cash dividend?

   d. What is the expected annual dividend yield, using your estimate of the ex-dividend price and the 12.5 cents quarterly cash dividend?

   e. If expected annual earnings per share are $3, what is the annual expected dividend payout?

4. On Thursday, August 16, 19XX, U.S. Bancorp, a Portland, Oregon, based bank holding company, declared a 20 percent common stock dividend payable on September 14 to stockholders of record on August 27. It was also announced that the cash dividend payment of $0.25 a share per quarter, payable on October 5 to stockholders of record on September 17, would remain the same.

   a. By how much did the quarterly dividend increase?

   b. What would you expect the price of shares to be after the stock dividend, given that on the date of the announcement they were selling at 24 ¼?

   c. Are the shareholders necessarily any better off? That is, does their wealth increase as a result of the stock dividend?

194

5. On August 15, 19XX, Jiffy Lube International, a fast-service automobile lubrication and oil change franchiser, announced a 1-for-10 reverse split, the event to occur on September 6, subject to shareholder approval. The stock's closing price on August 14 was 1 3/8. If nothing changes, at what price would you expect the stock to sell after the stock split is made effective on September 6?

6. Regression analysis reveals that the changes in MTY's annual dividend can be explained by the equation: $D_t - D_{t-1} = 0.18\,E_t - 0.30\,D_{t-1}$. What does this reveal about MTYs target payout ratio, and how far each year does the current dividend adjust towards it?

Essay Questions

1. Explain the mechanics of paying dividends.

2. "Stock repurchases can add value to the firm, even though dividends do not." Discuss.

3. Compare and contrast the middle-of-the-roaders' view and the MM irrelevance proposition.

4. "This dividend controversy stuff really bothers me. First off, I'm not even sure what the controversy is about. Second, everybody knows that dividend policy is really important. Finally, as investors, let's face it, it's the after-tax return that really counts!" Discuss.

5. How can it be said that cash dividends are financially equivalent to stock issues, once investment and financing policies are fixed? Explain fully.

ANSWERS TO EXERCISES

Fill-in Questions

1. Payment date
2. Dividend policy
3. Record date
4. With dividend; ex-dividend
5. Legal capital
6. Announcement date
7. Regular cash dividends; special dividends
8. Stock dividends
9. Payout ratio
10. Target payout ratio
11. Repurchase
12. Classic

Problems
1. Announcement date, ex-dividend date, record date, and payment date.

2. a. $30.00 x 2 = $60.00.
   b. Yes.
   c. 100%, so that two additional shares are outstanding for every old share.
   d. Before: [($0.125 x 4)/$59.75] x 100 = 0.84%;
      After: [($0.125 x 4)/$29. 875] x 100 = 1.67%.

e. [($0.125 x 4)/$1.95] x 100 = 25.6%.

f. No, this is not an unusual event. Invariably, large deviations from the usual contain valuable information.

3. a. ($16.50 - $.125)/1.10 = $14.89, or $14.875 to the nearest eighth of a dollar.

b. Tuesday, August 20, 1991.

c. 10 percent.

d. ($0.125 x 4)/$14.875 = 3.36%.

e. $0.50/$3.00 = 16.7 percent.

4. a. The cash dividend increase was also 20%. Think of it this way: if you had one share before the split, you received $1.00 a year in cash dividends; afterward, you have 1.2 shares, on which you receive $0.25 a share for a total of 1.2 x $0.25 x 4 = $1.20; an increase of 20%.

b. One would expect the stock to decline by $24.25 + 1.2= $29.21, or 20¾ to the nearest eighth.

c. The shareholders, all else the same, are not necessarily better off. If the dividend increase were expected, that would be built into the dividend discount model and reflected in share prices. If the dividend increase were unexpected, there might well be positive wealth effects for shareholders because the unexpected increase in dividends may signal from management sustainable earning power to cover not only the increase in dividends but also all other corporate needs. The share price closed down one-eighth on the day of the announcement, suggesting that the dividend increase was expected.

5. 10 x $1.375 = $13.75.

6. The equation can be rearranged as: $D_t - D_{t-1} = 0.30 (0.60 E_t - D_{t-1})$; so, we see that the target payout ratio is 60% and the dividend adjusts 30% of the way towards this each year.

17

Does Debt Policy Matter?

INTR0DUCTION

This chapter describes the classic Modigliani and Miller (MM) propositions concerning the capital structure of business firms under perfect market conditions. MM's proposition I states that the value of a firm is unaffected by the financing mix of debt and equity used by the firm. Proposition II, which is the corollary of the first proposition, states that the required rate of return on the equity increases with an increase in proportion to debt such that the weighted-average cost of capital does not change. The implication of these two propositions is that the choice of debt-equity mix or capital structure is irrelevant and has no effect on the value of the firm. Debt policy does not matter and investment and financing decisions can be separated.

The chapter focuses on MM's arguments that debt policy does not matter, the conditions under which their case is made, and the counter argument put forth by the traditional view that leverage has some intrinsic advantage. MM views are clearly difficult to challenge, once the perfect market conditions are accepted. Deviations from these conditions are considered in the following chapter. The primary logic of the MM propositions are based on the view that the firm's value is based only on the stream of cash flows produced by its assets. The claims to this cash flow can be packaged in different ways, but unless there are market imperfections, which permit deviations from the perfect market conditions, arbitrage across these claims will ensure that the value of the firm is unaffected by the capital structure changes.

In practice, capital structure matters because deviations from perfect market conditions are present in the real world. These deviations are discussed in Chapter 18. The significance of the MM propositions is not because they depict a realistic picture of the world, but a clear understanding of the propositions enable you to understand why capital structure decisions are important and why one capital structure may be better than another.

KEY CONCEPTS IN THE CHAPTER

Leverage and its Effects in Perfect Markets: Under perfect market conditions, financial leverage can have no effect on the value of the firm. MM presents simple arguments to prove this point. Imagine two firms [U (unlevered) and L (for unleveraged)] with identical operating cash flows but with different capital structures. Owning one percent of firm U will be equivalent in terms of claims to cash flows to owning one percent of both the debt and equity of firm, L. Ownership of one percent of each firm gives claims to identical cash flows. Therefore, the values of these claims should be identical. Hence, $V_U = V_L$. An alternate approach is to compare ownership of one percent of the equity of the leveraged firm to ownership of one percent of the unleveraged firm and finance it by borrowing an amount equal to one percent of the leveraged firm's debt. Again, the claims are identical and it leads to the result - $V_U = V_L$. It follows that under these conditions, debt policy is irrelevant. This is proposition I.

Proposition I is essentially a restatement of the *value additvity principle* (see chapter 7): PV (A+B) = PV(A) + PV(B). Proposition I applies this in reverse. It can be called a *law of conservation of value*. The value of an asset is based on the cash flows produced by the asset and is not affected by the nature of claims against it.

MM's arguments supporting proposition I assume that both firms and individuals can borrow at the risk-free interest rate. This assumption is not crucial to the proposition. A fact, which might appear to give corporate debt some advantage, is that corporate stockholders have limited liability and thus can borrow with limited liability. Individuals cannot, on their own, have limited liability. Thus, corporate debt might have some advantage over personal debt. However, the advantage is unlikely to be of any significant value now since there are any number of corporations that can and have issued limited liability debt. In other words, any demand for limited liability debt would have been fully met by now.

Leverage and Returns: Proposition I leads to proposition II, which gives the relationship of returns on the debt, equity, and the asset return. If proposition I is to hold, the asset return, r_A is unaffected by leverage. This means that when the firm borrows, the required rate of return demanded by the shareholders increases as their risk increases. Proposition II states that the expected return on equity increases in proportion to the debt-equity ratio, expressed in market value. The rate of increase in return depends on the difference between the return on assets and the return on debt. The relationship can be expressed as follows:

$$r_A = [D/(D + E) \text{ X } r_D] + [E/(D + E) \text{ X } r_E].$$

Rearranging, r_E is given by:

$$r_E = r_A + (D/E)(r_A - r_D)$$

The essential implication of proposition II is that the increased return given by the equity in a leveraged firm reflects the increased risk. Therefore, the shareholders will demand a higher *required* rate of return. Or, the higher expected rate of return for the equity is simply the reflection of the higher risk involved and will be exactly matched by the higher required rate of return by the stockholders. Thus, the higher return is not going to result in a higher value of the stock.

Leverage and Beta: The effect of leverage on beta is similar to the effect on expected return. The relationship can be stated as follows:

Beta of the firm's assets:

$$\beta_A = [D/(D+E) \times \beta_D] + [E/(D+E) \times \beta_E]$$

Rearrange to obtain the beta of the equity of a leveraged firm.

$$\beta_E = \beta_A + D/E(\beta_A - \beta_D)$$

This is an alternative explanation of why equity investors require higher returns as debt increases. Proposition II is consistent with CAPM.

The Traditional View: Prior to MM's work, the traditional wisdom was that some leverage was beneficial and by leveraging, a firm increased the return on equity. The traditional position used the *weighted-average cost of capital,* which is the expected return on the portfolio of all the company's securities. Weighted-average cost of capital is used to compute net present values of project cash flows when the project being evaluated does not differ from the firm's business risk. If leverage lowers the weighted-average cost of capital, then (assuming that the leverage *does not lower* cash flows correspondingly) the value of the firm will increase.

$$r_A = (D/V \times r_D) + (E/V \times r_E)$$

The traditional position held that increasing leverage resulted in lower weighted-average cost of capital because an increase in the cost of equity, if at all, is not proportionate to the increase in leverage. The traditional view, if correct, has the following implications:

- Proposition II does not hold or the expected return on equity does not increase as a firm borrows more.

- The weighted-average cost of capital declines at first as the debt-equity ratio increases and then rises.

- There is an optimal D/E ratio that exists, that is, where the cost of capital is lowest.

A word of caution is in order. The firm should try to *maximize* the value of the firm. This is not always equivalent to having the *lowest cost of capital.* The two goals will be equivalent *only* if the operating income is not affected by the change in leverage.

Beware of the managers who make the simplistic argument that they can enhance the firm's value by lowering the cost of capital, by borrowing more as the cost of debt is lower than the cost of equity. This argument ignores proposition II.

The traditional view made two arguments to support their claim. The first one essentially said that the shareholders did not increase their *required* rate of return in proportion to the rise in leverage. This argument implied some irrationality on the part of the shareholders. If some debt is good, more debt must be even better, and the optimal leverage would be one hundred percent debt. The second argument used possible imperfections in the market and the advantage for corporate debt over personal debt suggesting that individuals could not borrow at the same rate as corporations. It is true that some individuals face higher borrowing cost on account of transaction costs (lack of economies of scale). Such individuals might find it advantageous to borrow through a corporation. However, any such demand for corporate debt must be fully satisfied now. In other words, trying to make money by leveraging now is like trying to make money selling automobiles or personal computers. You are late by a few decades.

Essentially, borrowing costs should be a function of the risk of the borrower or more specifically, the use to which the borrowed money is put (or to be more exact, how the loan is backed or secured). Most individuals can get mortgage loans or margin loans from their broker at very competitive rates.

To sum up, the traditional view lacks support and it is not backed by valid arguments. One has to look elsewhere for weaknesses in MM's position. If you can find deviations from the perfect market framework used by MM, you can find situations where their propositions will not hold. Many of these deviations are created by government regulations. Chapter 18 focuses on the practical implications of the market imperfections for corporate debt policy.

It is possible that there may be unsatisfied clienteles demanding specially designed securities with unique features. If a firm can design and structure a package of securities that exploits these needs, it can profit from it and you will find an exception to MM's proposition I. Of course, investment bankers are trying to do this all the time and it is very unlikely that there is any unsatisfied demand for the garden-variety or plain vanilla debt security. The next several chapters describe different type of securities invented by investment bankers and companies. It is however, hard to see that a firm's value can be increased greatly by these innovations in the absence of some government created imperfection.

WORKED EXAMPLES

1. Grey Bird Corp. operates in perfect capital markets with no corporate or personal taxes. The company has 25 percent debt and 75 percent equity in its capital structure. The expected return on debt is 12 percent and the rate of return on equity is 16 percent. Calculate its expected return on assets.

SOLUTION

$$r_A = \frac{ExpectedOperatingIncome}{MarketValueofAllSecurities}$$

= (proportion in debt X expected return on debt) + (proportion in equity X expected return on equity)

200

$$= \text{(weight of debt X cost of debt)} + \text{(weight of equity X cost of equity)}$$
$$= W_D r_D + W_E r_E$$
$$= [D/(D + E) \text{ X } r_D] + [E/(D + E) \text{ X } r_E]$$
$$= (0.25 \text{ X } 0.12) + (0.75 \text{ X } 0.16)$$
$$= 0.03 + 0.12$$
$$= 0.15 = 15 \text{ percent}$$

2. Tricky Dick Inc. has an operating income is $9,000, and the market value of all its all-equity-financed securities is $50,000. If the company decides to sell $15,000 of debt and retire an equal amount of equity, how will the rate of return for equity change? Assume that it operates in perfect capital markets with no corporate or personal taxes, and that the expected return on debt is 12 percent.

SOLUTION

The return on assets is give by:

$$r_A = \text{expected operating income/market value of all securities}$$
$$= \$9,000/\$50,000$$
$$= 0.18 = 18 \text{ percent}$$

In an all-equity-financed firm, the return on equity r_E is equal to the return on assets; so

$$r_E = r_A = 18 \text{ percent}$$

While borrowing changes the return on equity, it will not change the return on assets. This will remain the same because the value of the firm does not change and the expected operating income does not change. Therefore, the return on equity is:

$$r_E = r_A + (D/E)(r_A - r_D)$$
$$= 0.18 + (\$15,000/\$35,000)(0.18 - 0.12)$$
$$= 0.18 + 0.4286(0.06)$$
$$= 0.18 + 0.0257$$
$$= 0.2057 = 20.57 \text{ percent}$$

3. Use the information given in problem 2 and assume that the beta of the firm is 1.2 before the debt financing and the beta of the debt is 0.5. What is the beta of the equity with the debt financing given in problem 2? What will the beta of the equity be if the debt-equity ratio were 30, 50, 60, and 70 percent?

SOLUTION

The beta of the equity without any debt financing is the same as the beta of the firm because no other securities are outstanding. After the financing, the beta of the equity changes as follows:

$$\beta_E = \beta_A + (D/E)(\beta_A - \beta_D)$$
$$= 1.2 + 0.4286(1.2 - 0.5)$$
$$= 1.2 + 0.3 = 1.5$$

For the other debt proportions, β_E is given in the table below.

D/E (%)	β_E
30	1.41
50	1.55
60	1.62
70	1.69

4. If beta of equity with no debt is 1.2. Calculate the equity betas for different debt levels for the following values of beta for debt: 0, 1.2 and 0.5. Compare these results with those of problem 3.

SOLUTION

The values for β_E for different debt/equity ratios and different β_D are given in the table below.

D/E (%)	β_E for different value of β_D		
	$\beta_D = 0$	$\beta_D = 1.2$	$\beta_D = 0.5$
0	1.20	1.20	1.20
5	1.26	1.20	1.24
10	1.32	1.20	1.27
20	1.44	1.20	1.34
40	1.68	1.20	1.48
60	1.92	1.20	1.62
80	2.16	1.20	1.76
100	2.40	1.20	1.90

While the data above are somewhat contrived, several interesting results emerge. You can clearly see that the increase in the risk or beta of the equity with increased debt levels is a function of the beta or risk of the debt itself. First, when the beta of the debt is equal to the beta of the firm, when it is all-equity-financed, for all practical purposes, the company has issued another dose of equity and not debt. Consequently, the beta of the equity does not change. If the company were able to issue debt at the zero-beta level, the risk-free rate, the betas of the equity would tend to increase substantially with additional debt. In practice and in most cases, the beta of corporate debt is greater than zero but less than the beta of the all-equity-financed firm.

5. Jane Black, the financial manager of Leverage Unlimited thinks she can increase shareholder value by increasing the leverage of the company. The company is currently all equity

financed and is earning 20 percent. The company can borrow at 10 percent and the beta of the debt is at 0.4. The beta of equity before borrowing is 1.2. There are 10,000 shares outstanding and the price-earnings ratio of the common shares is 5 on an operating income of $25,000. The company can be expected to continue to generate that amount of operating income after the debt financing. Ms. Black feels that the leverage will substantially raise the value of the firm and wants to buy back half the shares of the company. Formulate a response to Ms. Black assuming operation in perfect capital markets with no corporate or personal taxes.

SOLUTION

First, estimate the value of the firm before the debt financing. The operating earnings are capitalized at 20 percent, so the value of the firm when it is all-equity-financed is $125,000 ($25,000/0.20). The value per share is $12.50; earnings per share are $2.50 ($25,000/10,000 shares); with the price-earnings ratio being 5.0 times ($12.50/$2.50).

Next, determine the earnings per share after the debt financing. The company must sell $62,500 of debt at the going market rate of 10 percent in order to repurchase an equivalent amount of equity ($125,000/2). Remember, because the operating income remains unchanged, the firm's total value remains unchanged at $125,000.

The equity earnings change, however, as follows:

Operating income	$25,000
less interest	6,250
Equity earnings	$18,750

With 5,000 shares now outstanding, earnings per share increase to $3.75 ($18,750/5000 shares). Ms. Black assumes that she can still get the same price-earnings ratio of 5. Then, the shares have a market price of $18.75 (5 x $3.75). But going into debt entails additional risk to the shareholders. The beta will increase substantially. Using the formula:

$$\beta_E = \beta_A + D/E(\beta_A - \beta_D)$$

Before borrowing:

$$\beta = 1.2 + 0.0(1.2 - 0) = 1.2$$

After borrowing:

$$\beta = 1.2 + 1.0(1.2 - 0.4) = 1.2 + 0.8 = 2.0$$

Risk increases by two-thirds. With increased risk, the required rate of return on equity increases too. Assuming that the return on asset stays same, we can calculate the required return as follows:

$$r_E = r_A + (D/E)(r_A - r_D)$$
$$= 0.20 + 1.0(0.20 - 0.10)$$
$$= 0.20 + 0.10$$
$$= 0.30 \text{ or } 30 \text{ percent}$$

The value of the shares will then be: $3.75/0.30 = $12.50

Thus, there is no change in the value of the stock and leverage does not increase the value of the stock. Any increase in earnings is fully neutralized by the corresponding increase in risk and required rate of return. The price-earnings ratio will go down and the market price of the shares will remain the same.

SUMMARY

This chapter presents the well-known Modigliani-Miller propositions on debt policy under perfect market conditions. Proposition I states that a firm's value is unaffected by changes in leverage. Proposition II states that the risk of equity increases in proportion to the debt-equity ratio. This will cause an increase in the required rate of return demanded by investors. Essentially, under perfect market conditions, debt policy is irrelevant and the firm's value is not affected by changes in leverage. The value of a firm depends only on the cash flows produced by its assets. While financial leverage tends to magnify returns to common stockholders, their risk is increased too. Therefore, they require higher returns on their shares; thus, the value of a share remains unchanged.

Proposition I is very general and applies to all types of securities (short-term debt vs. long term debt, equity vs. preferred stock, etc.) and one can say that no combination of securities is better than any other. The MM propositions have replaced the traditional view that the cost of capital will tend to decrease initially as debt is added to the capital structure but that it will increase only after a market-determined intolerable-threshold level of risk is passed. At that point, the cost of equity and the cost of debt increase significantly. The traditional view cannot be supported unless one is willing to accept irrational behavior on the part of investors or the presence of market imperfections.

MM's propositions cannot be refuted once the perfect market conditions are accepted. Any violation of MM's propositions can only be found in market imperfections. These market imperfections are often created by government regulations (differential tax treatment of income streams, for example) and can create profitable opportunities for firms. It is also possible that there are clienteles for specific types of securities such as money market mutual funds and floating-rate notes. However, the demands by clienteles are often quickly met by an adequate supply of these securities and a firm getting into these markets now is unlikely to benefit.

LIST OF TERMS

Capital structure

Financial leverage

Gearing

Law of conservation of value

Proposition I

Proposition II

Separation of investment and financing

Value additivity

Weighted-average cost of capital

EXERCISES

Fill-in Questions

1. _____ is another term used to describe financial leverage.

2. _____ is the term used to describe the mix of debt and equity used by a firm.

3. _____ states that the value of the firm is not changed by the mix of debt and equity.

4. A firm that borrows is said to engage in _____.

5. The _____ states that the value of an asset is preserved regardless of the nature of the claim on it.

6. The _____ is the sum of the returns on debt and equity each weighted by its percentage in the capital structure.

7. _____ states that the expected return on the common stock of a financially leveraged firm increases in proportion to the debt ratio.

8. Proposition I of Modigliani and Miller permits _____ decisions.

9. Proposition I is a restatement of the _____ principle learned in Chapter 7.

Problems

1. JMH Corp. is operating in perfect market conditions with no corporate or personal taxes. The company's debt has an expected return of 11 percent and the return on equity is 16 percent. The debt to assets ratio is 40 percent. Calculate the return on assets.

2. Use the information given in problem 1. How will the return on equity change if the debt is increased to 60 percent?

3. What is the expected return on assets for a firm that is 60 percent debt-financed and pays an expected return on debt of 9 percent and has a required return on equity of 20 percent? Assume the firm operates in perfect capital markets with no corporate or personal income taxes.

4. Your firm's expected operating income is $5,000, and the market value of its outstanding securities is $25,000 when it is all-equity-financed. Assuming that the firm operates in perfect capital markets with no corporate or personal taxes, calculate the required return on equity when the firm sells enough debt to repurchase half of the outstanding equity for each of the following rates of return on debt: (a) 8 percent, (b) 10 percent, and (c) 12 percent.

5. Using the data in problem 4 above, a beta for the firm of 1.4, and a beta for the debt of 0.5, what is the beta of the equity after the financing?

6. The financial manager of Jumping Jack, Inc. estimates that she will increase the earnings per share of her presently all-equity-financed firm if she borrows at the going market rate of 8 percent. She estimates the debt's beta to be 0.3 and the beta of the all-equity firm is 0.8. A return of 12.5 percent is expected on the all-equity firm, the price-earnings ratio of 8 is expected to persist, expected operating income is $300,000, and 100,000 shares are outstanding. She plans to replace 40 percent of her equity with debt. How will the values of the shares change?

Essay Questions

1. Explain the Modigliani and Miller's propositions I and II and their implications for financial managers.

2. Discuss the following argument often heard in defense of leverage. "Cost of debt is definitely less than the cost of equity. By using the cheaper source of funds, a firm can increase the return available to its equity holders and thereby increase their value."

3. "Modigliani and Miller propositions I and II have very little practical appeal as they assume the so called perfect market conditions, which do not exist." Give a detailed response to that statement.

4. How may individual investors augment or undo the debt policy of firms in which they wish to invest? Explain fully. Also explain why this concept is important to the Modigliani-Miller position regarding debt policy.

5. Demonstrate how the beta of a firm is dependent on the beta of the capital structure components.

ANSWERS TO EXERCISES

Fill-in Questions

1. Gearing
2. Capital structure
3. Proposition I
4. Financial leverage
5. Law of conservation of value

6. Weighted-average cost of capital
7. Proposition II
8. Separation of financing and investment
9. Value additivity

Problems

1. $(0.4 \times 0.11) + (0.6 \times 0.16) = 14$ percent

2. $r_E = r_A + D/E\,(r_A - r_D) = 0.14 + 1.5(0.14 - 0.11) = 18.5$ percent

3. $(0.6 \times 0.09) + (0.4 \times 0.2) = 13.4$ percent

4. $r_A = \$5,000/\$25,000 = 20$ percent. $r_E = r_A + D/E(r_A - r_D)$.
   a. When $r_D = 8$ percent, $r_E = 0.20 + [(0.5/0.5)(0.20 - 0.08)] = 32$
   b. When $r_D = 10$ percent, $r_E = 30$ percent
   c. When $r_D = 12$ percent, $r_E = 28$ percent.

5. $\beta_E = \beta_A + D/E(\beta_A - \beta_D) = 1.5 + 1.0(1.5 - 0.6) = 2.40$

6. The analysis is the same as that for problem 5 of the Worked Examples.

   First, calculate the value of the all-equity firm:

   > Value = $300,000/12.5$ percent = $2,400,000
   > Value per share = $2,400,000/100,000$ shares = $24
   > Earnings per share = $300,000/100,000 = $3

   Then, compute the effect of debt financing on earnings per share:

   > Amount of required debt: $0.4(\$2,400,000) = \$960,000$

Operating income	= $300,000
less interest (0.08 X $960,000)	= <u>76,800</u>
Equity earnings	= $223,200

   > Earnings per share: $223,200/60,000 = $3.72

Now, calculate the beta of equity after debt financing:

Before-debt financing: 0.8; after:

$$\beta_E = \beta_A + D/E(\beta_A - \beta_D)$$
$$= 0.8 + 0.4/0.6(0.8 - 0.3)$$
$$= 1.133$$

Now, we can calculate the return on equity, after debt financing:

$$r_E = r_A + (D/E)(r_A - r_D)$$
$$= 0.125 + (0.4/0.6)(0.125 - 0.08)$$
$$= 15.5 \text{ percent}$$

Market price of equity after debt financing can be calculated as below:

Market price per share = $3.72/0.155 = $24

Value of equity = market price per share X number of shares
= $24 X 60,000 = $1,440,000

Value of firm after debt financing = Debt + Equity
= $960,000 + 1,440,000
= $2,400,000

The value of the firm is unaffected by the leverage.

18

How Much Should a Firm Borrow?

INTRODUCTION

Chapter 17 presented the view of debt policy under the perfect market conditions. The view is that debt policy does not matter. We know, however, that in the real world debt policy matters because there are a number of deviations from the perfect market conditions assumed in MM's theoretical framework. While capital markets work reasonably well, there are the following to consider: corporate and personal income taxes, the probability of bankruptcy and the costs associated with it, costs of other forms of financial distress, and differing goals and conflicts of interests among lenders and shareholders. These factors cause the debt policy to assume practical relevance and importance. This chapter provides the practical world's view of debt policy. The MM analysis enables us to understand the significance of these deviations from the perfect market conditions and their impact on corporate debt policy.

The chapter presents two broad theories to explain capital structures of corporations. The first theory, known as the *trade-off theory*, suggests that corporations can arrive at an optimal debt ratio by comparing the positive and negative aspects of borrowing. The primary positive side or benefit of borrowing is that interest payments to lenders are tax-deductible. Thus, the government subsidizes part of the payments to the lenders. The negative side of borrowing comes from the costs associated with bankruptcy and financial distress.

The second theory is known as the *pecking order theory* and is based on the observed (and somewhat stylized) behavior of financial managers. Financial managers appear to prefer a hierarchy of financing sources and their order of preference runs as follows: first choice is internal funds (retained earnings), followed by external debt financing, and external equity being the last choice. This behavior can be explained by *information asymmetry* between managers and investors.

KEY CONCEPTS IN THE CHAPTER

Corporate Taxes and Debt Policy: One of the most important deviations from the classic MM framework is the presence of corporate income taxes and the differential treatment meted out to interest payments on debt. Firms are allowed to deduct interest payments from their income subject to taxation. This creates a subsidy for borrowing and effectively expands the corporate pie available for distribution to investors (stockholders and bondholders). If a firm borrows D dollars at an interest rate of r_D the firm reduces its annual tax bill by $T_c(r_D D)$, where T_c is the corporate tax rate. If the debt is permanent, then the present value of this tax shield is:

$$T_c(r_D D)/r_D = T_c D$$

Thus, the firm's value can be increased by borrowing and the increase in value will equal $T_c D$. We can modify the MM proposition I to the following expression:

Value of firm = Value of all-equity-financed firm + $T_c D$

The basic problem with this is that it leads to an optimal debt ratio of one hundred percent. This, of course, does not make any sense.

Debt Policy and Corporate and Personal Taxes: The issue of taxes gets complicated when personal taxes are also considered. In a world where both corporations and individuals are taxed on their income, the firm does well by its investors when it minimizes not just the corporate taxes but the total taxes paid by the firm and its investors. Consider a firm with both debt and equity. Each dollar of operating income (income before taxes and interests) can be paid out either as equity income or as interest income. Let the tax rates on interest income and equity income be T_p and T_{pE} respectively. There are two ways you can pay the operating income to the investor – either as interest to the bondholder or as dividend to the stockholder. If it is paid out as dividends, the effective cash flow to the stockholder will be as follows:

Operating income	=	$1
less corporate taxes	=	$1 - T_c$
Personal tax on equity income	=	$T_{pE}(1 - T_c)$
Net of all taxes	=	$(1 - T_{pE})(1 - T_c)$

When a dollar of operating income is paid out to the bondholder, the firm saves corporate taxes and the bondholder gets $(1 - T_p)$. Under these conditions, the debt policy will be irrelevant, if:

$$1 - T_p = (1 - T_{pE})(1 - T_c)$$

This can happen only if the corporate tax rate, T_c, is less than T_p and T_{pE} is very small. This is what Merton Miller used to suggest that debt policy could very well be irrelevant. Miller suggested that the effective tax on equity income is very low as most of the income could be in the form of capital gains.

Miller extended the analysis to derive conditions for aggregate market equilibrium for corporate debt policy. Initially, corporations have a strong incentive to borrow. As borrowing begins, investors have to be induced to hold corporate debt instead of stocks. Tax-exempt investors are tapped first, leaving personal taxes unchanged and savings on corporate taxes. As more is borrowed, investors have to be persuaded to migrate from stocks to bonds; higher bond returns are offered in order to offset the loss on personal taxes. This migration stops when, at the margin, corporate tax savings equal personal tax losses. The implication of Miller's analysis is: while there is an aggregate equilibrium debt-equity ratio for the corporate world, any capital structure is irrelevant.

Miller's argument had some validity before the 1986 Tax Law changes when the tax on capital gains were low relative to the tax on interest income. The changes made in 1986 effectively reduced the personal tax rates on interest income and raised the tax on capital gains. It should be mentioned that more recent changes have somewhat reduced the advantage to debt as the effective tax on capital gains has been reduced to 20 percent. However, considering the fact that part of the equity income comes as dividends, which are taxed at higher rates, debt will continue to have some advantage over equity in terms of taxes. A moderate tax advantage to corporate borrowing exists for companies that are reasonably sure they can use the corporate tax shelter.

A practical rule on debt policy would be to structure debt and equity so that income goes to those who are taxed the least. In general, companies, which are unsure that the corporate tax shield will be used to its full advantage, have less incentive to borrow.

Financial Distress and Debt Policy: The prospect of *financial distress* concerns investors and reduces the present value of the firm. Financial distress occurs when the firm cannot meet its obligations to the creditors. The ultimate in financial distress is *bankruptcy* and liquidation of the business. The risk and cost of financial distress increase as borrowing increases. Financial distress can be costly and leads to a loss in the value of the business. The fear of the prospect of financial distress affects the market value of the levered firm's stocks and bonds. The value of the firm can be written as:

$$\text{Value of firm} = \text{value if all-equity-financed} + PV \text{ (tax shield)} - PV(\text{costs of financial distress})$$

Financial distress costs include *bankruptcy costs*, costs of operating under the cloud of bankruptcy, and *agency costs*. Bankruptcy is the legal mechanism allowing creditors to take over the assets of the firm and control the business. Bankruptcy costs are the costs of using the system. These direct costs include the legal and accounting costs. These costs can be large and reduce the total payoff to shareholders and creditors. Evidence suggests that bankruptcy costs are large absolutely but nominal relative to firm value. Smaller firms can have a much higher percentage of costs relative to their size.

Other financial distress costs vary with asset types and the nature of the firm. These costs arise from the difficulties of running a bankrupt firm. An airline facing potential bankruptcy will find it very difficult to hire able pilots. Market price adjustments when a firm enters bankruptcy are a significant cost to investors.

Agency costs are incurred when non-bankrupt, but financially troubled firms create conflicts of interest between creditors and shareholders. Stockholders can "play" different games that can be costly to the lenders. These games include:

- Risk shifting or investing in risky but negative NPV projects,
- Refusing to contribute equity capital,

211

- Cash in and run or paying themselves cash dividends,
- Playing for time, and
- Bait and switch or issuing progressively more and riskier debt.

Lenders anticipate these sub-optimal behaviors on the part of the stockholders and attempt to rein-in the behavior by including strict conditions in debt contracts. These, in turn, restrict stockholder flexibility and add to the costs.

The Trade-off Theory: The trade-off theory postulates that firms balance the benefits (tax-shield) and costs (financial distress costs) and arrives at an optimal debt ratio. Thus, the optimal debt ratio reflects a trade-off between tax shields and the costs of financial distress. The trade-off theory suggests that firms may have different target debt ratios. The optimal debt ratio will be a function of the type of assets and the ability of the firm to use the tax-shield provided by debt. Firms with assets, which are tangible and easily transferable to others, can be expected to borrow more. Examples of this type of firms include: airlines, retailers, and banks. On the other hand, firms with high levels of intangible assets, which can lose value in financial distress, will not use much debt. Examples: pharmaceutical companies, high tech firms, and software companies.

Empirical studies find broad support for the trade-off theory. However, many profitable companies--those that would tend to benefit the most from tax shields--borrow the least.

The Pecking Order Theory of Financing Choices: The pecking order theory of capital structure is fashioned from observed practice of companies. Firms appear to have a preferred order of financing choices—internal equity (retained earnings) being the most preferred and external equity being the least preferred. A formal framework for the theory uses *asymmetric information* between the manager and the investor as the basis for the theory. Given asymmetric information, it is rational for the manager to prefer the use of retained earnings first. The manager would also prefer to issue debt rather than common stock, as the common would be potentially under-priced.

The pecking order theory also suggests that managers would like to maintain a *financial slack*, which would provide flexibility of means for meeting future financing needs. Thus, they would hold reserves of marketable securities and have spare borrowing capacity. Firms also adapt their target dividend ratios to their investment opportunities while trying to avoid sudden changes in dividends.

WORKED EXAMPLES

1. Two firms are identical in all respects except that one firm is 100 percent financed by common stock and the other is 50 percent equity-financed and 50 percent debt-financed at 8 percent a year. The balance sheets of the two firms are as follows:

212

	ALL EQUITY FIRM			EQUITY AND DEBT FIRM		
Assets	$10,000	Equity	$10,000	Assets	$10,000	Debt (8%)	$5,000
						Equity	5,000
Total	$10,000	Total	$10,000	Total	$10,000	Total	$10,000

Assume that the company has an operating income of $1,500. Show that the interest paid on debt is a tax shield.

SOLUTION

The income statements for the two firms can be shown as below:

	ALL EQUITY FIRM	EQUITY AND DEBT FIRM
Earnings before interest and taxes	1,500	$1,500
Interest expenses		400
Pretax income	1,500	1,100
Tax at 35 percent	525	385
Net income to stockholders	$ 975	$ 715
Total income to bond and stockholders	$975	$400 + $715 = $1,115
Interest tax shield (0.35 x interest)	$0	0.35 x $400 = $140

The interest tax shield is the difference between the streams of payments received by the investors of the two firms.

2. What is the present value of the tax shield as calculated in problem 1?

SOLUTION

Assume that the risk of the investment in the tax shield requires a rate of return equal to that paid on the debt, namely, 8 percent. If the financing is considered permanent, the problem is one of solving for the present value of a perpetuity.

Present value of tax shield = $140/0.08 = $1,750

Because the total amount of the debt is $5,000, the present value of the tax shield is the amount of the total debt that the government underwrites when it allows interest to be deducted as an expense. The difference between the total debt and the federal subsidy, $3,250 ($5,000- $1750), is the amount the company underwrites. Also, note that the present value of the tax shield is independent of the return on the debt. The cash difference between taxes paid, $140 ($525 - $385), makes going into debt a profitable investment, worth $1,750. Restated,

Present value of tax shield = $\frac{\text{corporate tax rate x expected interest payment}}{\text{expected return on debt}}$

$$= T_c(r_D D)/r_D = T_c D$$
$$= 0.35 \times (0.08 \times \$5,000)/0.08$$
$$= 0.35 \times \$5,000$$
$$= \$1,750$$

3. Show how interest tax under the current tax laws may contribute to the value of XMZ Company's shareholders. The company has no long-term debt now and its balance sheet is shown below. Ignoring personal taxes, work out how much shareholders should benefit if the company borrowed $600 million of long-term debt and used it to repurchase stock.

Balance Sheets for XMZ Company ($ in millions)

Balance Sheet – Book Values				Balance Sheet – Market Values			
Net working capital	$300	Long-term debt	$0	Net working capital	$300	Long-term Debt	$0
Long-term assets	600	Equity	$900	Long-term assets	$3,150	Equity	$3,450
Total assets	$900	Total liabilities and equity	$900	Total assets	$3,450	Total liabilities and equity	$3,450

SOLUTION

The first step is to estimate the value of the firm as if it were to borrow $600 million in permanent long-term debt and use the proceeds to buy that much stock. Because of the tax shield effects, assuming a 35 percent tax rate, this financing scheme should increase the firm's value by the present value of the tax shield $T_c D$, which is the corporate tax rate T_c times the amount of permanent long-term debt D. In as much as the additional debt is $600 million, the market value of the firm should increase by 0.35 X $600 million = $210 million. If the MM theory, corrected for taxes, holds, the value of the firm must increase by $210 million to $3,660 (210 + 3,450) million. The new balance sheets are give below. The value of the equity declines by $390 (600-210) million, which is $(1 - T_c)(D)$ 0.65 X 600. The question remains: Are the shareholders better off? Analyze this in steps. Imagine that you bought the firm for $3,450 million, its value before issuing debt. You then "gave" part of your firm to debt-holders for $600 million. The value of your holdings is immediately reduced to $2,850 million. Then the market recognizes what has happened--you took advantage of the tax shield--and bids the value of the firm up to $3,660 million. Your holdings are now worth $3,660 - $600 = $3,060 million. Since you have also sold some shares back to the company for $600 million, you are $210 million better off than you started. This is the net advantage to shareholders for going into debt.

214

Balance Sheets for XMZ Company After Borrowing ($ in millions)

Balance Sheet – Book Values				Balance Sheet – Market Values			
Net working capital	$300	Long-term debt	$600	Net working capital	$300	Long-term debt	$600
Long-term assets	600	Equity	$300	Long-term assets	3,360	Equity	3,060
Total assets	$900	Total liabilities and equity	$900	Total assets	$3,660	Total liabilities and equity	$3,060

SUMMARY

This chapter's major point is that *debt policy does matter,* once taxes, the probability of bankruptcy, financial distress, and potential conflicts of interest among the firm's security holders are included. The chapter considers, one by one, the main deviations from the MM perfect market framework and arrives at practical implications for corporate debt policy. We end up with two theories of capital structure – the trade-off theory and the pecking order theory. It should be kept in mind that the two theories are not mutually exclusive and corporate practice can reflect both theories.

Corporate taxes combined with the tax-deductibility of interest are compelling reasons why debt policy counts. Interest on debt is deductible before corporate taxes are paid and that creates a tax shield, which enhances the after-tax value of the firm. Tax shields are valuable assets; their value being the present value of reduced taxes. Personal taxes introduce additional complications. Miller's analysis reflects these and suggests that the advantage to debt may not be that significant.

While tax shield encourages borrowing, nontrivial costs of financial distress are the costs to pay for the benefit of debt. Because promises made to creditors may be broken or honored only with substantial difficulty, a firm is not able to borrow as much as it may choose. Consequently, the prospective cost of financial distress reduces the value of the firm. Such costs include the cost of bankruptcy, as well as, such indirect costs of time and effort to resolve a financially distressed condition. Further, whenever financial distress arises, there are a variety of games in which stockholders may engage to minimize their risk exposure, such as risk shifting, refusing to contribute equity capital, taking cash out of the enterprise, and making decisions which defer the day of reckoning. These represent the agency costs of borrowing. To forestall the possibility of such maneuvers, restrictive provisions are often incorporated into bond contracts.

The trade-off theory of capital structure argues that a firm's debt-equity decision is really one of trading off interest tax shields against the cost of financial distress, and it partially helps to explain why companies have different debt-equity ratios. The pecking-order theory says that financial managers have a preferred, ordered set of financing options, and they go down that list in order of preference, the first being internal funds, then targeted but sticky cash dividends, and then external financing, the safest first, usually debt, and equity last.

Debt may or may not be a good alternative to equity financing. Factors to consider are the total tax liability to shareholders, a firm's business risk, the types of assets that produce operating income, and the need for financial slack.

LIST OF TERMS

Agency costs   Information asymmetry
Bankruptcy   Pecking order
Bankruptcy costs   Tax-deductible
Capital gains   Tax shield
Financial distress   Trade-off theory
Financial distress costs   Value of all-equity firm
Financial slack

EXERCISES

Fill-in Questions

1. The main benefit of corporate debt is that the interest is a(n) _____ expense.

2. An investor willing to lend at a before-tax return of 10 percent must be willing to lend at an after-tax return of _____ if her marginal income tax rate is 36 percent.

3. In Merton Miller's "debt and taxes" scheme of the financial world, migrations between stocks and bonds continue to take place up to the point where _____ tax losses are just equal to _____ tax savings.

4. _____ between managers and investors forms the basis for the pecking order theory.

5. The direct costs of _____ consist of the present value of administrative, court, and legal fees, which reduce the total payoff to shareholders and bondholders.

6. The indirect costs of bankruptcy, which arise out of conflicts of interest, are called _____.

7. In a financially distressed firm, stockholders (gain, lose) _____ when the business risk is increased.

8. In a financially distressed firm, a project whose net present value is $200 will add (exactly, less than, more than) _____ $200 to the value of shareholders.

9. The bondholders of a financially distressed firm have (more, less) _____ to gain from investments which increase firm value, the greater the probability of default.

10. The effective rate of tax on _____ is often lower than the statutory rate since gains remain untaxed until they are realized.

11. Firms should strive to maximize the (after-tax, before-tax) _____ income of shareholders.

12. If $1 - T_p$ is greater than $(1 - T_{pE})(1 - T_c)$, corporate borrowing is (better, worse) _____ than personal borrowing.

13. It pays companies to issue more debt as long as the corporate tax shield (exceeds, is less than) _____ the personal tax cost to the marginal lender.

14. The _____ of capital structure says firm attempt to find an optimal debt ratio by comparing the benefits and costs of leverage.

15. Firms whose assets are risky and mostly intangible tend to borrow (less, more) _____ than firms whose assets are tangible and relatively safe.

16. A preferred hirarchy of financing choices is called the _____ theory of capital structure.

17. _____ refers to the extent to which a firm has flexible opportunities for meeting its future financing needs.

Problems

1. Compute the present value of interest tax shields resulting from each of the following debt issues. Consider only corporate taxes, the marginal rate of which is 35 percent.
   a. A $1,000, 1-year loan at 9 percent.
   b. A 7-year loan of $1,000 at 9 percent. Assume principal is repaid at maturity.
   c. A $1,000 perpetuity at 8 percent.

2. The book and market value balance sheets of Right Lever, Inc. are given below. Assume that: (1) the MM theory holds except for taxes, (2) no growth, (3) the debt is permanent, (4) 35 percent corporate tax rate, and (5) the interest rate on debt is 8 percent.

Balance Sheets for Right Lever ($ in millions)

Balance Sheet – Book Values				Balance Sheet – Market Values			
Net working capital	$40	Long-term debt	$70	Net working capital	$40	Long-term debt	$70
Long-term assets	70	Equity	$40	Long-term assets	$110	Equity	$80
Total Assets	$110	Total liabilities and equity	$110	Total assets	$150	Total liabilities and equity	$150

    a. How can the market value of the firm be greater than its book value?

    b. Demonstrate the extent to which the stockholders would be better off if the company were to sell additional debt at 8 percent, using the proceeds to purchase $40 of stock.

    c. Demonstrate the effects of replacing $40 of permanent, 8 percent debt with equity.

3 Compute the total corporate and personal taxes paid on debt and equity income for each of the following cases. Assume a corporate income tax rate of 35 percent; realized capital gains and all cash dividends are taxed as ordinary income; the interest rate on debt is 10 percent; earnings before interest and taxes are $1,000; the levered firm borrows $1,000; and, where the condition calls for it, all earnings for shareholders are paid to them.

CASE	BONDHOLDERS' TAX BRACKET	STOCKHOLDERS' TAX BRACKET	FORM OF EQUITY INCOME
1	0	0	All dividends
2	0.15	0.15	All dividends
3	0.15	0.15	All unrealized capital gains
4	0.28	0.28	All dividends
5	0.28	0.28	All unrealized capital gains
6	0.36	0.36	All dividends
7	0.36	0.36	All unrealized capital gains

For each case, identify whether the levered or unlevered firm has the tax advantage? What implications do the differences you observe have for making financial decisions of the firm? For individual investors?

4. Jay Bright, Inc., has serious problems and is facing bankruptcy. Its market value balance sheet is as follows:

Net working capital	$500	Bonds	$650
Long-term assets	200	Equity	50
	$700		$700

You are brought in to evaluate the following actions the financial manager is contemplating. Present an objective evaluation of each action. Assume each action is independent of all other actions.

a. The company pays a cash dividend of $75.
b. The company sells its long-term assets for $100, collects $450 from its net working capital, closes its doors, and invests the cash of $550 in U.S. Treasury bills at the going rate of 8 percent.
c. The company is confronted with an investment opportunity, which has a net present value of $200 but decides not to undertake it.
d. The company is confronted with an investment project whose net present value is $200 and sells new equity to undertake it.
e. The company is confronted with an investment opportunity whose net present value is $200 and borrows $200 to undertake it.
f. The lenders agree to extend the due date of its debt from 1 year to 2 years. From 1 year to 5 years.
g. The lenders agree to extend the due date of its debt from 1 year to 2 years, provided the lenders control all working capital and investment decisions, as well as prohibiting the issuance of any further debt.

5. You are the financial manager of a Fortune 500 company. You are asked to demonstrate how interest tax shields may contribute to the value of the stockholders' equity. Assume that the company has a market value of about $30 billion, has about $2 billion of short-term debt, and very little long-term debt. Assume that debt can be issued at a rate equal to about 8 percent and that the corporation's income tax rate is 35 percent.

Essay Questions

1. Explain the trade-off theory of capital structure.

2. Explain MM's proposition I, as corrected for the presence of corporate income taxes.

3. Describe the pecking-order theory of capital structure. Compare the theory with the trade-off theory. Does it make sense for a company to follow the pecking order theory?

4. Select five Fortune 500 firms and describe their capital structure in terms of the two theories discussed in the chapter.

5. How can it be said that it may not be in the stockholders' self-interest to contribute fresh equity capital, even if that means foregoing positive net present value investment opportunities?

ANSWERS TO EXERCISES

Fill-in Questions

1. Tax-deductible
2. 6.4 percent
3. Personal; corporate
4. Information asymmetry
5. Financial distress
6. Agency costs
7. Gain
8. Less than
17. Financial slack

9. More
10. Capital gains
11. After-tax
12. Better
13. Exceeds
14. Trade-off theory
15. Less
16. Pecking order

Problems

1. a. Interest tax shield: $0.35(\$1,000 \times 0.09) = \$31.5$; PV(tax shield) $= \$31.5/1.09 = \$28.90$.

    b. Present value of tax shield $= \$31.5 \times$ Annuity factor for 7 years at 9 percent $= \$31.5 \times 5.033 = \$158.54$.

    c. $(0.35 \times \$1000 \times .08)/0.08 = \$350$. [Alternately, PV(tax shield) $= T_c \times D = 0.35 \times 41,000$]

2. a. Book values are based largely on historical costs, whereas market values are based on expected profitability. Companies earning profits higher than their cost of capital will typically have market values higher than book value.

    b. $T_cD = 0.35 \times \$40 = \$14.00$, the amount by which total assets increase. The decline in equity is $(1 - T_c)D = \$26.00$. The net gain for the shareholder can be summarized as below:

Amount received by shareholders	$40.00
Decline in shareholder value	26.00
Net gain to shareholders	$14.00

    Market value balance sheet after the debt issue:

Net working capital	$ 40.00	Debt	$110.00
Long-term assets	124.00	Equity	54.00
	$164.00		$164.00

220

c. Assets now decline by $14.00 and equity increases by $26.00. In sum,

Increase in shareholder value	26.00
Amount paid by shareholders	40.00
Net loss to shareholders	14.00

Market value valance sheet after the equity issue:

Net working capital	$ 40.00	Debt	$ 30.00
Long-term assets	96.00	Equity	106.00
	$136.00		$136.00

3. The details for case 5 are shown below. The results for all cases are summarized in the table below.

INCOME STATEMENTS

	TAX RATE	UNLEVERED FIRM	LEVERED FIRM
Earnings before interest and taxes		1,000	1,000
Interest		0	100
Pretax income		1,000	900
Corporate tax at	35%	350	315
Net income to stockholders		650	585
Total income to stockholders and bondholders (before tax)		650	685
Tax on firm		350	315
Tax on bondholders at	28%	0	28
Tax on stockholders	0%	0	0
Total income to stockholders and bondholders (after tax)		650	657
Total taxes paid:		350	343

Advantage to debt = $7 (on $1,000 debt at 10 percent interest)

The tax advantage to debt for the different cases is given in the table below.

221

Cases	Corporate Tax rate	Tax on bondholders	Tax on stockholders	Total Taxes Paid		Advantage to Debt
				Unlevered Firm	Levered Firm	
1	0.35	0	0	$350	$315	$35
2	0.35	0.15	0.15	$447.5	$417.75	$29.75
3	0.35	0.15	0	$350	$330	$20
4	0.35	0.28	0.28	$532	$506.8	$25.2
5	0.35	0.28	0	$350	$343	$7
6	0.35	0.36	0.36	$584	$561.6	$22.4
7	0.35	0.36	0	$350	$351	-$1.0

You can also calculate the effective advantage to debt as the difference between $1-T_p$ and $(1-T_{pE})$ x $(1-T_C)$, where T_p is the personal tax rate on interest income and T_{pE} is the personal tax rate on equity income and T_C is the corporate tax rate.

4. a. Bond value falls, stockholders gain.
    b. Bondholders will get $550; stockholders will get nothing.
    c. Everyone loses.
    d. Bondholders gain because the debt ratio improves; stockholders also gain.
    e. Bondholders could gain or lose, depending on the risk of the project.
    f. Bondholders lose in both instances.
    g. Bondholders may win in this case.

5. One billion dollars of debt, at an interest rate of 8 percent, enables the firm to reduce it annual tax bill by $28 million ($1,000 X 0.08 X 0.35). If the debt is permanent, the present value of this debt will be $350 million ($28/0.08). Assuming the effect of financial distress costs to be negligible, the firm value will increase by about $350 million.

19

Financing and Valuation

INTRODUCTION

So far, we have treated investment and financing to be separate and have not considered any interaction between the two. This assumed the MM perfect market world where the investment decisions could be made without any reference to how the investments are financed. This chapter provides you with tools required to make investment decisions when they are affected by financing decisions. The chapter gives useful and practical pointers to deal with capital budgeting situations where investment and financing decisions interact. The chapter also explains how to handle the cash flows which are very safe or of low risk.

The chapter describes two equivalent approaches to incorporating the effects of financing interactions. The first approach uses the popular and widely used tool of the weighted-average cost of capital (WACC). WACC incorporates the effect of tax shields into the discount rate used to value the cash flows produced by a project. WACC is typically calculated using actual market data and balance sheets for companies or industries. Usually, WACC works quite well, if you know its limitations and potential pitfalls.

The second approach adds the present value of the financing effects to the base-case net present value and calculates the *adjusted present value or APV* of the project. The modified MM proposition I described in Chapter 18 is an example of the APV approach. The approach is very general and can be useful in cases where WACC does not work very well because the assumptions for the correct use of WACC are violated. The APV approach is also useful in cases where the project or the investment decision involves special or subsidized financing or costs of issuing securities needed to finance the project.

Before we begin the lessons of this chapter, it might be useful to have a quick review of the investment decision making process we have used so far. The following steps are involved in evaluating investment opportunities:

- Forecast the project's incremental after-tax cash flows.
- Assess the project's risk.
- Estimate the opportunity cost of capital.
- Calculate NPV, using the discounted-cash-flow formula.

Remember that the opportunity cost of capital reflects the projects business risk and does not include any effect of financial leverage. This chapter tells you how to incorporate the effect of borrowing.

KEY CONCEPTS IN THE CHAPTER

The Weighted-Average Cost of Capital: The weighted average cost of capital, (or more exactly, the after-tax weighted average cost of capital) incorporates the tax deductibility of borrowing into the discount rate used to evaluate project cash flows. Thus, WACC is the adjusted discount rate or cost of capital. The formula for WACC is:

$$WACC = r_D(1 - T_c)D/V + r_E(E/V)$$

where, r_D = Before-tax cost of debt,
r_E = Cost of equity
T_c = Marginal tax rate for the firm
D/V = Debt to assets ratio
E/V = Equity ratio

It is simply the cost of the source of funds weighted by the percentage of each source in the balance sheet. The formula is general and can easily be adapted to include preferred stock or even separate costs for short-term and long-term debts. For example, if a firm uses preferred stock in its financial mix, the WACC can be written as:

$$WACC = r_d(1 - T_c)D/V + r_P(P/V) + r_E(E/V),$$

where r_P is the cost of preferred stock and P/V is the ratio of preferred stock to assets.

In practice, WACC is typically calculated using actual balance sheet data for firms and all the variables used in the formula refers to the whole firm. Therefore, when it is directly used to evaluate projects, the following points should be kept in mind:

- WACC calculated from actual company data should be used for project evaluation only when the project is a carbon copy of the firm or represents the same average risk as the firm.
- The project supports the same debt ratio as the firm.
- WACC assumes that the debt ratio (D/V) is maintained by regular re-balancing.
- The debt ratio and equity ratio should be based on market values, rather than book values.
- When computing WACC from actual numbers, care has to be taken for properly adjusting or accounting for current liabilities, short-term debt, and deferred taxes. The usual approach is to net these out of the balance sheet. However, if the short-term debt is part of the permanent financing mix used by the firm, it should probably be included in the WACC.
- Industry costs might be better than individual firms' cost when used for project analysis, especially by firms outside the industry.
- Immediate source of funds for the project is of no relevance for computing the WACC.

WACC is very useful when it is properly used. It can be adjusted for changes in debt ratios or business risk changes by applying the equations from MM's propositions I and II. (See worked example 3.) The adjustments can be used for betas also using the following equations from chapter 9:

$$\beta_{asset} = \beta_{debt} (D/V) + \beta_{equity} (E/V)$$
$$\beta_{equity} = \beta_{asset} + (\beta_{asset} - \beta_{debt})D/E$$

These leverage adjustments should be kept within reasonable limits and should not be used for large changes in debt ratio.

Adjusted Present Value: Adjusted present value (APV) is an alternative to using the WACC. Technically, the APV is more general and can be used in cases where the WACC may not be able to capture all the side effects of financing decisions. The general expression for APV can be written as below:

APV = base-case NPV + sum of present values of all financing side-effects

The base-case NPV is the NPV of the project cash flows using the opportunity cost of capital. That is, you are assuming that the project is an all equity-financed mini-firm. Here are the steps involved in computing the APV.

- First, calculate the base-case NPV, i.e. without financing side effects.
- Identify the financing side effects. The effects can be from: issue costs, tax shields, special interest loans, etc.
- Compute the present values of all the side effects using the appropriate discount rates.
- Add the present values of the side effects to the base-case NPV to get the APV.

Generally, issue costs reduce the project's NPV, while tax shields or special financing deals add to the NPV. Care has to be taken when computing the present value of tax shields. The amount supported by the debt has to be estimated. The tax shield is also a function of the following financing rules. The two financing rules are: 1) Debt is fixed in dollar terms and 2) Debt is constantly re-balanced. The WACC approach follows the latter assumption. Following rule 1 generally gives a higher value for the present value of the tax shield and therefore a higher APV.

APV and Hurdle Rates: Using APV, we can work backwards to compute the hurdle rate that has to be cleared by the project cash flows in order to be acceptable. This will be the internal rate of return for which the project's APV = 0. This rate is called the *adjusted cost of capital* or discount rate (r^*) and can be used as the hurdle rate for projects with comparable risk and similar debt capacity. The project is acceptable if it gives positive NPV when the cash flows are discounted using the adjusted cost of capital.

Opportunity Cost of Capital, Adjusted Discount Rate, and WACC: The opportunity cost of capital is a return measure based on pure business risk and is not affected by the financial leverage carried by the project. It is the expected return offered by capital markets on comparable risk projects. This should be the discount rate used if the project is all-equity financed. An *adjusted discount rate* or *hurdle rate* can be computed using the APV. This rate will reflect the financing side effects measured by the APV. WACC is an *adjusted cost of capital* that captures the benefit of tax shields. Be careful when you use these terms, because strictly, they are not interchangeable.

Discounting Safe, Nominal Cash Flows: Safe, nominal cash flows are comparable to debt related cash flows. This is because the firm is committed to making the stipulated dollar cash flows. The correct discount rate to use, in such cases, is the after-tax unsubsidized borrowing rate.

This rule is useful in the evaluation of special or subsidized financing deals. Such deals could be viewed as equivalent loans. That is:

Equivalent loan = Present value of the cash flows needed to service the debt.

Again, this present value is calculated using the firm's after-tax borrowing rate. Thus, any subsidized loan at interest rates below the market rate will be like signing up for an equivalent loan less than the amount you are really able to borrow. The difference between the actual amount borrowed and the equivalent loan is the NPV of the special financing deal.

WORKED EXAMPLES

1. Riders and Bikers Corp. (RBC) has a total market value of $10 million. The market value of equity is $6 million and the company carries debt valued at $4 million. The before-tax cost of debt is 8 percent and the cost of equity is estimated at 13 percent. The marginal tax rate is 35 percent. Estimate the weighted-average cost of capital for the company.

SOLUTION

The weighted average cost of capital = $r_D(1 - T_C)D/V + r_E E/V$
D = $4 million, E = $6 million, V = D + E = $10 million
D/E = 0.40, V/E = 0.6

Substituting these and other values into the equation for WACC,

$$WACC = 0.08(0.65)0.4 + 0.13 (0.6)$$
$$= 0.0208 + 0.078$$
$$= 0.0988 = 9.88 \text{ percent}$$

2. RBC is considering a project, which is expected to produce $600,000 in annual after-tax cash flows for the next 5 years. The project has the same risk as the company's existing operations and is expected to support the same debt capacity. What is the NPV of the project if the estimated investment required for the project is $2.25 million?

SOLUTION

NPV of the project = -2.25 + PV ($0.6 X annuity factor for 5 years and 9.88 percent)
Using a calculator, PV of $0.6 million for 5 years: N = 5, I = 9.88, PMT = $0.600, FV = 0, PV = solve = $2.2815 million. NPV = -2.25 + 2.2815 = $0.0315 million.

3. RBC is planning to spend large amounts of money on R & D over the next few years and feels that it may not be able to use all the tax shields generated by a 40 percent debt ratio. The company considers lowering the debt to 20 ratio percent. How will this change its WACC and cost of equity? Assume that the lower debt ratio will reduce the before-tax cost of debt to 7.8 percent.

SOLUTION

The problem can be solved by using the "three step" process of unlevering and relevering the WACC.

Step 1: Unlever the WACC to calculate the opportunity cost of capital, r.
$r = r_D D/V + r_E E/V = 0.08(0.4) + 0.13(0.6) = 0.11 = 11$ percent

Step 2: Calculate the cost of equity at 20 percent debt ratio.
$r_E = r + (r_A - r_D)D/E = 0.11 + (0.11 - 0.078)0.2/0.8 = 0.118 = 11.8$ percent

Step 3: Calculate the new WACC.
$WACC = 0.078(1 - 0.35)0.2 + 0.118(0.8) = 10.45$ percent

4. You are engaged as a financial consultant to estimate the value of a privately held firm, which earns $500,000 a year. You are to assume that the cash flows will continue indefinitely at that level. Because you estimate the risk of the private firm to be about that of the public ones comparable in business risk, the weighted-average cost of capital seems like a suitable approach. Average data of the industry is available. The firm's marginal tax rate is 34 percent. The weighted-average bond yield of the comparable companies is 12.2 percent. The risk of the comparable companies approximated a portfolio beta of 1.2. The yield on your benchmark default-free asset is 8 percent. You use the historical arithmetic-average equity risk premium of 8.6 percent. The expected return for an asset whose beta risk is 1.0 is, then, 16.6 percent. Adjusted for the 1.2 risk of your firm, your estimated average cost of equity is 1.2 x 16.6 percent = 19.92 percent.

SOLUTION

The formula for the weighted-average cost of capital is:

$$\text{WACC} = r_D(1 - T_c)D/V + r_E(E/V)$$

where, r_D = the firm's current borrowing rate
T_c = the marginal corporate income tax
r_E = the expected rate of return on the firm's stock (a function of the firm's business risk and its debt ratio)
D,E = the market values of currently outstanding debt and equity
$V = D + E$ = the total market value of the firm

The weighted-average cost of capital for the firm is therefore:

$$\text{WACC} = 0.122(1 - 0.34)0.4 + 0.1992(0.6)$$
$$= 0.032208 + 0.1195$$
$$= 0.1517 = 15.17 \text{ percent}$$

The value of the firm = $500,000/0.1517 = $3.3 million

5. What-Not, Inc., is considering an investment project which will generate a level after-tax cash flow of $500,000 a year in the next 5 years. Returns on comparable risk investment opportunities are 14 percent. The investment requires a cash outlay of $1.5 million. Compute the net present value of this project.

SOLUTION

This straightforward capital budgeting problem requires you to find the present value of $500,000 a year for each of 5 years, using the discount rate of 14 percent. The cash outlay is then deducted from the present value of that stream of cash to obtain NPV. The calculations are:

$$NPV = -1,500,000 + \sum_{t=1}^{5} \frac{\$500,000}{(1.14)^t}$$
$$= -\$1,500,000 + (\$500,000 \times 3.433)$$
$$= -\$1,500,000 + \$1,716,500$$
$$= \$216,500$$

6. What-Not, Inc., (problem 5 above) does not have the cash available to undertake the project. Therefore, it is investigating the possibility of selling stock. The financial manager discovered that for issues of that size, the effective cost to the firm would be 16 percent of the gross proceeds to the company. How much must the company raise in order to net $1.5 million, and what impact does the cost of issuing common stock have on the project's NPV?

228

SOLUTION

This is a problem of determining the adjusted present value (APV) of the investment, taking into account the costs incurred when external financing is needed. First, find the amount of money that must be raised so that the company obtains the needed $1.5 million. The company will receive only 84 percent of the amount raised. Thus, the amount of money (gross proceeds) to be raised equals:

Gross proceeds of the issue = $1,500,000/0.84 = $1,785,714

Issue costs = $1,785,714 - $1,500,000 = $285,714

Because this is an additional cash outlay prompted by this project, it must be included in the analysis. The APV will be:

APV = base-case NPV - issue cost
    = $216,500 - $285,714
    = -$69,214

The issue cost makes the project unacceptable.

7. What-Not, Inc., is comfortable with a 65 percent target debt ratio. It borrows at the rate of 12 percent, pays the principal in equal yearly installments, and pays interest based on the unpaid balance. Debt issue costs are 5 percent of the gross proceeds, and equity issue costs are those of problem 6. The tax on the corporation, bondholders, and shareholders is 30 percent. What does this do to APV?

SOLUTION

This extension of the basic problem requires you to incorporate the present value of the interest tax shield to make it complete. Let's go through it in steps.

Step 1. We already know the value of the base case is $216,500.

Step 2. Determine the issue cost. To calculate the issue cost of debt, determine how much will be needed. It is $975,000(0.65 X $1,500,000). Next, determine how much should be raised to obtain that amount: It is $1,026,316($975,000/0.95). The issue cost is determined by taking the difference between the amount that must he raised and the amount that is actually used: It is $51,316($1,026,316 - $975,000). The issue costs of equity are similarly determined. The amount needed is $525,000 ($1.5 million X 35 percent). The amount to be raised is $625,000 ($525,000/0.84). The issue cost is $100,000($625,000 - $525,000).

Step 3. Determine the present value of the interest tax shield. Before you can do that, however, you must determine the annual installment payments, the annual interest payable in each year,

229

the annual tax shelter, and the present value of the annual tax shelter. The annual installments are $205,263($1,026,316/5 years) plus interest on the remaining balance. The table is as follows. (Because the debt is not subsidized, it is evaluated at the 12 percent borrowing rate.)

YEAR	DEBT OUTSTANDING AT START OF YEAR	INTEREST	INTEREST TAX SHIELD	PRESENT VALUE TAX SHIELD
1	$1,026,316	$123,158	$36,947	$32,989
2	821,053	98,526	29,558	23,563
3	615,790	73,895	22,168	15,779
4	410,527	49,263	14,779	9,392
5	205,264	24,632	7,390	4,193
				$85,916

Combine all the PVs to obtain APV.

$$\text{APV} = \text{base-case PV} - \text{PV of issue cost} + \text{PV of tax shield}$$
$$= \$216,500 - (\$51,316 + \$100,000) + \$85,916$$
$$= \$151,100$$

Accept the project.

8. Forever and Ever Company is considering an investment project that costs $2 million and is expected to generate savings of $295,000 a year forever. The business risk of this project warrants a rate of return of 15 percent. Calculate the net present value of the project, assuming no tax shields. Then, calculate the project's NPV, assuming tax shields that arise because additional 12 percent debt may be issued in amounts equal to 30 percent of the cost of the project. The overall tax rate is 30 percent. Finally, determine the minimum acceptable base-case NPV, as well as, the minimum internal rate of return.

SOLUTION

The solution to this problem is straightforward. The base-case NPV is:

$$\text{Base-case NPV} = \text{cash outlay} + \text{present value of a perpetuity}$$
$$= -\$2,000,000 + (\$295,000/0.15)$$
$$= -\$2,000,000 + \$1,966,667$$
$$= -\$33,333$$

The project cannot be accepted as it is.

We need to calculate the effects of the financing scheme. A total of $600,000 ($2 million X 30 percent) is borrowed at the 12 percent rate. The tax shield is:

$$\text{Tax shield} = \text{debt X interest X tax rate} = \$600,000 \times 0.12 \times 0.30 = \$21,600$$

230

This annual tax shield lasts forever. So, to find the present value of this perpetuity, divide it by the required rate of return of 12 percent, the resulting answer being $180,000. Now, the project is acceptable. It has a positive APV.

$$APV = \text{base-case NPV} + \text{PV tax shield}$$
$$= -\$33,333 + \$180,000$$
$$= \$146,667$$

To find the minimum acceptable level of income for the project alone, that is, without the tax shield, we need to calculate the annual income needed to make the project acceptable. To find the minimum level of income *net* of the tax effects (of -$180,000):

$$-\$180,000 = -\$2,000,000 + (\text{annual income}/0.15)$$

Solving for annual income, we obtain:

$$\text{Annual income} = (\$2,000,000 - \$180,000) \times 0.15 = \$273,000$$

This is the minimum annual income this project must generate in order to make it acceptable. The minimum acceptable rate of return is:

$$\$273,000/\$2,000,000 = 0.1365 = 13.65 \text{ percent}$$

9. ABC Corp. is planning an investment in a European country. The local government has offered ABC a subsidized loan of $12 million for a term of 3 years. The loan will carry an interest rate of 3 percent annually. ABC's current borrowing rate is 8 percent. The company's marginal tax rate is 30 percent. ABC will pay interest only during the three years and the entire principal amount is repaid at the end of 3 years. The investment project has a base NPV of negative $600,000. Should ABC invest in the project?

SOLUTION

The after-tax unsubsidized borrowing rate is 5.6 percent. $[0.08(1 - 0.30)]$. This is the rate at which the loan cash flows are to be discounted. The table below gives the cash flows and their discounted values.

Period	0	1	2	3
Cash flow (in thousands)	12,000	-360	-360	-12,360
Tax shield		108	108	108
After-tax cash flow	12,000	-252	-252	-12,252
Marginal tax rate	30%			
Present value of outlays		-239	-226	-10,404
Sum of present values	10,869			
NPV of loan financing	1,131			

APV of the project = -$600,000 + $1,131,000 = $531,000.

Accept the project.

SUMMARY

This chapter enables us to deal with the all too common cases of investment and financing interactions. We had investment decisions from chapters 2 through 12 and in all cases it was assumed that investment and financing could be clearly separated. However, when financing decisions give rise to side effects such as tax shields, they have to be accounted for. The chapter describes two basic approaches to deal with this problem. The first approach is to adjust the discount rate used to evaluate the cash flows. The second approach evaluates the financing effects and adds the present values of these effects to the all-equity financed project NPV.

The weighted-average cost of capital represents the first approach and is typically calculated using company balance sheets valued at market values of debt and equity. The weighted-average cost of capital approach to adjusting discount rates says the proper discount rate used to evaluate projects of risk identical to that of the firm is the market value weighted cost of capital. WACC is popular and is fairly easily computed.

As long its limitations are understood, WACC is very useful. Care has to be taken to use it right. Remember, that WACC computed from actual company balance sheets should be used only for projects that resemble the company as a whole pretty closely. WACC also assumes that the debt is maintained by regular re-balancing of the sources of funds.

WACC is flexible and versatile and can be adjusted for changes in leverage and business risk. WACC is an adjusted cost of capital, which captures the tax shield benefit of debt. The CAPM can be used to adjust or compute the cost of equity for changes in business risk or leverage.

The adjusted present value approach is an alternative to using the WACC. The APV is simply the base-case NPV of the project, which is assumed to be all-equity financed plus the present value of all financing side effects. APV can be adapted to deal with different types of side effects such as issue costs, tax shields, special financing deals, etc. While computing APV, care has to be taken to ensure the proper assumptions about financing. In general, the true value of the tax shield is invariably less than that implied by the corporate marginal tax rate.

As an alternative to APV, a single adjusted discount rate or cost of capital is often computed reflecting the present values of financing side effects. With this adjusted discount rate, one can calculate the APV directly discounting the project cash flows at the adjusted discount rate. WACC is but an example of an adjusted discount rate.

The chapter also presents rules for evaluating safe, nominal cash flows. The proper discount rate to use in such cases is the after-tax borrowing rate. The cash flows may be viewed as the amount

232

of money needed to service an equivalent amount of debt. Two common examples of this type of cash flows are depreciation tax shields and payouts that are fixed by contract. The procedure of treating cash flows as debt-equivalent loans is consistent with adjusted-discount-rate approaches. The approach can be very useful in evaluating subsidies and special financing deals which go with some projects.

LIST OF TERMS

Adjusted cost of capital	Hurdle rate
Adjusted discount rate	Opportunity cost of capital
Adjusted net present value	Subsidized financing
Base-case NPV	Target debt ratios
Business risk	Value additivity
Corporate debt capacity	Weighted-average cost of capital

EXERCISES

Fill-in Questions

1. The adjusted net present value is equal to _____ plus the present value of the effects of financing decisions.

2. The _____ is the discount rate, which reflects only the business risk of the project and is used to calculate the base-case NPV.

3. The opportunity cost of capital depends on the _____ of the investment project to be undertaken.

4. The _____ is an opportunity cost or _____ adjusted for the financing effects.

5. The adjusted net present value analysis of a project has to take into account the change in _____ of the firm brought about by the project.

6. _____ is normally computed using the firm's market value balance sheets or the firm's _____.

7. The use of APV assumes that _____ holds.

8. The APV approach can be used to evaluate the value of _____.

Problems

1. The balance sheet of Bush and Forbes Corp. shows a debt ratio (debt to assets) of 35 percent. The company's cost of debt (before tax) is 8 percent and the beta of the company stock is 1.5.

The risk free rate is 5 percent and the expected market risk premium is 8.5 percent. The marginal tax rate is 30 percent. Calculate the weighted-average cost of capital for the firm.

2. Mr. Forbes, the CFO of the firm, suggests the company needs to increase debt to 45 percent of assets. The cost of debt will increase to 9 percent. What will be the effect this will have on the WACC?

3. If-Not, Inc. is evaluating a $1 million investment project, which is expected to generate level, after-tax cash flows of $300,000 a year in each of the next 6 years. Rates of return obtainable on investments of comparable risk are 12 percent. Compute the net present value of this project.

4. If-Not, Inc. will finance the project in problem 3 entirely by the sale of stock. The cost of floating the stock is 12 percent of the gross proceeds. How much must the company raise, and what impact does the flotation costs have on the net present value of the project?

5. The Perpetual Motion Company is evaluating a $6 million plant expansion, which it estimates will generate $750,000 in after-tax cash, year in and year out, perpetually. The return obtainable on investments of comparable risk is 13 percent.

   a. Calculate the net present value of the project, assuming no tax shields.
   b. Calculate the project's net present value, assuming tax shields produced by the issuance of 9 percent debt in amounts equal to 40 percent of the project's cost. The company's marginal tax rate is 34 percent.
   c. Determine the minimum acceptable base-case NPV.
   d. Determine the minimum acceptable internal rate of return.

6. Using the data in problem 5, calculate the weighted-average cost of capital.

7. You are considering a project in an East European country. The project has an investment of $4 million. The government of the country offers a special incentive package for investments in the country, which includes tax rebates amounting to 10 percent of the initial investment for each of the first two years. The project is expected to generate enough taxable income during the first two years to fully use the tax rebate. Your company's borrowing rate is 10 percent and its tax rate is 30 percent. What is the value of the tax rebate?

Essay Questions

1. Describe the differences between opportunity cost of capital and weighted average cost of capital. What are the primary assumptions you make when you use the weighted-average cost of capital based on actual values from a corporate balance sheet?

2. Explain the APV approach to evaluating the financing effects. Are there cases where the financing side effects can be negative?

3. Your company has been offered a special loan by a state government to induce your company to invest in their state. Describe how you will calculate the value of this offer.

4. Discuss the following statement – "Any safe or low risk cash flow should be evaluate using the risk-free rate, as these cash flows are certain and have no risk."

5. Why is it often better to use industry weighted average cost of capital than individual firm's cost of capital?

ANSWERS TO EXERCISES

Fill-in Questions

1. Base-case net present
2. Opportunity cost of capital
3. Business Risk
4. Adjusted cost of capital (or adjusted discount rate), hurdle rate
5. debt capacity
6. Weighted average cost of capital, target debt ratio
7. Value additivity
8. Subsidized financing

Problems

1. Cost of equity = $r_E = r_f + \beta(r_m - r_f) = 5 + 1.5(8.5) = 17.75$ percent
   Cost debt = $r_D = 8$ percent
   WACC = $0.08(1 - 0.30)0.35 + 0.1775(0.65)$
   $\qquad = 0.0196 + 0.1154$
   $\qquad = 13.50$ percent

2. Use the three step process to unlever and relever the WACC.

   Step 1: Unlever the WACC to calculate the opportunity cost of capital, r.
   $\qquad r = r_D D/V + r_E E/V = 0.08(0.35) + 0.1775(0.65) = 0.1434 = 14.34$ percent

   Step 2: Calculate the cost of equity at the 45 percent debt ratio.
   $\qquad r_E = r + (r_A - r_D)D/E = 0.1434 + (0.1434 - 0.09)0.45/0.55 = 0.1871 = 18.71$ percent

   Step 3: Calculate the new WACC.
   $\qquad$ WACC = $0.09(1 - 0.3)0.45 + 0.1871(0.55) = 0.1313 = 13.13$ percent

3. $NPV = -\$1,000,000 + \$300,000(4.111)$
   $= -\$1,000,000 + \$1,233,300$
   $= \$233,300$

4. Proceeds needed: $\$1,000,000/(1 - 0.12) = \$1,136,364$
   Issue cost: $\$1,136,364 - \$1,000,000 = \$136,364$
   APV = base-case NPV - issue cost
   $= \$233,300 - \$136,364 = \$96,936$

5. a. Base-case NPV $= -\$6,000,000 + \$750,000/0.13$
      $= -\$6,000,000 + \$5,769,231$
      $= -\$230,769$

   b. Amount borrowed: $\$6,000,000 \times 0.4 = \$2,400,000$
      Tax shield $= \$2,400,000 \times 0.09 \times 0.34 = \$73,440$
      APV = base-case NPV + PV of tax shield
         $= -\$230,769 + (\$73,440/0.09)$
         $= -\$230,769 + \$816,000$
         $= \$585,231$

   c. Base-case NPV = cash outlay + (annual income/required rate of return)
      Annual income = (cash outlay - minimum base case NPV) $\times$ required return
         $= (\$6,000,000 - \$816,000) \times 0.13$
         $= \$673,920$

   d. Minimum return $= \$673,920/\$6,000,000 = 11.23\%$

6. Before we can calculate the weighted-average costs of capital, we need to first calculate the r_E using the equation:

   $r_E = r + (r - r_D)D/E$
   $r_E = 0.13 + (0.13 - 0.09)0.4/0.6$
   $ = 0.13 + 2.67 = 0.1367 = 15.67$ percent

   $WACC = r_D(1 - T_c)D/V + r_E(E/V)$
   $ = 0.09(1 - 0.34)0.4 + 0.1567(0.6)$
   $ = 11.78$ percent.

7. The value of the incentive package can be calculated by discounting the resulting cash flows by your after-tax borrowing cost. Your after-tax borrowing rate r^* is:

   $r^* = r_D(1 - T_C)$
   $ = 0.10(1 - 0.3) = 0.07 = 7$ percent.

236

The cash flows from the package will be $1 million for each of the first two years.
Present value = $0.4 million(annuity factor for 2 years at 7 percent)
            = $0.4 X 1.808 million
            = $0.7232 million

20

Spotting and Valuing of Options

INTRODUCTION

This chapter starts a new section comprising three chapters, which deals with options. Options are important innovations of modern finance and an understanding of the theory and practice of option valuation and applications will help the financial manager do his or her job better. Chapter 20 provides an overview of the two basic options, *calls* and *puts*, and explains the valuation of options from the first principles. The chapter helps you understand the working of options through *position diagrams* which shows the pay-off of different positions in calls, puts, or shares held by an investor. The Black and Scholes option valuation model is presented in simple, straightforward terms and illustrated with a clear worked out example. Although this chapter focuses primarily on exchange traded options on stocks; the concepts and valuation principles are general and can be extended to options on different assets and liabilities. Chapter 21 deals with the applications of option theory and chapter 22 describes warrants and convertible bonds, which are often used by many corporations to raise money.

Most of the stock options are traded in exchanges and are not controlled by the corporations on whose stocks these options are based. These options do not directly affect the companies or their balance sheets. However, a financial manager needs to understand options and their valuation as these are very useful in managing and understanding risk associated with many management decisions. Nearly all corporate securities are options themselves or have some kind of options embedded in them. Financial managers will have to deal with options related to commodities, exchange rates, and interest rates. Corporate bonds often have call features and other options attached to them. Options are also part of many capital budgeting decisions, which involve *embedded* options to expand, abandon, or, in other ways, modify the project cash flows. A clear understanding of the principles of option valuation will help the manager understand the trade-off involved and arrive at the optimal decision.

KEY CONCEPTS IN THE CHAPTER

Calls and Puts: There are two basic options: *calls* and *puts*. A call option gives its owner the right to buy an asset at a specified exercise, or strike, price during a specified period. A put option gives its owner the right to sell an asset at a specified exercise price during a specified period. A *European* option is exercisable only at maturity while an *American* option is exercisable any time before its expiration date. Here are some terms associated with options.

- *Underlying asset* – e.g. an option on one share of IBM.
- *Type of option* – call or put.

239

- *Exercise price* or *strike price* – the price at which the buyer of the option gets the right to buy (call) or sell (put) the asset to the seller of the option. The seller of the option is often called the *writer* of the option.
- *Maturity* or *expiration date* – the date till (American) or on (European) which the option can be exercised.
- *Option premium* – This is the price paid to buy the option.
- *Asset price* – The price of the underlying asset.
- *In-the-money* or *out-of-the-money* – An option is said to be in-the-money if the exercise of the option makes money for you at that moment. A call option will be in-the-money if the share price is above the exercise price and a put option will be in-the-money if the share price is below the exercise price.

Calls, Puts, Shares, and Combinations: Position diagrams are key to understanding the pay-off from an option, or for that matter, holding any asset. Learn to draw the position diagrams for the simple options and assets first and then graduate to the different combinations of options and assets. In general, one observes the potential pay-off from holding the option versus the potential pay-off from holding the stock. By comparing the pay-off of different combinations, you soon realize that it is possible to create a combination equivalent to a call or a put.

Studying different combinations of options enable us to understand options and their pay-offs better. Study the diagrams given in figure 20.4. Consider the following: a call, a put, a share and a deposit equal to the present value of the exercise price. Of these four, only three can have independent values. In other words, you can always create the fourth asset or security by a combination of the other three. This helps in the valuation of options. The relationship among these four assets is called the *put-call parity*. This can be expressed as:

Value of a call + present value of exercise price = value of put + share price

We can rearrange this in several different ways to express the value of a call or a put in terms of the other three.

Value of call = Value of put + share price - present value of exercise price

Value of put = value of call - value of share + present value of exercise price

The relationship can be stated in words in different ways:

- Buying a call and investing the present value of the exercise price in a safe asset is identical in pay-off to buying a put and buying the share.
- Buying a call and selling a put is identical in pay-off to buying a share and borrowing the present value of the exercise price.
- Buying a put is identical in pay-off to buying a call, selling a share, and investing the present value of the exercise price.

240

Bonds and Stocks as Options: Study the Circular File Company example given in the chapter. The analysis leads to the conclusion that whenever a firm borrows, the lender, in effect, acquires the company, and shareholders obtain a call option to buy it back by paying off the debt. The shareholders will walk away if the assets of the firm are worth less than the promised payment to the bondholders. Again, there are different ways of looking at the stockholder-bondholder relationship in the options framework.

-   Bond value = asset value - value of call
-   Bond value = present value of promised payments to bondholders - value of put
-   Stock value = value of call (Exercise price = promised payment to bondholders)
-   Firm value = asset value

In general, we can say that the bondholders have bought a safe bond and then sold a put option to the stockholders. The stockholders will exercise this right if the value of the assets go down below the face value of the bonds.

Identifying Options: Options are not always easy to identify. Warrants and conversion features are obvious options. As long as there is a pay-off, which is contingent on another asset, an option is present. You have come across a number of options in everyday life, which might not have been obvious. Some examples include:

-   The right to drop a course within the first two or three weeks for a full refund of fees paid.
-   A money-back guarantee on articles purchased.
-   The right to get a ticket for your university's homecoming foot-ball game.
-   A fully refundable air ticket.

Try identifying the options in the above.

Valuing Options: Before attempting formal valuation of options, we can understand the determinants of the value of an option. Review figure 20-9, which shows the value of a call option at different values of the stock price. Note that the figure applies to an option that has some time to expiration, so that the option has a "time premium." The value of a call at expiration is simply the difference between the stock price and the exercise price, with a minimum value of zero. As long as there is time left to maturity and potential volatility in the option, an option will have value above the value at expiration. There are upper and lower bounds to which an option can rise or fall. The option will never be worth more than the price of the stock. The option will never be worth less than zero. An option value equals zero when the value of the underlying asset is equal to or less than the exercise price. Option values tend to increase as the value of the underlying asset exceeds the exercise price. Here are some additional facts on a call option value:

-   The value of an option increases as the stock price increases, if the exercise price is held constant.

241

- When the stock price becomes large, the option price approaches the stock price less the present value of the exercise price.
- The value of an option increases with the rate of interest and the time to maturity (the product of r_f and t).
- The value of an option increases with both the variability of the share and the time to

    expiration (that is, $\sigma\sqrt{t}$). This is because the probability of large stock price changes during the remaining life of an option depends on the variability of the stock price per period (standard deviation) and the number of periods until the option expires.

The table below summarizes the effect of changes in the key variables on the value of a call option.

Variables	Change in the value of a call option when the variable increases
Stock price (P)	Positive
Exercise Price (EX)	Negative
Interest rate (r_f)	Positive
Time to expiration (t)	Positive
Volatility (σ)	Positive

Model for Option Valuation: So far, discounted cash flows have been the basic approach we have used for valuation. However, discounted cash flows will not work for options, because:

- Difficulty in forecasting cash flows from an option, though it is possible to do.
- Impossible to find the correct opportunity cost of capital because an option's risk changes every time its price changes. An in-the-money option is safer than one out-of-the-money and a stock price increase raises option prices and reduces risk, and vice versa, each time stock prices change.
- Options are always riskier than the underlying stock because they have higher betas and higher standard deviations of return.

The problem of option valuation was finally solved by creating an option equivalent portfolio by combining common stock and borrowing. This portfolio is constructed such that it gives the same pay-off as the option. Thus, the value of the option can be written as:

Value of call = value of the number of shares in the equivalent portfolio – borrowed amount.

The number of shares needed to replicate one call is the *hedge ratio* or *option delta*. An equivalent, but alternative, approach is to assume that the investors are *risk-neutral*. With this assumption, we can get the investors to be satisfied with the risk-free rate of return on their stock investment. We can now estimate the *probability of stock price* going up or down and thereby

242

calculate the value of the option. This probability is not the real probability, but a synthetic construct, which enables us to value the option.

The above approaches to valuation are somewhat simplistic and assume that the stock will have just two possible values (one up and one down) in the next period. This method is know as the *binomial* method. While in theory, we can extend the binomial method by assuming shorter time intervals and then replicate the process. That is, we can break down a one month option into a series of 30 one day options and ultimately into shorter and shorter intervals so that you end up with continuous changes. Black and Scholes achieved this theoretically and derived a formula for the value of an option. The formula can be written as :

$$\text{Value of option} = [\text{delta x share price}] - [\text{bank loan}]$$
$$= [N(d_1) \times P] - [N(d_2) \times PV(EX)]$$

where:

$$d_1 = \frac{\log[P \, / \, PV(EX)]}{\sigma\sqrt{t}} + \frac{\sigma\sqrt{t}}{2}$$

$$d_2 = d_1 - \sigma\sqrt{t}$$

$N(d)$ = cumulative normal probability density function
EX = exercise price of option
PV(EX) is calculated by discounting at risk-free interest rate for t-periods in the usual way.
t = number of periods to exercise date
P = price of stock now
σ = standard deviation per period of (continuously compounded) rate of return on stock

Notice that the Black-Scholes formula has all the properties we expected. It increases with P, σ, and t, and decreases with PV(EX). It also increases smoothly as a function of P from C = 0 for small P up to P – PV(EX) for large P.

Using Black-Scholes Model: Using Black-Scholes model is not particularly difficult, once the values of the variables are known. See the worked examples and the problems at the end. $N(d_1)$ and $N(d_2)$ can be calculated from the tables for the probability tables for normal distribution (Appendix Table 6 in the Brealey and Myers book). Alternately, you can use the NORMDIST function in the Excel spreadsheet program. For example, if you want to find the value for $N(d_1)$ where $d_1 = 0.501$, type in "= NORMDIST(0.501, 0,1, TRUE)" in the EXCEL spreadsheet, you will get the value $N(d_1) = 0.308$. Once you get the values of $N(d_1)$ and $N(d_2)$, you can substitute these in the Black-Scholes formula and get the option value. See worked examples 4 and 5. The values for $N(d_1)$ and $N(d_2)$ for all the solutions were calculated using the EXCEL spreadsheet program.

WORKED EXAMPLES

1. Find the value of a call option, given that the present value of the exercise price is $35, the value of the put is $10, and the share price is $33.

SOLUTION

To answer this exercise, use the formula:

$$\text{Value of call} + \text{present value of exercise price} = \text{value of put} + \text{share price},$$

$$\text{Value of call} = \text{value of put} + \text{share price} - \text{present value of exercise price}$$
$$= \$10 + \$33 - \$35$$
$$= \$8$$

2. Find the implied present value of the exercise price of a 13-week call, given that the value of the call option is $8, the value of the put option is $5, and the market price is $20.

SOLUTION

Rearrange equation (1) to solve for the present value of the exercise price.

$$\text{Present value of exercise price} = \text{value of put} + \text{share price} - \text{value of call}$$
$$= \$5 + \$20 - \$8$$
$$= \$17$$

3. Recent quotations for options on IBM shares are given below. IBM stocks were selling at $129.25 and the call money rate (charged to brokers on stock exchange collateral) was 6.25 percent.

Strike Price	Call Price	Put Price
$125	$10.75	$5.75
130	8.15	8.25

a. Which options are in-the-money and which is out-of-the-money?
b. Assume that there is exactly 50 days to expiry. What values would put call parity imply for European puts? What reasons might account for the traded ones being worth slightly more?

244

SOLUTION

a. The $125 call and the $130 put are in-the-money. The other options are out-of-the-money.

b. The 50 day discount factor for the 6.25 percent call money rate is 0.992 $[(1/1.0625)^{50/365}]$. The values of European puts are given by:

Value of put = PV (exercise price) + V(call) – share price
V ($125 put) = $125 X 0.992 + 10.75 - $129.25 = $5.50
V($130 put) = $130 X 0.992 + 8.15 - $129.25 = $7.86

The traded options are American, and the early exercise feature of the puts is valuable, and increasingly so as they are more in-the-money.

4. Use the Black-Scholes model to evaluate the $130 IBM call option from problem 3. Assume a standard deviation of 26 percent.

SOLUTION

Summary of data needed:

Price of stock = $129.25
Exercise price = $130
Standard deviation = 26 percent
Years to maturity = 50/365 = 0.137 years
Interest rate = 6.25 percent

Black-Scholes formula: V (call) = $N(d_1)$ x P – $N(d_2)$ x PV (EX)

$$d_1 = \frac{\log[P / PV(EX)]}{\sigma\sqrt{t}} + \frac{\sigma\sqrt{t}}{2}$$
$$d_2 = d_1 - \sigma\sqrt{t}$$
$$d_1 = \frac{\log[\$129.25 / \$130 x 0.992)}{0.26\sqrt{0.137}} + \frac{0.26\sqrt{0.137}}{2}$$

$d_1 = 0.071$, $d_2 = -0.025$
$N(d_1) = 0.528$
$N(d_2) = 0.490$
Value of call = 0.528 X $129.25 – 0.490 X $130 X 0.992 = $5.05

The market price for the call is much higher for two reasons:

245

- The option is an American option.
- The implied volatility is probably higher than 26 percent.

5. Karl Cahn Partners, a private take-over specialist firm, has embarked on an acquisition strategy to buy several other privately held companies. It presently has an opportunity to buy RRK Inc., but needs another six months to complete its analysis. It has instructed the CFO to negotiate an option to buy RRK. What price should the CFO be willing to pay for the option? The estimated standard deviation of RRK is 0.60, the value of its shares is $50 apiece, and the estimated equivalent to an exercise price is $70. Assume the interest rate is 7 percent.

SOLUTION

Summary of data:

Price of stock = $50
Exercise price = $70
Standard deviation = 60 percent
Years to maturity = 0.5 years
Interest rate = 7 percent

$d_1 = -0.501$, $N(d_1) = 0.308$
$d_2 = -0.925$, $N(d_2) = 0.177$
$V \text{ (call)} = N(d_1) P - N(d_2) \times PV(EX)$
$\qquad = 0.308 \times \$50 - 0.177 \times \$70/1.07^{0.5}$
$\qquad = \$15.40 - \$11.98 = \$3.42$

6. Assume that the firm to be acquired views the conditions set forth in problem 5 as a put option and that it agrees with the estimated value of the call. How much is it worth to the firm?

SOLUTION

Use the put-call parity, beginning with:

Present value of exercise price = value of put + share price - value of call
Value of put = present value of exercise price - share price + value of call
$\qquad = \$70/(1.07^{0.5}) - 50.00 + 3.42$
$\qquad = \$67.67 - \$50 + \$3.42 = \$21.09$

7. XYZ, Inc., has a 1-year option to acquire a publicly traded company, ABC Corp. Here are the assumptions the CFO made to analyze how to construct option equivalents.

- Exercise price	$60
- Current price of ABC stock	$70
- Price may move only up or down:	
Estimated low price	$45
Estimated high price	$110
- 1-year interest rate	6%

Demonstrate how to replicate the pay-off from a call option.

SOLUTION

The pay-off for the call option for the high and low values of the stock and for a portfolio of equivalent stock + loan combination are given in the table below. The number of stocks required to duplicate the option pay-off is calculated using the hedge ratio or option delta formula.

$$\text{Hedge ratio} = \text{option delta} = \frac{\underline{\text{spread of possible option values}}}{\text{spread of possible share values}}$$
$$= \$40/\$65 = 0.6154$$

Thus, if you buy 0.6154 shares and borrow $26.12 (present value of the difference between the value of 0.6154 shares and the call option at the low stock price value), the pay-off for the option is duplicated. See the table below.

	Low stock price = $45	High stock price = $110
Value of 1 call option	0	$40
0.6154 stock	$27.69	$67.69
Loan + Interest on a loan of $26.12	$27.69	$27.69
Total pay-off	0	$40

$$1 \text{ call option} = 0.6154 \text{ X stock price} - \text{bank loan of } \$26.12$$
$$= 0.6154 \text{ X } \$70 - \$26.12$$
$$= \$16.96$$

8. Here is another Black-Scholes problem. Data for an option valuation problem are given below. Explain the option valuation model and compute the value of the option. Show all steps.

Time	3 years
Standard deviation of continuously compounded return on asset	0.635
Current asset price	$100
Option exercise price	$120
Interest rate	8 %

SOLUTION

Basic Black-Scholes model can be written in a way similar to the approach shown in problem 7 above.

$$\text{Value of option} = [\text{delta x share price}] - [\text{bank loan}]$$
$$= [N(d_1) \times P] - [N(d_2) \times PV(EX)]$$

where:

$$d_1 = \frac{\log[P / PV(EX)]}{\sigma\sqrt{t}} + \frac{\sigma\sqrt{t}}{2}$$

$$d_2 = d_1 - \sigma\sqrt{t}$$

$N(d)$ = cumulative normal probability density function

EX = Exercise price of option = \$120

t = number of periods to exercise date = 3 years

P = price of stock now = \$100

σ = standard deviation per period = 0.635

$d_1 = 0.598$, $N(d_1) = 0.725$
$d_2 = -0.501$, $N(d_2) = 0.308$

$$\text{Value of call} = 0.725 \times \$100 - 0.308 \times \$120/1.08^3$$
$$= \$72.5 - \$29.34 = \$43.16$$

$$\text{Value of put} = \text{Value of call} + PV(EX) - \text{stock price}$$
$$= \$43.16 + \$95.26 - \$100 = \$38.42$$

SUMMARY

This chapter introduces options in a more formal setting and explains option valuation techniques. The position diagrams are valuable tools, which can help you identify the pay-offs of owning different assets, particularly options. Learn to use the position diagrams to identify options.

The chapter is the beginning of the coverage of options in the book and describes the two basic types of options – calls and puts. The chapter explains the various characteristics of options and presents a step-by-step approach of the simple binomial option valuation method. The chapter also presents the more rigorous Black-Scholes model. The model is not too difficult to apply, once you learn how to calculate the normal probability distribution values required in the formula. You also learn the effects of the changes in the different variables affecting the value of an option. The value of a call option is a function of the exercise price, the stock price, the risk-free rate of interest, time to expiration, and the volatility of returns measured by the standard deviation of returns. While a higher exercise price would mean a lower option (call) value, all the other variables have a positive relationship with the value of a call. Note that the value of the option is not affected by the expected return on the stock.

Options are an important part of modern corporate finance. Most corporate securities are either options or have options embedded in them. The corporate financial manager will have a number of uses for options. Some of these include: capital budgeting decisions, financing decisions, and risk management. A good understanding of the way options work and the knowledge of how to value them will be very useful for a corporate financial manager.

LIST OF TERMS

American option	Out of the money
Binomial method	Position diagram
Black-Scholes	Put option
Call option	Put-call parity
European option	Risk neutral method
Exercise price	Strike price
Hedge ratio	Volatility
In-the-money	Warrants
Option delta	

EXERCISES

Fill-in Questions

1. A(n) _____ gives its owner the right (without the obligation) to buy an asset at a specified exercise price, or _____ price.

2. A(n) _____ gives its owner the right to sell stock at a specified price.

3. _____ call options may be exercised only on the expiration day, whereas _____ call options may be exercised on or before the expiration day.

4. For European options, the value of a call option plus the present value of the _____ equals the value of the _____ plus the share price.

5. The best way to show the effect of using combinations of options is to draw a _____.

6. When a firm borrows, (shareholders, creditors) _____ acquire the company and (shareholders, creditors) _____ obtain an option to buy it back.

7. The value of limited liability lies in the option to default and is the value of a (put, call) _____ option on the firm's assets with an exercise price equal to the promised payment to (creditors, owners) _____.

8. If the following variables decrease, the changes in the call option prices are (positive, negative):

    Stock price   _____
    Exercise price   _____
    Interest rate   _____
    Time to expiration   _____
    Stock price volatility   _____

9. The number of shares needed to create the option equivalents from buying and selling common stocks and borrowing is called the _____ or _____.

10. When an asset's value exceeds the strike price, then the call option on it is said to be (in, out of) _____ the money and the put option is said to be (in, out of) _____ the money.

11. This relationship -- value of call + present value of exercise price = value of put + share price --is called _____.

12. The _____ method shows how to replicate the outcomes from an option for the evolution of the stock price.

13. In the language of option pricing, the annualized standard deviation of the return on the underlying asset is called its _____.

Problems

1. Find the value of a call option, given that the present value of the exercise price is $26, the value of the put is $2, and the share price is $30.

2. Find the implied present value of the exercise price of a 26-week call, given the value of the call option is $1, the value of the put option is $7, and the market price is $35.

3. Use the Black-Scholes model to evaluate the following IBM option: exercise price = $135, stock price $130, volatility = 26 percent, time to expiration = 3 months, and the risk-free interest rate = 6.25 percent.

250

4. Private, Inc., has an opportunity to buy another privately held company. One deal in particular intrigues the company, but it needs more time to evaluate the deal. It wants a 6 month option to buy the company. How much is the option worth to Private, Inc., given that the estimated standard deviation of the firm to be acquired is 0.71, the value of each share is $34.50, and the estimated equivalent to an exercise price is $60? Assume the risk-free rate is 9 percent.

5. Assume that the firm to be acquired views the conditions set forth in problem 4 as a put option and that it agrees with the estimated value of the call. How much is it worth to the firm?

6. Use the following information to create option equivalents from common stocks and borrowing and show how to replicate a call option. Use the results to value the call.

   - Exercise price $80
   - Current price of share $100
   - Price may move only up or down:
     - Estimated low price $90
     - Estimated high price $140
   - 1-year interest rate   10%

7. Identify the options involved in the following:

   a. The CEO of Crazy Fox gets 10,000 shares when he is hired. He can sell the shares back to the company at a price of $40 if he is fired within the next two years.

   b. A cereal manufacturer has a contract to buy corn and wheat with an agricultural trading company. The transactions would normally be at market prices. However, the contract stipulates a minimum price the cereal company will pay if the market price falls below that price. The contract also stipulates a ceiling price, if the market price goes above that price.

Essay Questions

1. Explain the following statement – "Shares of a limited liability corporation can be viewed as call options or put options depending on how you look at them."

2. Explain why financial managers should be interested in options, since they are traded on the Chicago Board Options Exchange, and the means by which to place a value on such options.

3. Explain the technique of creating option-equivalent combinations using stocks and bank loans.

4. List and explain the key elements, which determine the value of options.

ANSWERS TO EXERCISES

Fill-in Questions

1. Call options; strike
2. Put option
3. European, American
4. Exercise price; put option
5. Position diagram
6. Creditors; shareholders
7. Put; creditors

8. Negative, positive, negative, negative, negative
9. Hedge ratio; option delta
10. In; out of
11. Put-call parity
12. Binomial
13. Volatility

Problems

1. Value of call = value of put + share price - PV of exercise price
$$= \$2 + \$30 - \$26$$
$$= \$6$$

2. PV of exercise price = value of put + share price - value of call
$$= \$7 + \$35 - \$1$$
$$= \$4$$

3. $d_1 = \log[P/PV(EX)]/\sigma\sqrt{t} + (\sigma\sqrt{t})/2$
$$= -0.1087$$

$d_2 = d_1 - \sigma\sqrt{t} = -0.2387$

$N(d_1) = 0.4567$, $N(d_2) = 0.4057$
Value of call $= N(d_1) \times P - N(d_2) \times PV(EX)$
$$= 0.4567 \times \$130 - 0.4057 \times 132.97$$
$$= \$5.43$$

4. $d_1 = -0.765$, $d_1 = -1.267$
$N(d_1) = 0.2221$, $N(d_2) = 0.1023$
Value of call $= 0.2213 \times \$34.50 - 0.1023 \times \$57.47$
$$= \$1.76$$

5. Using the put-call parity:
$V(put) = V(call) + PV(EX) - $ share price

252

$$= \$1.76 + 57.47 - \$34.50$$
$$= \$24.73.$$

6. The hedge ratio, also called the option delta, tells us the number of shares needed to replicate 1 call.

$$\text{Hedge ratio} = \text{option delta}$$
$$= \frac{\text{spreads of possible option values}}{\text{spread of possible share values}}$$
$$= (\$60 - \$10)/(\$140 - \$90)$$
$$= 1$$

Using this ratio, we can replicate the option pay-off with 1 share plus borrowing the present value of $80 ($90 −$10). Present value = loan amount = $80/1.1 = $72.73. The table below gives the pay-off of the option and the stock plus borrowing combination.

	Low stock price = $90	High stock price = $140
Value of 1 call option	10	$60
1 stock	$90	$140
Loan + Interest on a loan of $72.73	$80	$60
Total pay-off	$10	$40

$$1 \text{ call option} = 1 \times \text{stock price} - \text{bank loan of } \$72.73$$
$$= \$100 - \$72.73$$
$$= \$27.27$$

7. a. European put options with exercise price of $40, time to expiration of 2 years.

b. The two parties have sold each other a call option and a put option. The cereal manufacturer has bought a call option (sold by the trading firm) with the exercise price equal to the ceiling price. The agricultural trading firm has a put option (sold by the cereal manufacturer) with the exercise price equal to the minimum price.

21
Real Options

INTRODUCTION

This chapter uses and extends the lessons learned in chapter 20 to evaluate the many different types of real options often encountered by the corporate financial manager. Real options can be very valuable and can add value to the firm, if they are understood correctly and acted upon. The four common real options typically found in many capital investment projects are:

- The option to make follow-on investments.
- The option to abandon a project.
- The option to wait before investing.
- The option to change either the output or the production methods.

These options need to be considered as part of the capital investment project and included in the value of the project. The chapter provides a number of examples of valuing these options using the binomial method. The chapter also includes applications of the general binomial method and reviews the application of the binomial option-pricing model to American options. Remember that the Black-Scholes model was derived for the European call option.

The options approach to valuation of the special situations associated with capital budgeting decisions is necessitated by the fact that simple discounted cash flow (DCF) analysis does not work very well in these cases. The DCF analysis is designed for analyzing investments, which do not change their nature during the life of the project. It is ideally suited for evaluating passive investments like bonds and stocks. Corporate assets are, on the other hand, actively managed by the manager and the projects can very often change their nature in terms of risk, cost structure, expansion, and abandonment possibilities. In view of these, many situations in corporate capital budgeting are best valued as options. The options approach allows for added rounds of decisions, beyond the initial decision point. These additional rounds of decisions give us the choice to capitalize on good fortune or to mitigate loss. The choice creates uncertainty, but it is the uncertainty, which often gives rise to the value of options.

KEY CONCEPTS IN THE CHAPTER

Follow-on Investment Opportunities: Many investment projects have follow-on investment opportunities attached to them. Capital budgeting projects are rarely finite, one of a kind investments with no connections to the future. The follow-on investment opportunities add value to the original project. This is true, even if the follow-on project does not look very attractive at the time the decision on the original project is taken. You can consider the follow-on project as

255

an out-of-the-money call option. Please read the Blitzen Computers example given in the Brealey-Myers text. Typical investments with follow-on projects include R & D projects and investments in new markets, foreign countries, and new technology. Remember that the uncertainties associated with the follow-on project actually make the value of options even more attractive.

As mentioned before, DCF analysis cannot do justice to the follow-on projects. This is because managers are actively involved in the management of both the initial project and the follow-on projects. The company will take up the follow-on projects only if they are found attractive or become in-the-money at the time the investment is called for.

The follow-on projects can be evaluated as call options. The investment required in the project is the exercise price and the present value of cash flows from the project is the asset price. The volatility of the project cash flows is to be measured as the standard deviation of the return on a stock with characteristics similar to that of the project. It may not be easy to find a stock with these characteristics, but the company's experience from the past might be of some help.

The Option to Abandon: The option to abandon a project, when things are not going as well as one expected, is a very valuable option that can enhance the value of the project. The abandonment option can be seen as a put option with the exercise price equal to the price one can get for the project's assets when they are sold. The abandonment option can be analyzed in terms of the possible project outcomes. For simplicity and convenience, we can assume that two mutually exclusive outcomes are possible: one is a success route; the other is a failure route. The option to bail out is worth something, especially if the bail out value exceeds the value of the project at that time. An abandonment option can be seen as an insurance policy.

The valuation of the abandonment option can be done using the binomial method and you need the following information:

- The present value of the project without the option to abandon,
- The exercise price – this would be the price you can get for the assets of the project if you decide to sell them,
- The maturity,
- The interest rate,
- Future value of the business with high demand, and
- Future value with low demand

You can use the binomial method with the risk-neutral approach. The binomial method assumes that the asset can take only one of two possible values: one higher value and one lower value. We can calculate the probability that the asset value will rise by pretending that the investors are risk-neutral and will be satisfied with the risk-free rate of interest. If the business is successful, the option to abandon will be worthless. If it is unsuccessful, the option will be in-the-money. The assets can be sold for the exercise price and the expected future value of the option will equal the difference between the value of the firm and the exercise price. The current value of

256

the option can be calculated from the expected future value of the option. This method for option valuation can be extended to more than one period. (See the worked example for details.)

The Timing Option: Many projects can be started now or some time in the future. The fact that the project has a positive net present value does not necessarily imply that now is the best time to initiate the project. Valuing the timing option is simple when there is no uncertainty. One can calculate the project's NPV at various dates of project commencement and pick the one date with the highest NPV. Of course, this will not work when there is uncertainty. The timing option exists, if the project's commencement can be delayed. The choice to delay the project gives rise to a valuable call option.

The call option associated with the timing of the project can also be valued using the binomial method and the risk-neutral technique. The present value of the cash flows from the project will be the asset value and the investment required for the project is the exercise price. Cash flows from the project are similar to dividends on a stock. By delaying the exercise of the option, you are loosing the current cash flows, but gaining the time premium of the option. This premium will be a function of the volatility and time.

Flexible Production Facilities: The ability to switch production facilities to manufacture different types of products is a very valuable option for manufacturing companies. In general, flexibility is very useful in manufacturing especially, when the nature of the demand for the company's products can change very quickly. The flexibility can be to switch machine set ups, sources of raw material or utility, or location of manufacturing from one country to another. These options are somewhat more complicated than the abandonment or follow-on options, but the principles learned in the chapter can be used to evaluate them.

Real Options and the General Binomial Method: Real options discussed throughout this chapter are not traded in the Chicago Board of Options. The parameters required for valuation of these options would have to be carefully evaluated and computed based on experience relating to the specific business or industry. The technique of binomial method and the risk-neutral approach can be very useful in valuing these options. The binomial method starts with the assumption that the value of the asset can take only one of two possible values. In order to make this a realistic assumption, the unit of time for each change in value can be made shorter and shorter. That is, it is far more realistic to say that there can be only two possible values over the next one month, than say, the next one-year. This will lead to 13 possible values at the end of the year. While doing this type of option valuation manually will be cumbersome, one can find computer programs that will make the computations less time consuming.

The General Binomial Method: The basic approach in the binomial method involves specifying two (and only two) possible asset value changes per unit of time under consideration. We then assume that the investors will be risk-neutral and will be satisfied with a rate of return equal to the risk-free interest rate. Given these conditions, it is easy to calculate the implied probability (p) that the asset will rise (the probability of a fall in value will be, of course, 1-p). We can find the pay-off for the option for the two asset values and calculate the expected value of the option.

There are generalized formulas to determine asset value changes based on the standard deviation of asset returns.

$$1 + \text{upside change} = u = e^{\sigma\sqrt{h}}$$

$$\text{updside change} = e^{\sigma\sqrt{h}} - 1$$
$$1 = \text{downside change} = d = 1/u$$
$$\text{Downside change} = (1/u) - 1$$

Where,

e = base for natural logs = 2.718
σ = standard deviation of (continuously compounded) annual returns on asset
h = interval as a fraction of a year

As the number of intervals is increased, the values you obtain from the binomial method should get closer and closer to the Black-Scholes value.

Option Valuation and Decision Trees: The application of the binomial method looks and feels a lot like the decision trees we have seen in the capital budgeting chapters. However, the binomial method is not another application of decision trees. Option pricing theory is needed to solve the problems described in this chapter. Discounted cash flows will not work because there is no single discount rate, which will capture the changing risk involved. The option theory is more powerful and will provide simpler solutions where decision trees cannot or become too complex.

Calls and Puts - American and European: The Black-Scholes model derived the value of the European call. Using the put-call parity, you can also derive the value of a European put.

Value of put = Value of call – Value of stock + PV(Exercise price)

For European calls on dividend-paying stocks, the value obtained by the Black-Scholes model will overstate the value of the option as part of the share value is composed of the present value of dividends, which the option holder does not receive. Therefore, the share price will need to be reduced to reflect the present value of the lost dividends.

Adjustments will be required for the American calls and puts. These are briefly described below:

American call--no dividends: In the absence of dividends, the value of a call option increases with the time to maturity. An American call should not be exercised before maturity. Therefore, the value of the American call will be same as that given by the Black-Scholes model for the European call.

American put--no dividends: It sometimes pays to exercise an American put before maturity in order to reinvest the exercise price. An American put is always more valuable than a European put. The Black-Scholes formula does not allow for early exercise and thus, cannot be used to value an American put exactly. We can use the step-by-step binomial method by checking at each point whether the option is worth exercising the option ahead of its maturity.

American calls on dividend-paying stocks: The fact that a stock pays dividends does not necessarily imply that the option should be exercised early. The dividend gain is to be compared with the interest lost by the early exercise. Again, the best approach to valuing the option is to use the step-by-step binomial method and check at each stage whether the option is more valuable if exercised just before the ex-dividend date or held for at least one more period.

WORKED EXAMPLES

1. Burgers & Burgers Corp. (BBC) is considering a new technology for a new hybrid burger with high protein and very low fat content. The net present value of the project is negative and is estimated at -$10 million. However, the company's chief food-technologist is keen on the project because the project will open up opportunities for the next generation of burgers, which are expected to be of zero fat content. The estimated NPV of the ZB (for Zero fat content burger) project is -$65 million. The other details of the ZB project are given below:

Investment decision must be made in 2002	
Investment required in 2002	= $250 million
PV of cash flows expected (in 2002)	= $185 million
Standard deviation for comparable projects	= 45 percent
Required rate of return for the typical high-tech burger projects	= 18 percent
Interest rate	= 8 percent

BBC's CEO, Ms. Holly Patch has asked you, the CFO, to help her decide on the investment. What would you do?

SOLUTION

The problem is an example of a project with a follow-on investment. The fact that the follow-on project has a negative NPV does not necessarily mean that it should be rejected. The follow-on project is a call option and has to be evaluated as such. We can use the Black-Scholes model to evaluate the value of the option.

$$d_1 = \log[P/PV(EX)]/\sigma\sqrt{t} + \sigma\sqrt{t}/2$$
$$d_2 = d_1 - \sigma\sqrt{t}$$

$P = \$185/(1.18)^2 = 132.86$ [This is the value of the cash flow from the project. This should be discounted using the required rate of return for the project]

$PV(EX) = \$250/(1.08)^2 = \$214.33$ [This is part of the option process and the rate used to find the PV should be the interest rate]

$\sigma = 0.45,\ t = 2$ years

$\sigma\sqrt{t} = 0.6364$

$d_1 = -0.4332;\qquad d_2 = -1.0696$

$N(d_1) = 0.3325\qquad N(d_2) = 0.1424$

Value of the call option $= N(d_1)P - N(d_2) \times PV(EX)$
$= 0.3325 \times \$132.86 - 0.1424 \times 214.33$
$= \$13.66$ million

The value of the option when added to the NPV of the project, gives a positive value for the project (-$10 million + $13.66 million = $3.66 million).

2. Figure 21-1 summarizes the possible payoffs from the new project being considered by ABC Inc. The project is worth $30 million based on the cash flows projected. If things go well, the project will be worth $45 million by the end of the first year. If things do not go well, the business will be worth only $20 million. The company can get $25 million for the plant and machinery in the worse case scenario. Calculate the value of the abandonment option. Assume an interest rate of 10 percent.

Value = $30 million

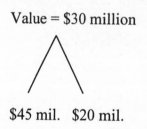

$45 mil. $20 mil.

Figure 21-1

SOLUTION

Using the risk-neutral approach, we can calculate the probability of a rise in the asset value. (Note: This is the notional probability in a risk-neutral world for option valuation; not the real probability. This value should not be used to calculate present value of the cash flows.)

The probability of a rise is:

$$p = (r - \text{down side change})/(\text{upside change} - \text{down side change});$$
where r = the interest rate = 0.10
upside change = (45/30) - 1 = 0.50
downside change = (20/30) - 1 = -0.33
p = 0.43/0.83 = 0.52

The value of the put option is zero for the upside change and $5 million for the downside change ($25 - $20). The expected future value of the put = 0.52 X 0 + 0.48 X $5 = $2.40 million
Current value = $2.40/1.10 = $2.182 million

3. Here is a project with the timing option. Green Bump Company has a project, which requires a cash outlay of $75 million. The company has the option to delay the project for up to 2 years. The project's current cash flow is $15 million, and the cost of capital is 15 percent. The company estimates that the project's cash flows may decrease by 20 percent or increase by 25 percent. Assume that the investment cannot be postponed beyond the end of the second year. The risk-neutral rate is 5 percent. Value the option.

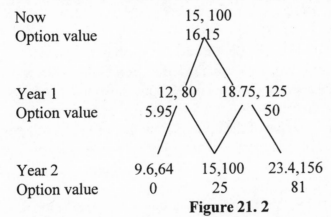

Now   15, 100
Option value   16, 15

Year 1   12, 80   18.75, 125
Option value   5.95   50

Year 2   9.6, 64   15, 100   23.4, 156
Option value   0   25   81

Figure 21. 2

Cash flows, end-of-year values and option values are in million dollars.

SOLUTION

Figure 21-2 shows the project's possible cash flows, end-of-year values and the option values at the different points in time. With a cash flow of $15 million, the value of the project is $100 million, when discounted at the market-required rate of 15 percent. If demand turns out to be low in year 1, the cash flow is only $12 million, and the remaining value of the project falls to 12/0.15 = $80 million. If demand is high in year 1, the cash flow is $18.75 and the value rises to 18.75/0.15 = $125 million. A second year of low demand would cause the cash flows to fall to $9.6 and the project value to fall to $64, and so on.

261

Notice that if you undertake the investment right away, you capture the first year's cash flow ($12 or $18.75). If you delay, you miss out on this cash flow, but you now have more information on how the project is likely to work out. In addition, that information has value.

If demand is high in the first year, the company has a cash flow of $18.75 million and a value of $125 million at the end of the first year. The total return is $(18.75 + 125)/100 - 1 = 0.4375$, or 44 percent. If demand is low, the cash flow is $12 and the year-end value is $80. Total return is $(12 + 80)/100 - 1 = -0.08$, or - 8 percent.

The probability of a rise is:

$$p = [0.05 - (- 0.08)]/[0.44 - (-0.08)]$$
$$= 0.25$$

The probability of a decline $= 1 - p = 1 - 0.25 = 0.75$

To find the call option value on the project with an exercise price of $75, begin at the end and work backwards. If the project value is $64, the option to invest is worthless. (Asset price is less than the exercise price.) At the other two points, the option is worth $25 million ($100 - $75), and $81 million ($156 - $75).

At the end of year 1, we need to calculate the option value as the higher of the following: i) value if the investment option is exercised ($5 million on the left branch ($80 - $75), and $50 on the right branch ($125 - $75) and ii) the expected value of the options from the end of year 2. The values are given in Figure 21-2. The value for the left branch for the options $= $5.95 = ($25 X 0.25)/1.05$. For the right branch, the value of the options from the next year will work out to $37.14 million $[($25 X 0.75 + $81 X 0.25)/1.05]$. This is lower than the value of the option if exercised at that point ($50 million $= $125 - 75).

The value of option now $= ($5.95 X 0.75 + $50 X 0.25)/1.05 = 16.15 million

This, however, is less than the value if the option is exercised now - $25 million $= $100 - 75. Thus, the company should go ahead and invest in the project right now.

4. Suppose you are offered a 1-year option to buy the Euro at the exchange rate of $1.10 = 1 Euro. You have the following additional information:

Maturity of option	$t = 1$
Exercise price	$E = \$1.10$
Current exchange rate (price) of Euro	$P = \$1.10$
Standard deviation of exchange-rate changes	$\sigma = .15$
Dollar interest rate	$r_\$ = .05$
Euro	$r_E = 0.10$

262

SOLUTION

To value the call option, you must first reduce the current price of the Euro by the amount of the lost interest.

Adjusted price of Euro, $P^* $ = current price/$(1 + r_E)$ = 1.10/1.10 = $ 1.0

Price/PV(exercise price) = $P^*/[E/(1 + r_s)]$ = 1/(1.10/1.05) = 0.9545

$d_1 = \log[P/PV(EX)]/\sigma o t + \sigma o t/2; \quad d_2 = d_1 - \sigma o t$

$\sigma = 0.15$, t = 1 year, $\sigma o t$ = 0.15

$d_1 = -0.2351 \quad\quad d_2 = -0.3851$

$N(d_1) = 0.4071 \quad\quad N(d_2) = 0.3500$

Value of the call option = $N(d_1)P - N(d_2) \times PV(EX)$

= 0.4071 X $1.0 – 0.3500 X 1.0476

= $0.0404 or 4.04 cents/Euro

SUMMARY

This chapter is an extension of chapter 20 and applies the lessons learned in the last chapter to real options faced by corporate financial managers. These real options are: the option for follow-on investment, the abandonment option, the timing option, and the option to vary production or other resources to achieve flexibility in production or manufacturing. These options can be valued using the binomial method with the risk-neutral approach. These options are extremely valuable and a manager's ability to understand and correctly value these options will enable him (her) to manage the corporate resources better.

The chapter also reviews the general binomial method, which is a very versatile tool in option valuation. By applying it over shorter and shorter periods, the binomial method approaches the Black-Scholes method in terms of accuracy. Valuation of American options and dividend paying European options are also explained.

While real options are not traded in the market, they can be valued using the same techniques applied to valuing traded options. Care and judgement will have to be used in obtaining the parameters required for valuation of these options.

LIST OF TERMS

Abandonment option

American option

Binomial

Call option

Currency option

European option

Flexible production facilities

Put option

Real options

Risk-neutral

Timing option

EXERCISES

Fill-in Questions

1. Capital budgeting decisions often involve _____ options.

2. A(n) _____ option is an insurance policy that pays off when the value of the asset is less than the option's _____ price.

3. An abandonment option is a(n) _____ option with an exercise price equal to the sales value of the assets.

4. Decisions concerning the timing of investments and the value of follow-on investments are examples of _____ options.

5. The _____ option is essentially one of choosing the optimal point for investment.

6. An option to buy British pounds at a stipulated exchange rate is a(n) _____ option.

7. Further real options may be provided by _____ where inputs or outputs may easily be varied.

8. As the number of intervals for analyzing options is increased from 1 to 52, the _____ method produces results that are very close to the _____ model.

9. Inasmuch as an American _____ (should, should not) _____ be exercised before maturity, its value is the same as a(n) _____ call, and the Black-Scholes formula (does, does not) _____ apply to both.

10. A(n) _____ put (is, is not) _____ always more valuable than a(n) _____ put.

Problems

1. MNK Corp. has a project with the following estimated values: $10 million by the end of the first year, if the things work out well.; and $2.7 million if things do not turn out well. In the latter case, the company can sell the assets for $3 million. There is a 50 percent chance that the business will succeed. Assets of comparable risk carry a required return of 23 percent.

   a. Based only on the above information, calculate the present value of the project. Round up as you go through the steps.)

264

b. Does this analysis incorporate the option embedded in process 2? Should it? Why? If so, what is the option worth? That is, what is the present value of the firm with the embedded option?

2. Refer to problem 1. Suppose now that in each 6-month period the firm may either rise in value by 40 percent or fall by 30 percent. Assume further that the company has the option to sell the project at the end of the year for $3 million. What option values emerge?

3. The percentage change for upside and downside changes in problem 1 work out to 92 and -48 percent. What is the implied volatility? How will the upside and downside value change if the period of analysis is six months and the implied volatility is the same.

4. You are offered a 1-year option to buy German Marks at $0.50/Mark. The current exchange rate is $0.55 You have the following information:

Maturity of option	$t = 1$
Standard deviation of exchange-rate changes	$\sigma = 0.16$
Dollar interest rate	$r_\$ = 0.05$
Mark interest rate	$r_M = 0.08$

What is the value of this currency option?

Essay Questions

1. What are real options? Describe two types of real options and tell how you would value them.

2. Describe the general binomial method. How does this method compare with the Black-Scholes model?

3. Explain the approach you would take to value an American call on a dividend paying stock.

4. "An American call option should never be exercised before its maturity." Discuss this statement.

ANSWERS TO EXERCISES
Fill-in Questions

1 Real
2 Put, exercise
3 Put
4 Call
5 Timing

6. Currency
7. Flexible production facilities
8. Binomial; Black-Scholes
9. Call option; should not; European; does
10. American; is; European

Problems

1. a. With a 50 percent chance that the business will succeed, the expected value in year 1 is (0.50 X 10) + (0.5 X 2.7) = $6.4 million. At a discount rate of 23 percent, the present value is 6.4/1.23 = $5.2 million. The rest of the problem deals with valuing a put option. Begin with a diagram such as Figure 21-3 and the following information.

Expected cash flow = [(probability of high demand X 10) + (probability of low demand X 2.7)]
= (0.5 X 10) + (0.5 X 2.7) = 6.4 million

PV = 6.4/1.23 = 5.2 million

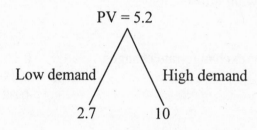

Figure 21-3

b. Present value of business without option to abandon $5.2 million
    Exercise price $3.0 million
    Maturity   1 year
    Interest rate   5 percent
    Better-case scenario: Future value with high demand $10.0 million
    Worse-case scenario: Future value with low demand $2.7 million

Percentage change in the value of the business:

Upside = (10.0/5.2) - 1 = 0.92 = 92%
Downside = (2.7/5.2) - 1 = 0.46 = - 48%

Next, calculate the probability that value will rise:

p = (r – downside change)/(upside change – downside change)
= [0.05 - (- 0.48)]/[0.92 - (-0.48)]
= 0.53/1.48 = 0.38
1 – p = 0.62

If the project is successful, the option to abandon = 0. If it is unsuccessful, the company can sell the assets and net 3.0 - 2.7 = 0.3 million.

266

The expected value of the option one period from now is:

(probability of rise X 0) + [(1 - probability of rise) X 0.3]
= (0.38 X 0) + (0.62 X 0.3)
= $186,000

The current value of the option to abandon is:

(expected future value)/(1 + interest rate) = 186,000/1.05 = $177,143

Value of business with abandonment option= value of business without abandonment option
+ value of option
= 5.2 + 0.177
= 5.38 million

2. Figure 21-4 shows the possible firm values by the year-end. When the firm is worth 2.548 million, the option is worth:

Exercise price - firm value = 3 - 2.548 = 452,000

p = (r – downside change)/(upside change – downside change)
= [0.05 - (- 0.30)]/[0.40 - (-0.30]
= .35/.70 = 0.5
$1 - p = 0.5$

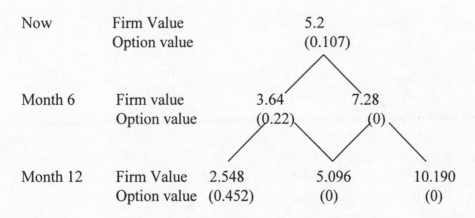

Now	Firm Value		5.2	
	Option value		(0.107)	
Month 6	Firm value	3.64		7.28
	Option value	(0.22)		(0)
Month 12	Firm Value	2.548	5.096	10.190
	Option value	(0.452)	(0)	(0)

Figure 21-4

Figures in parentheses show the values of an option to sell the firm's assets for $3 million.

In month 6, firm value is 3.64 million, and there is a 50-50 chance that, at the end of the year, the option will be worthless or worth 452,000. Thus,

Expected value of option at end of year = (0.5 X 0) + (0.5 X 0.452) = .226
Value at month 6 = .226/1.025 = .220

Option Value Now

Figure 21-4 contains values in parentheses for each step. The expected value of the option in month 6 is [(Probability of rise) X 0] + [(1 - probability of rise) X 220] = (0.5 X 0) + (0.5 X 220) = 110

Value today = (expected value of option at month 6)/(1 + interest rate)
= 110/1.025
= 107

3. Upside change = u = 0.92; 1 + u = 1.92 = $e^{\sigma\sqrt{h}}$

h = 1; Taking Log of both sides; log(1.92) = $\sigma\sqrt{h}$ = 0.652; σ = 0.652 = 65.2 percent.

The implied volatility or standard deviation of the annual returns is 65.2 percent.

The upside and downside changes for 6-month intervals are:

Upside change (6-month interval) = $e^{0.652\sqrt{0.5}}$ - 1 = 1.586 - 1 = 0.59
Downside change = (1/u) - 1 = 1/1.586 - 1 = 0.631 - 1 = -0.37

4. To value the call option, you must first reduce the current price of the Mark by the amount of the lost interest.

Adjusted price of Mark, P^* = current price/(1 + r_M) = 0.55/1.08 = $0.5093
Price/PV(exercise price) = P^*/[E/(1 + r_s)] = 0.5093/(0.50/1.05) = 1.0695
d_1 = log[P/PV(EX)]/σot + σot/2; d_2 = d_1 - σot
σ = 0.15, t = 1 year, σot = 0.15
d_1 = 0.4999 d_2 = 0.3399
$N(d_1)$ = 0.6914 $N(d_2)$ = 0.6330

Value of the call option = $N(d_1)P - N(d_2)$ X PV(EX)
= 0.6914 X $0.5093 – 0.6333 X 0.4762
= $0.051 or 5.1 cents/Mark

22

Warrants and Convertibles

INTRODUCTION

Corporations have always been on the lookout for new types of securities. Warrants and convertible securities are among the earliest of corporate financial innovations. The most common warrant is a long-term call option that is attached to a bond or a stock issue. It usually gives its holder an option to *buy for cash* another security of the company, usually its common stock. The typical convertible security is a long-term option that is attached to a bond or a preferred stock and it gives its holder the option to exchange the bond or preferred stock for another security of the company, usually common stock.

Compared with convertible securities, warrants are typically of shorter duration, are detachable from the securities from which they are issued, and carry an exercise price, which requires a cash payment when used. The Black-Scholes option valuation formula may be used to place a value on warrants, but care must be taken to allow for the effects of dividends and changes in the number of shares outstanding. Warrants are frequently issued with private placement bonds and occasionally with public bond issues. They are also occasionally used as compensation for investment bankers and as part of restructuring packages for firms reorganizing after bankruptcy.

The value of a convertible bond is equal to the value of the bond component plus the value of the option component. Both convertible bonds and the warrants are not entitled to receive any cash dividends till they are exercised. Their exercise prices are automatically adjusted for any stock split or stock dividends. Corporations usually have call options on the convertible bonds they issue. This allows them to call the bonds in order to force conversion of the bonds. The optimal rule for calling convertible securities would be to call them when, and only when, the value of the convertible security reaches the call price.

KEY CONCEPTS IN THE CHAPTER

Warrants: Warrants are usually detachable, meaning that they may be exercised apart from the security with which they were offered. Warrant holders are not entitled to vote, nor do they receive cash dividends. Their interest in the company is usually protected against stock splits and stock dividends. Often, the exercise price is stepped up over the life of the warrant. Usually, the life of a warrant is shorter than the conversion feature of a convertible bond. The Black-Scholes options valuation formula may be used to place a value on a warrant, provided it contains no unusual features and does not pay cash dividends. Cash dividends and dilution arising from the additional shares potentially outstanding, however, present difficulties in using

269

the Black-Scholes model. Consequently, adjustments for dilution are required. The binomial method is used to avoid the cash dividend problem.

Valuation of Warrants: Warrants are American call options and can be valued using the Black-Scholes model. Like any other American option, the value depends on the share price, exercise price, the volatility, the interest rate, and the time to maturity. Warrant valuation needs to be adjusted for the fact that the exercise of the warrant results in an increase in the number of shares outstanding. This causes dilution and needs to be adjusted for.

The value of a warrant at maturity can be written as:

$$\text{Value at maturity} = \frac{1}{(1+q)} \max imum(\frac{V}{N} - EX, 0),$$

Where q = number of warrants issued per share outstanding
  N = number of shares outstanding
  EX = exercise price of the warrant
  V = value of the equity of the firm *after the issue* of the warrant

In effect, the warrant is worth $1/(1+q)$ times the value of a call option written on the stock of an alternate firm with the same equity V and outstanding shares N, but with no warrants. This would require calculating the value of the share price of this notional firm and also adjust the volatility (standard deviation) of its equity to reflect the balance sheet of the notional firm. The worked example problem 1 shows the calculations involved.

Convertible Bonds: Convertible bonds resemble warrants because they are options to acquire common stock. The warrant and conversion options differ in that warrants are exercised by the payment of cash to the issuing firm, whereas holders of convertible securities exchange them for common stock on predetermined terms. The value of convertible bonds consists of the value of the bond as a bond and the value of the conversion feature, itself being evaluated as an option. Thus, the price of convertible securities has two lower bounds: the value as a security standing apart from the conversion feature and the value of the conversion feature itself. The conversion option is evaluated just as warrants are, making certain to adjust for cash dividends and potential dilution. The bonds are evaluated as all bonds are. Here are the terms commonly used with convertible bonds:

- *Conversion price*: the price at which the bond is convertible
- *Conversion ratio*: the number of shares received in exchange for each bond
- *Conversion value:* the value of the bond if converted = conversion ratio X share price.

Remember that the value of a convertible bond depends on the value of the bond portion and the value of the convertible (option) portion. The bonds value like that of any other bond is simply the present value of the coupon payments and the face value. This establishes a floor. The other floor is the conversion value. Low firm value and low bond values go together. Problem 2 of the worked examples gives an example of convertible valuation.

Convertible securities come in different forms. These include complicated securities like a Liquid Yield Option Note (LYON), which is a zero coupon convertible bond, which is also callable and putable (meaning the bondholder can sell it back to the issuer at a specified price). In recent years, some issuers have issued convertible preferred or bonds, which are automatically converted (mandatory convertible).

Forced Conversion: Convertible bonds always carry the *call feature* that permits the issuer to call the bond at a specified price, and typically, a few years after bond issue. This feature enables the firms to force conversion by calling the bonds for redemption. Ideally, the firms should do this once the bond's conversion value exceeds the call price. Empirical evidence indicates that financial managers do not consistently follow the optimal rule. They appear to wait a while and it is not uncommon to find convertible bonds with conversion values far exceeding their call price.

The Difference Between Warrants and Convertibles: While warrants and convertibles share many similarities, they are different in many ways. Here is a list.

- Warrants are usually issued privately; convertibles are usually issued publicly.
- Warrants are usually detachable and exercisable alone; when a convertible bond is exercised, both the bond and the option are given up.
- Warrants may be issued alone; convertible securities always consist of the security and the conversion option.
- Warrants are exercised for cash; convertible securities are not.
- The cash receipts from exercised warrants may be taxable; there are no unusual tax features with convertible securities.

Rationale for Issuing Warrants and Convertibles: Why do companies issue warrants and convertibles? You will hear reasons like: they lower interest costs or they allow a firm to issue stocks at a higher price. These do not make sense and assume inefficient markets and incorrect pricing of the securities. The real reasons could be more complex. Typically, convertibles and warrants are issued by smaller and more risky firms, who have trouble getting unsecured and subordinated debt at reasonable costs. The market, on account of asymmetric information, tends to overestimate the risk of these firms. By offering convertibles or warrants, the firm is giving a piece of the action and is thus able to lower its agency costs. These securities do a better job of assuring the investors that the management will not act against bondholders' interest. Since the lenders participate in any gains accruing to the shareholders from excess risk-taking or other actions not in the interests of the bondholders, lenders are less concerned about the management "misbehavior."

WORKED EXAMPLES

1. The table below contains information about Leisure Products, Inc.'s recently issued subordinated debenture bonds with detachable warrants.

   a. Calculate the cost of the warrants.
   b. Calculate the call option value without the dilution effects.
   c. Calculate the call option value with the dilution effects. (Assume the alternative firm's standard deviation of stock price changes is 53 percent.)

Details of Warrants Issued by Leisure Products, Inc.

Item	Value
Amount of loan	$60,000,000
Debt value without warrants	$46,500,000
Number of shares outstanding (N)	9,000,000
Current stock price	$32.00
Value of firm before debt issue	$318,000,000
Existing loans	$30,000,000
Number of warrants issued/share outstanding (q)	0.10
Total number of warrants issued	900,000
Exercise price of warrants (EX)	$40.25
Years to expiration of warrants (t)	6
Annual standard deviation of stock price changes	0.51
Rate of interest	10.00%

SOLUTION

1. a. Cost of warrants = total amount of loan - value of loan without warrants
   $$= \$60 \text{ million} - \$46.5 \text{ million} = \$13.5 \text{ million}$$
   $$= \$15.00 \text{ per warrant}$$

   b. Since we are not concerned about the dilution effect, we calculate the value of the option as if it were a regular call option on the stock.

   $$\sigma\sqrt{t} = 0.51\sqrt{6} = 1.25, \quad PV(EX) = \frac{\$40.25}{(1.1)^6} = \$22.72$$

   Share price/PV(EX) = $32/[$40.25/(1.1)^6 = 1.41$

   $d_1 = \log[P/PV(EX)]/\sigma\sqrt{t} + \sigma\sqrt{t}/2$
   $\quad = \log[\$32/22.72]/1.25 + 1.25/2 = 0.899$
   $d_2 = d_1 - \sigma\sqrt{t} = -0.351$

$N(d_1) = 0.8157;$ $N(d_2) = 0.3628$ (values obtained using the Excel spread-sheet. You can also use the appendix Table in the book)

Value of call option value $= N(d_1) \times P - N(d_2) \times PV(EX)$
$$= 0.8157 \times \$32 - 0.3628 \times \$22.72$$
$$= \$17.86$$

c. To calculate the value of the warrant with the dilution effect, we use the value of the stock of the alternate firm where the stock price $= V/N$. The value of the warrant is $1/1+q$ times this option value.

Equity (V) of the alternate firm = original firm's total assets - value of loans
$$= \$378 \text{ million} - \$76.5 \text{ million}$$
$$= \$301.5 \text{ million}$$

Current share of alternative firm $= V/N$
$$= \$301.5 \text{ million}/9 \text{ million shares}$$
$$= \$33.50 \text{ per share}$$

$\sigma\sqrt{t} = 0.53\sqrt{6} = 1.30$

Share price/PV(EX) $= \$33.50/[\$40.25/(1.1)^6] = 1.474$

$d_1 = \log[\$33.5/22.72]/1.30 + 1.30/2 = 0.9484$
$d_2 = d_1 - \sigma\sqrt{t} = -0.3516$
$N(d_1) = 0.8285;$ $N(d_2) = 0.3626$

Value of call option value $= N(d_1) \times P - N(d_2) \times PV(EX)$
$$= 0.8285 \times \$33.50 - 0.3626 \times \$22.72$$
$$= \$19.52$$

Dilution factor $= 1/1+q = 1/1.1$
Warrant value of original firm with dilution $= [1/(1 + q)] \times$ value of call on alternative firm
$$= (1/1.1) \times \$19.52$$
$$= \$17.75$$

2. Flying Colors Airlines issued a 5.5 percent convertible bond, which matures 25 years from now. The conversion price is $36, and the bonds are callable at 106.25. The market price of the common stock is $42 per share.

a. What is the conversion ratio of the bonds?
b. If the conversion ratio were 33.33, what would be the conversion price?

273

c. At the current market price for common shares, what is the conversion value of the convertible? Explain your answer.
d. If bonds of comparable risk to those of Flying Colors were selling to return 10 percent, at what price would you expect the bond to be selling if it did not have the conversion feature? Assume interest is payable annually.
e. Based on your answer in d, what part of the bond's total value is ascribable to the value of the bond alone and what part is ascribable to the conversion feature? Explain fully.
f. Should the financial manager call the bonds? Why or why not?

SOLUTION

2. a. Conversion ratio = face value of convertible security
$$\frac{}{\text{conversion price}}$$
   = $1,000/$36
   = 27.78 shares

b. Using the formula for the conversion ratio in (a) immediately above, the setup is:

   33.33 = $1,000/conversion price
   Conversion price = $1,000/33.33
   = $30

c. Conversion value of the convertible:

   Security = conversion ratio X market price of common shares
   = 27.78 shares X $42 per share
   = $1,166.76

In other words, one convertible bond may be exchanged for $1,166.76 worth of common stock and must be worth at least this value.

d. Using present-value tables, we obtain the PV of $55 a year for 25 years as 10 percent and the present value of $1,000 to be received at the end of the twenty-fifth year:

   9.077 X $55 = $499.24
   0.092 X $1,000 =   92.00
                    $591.24

e. Conversion value of bond $1,166.76
   Value of bond alone   591.24
   Value of conversion feature $ 575.52

f. Yes, because the conversion value exceeds the call price.

274

SUMMARY

Warrants and convertibles are a class of hybrid securities issued by firms. Warrants are often sold with a package of other securities, typically bonds. Both are call options and can be valued using the Black-Scholes model after making adjustments for the fact that, on exercise, they cause dilution by increasing the number of shares of the firm. The types of the hybrid securities have proliferated into a menagerie of convertibles or option-type securities with names like LYON. The motives for issuing convertibles and warrants can be traced to information asymmetry between the firm's management and the lenders. Many of the firms, which issue these types of securities are either small, young companies or companies with relatively higher risk compared to firms able to issue unsecured straight bonds. Convertibles and warrants allow the lenders to participate in the firm's future prospects without having to be equity holders. This type of arrangement protects the bondholders' interests better. Thus, they reduce the bondholder-shareholder conflict in an efficient way.

LIST OF TERMS

Bond value	Fully Diluted
Conversion price	Liquid yield option note (LYON)
Conversion ratio	Mandatory Convertible
Convertible bond	Non-detachable warrants
Detachable warrant	Warrant

EXERCISES

Fill-in Questions

1. A(n) _____ gives its owner the right to (buy, exchange) _____ for cash, whereas a convertible security gives its owner the right to (buy, exchange) _____ the bond for stock.

2. A(n) _____ is a zero coupon, convertible bond which is callable and putable.

3. A warrant which is sold originally with bonds but which may be resold apart from the bonds is called a(n) _____ warrant.

4. If the Whozits Corporation has a number of $1,000 convertible bonds outstanding, each of which is convertible to 40 shares of common stock, the (conversion ratio, conversion price) _____ is _____ dollars and the (conversion ratio, conversion price)_____ is _____ shares.

5. The value of a convertible bond depends on both its _____ and its _____.

6. A _____ is automatically converted into the firm's shares at the end of a certain date.

7. According to accounting guidelines, firms with a significant number of warrants outstanding have to report their earnings on a _____ basis.

Problems

1. The table below contains information about Jumble, Inc.'s recently issued bonds with detachable warrants.

   a. Calculate the cost of the warrants.
   b. Calculate the call option value without the dilution effects.
   c. Calculate the call option value with the dilution effects. (Assume the alternative firm's standard deviation of stock price changes is 45 percent.)

Jumble, Inc. – Details of Warrants

Item	Value
Amount of loan	$15,000,000
Debt value without warrants	$12,000,000
Number of shares outstanding	2,000,000
Current stock price	$28.00
Value of firm before debt issue	$66,000,000
Existing loans	$10,000,000
Number of warrants issued per share outstanding	0.15
Total number of warrants issued	300,000
Exercise price of warrants	$29.25
Years to expiration of warrants	4
Annual standard deviation of stock price changes	0.40
Rate of interest	11.80%

2. City-Buy, Inc., issued an 8 percent convertible, subordinated debenture bond nine years ago at a price of 99.95. The bonds mature in 20 years and contain a sinking fund, which begins next year, and which requires annual cash payments equal to 5 percent of the outstanding face amount of bonds. The conversion price at the time of issuance was $35 and is stepped up as follows: $40 - five years after issuance, $45 - ten years after issuance, and $50 - thereafter. The bonds are presently callable at 105, and the common stock's current price is $55 a share.

   a. What is the bond's present conversion ratio?
   b. What is the conversion ratio in each of the other periods?
   c. At the current market price for common shares, what is the conversion value of the convertibles? Explain fully.

d. If the market price of the common shares declined to $25 a share and comparable bonds were selling to return 8 percent, what is the lowest price at which you would expect the bonds to sell?

e. If the market price of the common shares were $50 and comparable bonds were selling to return 11 percent, at what price would you expect the bonds to be selling if they did not contain the conversion feature? Assume interest is payable annually.

f. Based on your answer in part e, what part of the bond's minimum value is ascribable to the value of the bond alone and what part is ascribable to the conversion feature? Explain fully.

g. Is it financially smart to call in the bonds, given the conditions in part e above?

Essay Questions

1. Explain how you would use the Black-Scholes model to value a warrant.

2. Compare the major characteristics of a convertible bond with a bond possessing a detachable warrant.

3. It has been well stated that convertible bonds have a floor or lower limit to their price. What is this floor and how is it determined? Is there more than one floor? Is there also an upper bound? If so, what is it and how is it determined?

4. "The way I see it, financial managers should call in outstanding convertible bonds when their value reaches the call price. Yet, empirical evidence suggests that many financial managers don't do this. And I would like to know how come." Explain.

5. Discuss the following statement: "Convertible bonds have lower interest costs and therefore they are better than straight bonds. Even when the bond is converted, the conversion comes at a premium compared to the current stock price. Under the circumstances, I do not see why more companies are not issuing convertibles."

ANSWERS TO EXERCISES

Fill-in Questions

1. Warrant; buy; exchange
2. Liquid yield option note
3. Detachable
4. Conversion price; 25; conversion ratio; 40

5. Bond value; conversion value
6. Mandatory convertible
7. Fully diluted

Problems

1. a. Cost of warrants = $15 million - $12 million
                                    = $3 million
                                    = $10.00 per warrant

    b. $\sigma\sqrt{t} = 0.40\sqrt{4} = 0.80$
        $PV(EX) = \$29.25/(1.118)^4 = \$18.72$

        Share price/$PV(EX) = \$28.00/[\$29.25/(1.118)^4] = 1.50$

        $d_1 = \log[\$28/18.72]/0.80 + 0.80/2 = 0.9068$
        $d_2 = d_1 - \sigma\sqrt{t} = 0.1068$
        $N(d_1) = 0.8177; \quad N(d_2) = 0.5425$

        Value of call option = $N(d_1) \times P - N(d_2) \times PV(EX)$
                                    $= 0.8177 \times \$28 - 0.5425 \times 18.72$
                                    $= \$12.74$

    c. Dilution factor = $1/(1 +q) = 1/1.15$
        Current equity value V = $56 million + $3 million = $59 million
        Current share price of alternative firm = $59/2 = $29.50 per share

        $\sigma\sqrt{t} = 0.45\sqrt{4} = 0.90$

        Share price/$PV(EX) = \$29.50/[\$29.25/(1.118)^4] = 1.576$

        $d_1 = \log[\$29.5/18.72]/0.90 + 0.90/2 = 0.9554$
        $d_2 = d_1 - \sigma\sqrt{t} = 0.0554; \quad N(d_1) = 0.8303; \quad N(d_2) = 0.5221$

        Value of call option = $N(d_1) \times P - N(d_2) \times PV(EX)$
                                    $= 0.8303 \times \$29.5 - 0.5221 \times \$18.72$
                                    $= \$14.72$

        Warrant value of original firm with dilution = $(1/1.15) \times \$14.71 = \$12.79$

2. a. Conversion ratio = face value/conversion price
                                    = 1,000/40
                                    = 25
    b. 1,000/35 = 28.57
        1,000/40 = 25.00
        1,000/45 = 22.22
        1,000/50 = 20.00

c. Conversion value is $55 X 25 = $1,375

d. $1,000

e. (7.963 X $80) + (0.124 X $1,000) = $761.04

f. $1,375 - $761.04 = $613.96 is ascribable to the conversion feature.

g. Yes

23
Valuing Debt

INTRODUCTION

This chapter provides fundamental insights into the valuation of debt. The five sections of the chapter describe: i) the relationship of nominal rates and real interest rates, ii) the term structure (variation of interest for different maturities) of interest rates, iii) the concept of duration and how it affects the bond values when interest rates change, iv) the theories of term structure, and v) the risk structure and debt value. The chapter is important and gives you answers to some vexing questions you would have on interest rates, debt values and their changes from time to time. Financial managers have to deal with the valuation of debt at some point or other and it is necessary that they understand the basic theoretical principles, which explain the relationship among the term structure, risk structure, and debt values.

The chapter begins with Irving Fisher's classical theory of interest. Fisher postulated that real rates of return are determined by the equilibration of the supply of and demand for real capital and are reasonably constant over time, and therefore, changes in nominal rates essentially reflect changes in inflation expectations. This insight has been fundamental to our understanding of changes in interest rates over time. While economists debate Fisher's theory, it appears that the broad relationship of inflation, nominal interest rates, and real interest rates support Fisher's ideas.

KEY CONCEPTS IN THE CHAPTER

Real and Nominal Interest Rates: Most debt securities promise a fixed *nominal* interest rate. Fisher postulated that real rates are not affected by changes in inflation. According to Fisher, the relationship between real interest rates and nominal or money rates of interest rate is given by:

$$1 + r_{money} = (1 + r_{real})(1 + i)$$

Therefore, real rate = money rate - inflation rate (approximately)

A change in the expected inflation rate will cause the same change in the money rate or *nominal interest rate*. Critics of Fisher's theory argue that real rates are affected by inflation rates. Historically, real rates have changed over time. Unfortunately, real rates are not observable. What is observed is the difference between nominal rates and inflation. Again, part of the problem is Fisher's theory is in terms of expected inflation, which cannot be observed. Empirical studies indicate that inflation expectations have been the principal causes of nominal interest rate changes. Fisher's theory appears to hold in broad approximation. Remember that the real rate is an expected rate. Actual rates may be different from what you expected to get when you bought a T-bill or some other investment. Also, the real rate may vary over time.

Spot Rates, Term Structure, and Yield to Maturity: The spot rate is the rate of interest obtainable on a bond at the present, or spot, time period. The series of spot rates of different maturities results in a term structure of interest rates; typically, the term structure is upward sloping, with long-term rates higher than short-term rates. The term structure is a series of spot rates $r_1, r_2, r_3, \ldots$. Safe cash flows are valued as:

$$PV = \frac{C_1}{(1+r_1)} + \frac{C_2}{(1+r_2)^2} + \frac{C_3}{(1+r_3)^3} + \ldots,$$

where r_I is the spot rate for the "ith" year.

This is how each bond is valued in the market. However, we use the yield to maturity as a summary measure. The yield to maturity is an internal rate of return and unambiguous and easy to calculate. The problems with yield to maturity include:

- Assumes that yield to maturity does not change,
- Assumes a constant reinvestment rate of return, and
- Yield to maturity does not determine price; it is vice versa.

The term structure of government bonds can be estimated using a series of zero coupon "strips". This is the yield curve you see in the Wall Street Journal every day. This provides the spot rates for different maturities.

Duration and Volatility: The prices of long-term bonds vary more than short-term bonds. *Duration* and *volatility* are two useful measures, which enable us to formalize this relationship. Duration is the average time for the total cash flow to be realized from an asset, such as a bond. It is actually a weighted average, where the date to each cash flow is weighted by its present value. The other statistic, called volatility, is easily obtained from duration. In fact, it is just duration discounted by the one time period. Volatility measures the sensitivity of the asset price (in percent) to a (unit) change in its yield. Both of these measures are extremely important for understanding the riskiness of bonds and portfolios containing bonds.

$$\text{Duration} = \frac{1 \times PV(C_1)}{V} + \frac{2 \times PV(C_2)}{V} + \frac{3 \times PV(C_3)}{V} + \ldots$$

where V is the total value of the bond.

$$\text{Volatility (percent)} = \frac{\text{Duration}}{1 + \text{yield}}$$

Explaining the Term Structure: The three primary explanations of the upward-sloping term structure of interest rates are the expectations hypothesis, the liquidity preference theory, and the inflation premium theory. The expectations hypothesis says that the investor's expectations that future spot rates will be higher than the current spot rates explain an upward-sloping term structure. The liquidity preference theory says that a liquidity premium, which is the difference between forward rates and expected future spot rates, is required because of the uncertainty regarding the reinvestment rate when bonds mature. The inflation premium argument says that the typically upward-sloping term structure is attributable to the risk associated with the uncertainty about the inflation rate. None of these explanations is totally satisfactory, although the expectations hypothesis is the least satisfactory of all.

Term structure analysis is static; it catches a slice of time and fixes interest rates of like kind and quality bonds. Recent analyses incorporate interest rate changes. One system shows financial managers how to replicate one bond by using two others, given that interest rates may change.

Default Risk: Bonds have market-related risks and firm-specific default risks. When the value of bonds and the term structure of interest rates are determined, default risk must also be considered. The threat of default on bonds, similar in all respects except their expected ability to pay interest and principal, is another reason why different rates of return exist. Bonds are evaluated by financial services whose ratings are reasonably good predictors. The decade of the 1980s witnessed an explosion of so-called junk bonds, primarily by poor credit-worthy firms. The default rate has been high, and the market for them is thin, yet high-yielding debt instruments have always had their place in corporate finance.

Debt as Options: When option pricing is extended to debt analysis, corporate bonds become the equivalent to lending money with no chance of default while giving stockholders a put option on the firm's assets. Thus, the value of a bond consists of the value of a risk-free debt less the value of the put option. The value of the put equals the value of the limited liability of stockholder's right to walk away from the firm's debt in exchange for handing over the firm's assets to creditors. We have discussed this in chapter 20. The relationship can be written as:

Bond value = bond value with no chance of default - value of put

Guaranteed Debt: Government loan guarantees are valuable because they lift the onus of default from the borrower. A loan guarantee is valued as a put option on the firm's assets. The value of the loan without the guarantee is equal to the value assuming no chances whatsoever of a default less the value of the put.

WORKED EXAMPLES

1. Find the real rate of interest, given that the nominal rate is 7 percent and the inflation rate is 3 percent.

SOLUTION

The solution is obtained by using the formula:

$$1 + r_{money} = (1 + r_{real})(1 + i)$$

where

r_{money} = nominal or money rate of interest
r_{real} = real rate of interest
i = inflation rate

Substituting in the equation, we obtain:

$$1 + 0.07 = (1 + r_{real})(1 + 0.03)$$

We then solve for r_{real}:

$$1 + r_{real} = (1 + r_{money})/(1 + i)$$
$$= 1.07/1.03$$
$$= 1.0388$$
$$r_{real} = 0.0388 = 3.88 \text{ percent}$$

Any of the rates can be calculated given the other two rates.

2. Calculate the yield to maturity on a 10-year bond carrying a coupon rate of 7 percent. Assume that the interest is payable annually and the bond is selling at 97.

SOLUTION

The setup for the solution of this problem is similar to every other internal rate-of-return problem, for that is what solving for the yield of maturity is, an internal rate-of-return problem. Using the present value of an annuity formula allows you to find the present value of the 10 equal interest payments. You also have to calculate the present value of the maturity value of $1,000. Doing this by hand requires a hunt-and-peck method, because the object is to find the present value that sums to the present market price of $970. Here is the BA-II Plus calculator solution:

PV = price of the bond = -$970
FV = principal paid at maturity = $1,000
PMT = coupon payments = $70
N = Number of coupons = 10
I = yield to maturity = solve = 7.44 percent.

3. It is 1996 and you notice that the yields to maturity of your company's two bonds, 5s of 2000 and 9s of 2000, are selling at 87.44 and 100.71 respectively, which results in yields to maturity of 8.87 and 8.78 percent. Your financial manager is puzzled as to why two bonds of the same quality and same maturity do not have the same yield to maturity. What reasonable answer will you give?

SOLUTION

The answer lies in estimating the spot rates for each of the remaining years and taking the present value of the payments to be received. This is done in the table below using a set of assumed spot rates. Each year's coupon payments and the principal payments are discounted using the respective spot rates, not the yield to maturity. It clearly shows that the two bonds are valued correctly by the market. The yield to maturity is different because the two bonds have different cash flow patterns. The lower coupon bond has more of its cash flows coming later. Remember that the market uses spot rates for different periods (not the yield to maturity) to discount the cash flows for different years.

Yield to maturity is a measure of convenience used by us – not the one that actually gets into the discounted cash flow for the bonds.

Present Value of Two Comparable-Risk Bonds with Different Coupon Rates

Present-Value Calculations

Period t	Interest rate r_t	C_t	5s of 2000 PV at r_t	C_t	9s of 2000 PV at r_t
1	0.06	$ 50	$ 47.17	$ 90	$ 84.91
2	0.07	50	43.67	90	78.61
3	0.08	50	39.69	90	71.44
4	0.09	1050	743.85	1090	772.18
			$874.38		$1,007.14

4. Calculate the duration of 8 and 14 percent, 5-year Treasury bonds whose yields are 7.85 percent.

$$\text{Duration} = [1 \text{ X } PV(C_1)/V] + [2 \text{ X } PV(C_2)/V] + [3 \text{ X } PV(C_3)/V] + \ldots\ldots$$

SOLUTION

Yield   7.85%
Coupon 8.00%

Year	C_t	PV(C_t) at 7.85%	Proportion of Total Value [PV(C_t/V]	Proportion of Value x Time
1	80	74.18	0.0737	0.0737
2	80	68.78	0.0684	0.1368
3	80	63.77	0.0634	0.1902
4	80	59.13	0.0588	0.2352
5	1,080	740.16	0.7357	3.6785
Totals	1,400	1,006.02	1.00	4.3144

Yield   7.85%
Coupon 14.00%

Year	C_t	PV(C_t) at 7.85%	Proportion of Total Value [PV(C_t)/V]	Proportion of Value X Time
1	140	129.81	0.1041	0.1041
2	140	120.36	0.0966	0.1932
3	140	111.60	0.0895	0.2685
4	140	103.48	0.0830	0.3320
5	1,140	781.27	0.6268	3.1340
Totals	1,700	1,246.52	1.00	4.0318

5. What is the impact of a 0.5 percentage point increase and decrease in interest rates on the present value of each of the two bonds in problem 4? Compute their volatilities and compare with what you would have estimated from their duration.

SOLUTION

The yields are now 7.35 percent and 8.35 percent. The results of the computations are as follows:

	8% Bonds		14% Bonds	
	New Price	% Change	New Price	% Change
Yield falls to 7.35	1,026.40	2.026	1,270.13	1.894
Yield rises to 8.35	986.15	-1.975	1,223.51	-1.846
Difference	40.25	4.001	46.62	3.740

The percentage change is, for example, the present value of the 8 percent bond yielding 7.35 percent divided by the present value of the 8 percent bond yielding 7.85 percent; that is, percentage change [($1026.40/$1006.02) - 1] X 100 = 2.03 percent.

The volatility results for the two bonds are as follows:

Bond	Duration	Volatility (from duration)	Volatility (direct)
8 percent	4.3144	4.001	3.999
14 percent	4.0317	3.740	3.739

6. Determine the better financial strategy when confronted with a 2-year spot rate of 9 percent, a 1-year spot rate of 8 percent, and an expected spot rate on 1-year bonds 1 year from now of 10 percent. Assume you do not need your money for 2 years and are not bothered by risk.

SOLUTION

To find the answer, you want to know the expected return of each strategy. The setup is:

$$\$1,000(1 + r_1)[1 + E(_1r_2)] \text{ compared with } \$1,000(1 + r_2)^2$$

where

r_1 = 1-year spot rate
$E(_1r_2)$ = expected spot rate on 1-year bonds 1 year from now
r_2 = 2-year spot rate

Substituting the values above, we obtain:

$$\$1,000(1 + 0.08)(1 + 0.10) \quad \text{compared with} \quad \$1,000(1 + 0.09)^2$$
$$\$1,000(1.08)(1.10) \quad \text{compared with} \quad \$1,000(1.09)^2$$
$$\$1,000(1.188) \text{compared with} \quad \$1,000(1.1881)$$
$$\$1,188 \text{compared with} \$1,188.10$$

For all practical purposes, there is no difference between the two outcomes; therefore, you would be indifferent about this investment.

If you wish to lock in the final outcome of $1,188, say, because of your queasiness about the expected 1-year spot rate, choose the 9 percent, 2-year spot rate. You should also note that the implied forward rate is:
$$(1 + r_2)^2 = (1+r_1)(1 + f_2)$$

where f_2 is the implied forward rate. Substituting the above values, we obtain:

$$(1 + 0.09)_2 = (1 + 0.08)(1 + f_2)$$
$$(1.09)_2 = (1.08)(1 + f_2)$$
$$1.1881 = 1.08(1 + f_2)$$
$$1 + f_2 = 1.1881/1.08$$
$$= 1.1000$$
$$f_2 = 0.1000 = 10.00 \text{ percent}$$

287

As expected, the implicit forward rate is almost exactly equal to the expected future spot rate, again indicating a condition of relative indifference.

SUMMARY

This chapter explores the full complexities of valuing debt. The chapter attempts to answer fundamental questions on interest rates, term structure, and risk structure. It starts with the basic relationship between inflation and nominal interest rates. Irving Fisher's theory still forms the basis for the widely accepted rule of thumb:

$$\text{Real interest rate} = \text{Nominal interest rate} - \text{inflation.}$$

Keep in mind that only the nominal rate is observed and the other two are expectations. Fisher's theory should be seen as a broad approximation.

The three term structure theories are explored. The expectations theory ignores the possibility of risk and is thus not acceptable as it is. There appears to be a risk premium in the term structure; i. e. the forward interest rates are on average higher than future spot rates. This risk premium can be on account of inflation or general risk based on future uncertainty. New theories are taking a different approach and would probably gain currency as more work is done.

Bond values reflect present values of cash flows produced discounted by the series of spot rates over the bond's maturity. For convenience, the yield to maturity is used as a summary measure. It is important to understand that the yield to maturity is derived from the price of the bond and the other way around. Duration and volatility are useful measures of the sensitivity of a bond's value to changes in interest rates.

Lastly, the risk structure of bonds is explored. Bond ratings capture the default risk of corporate bonds fairly well. A risky bond can be seen as the combination of a risk-free bond less the value of a put given to the shareholders. Thus, the value of a government guarantee to a private corporation is the value of this put.

LIST OF TERMS

Clean price	Money rate of interest
Duration	Nominal interest rate
Expectations hypothesis	Promised yield
Forward rate	Real interest rate
Inflation premium	Spot rate
Junk bonds	Strips
Liquidity preference theory	Term structure of interest rates
Liquidity premium	Yield to maturity

EXERCISES

Fill-in Questions

1. _____ include a premium for anticipated inflation.

2. The nominal rate of interest must equal the _____ plus the _____.

3. If the money (nominal) rate of interest is 10 percent and the anticipated inflation rate is 10 percent, the real rate of interest is _____.

4. Under Fisher's scheme of interest rates, if the forecasted inflation rate is 5 percent and the real interest rate is 0.3 percent, the nominal interest rate is _____.

5. The real rate of interest is equal to the _____ minus the _____.

6. Any interest rate, which is fixed today, is called the _____.

7. The term structure of interest rates consists of a series of _____ on bonds of comparable risk.

8. A bond's internal rate of return is called _____.

9. When government bonds are repackaged into mini-bonds, each of which makes only one payment; they are known as _____.

10. _____ measures the average time that the total cash flow from an asset is realized over the life of that asset.

11. _____ measures the percentage change in the price of a bond or other asset corresponding to a unit change in its yield.

12. The _____ rate between two dates is the interest rate we can lock into between buying them today and by selling discount bonds for those two dates.

13. Ordinarily, the term structure of interest rates presents a condition in which the _____ rates are higher than the _____ rates, and therefore, the term structure slopes upward.

14. The _____ of the term structure of interest rates says the only reason for an upward-sloping term structure is that investors expect future spot rates to be higher than current spot rates.

15. The difference between forward rates and expected future spot rates is called _____.

16. The _____ theory of term structure of interest rates takes into account risk, whereas the explanation does not.

17. The _____ theory of the term structure of interest rates assumes that the risk from holding bonds comes only from uncertainty about expected inflation rates.

18. The history of bond ratings indicates that they are (good, poor) _____ indicators of overall quality.

19. When one assumes that bonds create options, the bond value is equal to the value of the bond, assuming no chance of default, minus _____.

20. A loan guarantee may be valued as a(n) _____ on the firm's assets.

21. High-yield bonds are also called _____ bonds and are usually rated at _____ or lower.

22. The _____ on junk bonds is typically much higher than the _____.

Problems

1. Find the real interest rate, given that the nominal rate is 9 percent and the inflation rate is 5 percent.

2. If the money rate of interest is 9.3 percent and the real rate is expected to be 5 percent, what is the implied inflation rate? How realistic is it to assume that the real rate will be 5 percent?

3. How different is your inflation estimate in Problem 2 if you use the approximate formula, subtracting one rate from the other?

4. Calculate the yield to maturity on a 15-year bond carrying a coupon rate of 9 percent. Assume that the interest is payable annually and the bond is selling at 92.

5. As the financial manager of Ink, Inc., you estimate the following spot interest rates on Treasury securities:

YEAR	SPOT INTEREST RATE,%
1	$r_1 = 4.00$
2	$r_2 = 5.00$
3	$r_3 = 5.60$
4	$r_4 = 7.20$
5	$r_5 = 6.50$

Your company's bonds have an 11 percent coupon rate, interest is payable annually, and they mature in exactly 5 years.

a. What is the present value of the bond?
b. Calculate the present values of the following Treasury issues: (1) 5 percent, 3-year bond; (2) 8 percent, 3-year bond; and (3) 6 percent, 5-year bond.
c. Determine the yield to maturity of each of the bonds.
d. What differences between the yields to maturity do you observe, and how might you explain them to the board of directors, who also happen to have noticed the differences?

6. Calculate the duration and volatilities of 9 and 13 percent, 5-year Treasury bonds whose yields are 8.00 percent.

7. Trace the impact of a 0.5 percentage point increase and decrease in interest rates on the present value of each of the two bonds in problem 6. Use this to compute their volatilities and compare with your answer from problem 6.

Essay Questions

1. Explain the term structure of interest rates and the theories that attempt to explain the term structure.

2. How are nominal rates of interest adjusted for the effects of inflation? Explain fully, using whatever equations you feel are necessary.

3. Explain the relationship between the price of a bond and the yield to maturity. Does the yield determine the price or is it the other way around? What really determines the price of a bond in the market?

4. Why are there bond ratings, and what influence do you think they have on the value of bonds?

5. Government guarantees do not cost the taxpayer anything as they are rarely invoked. Discuss.

6. How do you think bond-rating agencies determine the ratings they place on bonds?

ANSWERS TO EXERCISES

Fill-in Questions

1. Nominal interest rates
2. Real rate; inflation premium

12. Forward
13. Long; short

3. Zero
4. 5.3 percent
5. Nominal rate on Treasury bills;
    expected inflation rate
6. Spot rate
7. Spot rates
8. Yield to maturity
9. Strip
10. Duration
11. Volatility

14. Expectations hypothesis
15. Liquidity premium
16. Liquidity preference
17. Inflation premium
18. Good
19. Value of a put
20. Put option
21. Junk; B
22. Promised yield; expected yield

Problems

1. $1 + r_{real} = (1 + r_n)/(1 + i)$
    $= 1.09/1.05$
    $= 3.81$ percent

2. $1 + I = (1 + r_n/(1 + r_{real})$
    $= 1.093/1.05$
    $= 4.10$ percent

    Not very, because it is well above the historical (1926-1994) arithmetic average of 0.6 percent.

3. $i = r_n - r_{real}$
    $= 9.3$ percent $- 5.0$ percent
    $= 4.30$ percent, 20 basis points different.

4. 10.00 percent

5. a.

PERIOD	INTEREST RATE	CASH FLOW	PRESENT VALUE
1	4.00	110	105.77
2	5.00	110	99.77
3	5.60	110	93.41
4	7.20	110	83.29
5	6.50	1,110	810.17
			1,192.41

b.

	PERIOD	INTEREST RATE	CASH FLOW	PRESENT VALUE
(1)	1	4.00	50	48.08
	2	5.00	50	45.35
	3	5.60	1,050	891.66
				985.09
(2)	1	4.00	80	76.92
	2	5.00	80	72.56
	3	5.60	1,080	917.13
				1,066.61
(3)	1	4.00	60	57.69
	2	5.00	60	54.42
	3	5.60	60	50.95
	4	7.20	60	45.43
	5	6.50	1,060	773.67
				982.16

c. Using the prices above:

1	5.75%
2	5.50
3	6.43

6. Yield 8.00%
    Coupon 9.00%

Year	C_t	PV(C_t) at 8.00%	Proportion of Total Value [PV(C_t)/V]	Proportion of Value X Time
1	90	83.33	0.0801	0.0801
2	90	77.16	0.0742	0.1484
3	90	71.44	0.0687	0.2061
4	90	66.15	0.0636	0.2544
5	1,090	741.84	0.7134	3.5670
Totals	1,450	1,039.92	1.00	4.2560

Yield 8.00% Coupon 13.00%

Year	Ct	PV(C_t) at 8.00%	Proportion of Total Value [PV(C_t)/V]	Proportion of Value X Time
1	130	120.37	0.1003	0.1003
2	130	111.45	0.0929	0.1858
3	130	103.20	0.0860	0.2581
4	130	95.55	0.0797	0.3186
5	1,130	760.06	0.6411	3.2054
Totals	1,650	1,190.63	1.00	4.0682

293

Discounting by their yields, we find that the volatilities of the two bonds are:

9.00% bond: 3.941, 13% bond: 3.767.

7. The yields are now 7.50 and 8.50 percent. We obtain:

	9% Bonds		13% Bonds	
	New Price	% Change	New Price	% Change
Yield falls to 7.50	1,060.69	1.997	1,222.51	2.678
Yield rises to 8.50	1,019.70	-1.944	1,177.33	-1.117
Difference	40.99	3.941	45.18	3.767

The percentage change is, for example, the present value of the 9 percent bond yielding 7.50 percent divided by the present value of the 9 percent bond yielding 8.00 percent; that is, percentage change = (($1060.69/$1039.92) - 1] X 100 = 2.00 percent.

The volatility results for the two bonds are as follows:

Bond	Volatility (direct)	Volatility (from problem 5)
9 percent	3.941	3.941
13 percent	3.767	3.767

24

The Many Different Kinds of Debt

INTRODUCTION

This chapter describes the many different types of debt securities available for corporations and other borrowers. The number and variety of debt instruments, which are used in global finance today, are amazing. One might wonder, why so many different forms? The answer lies in the fact that selling securities to raise money is essentially a marketing problem (as Brealey and Myers have pointed out more than once) and investment bankers and corporations try to appeal to potential customers (lenders) in many different ways; just like an auto-manufacturer offers so many different models with different market segments in mind.

Debt is broadly differentiated as public issue bonds, private debt, asset-backed securities, and project financing. All are promissory notes, although each has characteristics peculiar to it. The bond contract contains the specific terms, called covenants; to which borrowers and lenders agree. Bonds contain such features as being fully registered, unsecured, subordinated, mortgage, collateral trust, a variety of repayment provisions, and restrictive provisions. Debt is either sold publicly or placed privately, the latter being less costly to issue, containing nonstandard features, and imposing more restrictive terms on the borrower. Debt securities can be issued within one's own country or overseas and in many different currencies. Financial innovation is alive and well in debt markets with corporations coming up with new types of debt all the time.

The chapter also describes the typical provisions and covenants seen in debt contracts and the rationale for these. Financial managers should have the general awareness and knowledge of the common provisions contained in debt contracts and understand the need for the same. While the details will be taken care of by the specialist, the manager's familiarity will help her (him) to understand why a certain kind of debt might be of better value for her (his) company in a certain situation. Here are a few points, which a manager should keep in mind:

- Each financial manager should know the type of debt and its covenants that are best for him or her or the company. There is no "one size fits all" approach in financing.
- Be aware of the major distinctions between debt sold to the public and privately placed debt. The former contract is more complex and the characteristics and formats are more standardized. However, the restrictive covenants of publicly sold debt are less severe than privately placed debt. Issue costs for the former is higher, but the interest rate may be somewhat less.

KEY CONCEPTS IN THE CHAPTER

The chapter is descriptive and explains the many terms and phrases commonly used in global bond markets. We summarize the main points of the different sections.

Domestic Bonds, Foreign Bonds, and Eurobonds: U.S. firms may borrow either domestically or in foreign bond markets. The international market for long-term debt, typically debt sold in many different countries, is called the Eurobond market. Among some of the nuances that concern financial managers is the currency in which the principal or interest will be paid and local security markets regulation (or lack thereof).

The Eurobond market started as an innovation to get around government regulations and is technically defined as bonds in a currency sold outside its "home" jurisdiction (e. g. Japanese Yen outside Japan). Today, this market has broadened and expanded with major currencies for borrowing being the U.S. dollar, the British pound, and the Japanese yen and the bonds are sold in different countries at the same time. It is quite likely that the new European currency (Euro) may become a dominant currency of borrowing. Be careful not to confuse an Euro bond (one denominated in Euro) with a Eurobond (can be in any currency).

The Bond Contract: All bonds are promissory notes or "IOUs." All publicly issued bonds are covered by bond indentures, which are included in the registration statement and whose main provisions are contained in the prospectuses. Foreign issuers of bonds (or stocks) are not required to disclose nearly as much information as U.S. publicly offered ones.

Bond prices are quoted as a percentage of their face value. Sometimes they are sold at a discount from their face value. Most often interest payments, called coupons, are fixed for the life of the bond, although recently, more and more floating-rate notes have been issued. Bonds may or may not be registered.

The details of the contract terms are found in the *indenture* or *trust deed*, a copy of which is in the registration statement and a condensed version of which is in the prospectus. Here is a brief summary of some of the more common terms.

Accrued interest is the interest accrued between the last coupon date and the date of sale of a bond. The buyer of the bond will pay this to the seller. The price, excluding the accrued interest, is the *clean price.*

Underwriting fee is the difference between the offering price to the public and the price to underwriters. Most bonds are underwritten. Underwriters provide the service of distributing the bonds and advice the firm on other matters related to the bond issue.

Coupon payments are the interest payments made usually semiannually in the U.S. Eurobonds pay annually.

296

Bearer securities are bonds (or other securities) which are not *registered* and possession of the certificate is the evidence of ownership. Almost all bonds in the U.S. are registered, but many Eurobonds and bonds in some foreign countries are issued in the bearer form.

Security and Seniority: The significance of the legal security and seniority of bonds depends largely on the extent to which assets and earnings are available to meet the legal obligations of semiannual interest payments as well as the repayment of principal when due. *Debenture* bonds are unsecured general credit of the company and have no legal security other than the general bill-paying ability of the company. *Secured debt*, by contrast, has a specific claim on specific assets and is often called m*ortgage* bonds. *Collateral trust* bonds have a claim on other securities. *Equipment trust certificates* are used to finance railroad rolling stock, trucks, ships, and aircraft. The ownership of the equipment remains with a *trustee*; the company makes an initial down payment and the balance is paid through a series of trust certificates. Ownership is transferred to the company only after the last certificates has been paid off. The repayment of the principal claims of some debt holders may be *subordinated* to those of other debt holders.

Asset-backed Securities: These are securities backed by cash flows from a group of assets. Typical examples of assets packaged include: home mortgages, car payments, credit card payments, etc. Companies combine a group of assets and sell the cash flows from these assets to a separate company and this company sells *mortgage pass through certificates*. The mortgage payments are passed on to the security holders. Often, companies issue a series of this type of securities called *collateralized mortgage obligations* (CMOs).

Repayment Provisions: Some of the key repayment provisions included in typical bond contracts are briefly summarized below:

Sinking fund requires issuers to repay some or the entire principal of the debt before maturity. Payment may be in cash or an equal face value amount of the bonds. Sinking fund requirements may be mandatory, optional, or both (i.e. 5 percent). Sinking fund provisions may mean a test of firm solvency, unless the firm is allowed to purchase them in the open market. This would be like lowering the bar progressively, as the bonds of a company in financial distress will be selling at a discount.

Call provision allows the borrower to call in (retire) its bonds, invariably at a premium, before they mature. The option generally starts a few years after the issue of the bond. This is a valuable option because when it is invoked under the proper conditions--when the market price equals the call--it tends to minimize the value of the bonds, which is equivalent to saying that it tends to maximize the value of the firm's stock.

Defeasance involves retiring bonds selling at a discount because the interest rate is high compared to the coupon rate on the bond. The company transfers the debt to a trust and provides the trust with a package of U.S. government bonds for the needed cash flow to pay the coupon and principal of the bonds. The company can take the debt off its balance sheet and book a profit as it costs the company less than the face value of the debt to retire the debt. Defeasance is good

297

for the bondholders as their debt is now effectively guaranteed by US Treasury bonds. The bondholders have gained at the cost of the company's stockholders. This is not one of the "smart" things you want to emulate!

Restrictive Covenants: Because the company has the valuable option to default on its bonds, restrictive bond provisions are the order of the day. Maintaining an adequate ratio of assets to debt, minimum working capital requirements, ensuring that all subsequent debt will be subordinated to existing debt, incorporating a negative pledge clause, restricting the amount of cash dividends paid, and requiring a minimum level of net worth are typical restrictive provisions, all of which are intended to enhance the security of bondholders. The leveraged buy-outs (LBOs) of the 1980s ushered in an era in which many restrictive covenants--especially the prohibition on the use of debt of equal or senior claim to that already outstanding and the easing of dividend restrictions--were forgone in exchange for higher than normal yields. Some common covenants seen in most bonds include the following:

- *Negative pledge clause* undertakes not to give greater security to other parties. For example, the company is not permitted to have any lien without equally securing the debt securities.
- *Restrictions* on debt issues and dividend payments unless certain conditions are satisfied.
- *Cross-default clause* will make default on one issue an act of default on all issues.
- *Affirmative covenants* require the company to do certain things to protect lenders. These range from the innocuous providing of copies of accounts to agreeing to maintain particular levels of working capital or net worth.

Project Finance: Project finance involves loans that finance particular projects through a parent company or one of its major subsidiaries. Project loans rely on the project itself for the repayment of principal and the payment of interest. Because that may not be sufficient security for lenders, tangible property, production payments, completion guarantees, and recourse to stockholders are commonly incorporated into the lending agreement. This type of financing is typically used for joint ventures, such as electric power companies, in which the project's outputs are split among the participants. Some of the features of project finance include the following: large projects, physically isolated from the parent, and provide tangible security for the lender. The main benefits of project finance are the sharing of risk with parties who are in the best position to share specific kinds of risk.

Innovations in the Bond Market: Bond market innovations keep flowing at an amazing pace. Some of them succeed and some fail. Many of the innovations appeal to specific clientele with specific needs. Some rise because of quirks in "the system:" the GMAC issuance of zero coupon bonds being a case in point. The regulation of the Japanese insurance industry created special types of yen bonds. When the innovation survives, it is usually because of economies of scale, widened investor choices, and changes that accommodate changing perceptions of investor risk.

WORKED EXAMPLES

1. If Jill-in-the-Box Corp.'s 8 percent debenture matures in 10 years and the yield on comparable risk bonds is 6 percent, at what price would you expect the bonds to be selling?

SOLUTION

The object here is to determine the present value of the bond, the formula for which is:

$$PV = \sum_{t=1}^{n} \frac{C_t}{(1+r)^t}$$

Where

        PV = present value
        C_t = per period cash flow
         r = required rate of return on assets of this risk level
        t = number of periods over which cash flows will be forthcoming

In as much as interest is paid semiannually, the interest cash flow per period is $40 ($80/2), the semiannual interest rate r is 3 percent (6 percent divided by 2), and the total number of periods t over which the cash flows will be forthcoming is 20 (2 X 10 years). The completed formula is:

$$PV = \sum \frac{40}{(1.03)^t} + \frac{1,000}{(1.03)^{20}}$$

Next, use the present value tables. The first term on the right-hand side of the equation is the present value of an annuity (Appendix Table 3) of $40 for 20 periods at 3 percent. The second term is the present value of a lump sum (Appendix Table 1) of $1,000 to be received at the end of the twentieth period. The arithmetic of the matter looks like this:

        PV = ($40)(14.88) + $1,000(0.554)
           = $595.20 + $554.00
           = $1,149.20

Alternately, using the BA II-Plus:

Solve for PV = _____, FV = $1,000, PMT = $40, n = 20, I = 3
          PV = $1,148.77 (This is more accurate.)

2. If the bonds in problem 1 are callable at 106, what should the financial manager do?

SOLUTION

The financial manager should call the bond because the present value of the bond ($1,148.77) is greater than the present value of the call price ($1,060.00). The cost ($60) is less than the benefit (148.77). If needed, a new issue of bonds may be sold at the going rate of 6 percent, thereby reducing the drain on cash and improving its interest coverage ratio, all to the benefit of the shareholders.

3. If the call provision of problem 2 exists, what is the maximum price you would expect the bond to achieve when bonds of comparable risk are selling to yield 6 percent?

SOLUTION

The bond will sell for no more than the call price, which is $1,060. The difference between the present value of the bond without the call provision and $1,060 is the value of the call provision (option), or $88.77.

4. Jill-in-the-Box Corp.'s bonds have a provision, which stipulates that the ratio of senior debt to total assets will never fall below 45 percent. Say the company is at the limit of that ratio and it wishes to issue still another $25 million in senior debt. How much additional equity capital must it raise to comply with this restrictive provision?

SOLUTION

The required ratio of 45 percent senior debt implies that equity must be 55 percent. So the ratio of senior debt to equity is 45 percent to 55 percent. If they desire to issue $25 million of new debt, the amount of new equity required, x, will be determined thus:

$$0.45/0.55 = \$25 \text{ million}/x$$
$$x = 25 \times 0.55/0.45 = \$30.556 \text{ million}$$

5. A security dealer in New York offers to sell you a bond currently yielding 8.5 percent. A dealer from London offers a Eurobond of equivalent risk and similar features at a yield of 8.6 percent. Which one would you buy?

SOLUTION

The New York bond will have interest semiannually and thus have an effective yield of 8.68 percent ($1.0425^2 - 1$). The Eurobonds interest is annually and the effective yield is the same as the quoted yield. The New York bond is better.

SUMMARY

The chapter gives you an overview of the global debt market with all the varieties and kinds of debt securities. There is also coverage of the contractual provisions of typical bond indentures. As a financial manager, you should be familiar with the bond market scene, the terms, and terminology so that you are able to evaluate any prospective debt offering you would like to make for your company. The chapter also covers the continuing innovation going on in the bond markets. The innovators attempt to create value by offering specialized products, which would appeal to different market segments. Innovation is also the result of trying to get around government regulations. Keep in mind that all innovations do not necessarily succeed. The trick is to understand which would create value and which is merely packaging old stuff in new colors.

LIST OF TERMS

Affirmative covenant
Call provision
Collateral trust bonds
Collateralized mortgage obligations
Cross-default clause
Debenture bonds
Defeasance
Equipment trust certificates
Eurobond
Floating-rate notes (FRN)

Indenture
Mortgage bonds
Mortgage pass-through certificates
Negative pledge clause
Original issue discount bonds
Pay-in-kind bonds (PIKs)
Project finance
Registered bonds
Sinking fund
Zero coupon bonds

EXERCISES

Fill-in Questions

1. The international market for foreign bonds is called the _____ market.

2. The document in a public issue of bonds which incorporates all the contract provisions between the borrower and lender, through an agreement with a trust company, is called a(n) _____.

3. Bondholders whose names appear on the records of the company as being owners of the bonds and to whom bond interest and principal will be paid hold _____ bonds, whereas those who must clip coupons in order to collect their interest and turn in the bond for repayment of principal hold _____ bonds.

4. A bond, which is unsecured and relies on the general credit of the corporation is called a(n) _____.

5. If an issue of bonds has a(n) _____, then if interest rates fall, the company may be able to retire them for less than their present value.

6. Provision for a periodic allocation of cash or bonds to retire debt before its maturity is called a _____.

7. The "me too" covenant in which a company undertakes not to give greater security to other parties is properly known as a _____.

8. If a company defaults to one set of creditors, then other bondholders are likely to be protected by a _____ clause.

9. Agreeing to provide copies of accounts to bondholders or to maintain a particular level of net worth are examples of _____.

10. Short-dated bonds, whose rate of interest is contingent on the rate of interest paid on Treasury bills, are called _____.

11. It is often attractive to use _____ to fund large projects which are physically isolated from the parent and can offer the lender tangible security.

12. Bonds, which have the option to pay interest in the form of either cash or more bonds, are called _____ bonds, the acronym for which is _____.

13. The _____ bonds do not pay any interests and are issued as _____.

14. The _____ are _____ and are created by companies packaging assets like home mortgages and car loans and the interest and principal payments are passed through to the investors.

15. _____ does not create stockholder value.

Problems

1. If Rudy Hill, Inc. 's 6 percent debenture bonds mature in 8 years and the yield on comparable-risk bonds is 10 percent, at what price would you expect the bonds to be selling, all else the same?

2. If Rudy Hill, Inc. has 10 percent mortgage bonds maturing in 9 years and comparable risk bonds are selling to yield 8 percent, at what price would you expect the bonds to be selling if they were non-callable? If they were callable at 105?

3. What is the value of the right to call a 10-year, 10 percent coupon bond at a price of 106 when bonds of comparable risk yield 6 percent?

4. Rudy Hill, Inc. 's bond indenture contains a provision stipulating that the ratio of senior debt to total assets must be kept at 35 percent at all times. If the company is at the limit of that ratio, determine how much more additional equity capital it must raise in order to float an additional $70 million of bonds.

Essay Questions

1. Differentiate between a debenture bond, a subordinated bond, and a mortgage bond.

2. In what sense, if any, may subordinated debt be viewed as equity capital?

3. Why does a call provision have value to the financial manager?

4. Explain what a sinking fund is and how it is most likely to work.

5. Why is the option to default on a corporate bond valuable? Explain fully.

6. When would innovations in the financial markets create value?

ANSWERS TO EXERCISES

Fill-in Questions

1. Eurobond
2. Indenture
3. Fully registered; bearer
4. Debenture
5. Call provision
6. Sinking fund
7. Negative pledge clause
8. Cross-default
9. Affirmative covenant
10. Floating-rate notes
11. Project finance
12. Pay-in-kind, PIK
13. Zero coupon; original issue discount
14. Mortgage pass-through certificates; collateralized mortgage obligations
15. Defeasance

Problems

1. Solve for PV, given: FV = $1,000, PMT = $30, n = 16, i = 5
   PV = $783.24

2. Solve for PV, given: FV = $1,000, PMT = $50, n = 18, i = 4
   PV = $1,126.59
   Value without the call = $1,126.59
   If callable   = $1,050.00

3. First find the value of the bond.
   Solve for PV, given: FV = $1,000, PMT = $50, n = 20, i = 3
   PV = Bond value = $1,297.55
   Call price = $1,060.00
   Bond value less call price = value of call provision
   Value of call provision = $1,297.55 - $1,060 = $237.55

4. 0.35/0.65 = $70 million/x; Equity needed = $70 X 0.65/0.35 = $130 million

25

Leasing

INTRODUCTION

The central focus of this chapter is the valuation of a lease to determine whether, and to what extent, it tends to enhance the value of the firm. Financial leases are leases that cover most of an asset's estimated economic life. These leases are non-cancelable by the lessee or cancelable only if the lessor is reimbursed for expected losses arising from forgone income. Financial leases are essentially considered as substitutes for buying the asset and financing the same by borrowing the money required. A continuing comparison between leasing and borrowing is made as financing alternatives. The decision rule that emerges is: a financial lease is superior to buying and borrowing if the financing provided by the lease exceeds the present value of the liability it creates.

KEY CONCEPTS IN THE CHAPTER

Terms to Know: Before you embark on an analysis of leases, you must know a variety of terms. The more important ones are summarized below:

Lessee is the renter or the user of the asset. Lessee contracts to make a series of payments to the lessor, and in return, gets to use the asset for the lease term.

Lessor is the legal owner and normally is entitled to the tax privileges of ownership like depreciation deductions or investment tax credits, if they are available. At the end of the lease period, the equipment reverts to the lessor.

Operating lease is a short-term lease, cancelable at the option of the lessee. These are usually engaged into for convenience and flexibility. Generally, this is not considered a substitute for ownership and long-term use of the asset.

Financial or full-payout leases are non-cancelable, long-term leases for most of the asset's useful life. Failure to make the lease payments can get the lessee into serious trouble, and in that sense, lease obligations are like debt obligations. This form of leasing is considered a source of financing and a substitute for debt.

Full-service or rental lease is one where the lessor maintains, insures, and pays taxes on the equipment. On the other hand, in a n*et lease* the lessee maintains, insures, and pays taxes on the property. *Sale and leaseback* is an arrangement where a firm sells an asset to the lessor and then leases it back from the buyer. *Leveraged leases* are financial leases where the lessor borrows part of the purchase price using the leased equipment as collateral.

Significance of Financial Leases: Financial leases are studied in depth because they are a source of financing; they displace debt. With financial leases, the lessee (the user) assumes the risks and rewards of ownership. Leasing displaces debt. The ownership of the asset makes a difference as to who gets the salvage value at the end of the lease period and who gets the tax privileges. When bankruptcy and reorganization occur, the lessee loses the asset's use, whereas the lessor does not. Financial leases will, normally, have to be reported in the balance sheet as equivalent ownership of the asset with the lease obligations capitalized and shown on the liability side.

Why Lease: Some motivations for leasing can make a lot of sense, while others appear dubious and imply market myopia and inefficiency. Those, which are rational and make sense include:

- Convenience,
- Cancellation options are valuable,
- Maintenance is provided,
- Tax shields may be advantageous, and
- Could help avoid alternative minimum tax.

Some dubious reasons for leasing include:

- Avoid capital expenditure controls,
- Preserves capital,
- Off-balance sheet financing; this may no longer be possible as leases must be capitalized and their estimated present values called as an asset and a liability, if they fall under certain guidelines, and
- Affects book income positively

The dubious reasons imply that markets and the investor could be fooled by appearances.

Operating Leases: Operating leases may make sense when an asset is required over an extended period and the lessor can buy and manage the asset cheaper than the lessee; for example, a truck-leasing company. The option to cancel the lease is sufficiently important to the lessee.

Valuing Financial Leases: Valuing financial leases are similar to valuing any set of cash flows. Essentially, you identify all the cash flows involved and then calculate the present values at the appropriate discount rates. Add up the present values to find the NPV; accept if the NPV is positive. For convenience, we will adopt the usual practice of analyzing a lease from the lessee's perspective. If you are interested in the lessor's perspective, all you need to do it is just reverse the signs – a positive cash flow to the lessee is negative for the lessor. The main cash flows resulting from a lease transaction are:

- At the start (time 0), the lessee saves the cost of purchasing the asset. This is the main positive cash flow for the lessee.

306

- During the lease term, the lessee promises to pay regular lease payments. These could be annual, or more frequent, and in some cases start, at time 0. The lease payments are tax-deductible.
- The lessee loses the tax privileges associated with ownership. This means that the tax deductions from depreciation are not available.
- At the end of the lease period, the lessee does not own the asset and thus, loses the remaining value of the asset.
- There may be other cash flows such as maintenance costs. These will have to be accounted for.

The basic approach to valuing the lease is to find the present value of all the above cash flows and sum them up. The only issue, which remains, is the discount rate to be used. The accepted practice is to use the after-tax borrowing rate to discount all the cash flows, except the salvage value. The salvage value may be discounted at the company cost of capital.

An alternate approach involves calculating the equivalent loan. The equivalent loan is the loan that exactly matches the lease liability at each point in time, i.e., commits the firm to exactly the same cash outflows as the lease would. Compare the financing by the lease with the financing provided by the equivalent loan and accept the lease if the value of the lease is positive.

Value of lease = cash flows from leasing - cash flows from equivalent loan

The main cash flow from leasing, in most cases, is simply the purchase price of the asset. The two approaches would give exactly the same answer. In general, a financial lease is superior to buying and borrowing if the financing provided by the lease exceeds the present value.

Financial leasing decisions are an example of the interaction between financing and investing decisions. Therefore, where subsidies arise, the adjusted net present value of the investment decision should be determined before a decision is made.

APV = NPV of the project + NPV of lease

What this suggests is that if the equipment for a project is available under lease financing, the project NPV should be adjusted to reflect any positive NPV coming out of the lease transaction. This could, in some cases, result in turning a negative NPV project into an acceptable project because of the benefits of the lease.

The evaluation methods discussed above will show that if all the factors are identical for the lessee and the lessor, then the values of the lease to the lessor and lessee would be equal (but of opposite signs). This would mean that it is not possible to have a mutually beneficial lease transaction if the lessee and the lessor have the same tax rates, the same cost of the asset, and the same discount rate. Thus, a lease would make sense only if the lessee and the lessor have different tax rates. Of course, it might also make sense if the cost of the asset or the discount rate is different; but then this is not a reason for leasing. Any such difference would qualify the

307

lessor to be a seller (lower cost of asset) of the asset or a lender (lower discount rate). In short, it is generally agreed that tax differentials drive financial leases in many cases.

WORKED EXAMPLES

1. Lean and Mean, Inc., is evaluating the lease of a minicomputer which, if purchased, would cost $150,000. Its estimated useful life is 5 years, at the end of which time it will be obsolete. The annual lease payments are $35,000, payable in six installments, the first being payable when the contract is signed. The company is in the 35 percent marginal income tax bracket. Set up a statement of cash-flow consequences of the lease contract. If Lean and Mean, Inc.'s before-tax borrowing rate on long-term debt is 12 percent, estimate the net present value (NPV) of the lease.

SOLUTION

The table below gives the cash flows and present values. Note that the depreciation schedule is contained in that portion of the table (from Chapter 6 of the text). Leasing displaces debt and the risk of the cash flows from leasing approximates the risk of the cash flows that would have been incurred had the firm borrowed. The current after-tax borrowing rate is the appropriate rate at which to evaluate the lease. That is $12(1 - 0.35) = 7.80$ percent. This is the rate used to calculate the present values. Discounting at this rate, we obtain a NPV of -$10,210.

Cash-Flows from the Lease Contract (Value of Lease to Lessee - $ 1,000)

	Year 0	Year 1	Year 2	Year 3	Year 4	Year 5
Cost of computer	150.00					
Lost depreciation tax shield	-10.50	-16.80	-10.08	-6.05	-6.05	-3.02
Lease payment	-35.00	-35.00	-35.00	-35.00	-35.00	-35.00
Tax shield of payment	12.25	12.25	12.25	12.25	12.25	12.25
Cash flow	116.75	-39.55	-32.83	-28.80	-28.80	-25.77
NPV at 7.80%	-10.21					
Tax depreciation rate	0.20	0.32	0.192	0.1152	0.1152	0.0576
Borrowing cost	12%					
Tax rate	0.35					
After-tax rate	7.80%					

Note that:
Lost depreciation tax shield = cost X depreciation rate X marginal tax rate
For year 1- Lost depreciation tax shield = 150 X 0.32 X 0.35 = 16.80

2. Calculate the equivalent loan of the lease given in problem 1.

308

SOLUTION

The equivalent loan is simply the present value of the lease cash outflows discounted at the after-tax borrowing rate. From the table above, present value of the cash out flows (exclude the cost of the computer) = $126.96. What this means is that for the same cash flows you are committing to the lease, you can actually get a loan of $126,960. As this is more than the cost of the computer, you are better off rejecting the lease.

NPV of lease = 116.75 - 126.96 = -10.21

3. What is the value of the above lease to the lessor?

SOLUTION

The cash flows to the lessor are the same as those to the lessee except the signs are reversed. Thus, the NPV to the lessor is a positive $10,210.

4. Assume the lessee's tax rate is zero. What is the value of the lease now?

SOLUTION

The table below shows the results. It is still a negative NPV deal, actually a little worse.

			Year			
	0	1	2	3	4	5
Cost of computer	150.00					
Lost depreciation tax shield	0.00	0.00	0.00	0.00	0.00	0.00
Lease payment	-35.00	-35.00	-35.00	-35.00	-35.00	-35.00
Tax shield of lease payment	0.00	0.00	0.00	0.00	0.00	0.00
Cash flow of lease	115.00	-35.00	-35.00	-35.00	-35.00	-35.00
NPV	-11.17					
Tax depreciation rate on cost	0.2000	0.3200	0.1920	0.1152	0.1152	0.0576
Required return	12.00%					
Marginal tax rate	0.00%					
After-tax discount rate	12.00%					

SUMMARY

This chapter provides an overview of the different types of leases. It then focuses on the evaluation of financial leases, which are considered a source of financing. Financial leasing can be considered as an alternative to buying the asset and borrowing the cost of the asset. Two equivalent approaches to evaluating financial leases were presented.

The evaluation of financial leases assumes the same format as the evaluation of any other cash flows. The direct cash flows are discounted at a tax-adjusted rate appropriate to the level of risk, which is typically and conveniently assumed to be the firm's present borrowing rate. The present borrowing rate is used because the lease displaces debt in the company's financial structure but has no effect on the required amount of equity financing.

The first approach to evaluating leases is to discount all the cash flows at the after-tax interest rate of the firm. The sum of these present values gives you the NPV of the lease transaction. The alternate approach computes the equivalent loan that would be supported by the cash outflows produced by the lease payments. If the equivalent loan is less than the financing required to purchase the asset, the lease would be a good deal.

LIST OF TERMS

Capital leases	Lessor (owner)
Direct lease	Leveraged leases
Equivalent loan	Net lease
Financial lease	Off-balance-sheet financing
Full-service lease	Operating lease
Lease	Sale and lease-back
Lessee	

EXERCISES

Fill-in Questions

1. The user of a leased asset is called the _____, whereas the owner of a leased asset is called the _____.

2. Leases which are short-term and cancelable during the contract period at the option of the _____ are called _____ leases.

3. Leases which are long-term or extend over the economic life of the asset and which cannot be canceled or can be canceled only if the _____ is reimbursed for losses are called _____ leases.

4. When the lessor promises to maintain and insure the leased assets and pay property taxes on it, they have taken out a(n) _____ lease.

5. When the _____ agrees to maintain the leased asset, insure it, and pay properly taxes due on it, the lease is known as a net lease.

6. When the lessee identifies the equipment to be used and arranges for the leasing company to buy it from the manufacturer, the signed contract is called a(n) _____ lease.

7. When a firm sells an asset it owns and leases it back to the buyer, the arrangement is known as _____.

8. When lessors borrow part of the purchase price of a leased asset and use the lease contract as security for the loan, the entire financing scheme is known as a(n) _____ lease.

9. Generally accepted accounting standards no longer allow _____ financing; rather, lease payments of _____ leases must be _____, which is to say that the present value of the lease payments must be estimated and shown as debt on the right-hand side of the balance sheet.

10. A(n) _____ is one that exactly matches the lease liability, or to put it another way, one which commits the firm to exactly the same cash outlays as a lease would.

Problems

1. H. L. Mean, Inc., decided to lease additional computer equipment for the next 5 years. The deal requires annual lease payments of $66,000 commencing on the day the contract is signed. Had the equipment been purchased, it would have cost $320,000. The company's marginal tax bracket is 35 percent, and its long-term borrowing rate is 10 percent. Calculate the net present value of the lease and its equivalent loan.

2. Provide an equivalent loan analysis for the situation of problem 1.

3. H. L. Mean, Inc.'s treasurer suddenly realizes that H. L. Mean, Inc. is unlikely to pay taxes in the next five years. How does this affect the NPV of the lease?

Essay Questions

1. How can it be said that financial leases are a source of financing? Explain fully.

2. What is meant by off-balance-sheet financing?

3. In what sense may lease payments be viewed as the equivalent of interest payments?

4. Some people say that long-term lease obligations should be regarded as debt, even though they may not appear on the balance sheet. What rationale can you give for this point of view?

5. List and explain some of the reasons that make leasing dubious and offer an explanation for each item.

6. Usually the direct cash flows from the lease are assumed to be safe and are discounted at roughly the same rate of interest as obtainable on a secured bond issued by the lessee. Why?

ANSWERS TO EXERCISES

Fill-in Questions

1. Lessee; lessor
2. Lessee; operating
3. Lessor; financial
4. Full-service
5. Lessee

6. Direct
7. Sale and lease-back
8. Leveraged
9. Off-balance-sheet; financial; capitalized
10. Equivalent loan

Problems

1. The analysis is provided in the table below. The NPV is negative (-$1,610). Reject the lease.

Cash Flow Analysis of the Lease (in $1,000s)

	Year 0	Year 1	Year 2	Year 3	Year 4	Year 5
Cost of computer	320.00					
Lost deprn tax shield	-22.40	-35.84	-21.50	-12.90	-12.90	-6.45
Lease payment	-66.00	-66.00	-66.00	-66.00	-66.00	-66.00
Tax shield of pmt	23.10	23.10	23.10	23.10	23.10	23.10
Cash flow	254.70	-78.74	-64.40	-55.80	-55.80	-49.35
NPV at 6.5%	-1.60					
Tax deprn rate	0.2	0.32	0.192	0.1152	0.1152	0.0576
Borrowing cost	10					
Tax rate	0.35					
After-tax rate	6.50					

2. The equivalent loan is equal to the present value of the cash out flows produced by the lease.

Equivalent Loan Analysis (in $1,000s)

	Year 0	Year 1	Year 2	Year 3	Year 4	Year 5
Lost deprn tax shield	-22.40	-35.84	-21.50	-12.90	-12.90	-6.45
Lease payment	-66.00	-66.00	-66.00	-66.00	-66.00	-66.00
Tax shield of pmt	23.10	23.10	23.10	23.10	23.10	23.10
Cash flow	-65.30	-78.74	-64.40	-55.80	-55.80	-49.35

Present value at 6.5% $321,601

Equivalent Loan = $321,601. Reject the lease.

3. The analysis is given in the table below. The NPV of the lease is positive at $3,810. The
    company's zero tax rate now makes the lease beneficial.

	Year 0	Year 1	Year 2	Year 3	Year 4	Year 5
			(in $ 1,000s)			
Cost of computer	320.00					
Lost deprn tax shield	0.00	0.00	0.00	0.00	0.00	0.00
Lease payment	-66.00	-66.00	-66.00	-66.00	-66.00	46.00
Tax shield of pmt.	0.00	0.00	0.00	0.00	0.00	0.00
Cash flow	254.00	-66.00	-66.00	-66.00	-66.00	-66.00
NPV at 10%	3.81					
Tax deprn rate	0.20	0.32	0.192	0.1152	0.1152	0.0576
Borrowing cost	10					
Tax rate	0					
After-tax rate	10.00					

26

Managing Risk

INTRODUCTION

Risk management through hedging is the focus of this chapter. Thanks to financial innovation and development of financial derivatives, corporate financial managers have considerable flexibility as to the kind of risk they want to be exposed to and the kind of risk they want to hedge. Hedging offsets risk and is accomplished with options, futures, and often with customer designed derivatives. One of the primary purposes of hedging is to control individual risks thereby controlling a firm's total risk. Such hedging techniques are part and parcel of today's financial manager's tasks. The point of hedging is to minimize the risks the manager is not equipped to handle. The object is to find the number of units of an asset that is needed to offset changes in the value of an obligation. Risk reduction of controllable risk allows financial managers to worry about the things that are worth worrying about and they are in the best position to handle.

KEY CONCEPTS IN THE CHAPTER

Insurance: Insurance as a way of reducing or hedging risk has been around for a long time. One simple way of hedging some kinds of risk is to go out and buy insurance. However, the kind of risk, which can be insured, is rather limited. Mostly it depends on the type of risk and the extent to which insurance companies have a relative advantage in dealing with it. It is unlikely that you will want to insure risks, which they find difficult to assess, or where the presence of insurance gives you less incentive to reduce the risk yourself.

Insurance companies have the following relative advantages:

- They are skilled at estimating risks.
- They are skilled at advising on reducing risk.
- They can pool (or diversify) risks.

Insurance companies also have some disadvantages. These include:

- They have to overcome their administrative costs, including legal costs of disputes.
- *Adverse selection* means that those at greater risk are more likely to insure.
- *Moral hazard* means that those who insure have less incentive to reduce their exposure to risk.

Homemade insurance like options or future contracts might work better in some cases.

Hedging with Futures: Futures, forwards, swaps, and options are ideal hedging tools. When a financial manager hedges with futures, he or she agrees to deliver or accept a specified "commodity" at a specified price, location, and time. Futures contracts allow one to hedge the risk of a present commodity by buying (the long hedge) or selling (the short hedge) the contract for future delivery. This is typically done against the present or spot price. Excess demand for or supply of futures contracts is absorbed by speculators. Futures contracts are important for the management of physical commodities, exchange rates, and interest rates. Futures contracts allow financial managers to fix today's prices on commodities that will not be available until some time in the future. Each day futures contracts are marked to market to determine profits or losses.

When financial futures are bought, one does not pay for the security immediately although margin is needed (one can earn interest on the purchase price). Any income that accrues on the futures contracts is not available to the purchaser. When one is dealing in commodity futures, payment is not made immediately for the entire contract, and interest may be earned. In addition, there are no storage fees for the purchaser of the contract, for the commodity is bought to be delivered in the future. The convenience yield is forgone, however, when one buys commodity futures because the commodity is not available for immediate use.

Setting up a futures hedge is similar to any other hedge: You identify your risk exposure. For example, let us say that you are expected to cotton fiber in November. You can find the futures contracts with the closest relationship to cotton and establish an offsetting position in the futures market. In this case, you can actually use cotton fiber futures and buy them for delivery in November. The hedge delta will be nearly 1. If the futures are not exactly identical to the actual exposure you have *basis risk*. When basis risk exists, delta may not be 1.0.

Here are some important points about futures and futures hedging:

- Futures contracts are available for many commodities, foreign currencies, stock indexes, interest rate instruments (T-bills and T bonds).
- Futures contracts are standardized as to the date, quantity, and specifications of the underlying asset.
- They are traded through organized exchanges and you are required to keep margin deposits as security for your position.
- Speculators are essential to futures contract markets because they take up the imbalances between futures contract supply and future contract demand.
- Spot prices are prices for immediate delivery of the contracts.
- As the delivery date for futures contracts approaches, the contracts become more and more like spot contracts and the prices approach the spot price.

Price of Futures: The price of a futures contract will have a definite relationship with the spot price of the same commodity or financial instrument. Financial futures, for example, differ from buying exactly the same item in the spot market in that the buyer does not pay for the security at the time the order is placed and can earn interest during the interim. The buyer also does not receive dividends or interest normally paid to the holder of the actual instrument. Thus we get:

$$\frac{\text{Futures price}}{(1+r_f)^t} = \text{spot price} - \text{PV(dividends or interest payments forgone)}$$

Foreign exchange futures are important to firms dealing in international markets. The price of a currency future will be related to the spot exchange rate as follows:

$$\frac{\text{Futures price of foreign currency}}{1+r_\$} = \text{spot price} - \text{PV(foregone interest on foreign currency}$$

$$\text{PV(forgone interest)} = (r_{fc} \times \text{spot price})I(1+r_{fc})$$

Commodity fixtures are more complicated than financial futures. The buyer of a commodity future earns interest on the money, which is the deferred payment and shifts the cost of storage to another party. However, the holder of the commodity futures contracts have no convenience yield. Thus the relationship between spot and future prices for commodities can be written as:

$$\frac{\text{Futures price}}{(1+r_f)^t} = \text{spot price} + \text{PV(storage costs)} - \text{PV(convenience yield)}$$

$$= \text{spot price} - \text{PV(net convenience yield)}$$

Forward Contracts: A high degree of liquidity exists in futures markets because futures contracts are standardized and mature on a limited number of specified dates each year. But what about financial managers who wish to customize futures contracts to suit their special needs or make deals that mature on dates other than those found on organized futures markets? The answer is to construct a forward contract, which is the equivalent of a homemade futures contract. The forward rate agreement (FRA) is one way to customize futures contracts. Most forward contracts arise from dealings in foreign exchange currency markets. A financial manager may manufacture a forward loan by borrowing short-term and lending long-term. Such homemade forward contracts may occur either in foreign exchange or in loans. For example, we can get a 1-year forward interest rate by borrowing for 2 years and lending (depositing the money) for one year. The relationship can be expressed as:

$$\text{1 year forward interest rate} = \frac{(1+2 \text{ year borrowing rate})^2}{1+ 1 \text{ year lending rate}} - 1$$

Swaps: Often financial managers who deal in international markets are better known in one country than another. Their firm may issue debt in the country in which it is well known, receive that currency, and then swap it for another country's currency. This is a currency swap. Swaps also exist on loans in which a fixed interest-rate loan is exchanged for a floating-rate loan, or a floating-rate loan is subsequently tied to different base rates.

How to Hedge: There are a number of general principles involved in hedging. The most important one is how to think about the relationship between the risk you want to reduce and the kinds of contracts available to hedge it with. It is likely that no contract will give a perfect hedge: There will generally be residual (or basis) risk between the risk and the hedge. Hedging commodity prices, exchange rates, interest rates, and stock market levels are all very similar. Many risks change continuously through time, so their hedges have to be adjusted as a dynamic hedge quite frequently through time.

Here are the steps involved in setting up a hedge:

- Find the relationship between the commodity or asset position (say, A) you want hedged and the futures contract (B). You can study the historic relationship between the two and it may be expressed as follows:

$$\text{Expected change in value of A} = a + \delta \text{ (change in value of B)}$$

- Delta (δ) measures the sensitivity of A to changes in the value of B.

- It is called the *hedge ratio*. It is the number of units of B which should be purchased to hedge the liability of A.

- Duration hedging is very similar. Duration measures sensitivity to a parallel shift in interest rates (chapter 23).

The Role and Use of Derivatives: Derivatives provide an extremely flexible set of instruments, which enable many kinds of risks to be hedged. They can also be used for speculative purposes, and this has brought some companies into serious trouble and caused questions to be asked about the derivatives markets themselves. The chapter provides some commonsense guidelines for making sure you only use derivatives in a way, which helps your company.

WORKED EXAMPLES

1. John B. Rosso has $20 million of Glory Be! stock and that he wants your help in determining how much of the Standard & Poor's 500 Index (S&P 500) he should buy in order to hedge the market-related risk to which he is exposed. The historical relation between the stock's change in price and the change in price of the market index is

$$\text{Monthly change in value of Wild Gyrations} = a + \delta \text{ (monthly changes in market index)}$$
$$= 0.05 + 1.5 \text{(monthly changes in market index)}$$

SOLUTION

To hedge the short sale, John must set aside $30,000,0000 (1.5 x $20,000,000). This minimizes his risk in this short position.

2. The S&P 500 stock index 6-month futures are trading at 1,250 and the spot S&P 500 index is at 1,226. The 6-month Treasury bill rate is 6 percent, and the average annual yield on stocks is 2 percent. Are these rates consistent?

SOLUTION

$$\frac{\text{Future price}}{(1+r_f)^t} = \text{spot price} - \text{PV(dividends)}$$

Semiannual T-bill yield = $(1.06)^{1/2}$ = 2.96%

Semiannual dividend yield = 2%/2 = 1%

Completing the formula, we have:

Futures price = 1,250/1.0296 = 1,214.06
Expected spot price = Spot price - PV(dividends)
= 1,226 - [(1,226 x 0.01)/1.0296]
= 1,214.09

The prices are very close. there is no arbitrage opportunity.

3. Handy Motor Company is able to borrow at an annual rate 8 percent for 2 years, using its automobile loans as collateral. The loans are made from Handy Acceptance Corporation, a wholly owned subsidiary. It estimates that its overall return from car loans is 12 percent, once the return on the loans, 6.9 percent, and economies realized from manufacturing costs are factored into the analysis. If the average automobile loan is 3 years in length, what forward interest rate is implied by this homemade forward contract?

SOLUTION

$$\text{Forward interest rate} = \frac{(1 + 3\text{ year rate})^3}{(1 + 2\text{ year rate})^2} - 1 = \frac{1.12^3}{1.08^2} - 1$$

= 23.85 percent

4. MPG Motor Company plans to build a parts plant in Germany. It finds it can get better financing terms if it borrows in the United States than in any other country. It issues $15 million of 5-year, 10 percent notes in the U.S. capital markets. Simultaneously, it enters into another agreement with its bank, the details of which are: (1) It is to swap its dollar liabilities (the U.S.

319

notes) into deutsche marks; (2) the bank pays MPG sufficient dollars to service the debt; and (3) MPG agrees to make annual payments in deutsche marks to the bank. What is the result of this currency swap?

SOLUTION

	Year 0		Years 1 - 4		Year 5	
	$	DM	$	DM	$	DM
Issue dollar notes	+15	0	-1.5	0	-16.5	0
Swap $s for DMs	-15	30.0	+1.5	-3	+16.5	-32.52
Net cash flow	0	30.0	0	-3	0	-32.52

MPG made a 10 percent loan an 8.35 percent loan by engaging in the swap: [(32.51/30.0) - 1] x 100 = 8.35 percent.

SUMMARY

Managers and businesses are in the business of taking risks. However, they are better of taking the risks they are equipped to handle and where they have expertise and skill. Hedging enables businesses to reduce the risk which take away from their basic business advantage. Managers can choose the risk they want to reduce or hedge. They can use either insurance or hedge with hedging tools available in the market.

The hedge is established by buying futures, forwards, swaps, or even options contracts. The use of all these is explained in the chapter. Because hedging mitigates the risk of individual assets, the firm's collective risk is also mitigated. Hedging tactics are important because they allow financial managers to concentrate their energies on decisions whose risks are not easily hedged or diversified away.

LIST OF TERMS

Adverse selection
Arbitrageurs
Basis risk
Convenience yield
Counterparty
Delta
Derivative instruments
Forward contract
Forward rate agreement (FRA)
Futures contract
Hedge

Hedge ratio
Immunized
Jump risk
Long hedge
Marked to market
Moral hazard
Net convenience yield
Short hedge
Spot price
Storage costs
Swap

EXERCISES

Fill-in Questions

1. A(n) _____ offsets risks by trading assets or liabilities for other assets.

2. _____ measures the sensitivity of an asset's value to changes in the value of the liability.

3. Such securities as futures, forwards, swaps, and options are called _____ instruments, because their value depends on the value of other assets.

4. The problem that insurance tends to be bought by those most at risk is called the problem of _____.

5. The problem that once you have insurance you have less incentive to reduce the risks you take is called _____.

6. _____ contracts are contracts to buy or sell commodities or securities in the future on terms fixed today which are bought and sold on organized exchanges.

7. Futures contracts are _____ daily to determine profits and losses.

8. The delta of the relationship between the risk and the hedging instrument establishes the _____ for the hedge.

9. When a hedge has been established, the position is said to have been _____ against that particular source of risk.

10. When the prices of two commodities are not likely to move exactly together, a perfect hedge is not possible. The remaining risk is called _____ and the hedge ratio is greater than, less than) _____ one.

11. Selling futures contracts is a(n) _____.

12. Buying futures contracts is a(n) _____.

13. Today's price of a commodity is called the _____.

14. The discounted futures price equals the spot price plus the present value of_____ and minus the present value of the _____.

15. The difference between the convenience yield and the storage cost is called the _____.

321

16. Financial managers who wish to trade in futures contracts which are non-standardized or which mature at dates other than those traded in the futures markets must use _____.

17. A(n) _____ is an agreement with a bank in which an interest rate today is locked in for a loan to be delivered from the bank at some future date.

18. If significant price differentials exist between forward and futures markets, _____ will buy and sell contracts so that such discrepancies will be eliminated.

19. Firms that issue debt in the country in which they are well known, receive that currency, and then exchange it for another country's currency are said to have engaged in a currency.

20. The persons or companies taking the two sides of a swap transaction are referred to as _____.

21. Many insurance risks are _____ and are probably the type of risk that would like to have covered by insurance rather than by hedging.

Problems

1. Grace Mully is your friend and she tells you how she shorted $30 million of MGK.com stocks. She wants your help in determining how much of the Standard & Poor's 500 Index (S&P 500) he should buy in order to hedge the market-related risk to which he is exposed. The index stands at 1,200. The historical relation between the stock's change in price and the change in price of the market index is

    Monthly change in value of Wild Gyrations = $a + \delta$(monthly changes in market index)
    $$= 0.35 + 2.2(\text{monthly changes in market index})$$

2. ABC Corp. able to borrow at 10 percent for 1 year, using its credit card receivables as collateral. It estimates that its overall return from the credit card loans is 14 percent, once the return on the loans. If the average automobile loan is 2 years in length, what forward interest rate is implied by this homemade forward contract?

3. RainDeer Corp. plans to modernize its German manufacturing facility. It finds it can get better financing terms if it issues $25 million of 6-year, 12 percent notes in the U.S. capital markets. Simultaneously, it enters into another agreement with its bank, the details of which are: (1) to swap its dollar liabilities (the U.S. notes) into deutsche marks; (2) for the bank to pay RainDeer sufficient dollars to service the debt; and (3) RainDeer agrees to make annual payments in deutsche marks to the bank. Demonstrate the "numbers" of this currency swap.

Essay Questions

1. Discuss the statement. " Managers are paid to take risk.".

2. Describe the difference between adverse selection and moral hazard, and explain why they cause problems for insurance companies.

3. Put in words how financial managers may hedge with financial futures, and use a typical example to demonstrate the concepts you raise.

4. Demonstrate how forward contracts may be constructed to suit a particular need you can think of.

5. Discuss the statement. "Derivatives have improved the hedging opportunities for managers."

6. Your company is a one of the largest packaged food producer in the world and consumes large quantities of corn, wheat, pork bellies, etc. Devise a hedging strategy for the firm, explaining why you might want to hedge the risk in your primary supplies.

ANSWERS TO EXERCISES

Fill-in Questions

1. Hedge
2. Delta
3. Derivative
4. Adverse selection
5. Moral hazard
6. Futures
7. Marked to market
8. Hedge ratio
9. Immunized
10. Basis risk; less than
11. Short hedge
12. Long hedge
13. Spot price
14. Storage costs; convenience yield
15. Net convenience yield
16. Forward contract
17. Forward rate agreement (FRA)
18. Arbitrageurs
19. Swap
20. Counterparties
21. Jump risk.

Problems

1. To hedge the short sale, she must set aside $66,000,000 (2.2 x $30,000,000).

2. Forward interest rate = $[(1.14)^2/1.10] - 1 = 18.15$ percent

3.

	Year 0		Years 1 - 5		Year 6	
	$	DM	$	DM	$	DM
Issue dollar notes	+25	0	-3.0	0	-28.0	0
Swap $5 for DMs	-25	50.0	+3.0	-5.55	+28.0	-53.20
Net cash flow	0	50.0	0	-5.55	0	-53.20

RainDeer made a 12 percent loan a 6.40 percent loan by engaging in the swap: [(53.20/50.0) - 1] x 100 = 6.40 percent.

27
Managing International Risks

INTRODUCTION

This chapter covers management of risks brought on by international exposure of one kind or another. Any firm dealing with overseas operations faces risk on three additional dimensions: Currency risk, interest rate differences and political risk. An understanding of the exchange markets is the first step in understanding exchange risk. The chapter begins with a description of the foreign exchange markets. It then goes on to explain the basic exchange rate relationships. This is followed by sections on hedging currency risk and political risk.

KEY CONEPTS IN THE CHAPTER

Foreign Exchange Markets: The foreign exchange market is global and has no central trading place. Trading takes place all over the world, though most of the trading is done in centers like New York, London, and Frankfurt. The daily volume of currency transactions in these markets exceeds over 1 trillion dollars. International banks and some large multinational corporations are the major players in currency markets. Transactions can be spot or forward. Spot transactions are for immediate delivery and forward transactions are completed at future points in time at prices agreed now.

An e*xchange rate* is the price of one currency in terms of another. A *direct quote* (for Americans) is the dollar price of 1 unit of the foreign currency. For example $0.53/D Marks and $1.54/British pound are direct quotes. An *indirect quote* is given as units of foreign currency needed to buy one dollar (e.g. DM 1.89 /$). Indirect quotes are commonly used for most currencies. The British pound sterling and the Euro are the exceptions and are quoted in direct terms. There is also an organized futures market for currencies. Futures are (as we saw in chapter 26) standardized forward contracts and are available only for the major currencies. You can also buy options on the futures contracts. Banks sell custom designed option contracts on currencies. There are also more complicated contracts combining features of a forward contract and options.

Some Basic Relationships: If individuals are not worried about risk and there are no barriers to international trade, exchange rates would be governed by four fundamental relationships. These relationships cover the current spot and forward exchange rates, the interest rates in the two countries, the inflation rates in the two countries, and the expected future spot rate. The four relationships are interdependent. The difference in interest rates between two currencies is equal to the difference in the expected inflation rates, which in turn is equal to the expected change in spot rate. This change in spot rate is equal to the difference between the forward and spot rates, which in turn is equal to the difference in interest rates between two different currencies. These relationships are based on the economic argument that the real rate of return on invested capital among all countries tends to equilibrate even though nominal interest rates may differ on account of inflation.

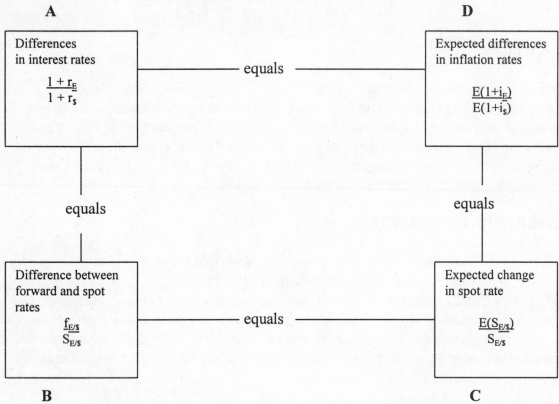

A

Differences
in interest rates

$$\frac{1 + r_E}{1 + r_\$}$$

— equals —

D

Expected differences
in inflation rates

$$\frac{E(1+i_E)}{E(1+i_\$)}$$

equals

equals

B

Difference between
forward and spot
rates

$$\frac{f_{E/\$}}{S_{E/\$}}$$

— equals —

C

Expected change
in spot rate

$$\frac{E(S_{E/\$})}{S_{E/\$}}$$

Figure 1 – Four basic Relationships for the Euro and the Dollar

These relationships are reviewed below.

<u>Interest rates and exchange rates (boxes A and B):</u> This is known as the *interest-rate parity*. The difference between interest rates must equal the differential between the forward and spot exchange rates. This relationship seems to hold pretty well when taxes and government regulations are absent. This is the case in international markets (Eurocurrency markets). If the relationship does not hold, one can make money by borrowing in one currency, lending in the other, and covering the exchange rate risk with forward contracts.

<u>The forward premium and changes in spot rates (boxes B and C):</u> This relationship (the *expectations theory*) implies that the expected change in spot rate should equal the current forward premium (or discount). This theory ignores risk. On average forward rate equals future spot rate. The relationship may not hold exactly and the forward price may be an over or underestimate.

<u>Changes in the exchange rate and inflation rates (boxes C and D):</u> This is the *law of one price*. If goods flow freely across borders, then the prices should roughly be equal across countries. This

is often called the *purchasing power parity* (PPP) implying that similar goods should be priced roughly the same in each country. This also means that the differences in inflation rates get reflected in exchange rates. That is if the inflation rate is 3 percent in the US and 2 percent in Germany, the mark will appreciate by about 1 percent or the number of marks required to buy a dollar will fall by about 1 percent. The PPP holds broadly in the long run, but short run deviations are not uncommon. The estimated differences in relative inflation rates can be seen as rough estimates of changes in spot rates of exchange.

Interest rates and inflation rates (boxes D and A): Capital tends to flow to its highest and best use and in equilibrium expected real return on capital should be the same in different countries. Thus the money rate of interest will reflect expected inflation and differences in money rates should equal the expected differences in inflation rates.

The four relationships in practice:

Interest-rate parity: Works well in international markets, but not so well in domestic markets because of government regulations and taxes.

The expectation theory of forward rates: On average the forward rate equals the future spot rate; however it often overshoots one way or the other. Forward rate is seen as a better predictor than exchange forecasting services.

The law of one price: Generally holds well over the long term. It is also seen that in cases where there are large differences in inflation are there as between Brazil and the US, the adjustment is more rapid.

Capital market equilibrium: High inflation countries have higher interest rates and real rates seem to converge, though in the short-term a disparity in real rates might exist especially where government regulations and taxes are significant factors. Part of the problem in testing this theory is that we cannot observe expected inflation rates and expected real rates.

Currency Risk: Most companies engage in some form of exchange risk hedging. Exchange risk is often classified as either *transaction exposure* or *economic exposure*. Transaction exposure the risk of unfavorable exchange rate movements affecting known commitments in foreign currency. For example, a company, which is expecting a payment in a foreign currency from an export transaction, is facing a transaction exposure. Transaction exposure can be easily hedged through different means as discussed below. Economic exposure is refers to the overall impact on the business from changes in exchange rates. This is harder to quantify and managing this risk should be part of the firm's overall global business strategy.

Transaction exposure can be hedged using futures or forward contracts. Hedging can also be done using options, which protect against adverse currency movements without affecting any possible gains form favorable movement of exchange rate. In theory one can also hedge by lending or borrowing in the foreign currency depending on the direction of the exposure (borrow if you are expecting a foreign currency cash flow in future; lend if you have to pay in foreign currency at a future date.) If the interest rate parity holds, hedging by forward/futures contracts or through lending/borrowing should give essentially the same results.

The main advantage of hedging transaction exposure is that the firm is free to concentrate on the main business. Hedging can also be done at a relatively low cost. Foreign exchange markets are reasonably efficient in the major currencies. This means that the cost of hedging is likely to be low. Remember that cost of hedging is not the difference between today's spot rate and forward rate, but the expected spot rate and the forward rate.

International Investment Decisions: Overseas investments are evaluated by discounting estimated cash flows at the opportunity cost of capital with adjustments for subsidized financing or other effects. There are two ways to calculate net present value. One converts the foreign currency into the home currency and discounts the cash flows at the domestic opportunity cost of capital. This method requires a forecast of foreign exchange rates. The other method discounts foreign investments at the foreign currency cost of capital and converts the result into the domestic currency. The latter method implicitly assumes that the currency flows are hedged. The two approaches to evaluating foreign projects are summarized below.

	Approach 1	Approach 2
Step 1	Estimate cash flows in foreign currency	Estimate cash flows in foreign currency
Step 2	Convert to home currency using forecasted exchange rates	Calculate present value using the foreign currency discount rate)
Step 3	Calculate present value using the domestic discount rate	Convert to home currency using the current spot rate

Approach 1 requires exchange rates forecast, while approach 2 does not. The forward rates could be used as the forecast for future spot rates.

The Cost of Capital for Foreign Investment: The cost of capital for foreign projects was discussed in chapter 9. The basic approach is to calculate the beta for the foreign project relative to the company's *home market index* and then calculate the home currency required rate of return. This rate of return can then be converted into the foreign required rate of return using the following relationship:

$$\frac{1 + \text{home currency return}}{1 + \text{home currency interest rate}} = \frac{1 + \text{foreign currency return}}{1 + \text{foreign currency interest rate}}$$

Remember that diversification is valuable and international diversification may be even more valuable. In general, it is wiser to adjust estimated cash flows for foreign risks than to adjust the discount rate.

Political Risk: In a general sense, political risk is not confined to foreign investments. Businesses always face the risk of unanticipated government action, which affect their business adversely. The important difference about foreign political risk, the risk arises from the fact that your company is a foreign company in that country and may be treated differently because it is a foreign company. The extreme case of political risk is the risk of expropriation. If foreign governments change the rules after you have made your investments, your business profitability gets affected.

The key to "managing" political risk is understanding the nature of the risk and then structure the business, its operations and financing in a way that the probability of adverse foreign government action is reduced or if any adverse action takes place, the effect on the business value is minimal.

WORKED EXAMPLES

1. The Wall Street Journal reported the following spot and forward rates:

	Spot Rates	6 - month forward rate
German Mark	DM1.93/$	1.90
Japanese Yen	Y122.1/$	118.8
British Pound	$1.558/pound	1.561

Calculate the forward premium (discount) for each of the currencies.

SOLUTION

The forward premium (discount) for each currency can be calculated as follows:

$$\text{Forward premium (discount)} = \frac{\text{spot rate} - \text{forward rate}}{\text{forward rate}} \times \frac{12}{\text{months to expiration}}$$

Please note that this is the formula used for indirect quotes. For direct quotes, the premium would be measured as a percent of the spot rate and the sign would be reversed. The premium is always reported as an annualized number.

$$\text{Premium for German mark} = \frac{1.93 - 1.90}{1.93} \times 2 = 3.11 \text{ percent}$$

$$\text{Premium for Japanese yen} = \frac{122.1 - 118.8}{12.1} \times 2 = 5.41 \text{ percent}$$

$$\text{Premium for British pound} = \frac{\text{forward rate - spot rate}}{\text{spot rate}} \times 2 = \frac{1.561 - 1.558}{1.558} \times 2$$

$$= 0.39 \text{ percent}$$

Note that the quote for the pound is in direct terms and the formula was reversed to reflect that.

2. Use the spot exchange rates given in problem 1 and check if the interest rate parity holds or not given the following 6 month interest rates:

US dollar interest rate	5.60 percent
Germany	2.50
Japan	1.00
Britain	5.25 percent

SOLUTION

According to interest rate parity, the relationship among the spot, forward and interest rates can be written as:

$$\frac{\text{forward rate}}{\text{spot rate}} = \frac{1 + \text{foreign interest rate}}{1 + \text{dollar interest rate}}$$

We can write the foreign interest rate $= \dfrac{\text{forward rate} \times (1 + \text{dollar interest rate})}{\text{spot rate}} - 1$

This is the formula for indirect quotes. For direct quotes, the spot rate becomes the numerator and the forward rate is the denominator. Also, note that the interest rate should be for the period of the forward contract. So the dollar rate should be: 5.6/2 = 2.8 percent

German interest rate as per interest parity = [(1.90x1.028)/1.93] – 1 = 1.2 percent/6 months
= 2.4 percent (annual)

Japanese interest rate = [(118.8 x 1.028)/122.1] – 1 = 0.022 percent/6 months
= 0.044 percent (annual)

The British interest rate = [(1.558x1.028)/1.561] – 1 = 2.6 percent (6 months)
= 5.2 percent (annual)

None of the interest rates reported matches the ones calculated by the interest rate parity. The British and the German rates are close enough to say that but for transaction costs, the interest parity holds. The Japanese rate deviates quite a bit from the one calculated by the interest rate parity.

3. The one-year dollar interest rate is 5.6 percent. The one-year spot and forward rate for the Euro is $1.02 and $1.04. Estimate the one-year Euro interest rate.

SOLUTION

Using the interest rate parity relationship, we can write the Euro interest rate as:

$$= [(1.02 \times 1.056)/1.04] - 1 = 3.57 \text{ percent}$$

4. The expected annual inflation in Mexico is 5 percent. The expected inflation for the US is 1.5 percent. If the spot rate for the peso is 3.4 peso/\$, estimate the expected 1-year future spot rate.

SOLUTION

$$\text{Expected spot rate} = \frac{(1 + \text{inflation rate for Mexico}) \times (1 + \text{spot rate})}{(1 + \text{inflation rate for US})} = \frac{1.05 \times 3.4}{1.015}$$
$$= 3.517 \text{ peso}$$

5. Dos Amigos Brewery (DAB) exports Mexican beer to the United States. They expect to receive a payment of \$525,000 in about 3 months time from their wholesaler in Texas. The spot and forward rates for peso are 3.4 peso/\$ and 3.52 peso/\$. DAB has banking relationship with a Houston bank and the bank is willing to lend money to DAB at the US prime rate of 8 percent. DAB's cost of funds in Mexico is 10 percent. Suggest two ways of hedging DAB's dollar exposure. Compare the cash flows resulting from each hedging approach.

SOUTION

DAB can hedge by either: i) selling dollar forward or borrowing from its bank and converting the dollars at the spot rate and pay back the bank using its dollar cash flow 3 months from now. The cash flows of the two approaches are shown below:

Hedging with forward contract:

DAB sells \$525,000 forward at 3.52 pesos/\$. Cash flow in 3 months = 525,000 x 3.52
$$= 1,848,000 \text{ pesos}$$

Present value of the cash flow (annual cost of 10%, quarterly cost = 2.5%) = 1,848,000/1.025
$$= 1,802,927 \text{ pesos}$$

Hedging through bank loans

DAB borrows the present value of \$525,000 to be received in 3 months. The loan amount is then converted into pesos now using the spot rate. The loan is paid off by the dollars received in 3 months. First, calculate the loan amount. Annual interest rate of 8 percent converts to 2 percent/quarter.

331

Loan amount   = $525,000/1.02 = $514,706
Peso cash flow = 514,706 x 3.4 = 1,750,000 pesos

DAB is better off with the forward contract hedging. Its loan rate in the US is too high relative to its cost of funds in Mexico. There appears to be a deviation from the interest rate parity.

SUMMARY

This chapter covered the basics of managing the risks associated with international operations. International operations add three additional elements of risk to a company's business: risk caused by changes in exchange rates, risk caused by different interest rates in different countries and political risk. Financial managers should understand the nature of each of these risks. The nature and complexity of each element of risk will be a function of the type of the business, the size of the firm and the nature of international operations.

Understanding the workings of foreign exchange market is a necessary first step to understanding exchange rate risk. There are four basic economic relationships, which govern the changes in exchange rates. These relationships link: the spot and forward exchange rates, the interest rates and the inflation rates. The relationships ignore investor' risk aversion, transaction costs, taxes and other form of government intervention and are therefore not empirically perfect. However, they are reasonable accounts of the relationships involved and are useful for anyone interested in the direction and magnitude of changes in exchange rates. Financial managers would do well to learn the four basic relationships or parity theories as they are often called.

Exchange rate changes affect cash flows of businesses involved in international operations. Businesses are exposed to two types of exchange risk: transaction exposure and economic exposure. Transaction exposure is the exposure given by known or committed transactions, is quantifiable and can be, in most cases, fully hedged. The cost of hedging should be seen in terms of expected future spot rates rather than current spot rates. Economic exposure, on the other hand, is the long and medium term impact on the firm's business caused by the changes of exchange rates. This is difficult to quantify and hedge. The best approach to managing economic exposure is to treat it as part of the firm's overall risk and develop strategies to control and minimize the impact of the exposure.

International capital investment decisions are no different from any other investment decision. You accept positive NPV projects. The only complexity is that you have cash flows in a foreign currency and these need to be evaluated using the "foreign discount' rate. Alternately, you can convert the cash flows into your home currency cash flows and use the home currency discount rate.

The last part of the chapter discusses political risk. Foreign operations are subject to an extra dimension of political risk because it is possible that a foreign company might be treated differently than a domestic firm in the same business. The key to managing political risk is to understand it fully and then design the business operations and financing structure to reflect and minimize the effect of any adverse political action. The nature and level of political risk is a function of not only the country involved but also the industry and the current economic and political situation in the country.

LIST OF TERMS

Direct quote
Economic exposure
Eurocurrency market
Expectations theory of exchange rates
Forward market
Indirect quote

Interest rate parity theory
Law of one price
Purchasing power parity
Spot rate of exchange
Transaction exposure

EXERCISES

Fill-in Questions

1. An exchange rate quotation for the price of a currency for immediate delivery is known as

   _____.

2. Financial managers who buy and sell currency for future delivery do it in the
   _____ market for foreign currencies.

3. The relationship between the interest-rate differential and the annual forward premium or discount is known as the _____

4. The _____ theory of exchange rates says that the percentage difference between forward exchange rates and spot exchange rates is equal to the expected change in the spot rate.

5. The _____ suggests that expected changes in the spot exchange rate is approximated by estimated differences in relative _____ rates.

6. The international market for short-term loans that is virtually free of government regulation is called the _____ market.

7. Most currency quotations are given as _____ quote, and give the number of units of foreign currency needed to buy one United States dollar.

8. The Euro and the British pound are normally quoted using the _____ quote, which gives the number of US dollars needed to buy one unit of foreign currency.

9. The risk from an exchange rate movement on currency receipts/payments already contracted is known as _____.

10. The risk from an exchange rate movement on the value of the entire business is known as _____.

Problems

1. Given below are quotes for the Mexican peso and the Euro. Calculate the forward premium or discount.

	Spot rate	3 month Forward rate
Peso	3.4 peso/$	3.52/$
Euro	$1.02/Euro	1.04/Euro

2. The current dollar interest rate is 5.6 percent. The spot and 1-year forward rate for French Franc is FF5.5/$ and FF5.3/$ respectively. Calculate the French interest rate assuming interest rate parity.

3. Robin Hood Plc. is a London based sports good manufacturer. They export archery equipment to the US. The company is expecting a payment of $250,000 in 3 months. The spot and forward rate for the pound is $1.56 and $1.54 respectively. Robin Hood has an opportunity cost of funds of 7.5percent. It can also borrow dollars from its New York bank at the rate of 8 percent. Suggest the best hedging approach for Robin Hood.

ANSWERS TO EXERCISES

Fill-in Questions

1. Spot rate
2. Forward
3. Interest-rate parity
4. Expectations theory
5. Purchasing power parity, inflation
6. Eurocurrency
7. Indirect
8. Direct
9. Transaction exposure
10. Economic exposure

Problems

1. The forward premium can be calculated using the following formula

$$\text{Forward premium (discount)} = \frac{\text{spot rate - forward rate}}{\text{forward rate}} \times \frac{12}{\text{months to expiration}}$$

For peso the premium or discount $= \frac{3.4 - 3.52}{3.52} \times 4 = -13.64$ percent

That is the peso is at a discount of 13.64 percent.

For the Euro, we would need to the modified formula to reflect the fact that it is a direct quote:

$$\text{Forward premium (discount)} = \frac{\text{forward rate - spot rate}}{\text{spot rate}} \times \frac{12}{\text{months to expiration}}$$

$$= \frac{1.04 - 1.02}{1.02} \times 4 = 7.84 \text{ percent}$$

The Euro is at a premium of 7.84 percent.

2. The French interest rate $= \frac{5.3 \times 1.056}{5.4} - 1 = 3.64$ percent

3. Robin Hood can hedge in two ways. See the worked example problem 5.

$$\text{Cash flow from forward hedging} = \frac{250,000}{1.54} \times \frac{1}{1.0875} = 159,350 \text{ pounds}$$

Hedging through dollar loan:
Loan amount = $250,000/1.02 = $245,098
Pound cash flow by conversion using spot rate = 245,098/1.56 = 157,114 pounds.

Forward hedging is better.

28

Financial Analysis and Planning

INTRODUCTION

This chapter shows us how to use a firm's financial data to analyze past performance and assess its current financial condition. Financial analysis involves using the accounting statements to measure and interpret past performance. Past performance, while no guarantee of future performance, can help us understand the future. The chapter demonstrates the use of financial ratios and discusses the limitations of financial analysis. Ratios are convenient summary measures and always have to be viewed with healthy skepticism. The ratios commonly used for financial analysis, however, help you to ask the right questions about a firm's financial performance.

The chapter also provides an introduction to financial planning. Growth and financial planning go hand in hand. Financial planning helps identify the financing requirements needed to fund growth and the need for external financing.

KEY CONCEPTS IN THE CHAPTER

Five classes of financial ratios are typically used in financial analysis. These are leverage ratios, liquidity ratios, efficiency ratios, profitability ratios, and market value ratios. Each of these classes is described briefly below.

Leverage Ratios: These ratios tell us about a firm's financial leverage. Book values are often used in place of market values. Several debt ratios are used. No generally satisfactory measure of earnings variability exists, although all financial analysts try to get a handle on it. Some commonly used leverage ratios are given below.

$$\text{Debt ratio} = (\text{long-term debt} + \text{value of leases})/(\text{long-term debt} + \text{value of leases} + \text{equity})$$

$$\text{Debt-equity ratio} = (\text{long-term debt} + \text{value of leases})/\text{equity}$$

$$\text{Times interest earned} = (\text{EBIT} + \text{depreciation})/\text{interest}$$

Liquidity Ratios: These ratios attempt to measure the short-run ability of the firm to meet its current liabilities. Reserve borrowing power may mean more than any of these ratios. Common liquidity ratios:

Net working capital to total assets = net working capital/total assets

Current = current assets/current liabilities

Quick Ratio = (cash + marketable securities + receivables)/current liabilities

Cash ratio = (cash + marketable securities)/current liabilities

Efficiency Ratios: These ratios measure how efficiently the firm uses its assets.

Sales to Assets (Asset Turnover) = sales/average total assets

Days in Inventory = (Average inventory/cost of goods sold) X 365

Average collection period = average receivables/average daily sales

Profitability: More ambiguity exists in these ratios than in any others. One ratio alone is likely to be misleading; the entire set, and trends, are likely to provide more insights.

Net profit margin = (EBIT - tax)/sales

Return on total assets = (EBIT - taxes)/average total assets

Return on equity = earnings available for common/average equity

Payout ratio = dividends per share/earnings per share

Market Value Ratios: These are often used to measure a firm's performance. Some analysts prefer them to other performance measures precisely because they use market data and because capital markets send information to a firm's management. Four market-based ratios are:

Price-earnings ratio = stock price/earnings per share

Dividend yield = dividend per share/stock price

Market-to-book = stock price/book value per share

Tobin's q = market value of assets/estimated replacement cost

Benchmarks: Ratios without benchmarks are not of much use. Among the options are: year by year for the same firm, one firm to a set of comparable firms, one firm to firms classified in the same industry, and industry-to-industry and one firm. Be cautious. Also be careful about which ratios you select; all ratios may be created equal, but some ratios are likely to be more equal than others.

Accounting Rules and Definitions: An important point to be kept in mind while conducting financial analysis is that the ratios are based on accounting information produced by the company's accountants. Accountants enjoy considerable discretion and flexibility as to the treatment of intangible assets as well as many other elements, which go into an accounting statement. When you calculate financial ratios and make comparisons, you need to look below the surface to see how particular items have been treated. Some of the items, which could make significant differences on ratios, depending on how they are treated include:

- Depreciation
- Deferred tax
- Intangible assets
- Goodwill
- Off-balance-sheet debt
- Pensions
- Derivatives
- Foreign accounting practices.

Applications of Financial Analysis: Financial analysis is used to evaluate the creditworthiness of borrowers. Evidence suggests that failed firms tend to have identifiable financial characteristics peculiar to themselves several years before they actually fail. Credit analysis of bonds indicates that financial analysis predicts a large percentage of bond ratings. Financial ratios have been used successfully to estimate a firm's market-related risk.

DuPont System: This shows the linkages among some profitability and efficiency ratios. The DuPont equations are expressed in terms of the return on assets (ROA) or the return on equity (ROE).

$$ROA = \frac{EBIT - tax}{assets} = \frac{sales}{assets} \, x \, \frac{EBIT - tax}{sales}$$

$$ROE = \frac{EBIT - tax - \mathrm{int}\, erest}{equity}$$

$$= \frac{assets}{equity} \, x \, \frac{sales}{assets} \, x \, \frac{EBIT - tax}{sales} \, x \, \frac{EBIT - tax - \mathrm{int}\, erest}{EBIT - tax}$$

Firms would like to earn high ROA. ROA is the product of the sales to assets ratio and profit margin. Generally, the ratios are determined by the type of industry the firm is in, the level of competition, and the firm's own competitive strength. ROE includes the effect of leverage also. Again, this is a function of the industry and firm's own choice of leverage.

Financial Planning: Financial plans project the funds requirement for the firm's projected growth plan. Normally, firms prepare alternate plans reflecting different scenarios. The primary objective of the financial plan is ensuring that the firm will have the needed funds to meet the expansion plans. The basic uses and sources relationship can be used to project the external funding requirement:

$$\text{External funds needed} = \text{operating cash flow} - \text{investment in fixed assets} - \text{investment in net working capital} - \text{dividends.}$$

These projections can be best carried out using spreadsheet programs. Sophisticated models are often used, though the models may not emphasize the tools of financial analysis such as present value, market risk, etc. The simple percentage of sales model can work very well in most cases.

Growth and External Financing: Two measures of growth are often used to indicate the level of growth that can be financed without having to resort to external financing. The first, *internal growth rate*, gives the growth rate that can be sustained without any external financing. This can be calculated as follows:

$$\text{Internal growth rate} = \text{retained earnings/assets}$$

This can be expressed in an alternate form, which gives greater insight into the measure:

$$\text{Internal growth rate} = (\text{retained earnings/net income}) \times (\text{net income/equity}) \times (\text{equity/assets})$$
$$= \text{plowback ratio} \times \text{return on equity} \times (\text{equity/assets})$$

The internal growth rate implies that the firm will not use *any external funding*. A more practical measure is the *sustainable growth rate*, which measures the growth that can be sustained without any *external equity* financing.

$$\text{Sustainable growth rate} = \text{plowback ratio} \times \text{return on equity}$$

WORKED EXAMPLES

1. For 1998, make a thorough financial ratio analysis of Great Tires, Inc. Use the data in the table below.

Great Tires, Inc.	1998	1997
Balance Sheet		
Cash & short-term securities	175	100
Receivables	500	350
Inventories	750	755
Other current assets	100	75
Total current assets	1,525	1,280

Plant and equipment	1,105	1,170
Other long-term assets	150	100
Total assets	2,780	2,550
Debt due	25	35
Payables	510	405
Other current liabilities	15	10
Total current liabilities	550	450
Long-term debt and capital leases	375	425
Other long-term liabilities	225	175
Preferred stock	250	250
Shareholders' equity	1,380	1,250
Total liabilities & equity	2,780	2,550

Income Statement

Net sales	3,465	3,210
Cost of goods sold	2,252	2,119
Other expenses	346	314
Depreciation	77	62
Earnings before interest and tax (EBIT)	790	715
Net interest	40	46
Tax	285	254
Net income	465	415
Preferred stock dividend	25	25
Earnings applicable to common stock	440	390
Common dividends	260	260
Earnings retained	180	130

Other Financial Information

Market value of equity	6,675
Average number of shares	100
Earnings per share	4.40
Dividends per share	2.60
Share price	66.75

SOLUTION

Leverage ratios:
 a. Debt ratio = ($375 + $225)/($375 + $225 + $1,380) = 30.3%
 b. Debt-equity ratio = ($375 + $225)/$1,380 = 43.5%
 c. Times interest earned = ($790 + $77)/$40 = 21.7 times

Liquidity ratios:
 a. Net working capital to total assets = ($1,525 - $550)/$2,780 = 35.1%
 b. Current = $1,525/$550 = 2.77
 c. Quick = ($175 + $500)/$550 = 1.23
 d. Cash = $175/$550 = 0.32
 e. Interval measure = ($175 + $500)/[($2,252 + $346)/365] = 94.8 days

Profitability or efficiency ratios:
 a. Sales to total assets = $3,465/[($2,780 + $2,550)/2] = 1.30
 b. Sales to net working capital = $3,465/{[($1,525 - $550) + ($1,280 - $450)]/2} = 3.84
 c. Net profit margin = ($790 - $285)/$3,465 = 14.6%
 d. Inventory turnover = $2,252/[($750 + $755)/2] = 3.0
 e. Average collection period = [($500 + $350)/2]/($3,465/365) = 44.8 days
 f. Return on total assets = ($790 - $285)/[($2,780 + $2,550)/2] = 18.9%
 g. Return on equity = $440/[($1,380 + $1,250)/2] = 33.5%
 h. Payout = $2.60/$4.40 = 59.1%
  (1) Plowback = 100% - 59.1% = 40.9%
  (2) Growth in equity from plowback = [($4.40 - $2.60)/$4.40] X ($4.40/$13.80) = 13.0%

Market value ratios:
 a. Price-earnings ratio = $66.75/$4.40 = 15.2 times
 b. Dividend yield = $2.60/$66.75 = 3.90%
 c. Market-to-book = $66.75/($1,380/100) = 4.8 times

2. The table below contains financial data for Green Grass Mulchers, Inc., manufacturer of the world-famous Green Thumbers. Calculate a complete set of financial ratios for the company and make a statement about the financial soundness of the firm.

Green Grass Mulchers, Inc.	1998	1997
Balance Sheet		
Cash & short-term securities	125	75
Receivables	438	300
Inventories	750	650
Other current assets	125	75
Total current assets	1,438	1,100
Plant and equipment	1,867	1,450

342

Other long-term assets	188	100
Total assets	3,493	2,650
Debt due	75	60
Payables	615	375
Other current liabilities	25	15
Total current liabilities	715	450
Long-term debt and capital leases	1,191	425
Other long-term liabilities	305	175
Preferred stock	150	150
Shareholders' equity	1,132	1,000
Total liabilities & equity	3,493	2,650

Income Statement

Net sales	3,985	3,586
Cost of goods sold	2,815	2,590
Other expenses	484	436
Depreciation	93	73
Earnings before interest and tax (EBIT)	593	487
Net interest	127	49
Tax	177	166
Net income	289	272
Preferred stock dividend	14	14
Earnings applicable to common stock	275	258
Common dividends	140	126
Earnings retained	135	132

Other Financial Information

Market value of equity	2,485	1,952
Average number of shares	70	70
Earnings per share	3.93	3.69
Dividends per share	2.00	1.80
Share price	35.50	27.88

SOLUTION

The ratios are shown in the table below. Also shown are data for the firm's past 5 years of operations and for the industry. The last two columns show deviations from the 5-year average and from the industry. Although hardly conclusive, these comparisons suggest that the company is doing okay, not much better on average and not much worse.

Green Grass Mulchers, Inc.

	1998	Prior 5-year Average	Industry Average	Deviations from. Firm Average	Industry Average
Leverage ratios:					
Debt ratio	56.9%	37.6%	30.7%	-19.3%	-26.2%
Debt-equity ratio	132.2%	57.0%	60.0%	-75.2%	-72.2%
Times interest earned	5.4	4.1	7.1	- 0.6	2.4
Liquidity ratios:					
Net working capital to total assets	20.7%	22.0%	30.0%	1.30%	9.30%
Current	2.01	2.25	2.35	0.24	0.34
Quick	0.79	0.83	1.01	0.04	0.22
Cash	0.17	0.17	0.24	0.00	0.07
Interval measure	62.3	54.8	110.1	-7.5	47.8
Profitability or efficiency ratios:					
Sales to total assets	1.30	1.63	1.34	0.33	0.04
Sales to net working capital	5.80	5.52	4.23	-0.28	-1.57
Net profit margin	10.4%	11.5%	10.3%	1.1%	-0.1%
Inventory turnover	4.0	3.8	3.4	-0.2	-0.6
Average collection period	33.8	35.1	31.6	1.3	-2.2
Return on total assets	13.5%	19.9%	17.9%	6.4%	4.4%
Return on equity	25.8%	21.3%	19.2%	-4.5%.	-6.6%
Payout	50.9%	54.7%	52.4%	3.8%	1.5%
Plowback	49.1%	45.3%	47.6%	-3.8%	-1.5%
Growth in equity from plowback	11.9%	10.9%	11.3%	-1.0%	-0.6%
Market value ratios:					
Price-earnings	9.0	14.4	10.5	5.4	1.5
Dividend yield	5.63%	3.01%	4.32%	-2.62%	-1.31%
Market-to-book	3.1	4.7	3.5	1.6	0.4

3. Brinkley Corp. had sales of $500 million last year and total assets of $400 million. The company earned a net income of $50 million and paid dividends of $25 million. The net equity for the firm was $200 million. Calculate the internal growth rate and the sustainable growth rate for the firm.

Net income = $50 million - $25 million = $25 million
Internal growth rate = Net income/Assets = $25 million/$400 million = 6.25 percent
Plowback ratio = $25 million/$50 million = 0.50
ROE = $50 million/$200 million = 25 percent
Sustainable growth rate = plowback ratio X ROE = 0.5 X 25 = 12.5 per cent.

SUMMARY

The chapter describes the five classes of financial ratios commonly used in financial analysis. Of course, financial analysis is a lot more than the ratios. The ratios should be used to analyze past performance, for assessing current financial standing, and to understand the future prospects. Remember that the ratios provide answers. Often, they provide the basis for asking questions. One has to be careful and selective in the use of financial ratios.

The chapter also provides a brief look into financial planning. Financial planning helps a firm prepare for meeting the financial needs for future growth. Simple percentage of sales model can work well. More sophisticated models are available, but they suffer from the limitation that they are not based on finance theory. Two useful growth measures, the internal growth rate and the sustainable growth, can tell you the extent of the growth that can be pursued with no external funding or no external equity financing.

LIST OF TERMS

Average collection period	Net profit margin
Current assets	Net working capital
Current liabilities	Payout ratio
Current ratio	Price-earnings ratio
Debt ratio	Quick ratio
Debt-equity ratio	Return on equity (ROE)
Dividend yield	Return on total assets (ROA)
Inflation premium	Sales-to-assets ratio
Internal growth rate	Sustainable growth rate
Leverage ratio	Tobin's q

EXERCISES

Fill-in Questions

1. The difference between current assets and current liabilities is called

   _____.

2. _____ measure the firm's financial leverage.

3. Long-term debt and the value of leases are included in the (numerator, denominator) _____ of both the _____ ratio and the _____ ratio.

4. Times interest earned is a (liquidity, profitability, leverage) _____ ratio.

5. Assets that are in cash or will be turned into cash in the near future are called _____.

6. Liabilities that are to be paid in the near future are called _____.

7. The _____ ratio is the same as the _____ ratio except inventories and "other current assets" are dropped from the numerator.

8. The extent to which a firm's assets are being turned over is captured by the _____ ratio.

9. _____ measures the percentage of sales, which finds its way into profits.

10. The speed with which customers pay their bills is measured by the _____.

11. One overall measure of financial performance is captured by the _____ ratio.

12. The _____ ratio is computed by relating earnings available to common to (average, ending, beginning) _____ equity.

13. Nuts, Inc.'s cash dividend per share was $2.40 and its earnings per share were $6.20, so its _____ ratio was 38.7 percent. Nuts, Inc.'s market price per share is $75.25, so its _____ ratio is 12.14 times and its _____ is 3.19 percent.

14. If Nuts, Inc.'s equities and liabilities have a market value of $175 million and a replacement cost of $160 million, its _____ is 1.09.

15. As with share prices, earnings seem to follow a(n) _____; there is almost no relationship between a company's earnings growth in one period and the rest.

346

16. If finished goods that would have produced a profit of $1,000 are sold at prices to reflect a 10 percent inflation rate, the incremental gain is called _____ and is $_____.

17. The growth that can be financed without resorting to any external equity financing is called the _____.

18. The growth rate that can be achieved without resorting to any external financing is the _____.

Problems

1. For 1998, make a thorough financial ratio analysis of Beauty, Inc. Use the data in the table below.

Beauty Inc.	1998	1997
Balance Sheet		
Cash & short-term securities	150	135
Receivables	480	435
Inventories	860	775
Other current assets	110	100
Total current assets	1,600	1,445
Plant and equipment	1,611	1,420
Other long-term assets	150	100
Total assets	3,361	2,965
Debt due	55	45
Payables	615	565
Other current liabilities	45	30
Total current liabilities	715	640
Long-term debt and capital leases	375	425
Other long-term liabilities	225	175
Preferred stock	100	100
Shareholders' equity	1,946	1,000
Total liabilities & equity	3,361	2,965
Income Statement		
Net Sales	5,750	5,180
Cost of goods sold	4,125	3,710
Other expenses	750	515

Depreciation	64	57
Earnings before interest and tax (EBIT)	811	898
Net interest	43	47
Tax	292	323
Net income	476	528
Preferred stock dividend	9	9
Earnings applicable to common stock	467	519
Common dividends	198	198
Earnings retained	269	321

Other Financial Information

Market value of equity	6,188
Average number of shares	110
Earnings per share	4.25
Dividends per share	1.80
Share price	56.25

2. The table below contains financial data for Garden Reach Shop, Inc., manufacturer of the Slow Release Plant Food. Calculate a complete set of financial ratios for the company, and make a statement about the financial soundness of the firm.

Garden Reach Shop, Inc.	1998	1997
Balance Sheet		
Cash & short-term securities	180	160
Receivables	520	475
Inventories	995	890
Other current assets	100	95
Total current assets	1,795	1,620
Plant and equipment	2,500	2,650
Other long-term assets	750	675
Total assets	5,045	4,945
Debt due	75	60
Payables	615	375
Other current liabilities	25	15
Total current liabilities	715	450
Long-term debt and capital leases	3,090	3,070
Other long-term liabilities	305	175
Preferred stock	250	250
Shareholders' equity	685	1,000
Total liabilities & equity	5,045	4,945

348

Income Statement

Net sales	6,750	5,925
Cost of goods sold	5,800	5,355
Other expenses	450	575
Depreciation	150	30
Earnings before interest and tax (EBIT))	350	-35
Net interest	416	397
Tax	-25	-164
Net income	-41	-268
Preferred stock dividend	33	33
Earnings applicable to common stock	-74	-301
Common dividends	0	14
Earnings retained	-74	-315

Other Financial Information

Market value of equity	167	840
Average number of shares	70	70
Earnings per share	-1.06	-4.30
Dividends per share	0.00	0.20
Share price	2.38	12.00

3. Green Grocers Corp. had sales of $220 million last year. The company' sales to assets ratio was 1.25. The net income for the year was $11 million. The company paid a dividend of $3 million. The ROE was 12.5 percent. Calculate the internal growth rate and the sustainable growth rate.

Essay Questions

1. Explain the use of the DuPont system.

2. Describe how a bank lending officer might use ratio analysis. Select five ratios that would be most useful for the purpose.

3. Discuss the statement – "Financial planning models have no finance in them."

4. What connection is there among the payout ratio, plowback, return on equity, and growth in equity? Explain fully.

5. What is the practical significance of internal growth rate and sustainable growth rate? Which, if any, should be the goal for growth for a company?

6. You are a newly hired financial analyst at an investment firm specializing in web commerce. Your first task is to review all the studies the firm produced and to recommend a system by which to compare individual companies. You are somewhat perplexed because the

"industry" is not well defined and most of the companies are new and small and do not have any earnings. What do you do? Do the ratios contained in the text help? Explain fully.

ANSWERS TO EXERCISES

Fill-in Questions

1. Net working capital
2. Leverage ratios
3. Numerator; debt; debt-equity
4. Leverage
5. Current assets
6. Current liabilities
7. Quick; current
8. Sales to assets
9. Net profit margin
10. Average collection period
11. Return on total assets
12. Return on equity; average
13. Payout; price-earnings; dividend yield
14. Tobin's q
15. Random walk
16. Inventory profit; $100
17. Sustainable growth rate
18. Internal growth rate

Problems

1. Beauty, Inc.
   Leverage ratios:
   a. Debt ratio = ($375 + $225)/($375 + $225 + $1,946) = 23.6%
   b. Debt-equity ratio = ($375 + $225)/$1,946 = 30.8%
   c. Times interest earned ($811 + $64)/$43 = 20.3 times

   Liquidity ratios:
   a. Net working capital to total assets = ($1,600- $715)/$3,361 = 26.3%
   b. Current = $1,600/$715 = 2.24
   c. Quick = ($150 + $480)/$715 = 0.88
   d. Cash = $150/$715 = 0.21
   e. Interval measure = ($150 + $480)/[($4,125 + $750)/365] = 47.2 days

   Profitability or efficiency ratios:
   a. Sales to total assets = $5,750/[($3,361 + $2,965)/2] = 1.82
   b. Sales to net working capital = $5,750/{[($1,600 - $715) + ($1,445 - $640)]/2} = 6.80
   c. Net profit margin = ($811 - $292)/$5,750 = 9.0%
   d. Inventory turnover = $4,125/[($860 + $775)/2] = 5.0
   e. Average collection period = [($480 + $435)/ 2]/($5,750/365) = 29.0 days
   f. Return on total assets = ($811 - $292)/[($3,361 + $2,965)/2] = 16.4%
   g. Return on equity = $467/[($1,946 + $1,625)/2] = 26.1%
   h. Payout = $1.80/$4.25 = 42.4%
      (1) Plowback = 100% - 42.4% = 57.6%
      (2) Growth in equity from plowback = [($4.25 - $1.80)/$4.25] X ($4.25/$17.69) = 13.8%

Market value ratios:
a. Price-earnings = $56.25/$4.25 = 13.2 times
b. Dividend yield = $1.80/$56.25 = 3.20%
c. Market-to-book = $56.25/($1,946/110) = 3.2 times

2. Garden Reach Shop, Inc.

	1998	Prior 5-year Average	Industry Average	Deviations from: Firm Average	Industry Average
Leverage ratios:					
Debt ratio	83.2%	37.6%	30.7%	-45.6%	-52.5%
Debt-equity ratio	495.6%	57.0%	60.0%	-438.6%	-435.6%
Times interest earned	1.2	4.1	7.1	3.3	6.3
Liquidity ratios:					
Net working capital to total assets	21.41%	22.0%	30.0%	0.59%	8.59%
Current	2.51	2.25	2.35	-0.26	-0.16
Quick	0.98	0~83	1.01	-0.15	0.03
Cash	0.25	0.17	0.24	-0.08	-0.01
Interval measure	40.9	54.80	110.10	13.9	69.2
Profitability or efficiency ratios:					
Sales to total assets	1.35	1.63	1.34	0.28	-0.01
Sales to net working capital	6.00	5.52	4.23	-0.48	-1.77
Net profit margin	5.6%	11.5%	10.3%	5.9%	4.7%
Inventory turnover	6.2	3.8	3.4	-2.4	-2.8
Average collection period	26.9	35.1	31.6	8.2	4.7
Return on total assets	7.5%	19.9%	17.9%	12.4%	10.4%
Return on equity	-8.8%	21.3%	19.2%	30.1%	28.0%
Payout	0.0%	54.7%	52.4%	54.7%	52.4%
Plowback	100.0%	45.3%	47.6%	-54.7%	-52.4%
Growth in equity from plowback	-10.8%	10.9%	11.3%	21.7%	22.1%
Market value ratios					
Price-earnings	-2.2	14.4	10.5	16.6	12.7
Dividend yield	0.00%	3.01%	4.32%	3.01%	4.32%
Market-to-book	0.3	4.7	3.5	4.4	3.2

3. Net income = $11 million
   Retained earnings = $11 million- $3 million = $8 million
   Assets = sales/(sales/asset ratio) = $220 million/1.25 = $176 million
   Internal growth rate = retained earnings/assets = $8 million/$176 million = 4.55 percent

Plowback ratio = $8 million/$11 million = 0.73
Sustainable growth rate = plowback X ROE = 0.73 X 12.5 = 9.13 percent

29

Short-Term Financial Planning

INTRODUCTION

This chapter focuses on short-term financial planning. Short-term financial decisions differ from long-term financial decisions in two important ways. First, they are easily reversed in most cases. Second, there is far less uncertainty about the decision variables as you are concerned with the next few months rather than years. This does not mean that short-term financial decisions are any less important. Short-term financial decisions are very important to the survival of the business. They ensure liquidity and short-term survival of the business. The analysis of short-term financial decisions is the focus of this chapter. The chapter is like an introduction to the next part of the book, which deals with the details of short-term assets and liability management.

Firms finance their operations from short-term and long-term sources. Although short-term financial decisions almost always involve short-lived assets, there is a linkage between short-term and long-term financing decisions arising from a firm's cumulative capital requirements. If you have a surplus of long-term financing, you would need less short-term funds. Ordinarily, financial managers try to match the maturity of capital sources with the life of the assets funded by them. For example, some minimum level of working capital is needed permanently in the business and is financed from permanent sources, whereas the seasonal increase in working capital typically is financed from short-lived sources.

KEY CONCEPTS IN THE CHAPTER

Components of Working Capital: *Current assets* and *current liabilities* together are known as working capital. The term *net working capital* is used to denote the difference between current assets and current liabilities. Current assets include cash and marketable securities, *accounts receivable* and *inventory*. Current liabilities include *accounts payable*, which reflects the credit obtained from suppliers, and any other short-term obligation including short-term loans.

Working capital management (sometimes also referred to short-term financial management) involves decisions on the levels and mix of current liabilities. Persons other than the financial manager will be actively involved in management decisions with respect to specific components of working capital. For example, the production manager has comparative advantage over the financial manager in determining how much to invest in inventories in order to minimize stockouts, storage costs, risks of spoilage and obsolescence, and the opportunity costs of tying up money in inventories. Details of management of current assets and liabilities are discussed in the next three chapters.

Links between Long- and Short-Term Financing Decisions: Businesses require funds for investments in fixed assets and current assets. Over time, the capital requirements tend to accumulate, steadily but mostly irregularly. These requirements are financed by either long- or short-term capital sources. The decision to use one type of funding necessarily affects the other. Usually many companies try to match the maturities of assets and financing. Financing of the seasonal requirements of current assets and the comfort level for surplus cash are discretionary decisions. Too much comfort level cash is not good.

Changes in Cash and Working Capital: The changes in cash and working capital can be traced through a uses and sources statement. The statement tells us the overall changes in cash and other assets and how they were financed. Note that profits and cash flows are not the same and that short-term liquidity measures are frequently used, most notably the current and quick ratios. The worked example shows how to prepare a uses and sources statement.

Cash Budgeting: A cash budget is a weekly, monthly, or quarterly forecast of cash inflows and outflows. The budget indicates deficient or excessive cash balances, and financing plans are formulated based on it. Remember that this is a budget of actual cash flows and not expenses booked in the ledger. The steps involved in preparing cash budgets are:

Step 1: Estimate cash inflows, which typically include:

- Prior receivables,
- Present sales,
- Estimated collections,
- Sale of assets, and
- Tax refunds.

Step 2: Estimate cash outflows, which include:

- Payments on accounts payable,
- Labor, administrative, and other expenses,
- Capital expenditures, and
- Taxes, interest, and dividends.

Sum the cash flows and find the net inflow. Estimate the amount that must be financed, including a minimum cash balance.

The Short-Term Financial Plan: The estimated financing needs from the cash-budget forms the basis for the short-term financing plan. Note that:

- Large cash flows may result because of seasonal considerations.
- The cash budget is a best guess, and the uncertainty of its elements should be evaluated.

By trial and error, each proposed plan is evaluated for its compatibility and costs and the need to maintain required ratios. Note that simulation and optimization models help, but rely heavily on the reality of their underlying assumptions.

Financial managers have two major options for financing short-term cash deficiencies:

- Borrow from banks, perhaps an unsecured line of credit with a compensating balance or
- Stretch out payments on accounts payable. This may be expensive, as trade credit is not free beyond the minimum period allowed.

Here are some typical questions, which need to be asked before finalizing the plan:

- Is the cash reserve too large?
- Are the current and quick ratios satisfactory?
- What are the intangible costs of stretching payables, such as lost discounts?
- Does the plan produce a financially sound result?
- Is long-term financing needed and not short-term?
- What about adjusting operating and investment plans?
- What about selling receivables to a commercial finance company?

WORKED EXAMPLES

1. The table below contains the balance sheets and income statement for Cards Galore, Inc. Complete a statement of sources and uses of cash and sources and uses of funds for 1998.

Cards Galore, Inc. Balance Sheet	1997	1998	Sources and Uses Impact
Current assets			
Cash	15	13	2
Marketable securities	5	0	5
Inventory	25	17	8
Accounts receivable	20	35	-15
Total current assets	65	65	0
Fixed assets			
Gross investment	75	85	-10
Less depreciation	-15	-17	2
Net fixed assets	60	68	-8
Total assets	125	133	8
Current liabilities			
Bank loans	10	15	5
Accounts payable	35	30	-5
Total current liabilities	45	45	0

355

Long-term debt	15	20	5
New worth (equity and retained earnings)	65	68	3
Total liabilities and net worth	125	133	8

Income Statement	1998	Sources and Uses Impact
Sales	300	
Operating expenses	245	
	55	
Depreciation	-2	2
	53	
Interest	-3	
Pretax income	50	
Tax at 34 percent	-17	
Net income	33	33
Note:		
Dividend	12	-12
Retained earnings	21	21

SOLUTION

The object of analyzing both these statements is to determine how management derived the funds and cash to finance its operations during this period. Because such information may be valuable for future financial planning, the method for composing such statements is important. To determine the sources and uses of cash, analyze the differences between the two balance sheet dates and the cash generated from operations.

Step 1: Compare the differences in each balance sheet account.

Step 2: Determine whether those differences increase or decrease the cash or funds of the firm.

Step 3: Under the caption "Sources," list all the items, which increased the amount of cash or funds. Under the caption "Uses," list all the items, which decreased cash or funds.

Step 4: Sum both sources and uses.

Step 5: Take the difference between sources and uses to determine the net change in the cash position of the firm.

By applying these steps to Cards Galore, Inc., the right-hand column of the table above indicates the impact each change has on the uses and sources of funds, plus or minus. These results are then summarized in the table below.

As you review the pluses and minuses of those statements, remember this: anything that increases the sources of funds is a plus; anything that uses funds is a negative. For example, a reduction of accounts payable is a use of funds because funds were needed to pay off the payables.

Cards Galore, Inc.
Sources and uses of funds and cash

Sources of funds
Sold marketable securities	5
Reduced inventories	8
Increased bank loan	5
Issued long-term debt	5
Cash from operations:	
Net income	33
Depreciation	2
Total sources	58

Uses of funds
Increased accounts receivable	15
Invested in fixed assets	8
Reduced accounts payable	5
Dividends	12
Total uses	40

Change in cash balance   18

2. Refer to problem 1. What are the changes in the net working capital that took place?

SOLUTION

The changes in net working capital are contained in the table below.

Cards Galore, Inc. - Changes in Net Working Capital

Sources:
Issued long-term debt	5
Cash from operations:	
Net income	33
Depreciation	2
Total	40

Uses:

Invested in fixed assets	8
Dividends	<u>12</u>
Total	20
Changes in net working capital	20

Because it is the difference between current assets and current liabilities, changes that result in net working capital account for factors other than the current assets and short-term liabilities; they stem from long-term financing and investment decisions, as well as from current operations.

3. Section A of the table below contains the 1998 sales forecast for Cards Galore, Inc. Use the following assumptions to construct a cash budget for the company:

- 85 percent of sales is realized in cash in the quarter sales are made.
- The remaining 15 percent of sales is collected in cash in the following quarter.
- The sales prior to the forecast first quarter were $88.3 million.
- Receivables carried into the first quarter were $17 million.
- Accounts payable is to be paid on time.
- All labor and administrative expenditures are paid when due.
- The capital expenditures are those indicated in the budget below
- The firm's financial manager feels "comfortable" with a cash cushion of $10 million.

Cash Budget For Cards Galore, Inc. (In Millions)

	First Quarter	Second Quarter	Third Quarter	Fourth Quarter
Section A Sales Forecast (in millions)				
Sales	92.5	80.5	135.8	165.2
Section B Sales and Collections Forecast (in millions)				
Receivables at start of period	17.0	17.7	15.9	24.2
Sales	92.5	80.5	135.8	165.2
Collections				
Sales in current period (85 percent)	78.6	68.4	115.4	140.4
Sales in last period (15percent)	13.2	13.9	12.1	20.4
Total collections	91.8	82.3	137.5	160.8
Receivables at end of period	17.7	15.9	24.2	28.6
Section C Cash Budget				
Sources of cash:				
Collections on accounts receivable	91.8	82.3	127.5	160.8
Other	6.0	10.0	0.0	0.0
Total sources	97.8	92.3	127.5	160.8
Uses of cash:				
Payments on accounts payable	84.0	36.0	48.0	80.0

Labor, administrative, and other expenses	35.0	35.0	35.0	35.0
Capital expenditures	20.0	10.0	0.0	0.0
Taxes, interest, and dividends	9.0	9.0	9.0	9.0
Total uses	148.0	90.0	92.0	124.0
Sources minus uses	-50.2	2.3	35.5	36.8

Section D Calculation of Short-Term Financing Needs

Cash at start of period	13.0	-37.2	-34.9	0.6
Changes in cash balance (sources - uses)	-50.2	2.3	35.5	36.8
Cash at end of period	-37.2	-34.9	0.6	37.4
Minimum operating cash balance	10.0	10.0	10.0	10.0
Cumulative short-term financing needs	-47.2	-44.9	-9.4	27.4

SOLUTION

To complete the 1998 cash budget, take the following steps:

- Formulate a statement of expected receivables.
- Formulate a cash budget in which the expected cash sources and cash uses are combined, with the end result being an estimate of the quarterly cash deficiency or excess.
- Sections B, C, and D of the table above contain the results.

SUMMARY

This chapter provided an overview of short-term financial planning. Short-term financial decisions are easier than the long-term financial decisions for the simple reason that they are often easily reversed. They are however, no less important. Short-term planning ensures liquidity and the very survival of the firm. The chapter included a uses and sources statement as a way of analyzing changes in working capital and evaluating the financial position of the firm.

A cash budget is a useful planning tool that helps in short-term financing decisions. Cash budget show the amount of financing needed at various times during the plan period. It also highlights the major inflows and outflows, which could create huge surpluses or deficits. The chapter leads to the next three chapters, which deals with the details of short-term assets and liability management.

LIST OF TERMS

Cash budget
Compensating balance
Line of credit
Matching maturities
Net working capital

Quick ratio
Sources and uses of cash
Sources and uses of funds
Stretching payables
Working capital

EXERCISES

Fill-in Questions

1. The concept of _____ is at work when short-lived assets are financed from short-term sources and long-lived assets are financed from long-term sources.

2. A forecast of cash inflows and cash outflows is called a(n) _____.

3. Changes in _____ are captured by the sources and uses of cash statement, whereas the sources and uses of funds statement captures changes in _____.

4. The percentage of a loan that must be retained on deposit is called a(n) _____.

5. A prearranged maximum borrowing capability at specified interest rates is known as a(n) _____.

6. Extending the payment dates for bills from suppliers is called _____.

Problems

1. Using the balance sheets and income statement given below for Bundle of Joy Corp., work out a complete sources and uses of cash and a sources and uses of funds statement for 1998.

Bundle Of Joy Corp.

Year-End Balance Sheets, In Millions	1997	1998
Current assets:		
Cash	$ 13	$ 2
Marketable securities	0	5
Inventory	17	22
Accounts receivable	35	48
Total current assets	$ 65	$ 77
Fixed assets:		
Gross investment	$ 85	$ 85
Less depreciation	-17	-19
Net fixed assets	68	66
Total assets	$133	$143
Current liabilities:		
Bank loans	$ 15	$13
Accounts payable	30	37
Total current liabilities	$ 45	$ 50
Long-term debt	$ 20	$18
Net worth (equity and retained earnings)	68	75
Total liabilities and net worth	$133	$143

Income Statement, In Millions

Sales	$320
Operating expenses	-289
	$ 31
Depreciation	-2
	$ 29
Interest	-3
Pretax income	$ 26
Tax at 50 percent	13
Net income	$ 13
Cash dividends	$6
Retained earnings	$7

2. Using the data for 1998 contained in problem 1, answer the following:

   a. The company's current liabilities were _____.
   b. The company's current assets were _____.
   c. The company's current ratio was _____.
   d. The company's quick ratio was _____.
   e. The company's net working capital was _____.

3. The table below contains 1998 data for Bundle of Joy Corp.

Cash Budget for Bundle of Joy Corp. (in millions)

	First Quarter	Second Quarter	Third Quarter	Fourth Quarter
Section A New Data (in millions)				
Sales forecast	85.0	75.0	100.0	150.0
Other sources of cash	5.0	6.0	7.0	10.0
Accounts payable	72.0	63.0	76.0	84.0
Labor, administrative, and other expenses	42.0	42.0	42.0	42.0
Capital expenditures	15.0	0.0	5.0	0.0
Taxes, interest, and dividends	19.0	19.0	19.0	19.0

In addition, the following assumptions are made:

1. 87 percent of sales is realized as cash in the quarter in which they are made.
2. The remaining 13 percent of sales is collected as cash the following quarter.
3. Sales prior to the first quarter of this forecasting period were $130 million.
4. Receivables carried into the first quarter were $17 million.
5. All accounts payable are paid when due.
6. All labor and administrative expenses are paid when due.

Construct a revised cash budget for 1998 and work out a financing scheme for Bundle of Joy Corp.

1998 Cash Budget for Bundle of Joy Corp. (in millions)

	First Quarter	Second Quarter	Third Quarter	Fourth Quarter
Sources of cash:				
Collections				
Other	$5.00	$6.00	$7.00	$10.00
Uses of cash:				
Accounts payable	72.00	63.00	76.00	84.00
Labor, administrative, and other expenses	42.00	42.00	42.00	42.00
Capital expenditures				
Taxes, interest, and dividends	19.00	19.00	19.00	19.00
Total uses				
Sources -- uses				
Short-term financing requirements:				
Cash at start of period				
Change in cash balance				
Cash at the end of period				
Minimum operating cash balance				
Cumulative short-term financing requirement				

Essay Questions

1. What is meant by matching maturities?

2. Discuss the following statement. "Short-term financial decisions are easily reversed; so they are no big deal, anyone can make them."

3. How might a financial manager trace changes in cash and working capital?

4. Explain the importance of the cash budget. What is the ideal budgeting period for a small "mom & pop" retail boutique?

ANSWERS TO EXERCISES

Fill-in Questions

1. Matching maturities
2. Cash budget
3. Cash; working capital
4. Compensating balance
5. Line of credit
6. Stretching payables

Problems

1. From the balance sheet:

Cash	-11
Marketable securities	-5
Inventory	-5
Accounts receivable	-3
Total current assets	-2
Gross investment	0
Depreciation	+2
Net fixed assets	+2
Total assets	-10
Bank loans	+2
Accounts payable	+7
Total current liabilities	+5
Long-term debt	-2
Net worth	+7
Total liabilities and net worth	+ 10

From the income statement:

Depreciation	+2
Net income	+13
Cash dividends	-6
Retained earnings	+7

Sources and uses of funds and cash:

Sources:

Depreciation	$2
Net income	13
Increased accounts payable	7
Total sources	$22

Uses:

Bought marketable securities	$5
Increased inventories	5
Increased receivables	13
Decreased bank loans	2
Reduced long-term debt	2
Dividends	6
Total uses	$33

Reduction in cash $11

2. a. $50
    b. $77
    c. $77/$50 = 1.54
    d. ($2 + $5 + $48)/$50 = 1.10
    e. $77 - $50 = $27

3. **Cash Budget For Bundle of Joy Corp** - Continued from the table given in the problem.

	First Quarter	Second Quarter	Third Quarter	Fourth Quarter
Section B Sales and Collections Forecast (in millions)				
Receivables at start of period	17.0	11.1	9.7	12.9
Sales	85.0	75.0	100.0	150.0
Collections				
Sales in current period (87 percent)	74.0	65.3	87.0	130.5
Sales in last period (13 percent)	16.9	11.1	9.8	13.0
Total collections	90.9	76.4	96.8	143.5
Receivables at end of period	11.1	9.7	12.9	19.4
Section C Cash Budget				
Sources of cash				
Collections on accounts receivable	90.9	76.4	96.8	143.5
Other	5.0	6.0	7.0	10.0
Total sources	95.9	82.4	103.8	153.5
Uses of cash				
Payments on accounts payable	72.0	63.0	76.0	84.0
Labor, administrative, and other expenses	42.0	42.0	42.0	42.0
Capital expenditures	15.0	0.0	5.0	0.0
Taxes, interest, and dividends	19.0	19.0	19.0	19.0
Total uses	148.0	124.0	142.0	145.0
Sources -- uses	-52.1	-41.6	-38.2	8.5

Section D Calculation of Short-Term Financing Needs

Cash at start of period	2.0	-50.1	-91.7	-129.9
Changes in cash balance (sources - uses)	-52.1	-41.6	-38.2	8.5
Cash at end of period	-50.1	-91.7	-129.9	-121.4
Minimum operating cash balance	8.0	8.0	8.0	8.0
Cumulative short-term financing needs	-58.1	-99.7	-137.9	-129.4

It should be obvious that if the present conditions persist, permanent additions to working capital are in order. Chances are retained earnings or a stock sale is best for this company. Short-term financing does not seem to be in order because of the seemingly chronic deficiency in cash flows.

30

Credit Management

INTRODUCTION

This is the first of the three chapters dealing with the details of short-term financial management and deals with the management of credit. As you study the nuts-and-bolts issues of credit management, remember that no clear-cut, scientific guidelines exist by which to make credit decisions. The five key components of credit management are:

- Terms of sale,
- Evidence of indebtedness,
- Credit analysis,
- The amount of credit to be extended, and
- Collection procedures.

The chapter discusses each of these and provides broad suggestions on managing credit.

KEY CONCEPTS IN THE CHAPTER

Terms of Sale: The terms of sale indicate the method by which customers pay for goods and services. Most goods and services are sold on credit, usually with a cash discount being offered if payment is received within a short time, but with the entire amount nonetheless due at the end of a specified period. Cash on delivery (COD) and cash before delivery (CBD) may be a good policy in certain cases, but in most industries credit is common. Industry practice plays an important part in determining the credit terms. A term of 2/10, net 30 means the customer will get a 2 percent discount if the bill is paid within 10 days from the invoice date and then the customer has 30 days to pay the bill in full. The discount terms may start from the end of the month in some cases. Credit terms can be part of an overall sales strategy and the sales manager will probably be part of the decision process.

Commercial Credit Instruments: A variety of commercial credit instruments facilitate the terms of sale. The chief commercial credit instrument is the open account, which is simply a record on the books of the firm indicating that credit is extended. Depending on the nature of the business and one's customers, other commercial credit instruments may be used, such as promissory notes, commercial drafts, bank acceptances, and letters of credit. A *commercial draft* is a Bill of Exchange and the customer *accepts* as record of debt before delivery of the goods. The actual payment may be immediate for a *sight draft* or after a period of credit for a *time draft*. The customer's acceptance creates a *trade acceptance,* which is either held to maturity or can be discounted for immediate payment when used as collateral for a loan.

Credit Analysis: Ordinarily, credit analysis precedes credit extension. To that end, financial managers may hire the services of a credit agency, such as Dun and Bradstreet, but that may not be enough. Financial ratio analysis is another method of checking customers' creditworthiness. Yet another method of analyzing the creditworthiness of customers is numerical credit scoring and risk indexes. The credit scores can be constructed using a company's past experience and can use traditional financial ratios such as current ratio, quick ratio, and return on assets. Altman's Z score is based on the statistical technique known as *multiple discriminant analysis*. Altman used multiple discriminant analysis to study the financial ratios of firms, which went bankrupt and compared them with the ratios of non-bankrupt firms. He developed an index of credit worthiness, called the Z score, given as:

$$Z = 3.3(\text{EBIT/total assets}) + 1.0(\text{sales/total assets})$$
$$+ 0.6(\text{market value of equity/book value of debt})$$
$$+ 1.4(\text{retained earnings/total assets})$$
$$+ 1.2(\text{working capital/total assets})$$

The cut-off Z score was able to clearly separate the bankrupt and non-bankrupt firms. Updated and modified versions of Z scores are available and can be used. Remember that the original Altman model was developed for predicting bankruptcy and not default on trade credit.

The Credit Decision: After the foregoing steps have been taken, the credit decision is made. In essence, every credit decision estimates the present value of the difference between revenues to be received and the cost expended for credit sales. This trade-off can be expressed as:

$$\text{Expected profit} = p \times PV(\text{REV - cost}) - (1 - p)PV(\text{cost})$$

Where p is the probability of payment.

Note that no credit manager pursues the credit search without limits; after all, there is a cost of searching for additional information. Usually the probability of default, as well as the size of the order, when compared with the gain from not extending credit, forms the basis for the analysis. Repeat orders, however, cannot be ignored without hazard. To cultivate prospective business, the financial manager looks beyond the immediate order in hand.

A reasonable credit policy is based on three principles. First, maximize expected profits, and do not minimize the number of bad accounts. Second, concentrate efforts on those accounts most likely to pose a threat to the financial welfare of the firm, either because of their size or because of their doubtful paying ability. Third, factor repeat orders into the overall decision because they have a bearing on long-run sales and production.

Collection Policy: After credit has been extended, a collection policy is enforced. By aging accounts receivable, those, which are delinquent, and the extent to which they are delinquent are identified and appropriate measures are taken. Another method of collecting accounts receivable is to sell them outright to firms that specialize in this practice. *Factors,* as they are called, may absorb the entire credit collection function or parts of it, for a fee. To further ensure that accounts receivables are collected, credit insurance may be bought. Factoring is particularly useful and efficient for smaller firms, who do not have the resources for extensive credit analysis.

WORKED EXAMPLES

1. Find the effective annual cost of forgoing taking cash discounts for each of the following terms of sale: 2/10, n/30; 5/20, n/45; 2/10, n/60; and 5/20, n/60.

SOLUTION

The object is first to determine the effective cost of the loan arising from not taking the cash discount. For convenience, let's deal in increments of $100 of sales, and let's take the case of 2/10, n/30. Recognize that during the first 10 days you obtain a "free ride" on the seller's credit (although it is not cost-free, the cost of the free ride most probably being built into the sale price). Also note that if you do not take the cash discount, in effect you are borrowing the difference between the total amount billed, $100, and the amount of the cash discount, $2, which, of course, is $98; it costs you $2 each time you borrow the $98. You are borrowing the $98 for 20 days. If you repeat this process throughout the year, you will borrow 18.25 times because there are 18.25 20-day periods in a 365-day year (365/20).

The cost of the 20-day, $2 loan is:

$$\text{Per period cost of loan} = \text{dollar cash discount/dollar amount of loan}$$
$$= \$2/\$98$$
$$= 0.0204 = 2.04 \text{ percent}$$

You are paying 2.04 percent for each of the 18.25 periods. The effective annual cost is the compound return on the 2.04 percent, namely,

$$\begin{aligned}
\text{Effective annual cost of} \quad &= [(1 + \text{per period rate})^{\text{number of periods per year}} - 1] \times 100 \\
\text{foregoing cash discounts} \\
&= [(1 + 0.0204)^{18.25} - 1] \times 100 \\
&= [(1.0204)^{18.25} - 1] \times 100 \\
&= (1.4456 - 1) \times 100 \\
&= 0.4456 \times 100 \\
&= 44.56 \text{ percent}
\end{aligned}$$

which is very expensive by anyone's standards. Note that it is incorrect to estimate the cost of not taking the discount by merely estimating the cost as 2 percent ($2/$100) and multiplying that by the number of periods to obtain an answer of 36.5 percent (2 percent x 18.25) because that procedure ignores the effective amount that is borrowed and the compounding effect of the forgone interest.

369

The calculations for the other terms of sale are as follows:

5/20, n/45: Per-period cost of loan = $5/$95
                             = 5.26 percent

Effective annual cost = $[(1.0526)^{365/25} - 1] \times 100$
                                  = $[(1.0526)^{14.6} - 1] \times 100$
                                  = $(2.1137 - 1) \times 100$
                                  = 111.37 percent

2/10, n/60: Per-period cost of loan = $2/$98
                             = 2.04 percent

Effective annual cost = $[1.0204)^{365/50} - 1] \times 100$
                                  = $[(1.0204)^{7.3} - 1] \times 100$
                                  = $(1.15884 - 1) \times 100$
                                  = 15.88 percent

5/20, n/60: Effective annual cost = $[(1 + 0.0526)^{365/40} \times 100$
                                  = $[(1.0526)^{9.125} - 1] \times 100$
                                  = $(1.5964 - 1) \times 100$
                                  = 0.5964×100
                                  = 59.64 percent

2. Use Altman's multiple discriminant analysis to estimate the Z scores for each of the firms listed below.

	A	B	C	D
EBIT	$200	$ 600	$ 50	$ 5
Total assets	400	400	400	400
Sales	400	1,900	1,200	200
Market price per share	20	100	50	5
Number of shares	100	100	100	100
Book value of debt	100	100	100	100
Retained earrings	50	100	25	50
Working capital	100	200	10	10

SOLUTION

The setup for this answer is as follows:
         Z = 3.3(EBIT/total assets) + 1.0(sales/total assets)
             + 0.6(market value of equity/book value of debt)
             + 1.4(retained earnings/total assets)
             + 1.2(working capital/total assets)

370

The solution for firm A is:

$$Z = 3.3(\$200/\$400) + 1.0(\$400/\$400)$$
$$+ 0.6[(\$20 \times 100)/\$100] + 1.4(\$40/\$400) + 1.2(\$100/\$400)$$
$$= (3.3)(0.5) + (1.0)(1.0) + (0.6)(20) + (1.4)(0.125) + (1.2)(0.25)$$
$$= 1.65 + 1 + 12 + 0.175 + 0.3$$
$$= 15.125$$

For firms B, C, and D the solutions are:

Firm B:
$$Z = 3.3(\$600/\$400) + 1.0(\$1,900/\$400)$$
$$+ 0.6[(\$100 \times 100)/\$100 + 1.4(\$100/\$400) + 1.2(\$200/\$400)$$
$$= 4.95 + 4.75 + 60 + 0.35 + 0.6$$
$$= 70.65$$

Firm C:
$$Z = 3.3(\$50/\$400) + 1.0(\$1,200/\$400)$$
$$+ 0.6[(\$50 \times 100)/\$100] + 1.4(\$25/\$400) + 1.2(\$10/\$400)$$
$$= 0.4125 + 3.0 + 30.0 + 0.0875 + 0.03$$
$$= 33.53$$

Firm D:
$$Z = 0.04125 + 0.5 + 3.0 + 0.175 + 0.03$$
$$= 3.74625$$

3. RamWay Corp.'s credit manager studied the bill-paying habits of its customers and discovered that 95 percent were prompt payers and 5 percent were slow payers. The records also showed that 15 percent of the slow payers and 2 percent of the prompt payers subsequently defaulted. The company now has 3,500 accounts on its books, none of which has yet defaulted. What is the total number of expected defaults, assuming no repeat business is on the horizon?

SOLUTION

To solve this problem, first categorize the number of prompt and slow payers. They are

Prompt payers = 3,500 X 0.95 = 3,325
Slow payers = 3,500 X 0.05 = 175

Next, multiply the probability of default for each class to obtain the expected number for each class.

Prompt payers: 3,325 X 0.02 =   66.5
Slow payers: 175 X 0.15 =   26.25
                              92.75

A total of 92.75 (say, 93) accounts (2.65 percent of the total) is expected to default.

4. Given the data in problem 3, revenues from sales of $1,800, and cost of the sales of $1,560, what is the expected profit (loss) from extending credit to slow payers?

SOLUTION

Expected profit $= p \times PV(\text{revenues} - \text{cost}) - (1 - p)(\text{cost})$
$= 0.85(\$1,800 - \$1,560) - 0.15(\$1,560)$
$= \$204 - \$234$
$= -\$30$

Clearly, it is not profitable to extend credit to slow payers.

5. Estimate how much RamWay would have to increase prices to make it just worthwhile to extend credit to slow payers in problem 4.

SOLUTION

Estimate the revenues (left-hand side) needed to cover the costs (right-hand) side:

$$0.85(\text{revenues} - \$1,560) = 0.15 \times \$1,560$$
$$0.85(\text{revenues} - \$1,326 = \$234$$
$$\text{Revenues} = (\$234 + \$1,326)/0.85 = \$1,835$$

At average revenues of about $1,835, a price increase of about 2 percent, the firm is likely to just break even from extending credit to all customers.

6. Is it worthwhile for the credit manager of RamWay Corp., to engage in a credit search to determine whether customers are slow or prompt payers if the cost of the search is $8, the probability of identifying a slow payer is 0.10, and the expected loss from a slow payer is $30?

SOLUTION

To answer this, set up the problem in this way:

Expected payoff
from credit check $=$ (probability of identifying a slow payer X gain from not extending credit) - cost of credit check
$= (0.10 \times \$30) - \$8$
$= \$3 - \$8$
$= -\$5$

It is not worthwhile to engage in the credit check.

372

7.   At what level of sales per customer would the credit manager in problem 6 be indifferent?

SOLUTION

If the expected loss from a slow payer were $80, the credit check would be worthwhile.

Set expected payoff from credit check $(0.10 \times X) - \$8$ equal to zero and solve for x, that is, $0.10X = 8$; $X = \$80$.

8.   We expect that one of our slow-paying customers in problems 3-7 will subsequently place a repeat order. If the customer pays on the first order, we estimate a probability of 0.90 of no default on the second order. Assuming investments of comparable risk return 15 percent, how would you evaluate the extension of credit?

SOLUTION

Let's take this in steps. First, calculate the expected profit on the initial order.

$$\begin{aligned}
\text{Expected profit on initial order} &= p_1 \times PV(\text{revenues - cost}) - (1 - p_1)PV \times (\text{cost}) \\
&= (0.85 \times \$240) - (0.15 \times \$1,560) \\
&= \$204 - \$234 \\
&= -\$30
\end{aligned}$$

Second,

$$\begin{aligned}
\text{Next year's expected} \\
\text{profit on repeat order} &= p_1 \times PV(\text{revenues - cost}) - (1 - p_2)PV \times (\text{cost}) \\
&= (0.90 \times \$240) - (0.10 \times \$1,560) \\
&= \$216 - \$156 \\
&= \$60
\end{aligned}$$

Third, calculate the present value of the total expected profit.

$$\begin{aligned}
\text{Total expected profit} &= \text{expected profit on initial order} + (\text{probability of payment} \\
&\quad \text{and repeat order} \times PV \text{ of next year's expected profit on} \\
&\quad \text{repeat order}) \\
&= -\$30 + 0.85PV(\$60) \\
&= -\$30 + [(0.85)(\$60)]/1.15 \\
&= -\$30 + \$44.35 \\
&= \$14.35
\end{aligned}$$

373

SUMMARY

The chapter deals with credit management. Credit management involves five steps:

- Deciding the terms of sale,
- Using the appropriate credit instruments,
- Designing the right credit analysis tools and techniques,
- Making the right credit decisions, and
- Managing the collection.

This is not an exact science and companies will have to use their experience and industry wisdom to design the best policy. Sophisticated credit scoring techniques may not be relevant or the right ones to use in every case. Credit policy is also part of the overall marketing and sales strategy and the sales/marketing managers should be part of the decision process.

LIST OF TERMS

Aging of receivables	Open account credit
Cash discount	Promissory note
Commercial draft	Sight draft
Factor	Time draft
Multiple-discriminant analysis	Trade acceptance

EXERCISES

Fi11-in Questions

1. _____ are often used to induce customers to pay their bills before the end of the free payment period.

2. When the buyer accepts the Bill of Exchange, you have a _____.

3. A _____ is a credit instrument used to get the buyer to acknowledge the credit before delivery.

4. A commercial draft may be a(n) _____ or a(n) _____, depending on when the payment is made.

5. A simple _____ note may be used to record the customer's indebtedness.

6. Ordinarily, a credit manager (does, does not) _____ subject each customer to the same credit analysis. Rather, efforts should be concentrated on the (large, small) _____ and doubtful orders.

7. A firm, usually part of a commercial bank, which purchases accounts receivable is called a(n) _____.

8. The statistical procedure known as _____ was used to estimate the likelihood of financial failure.

9. Most trade credit is _____ credit rather than CED or COD.

10. Financial managers are said to be _____ when they classify their credit sales according to the percentage of the total that pay their bills in 1, 2, 3, or more than 3 months.

Problems

1. Find the effective annual cost of not taking the cash discounts on the following terms of trade: 3/10, n/30; 3/10, n/45; 3/10, n/60; 4/10, n/30; 5/10, n/30; and 6/10, n/30. What general phenomena seem to be at work?

2. Use Altman's multiple-discriminant analysis to estimate the scores for each of the following companies:

	1	2	3	4
EBIT	$200	$400	$600	$800
Total assets	1,000	1,200	1,400	1,600
Sales	2,000	2,400	2,800	3,200
Market price per share	40	48	56	64
Number of shares	50	100	150	200
Book value of debt	400	500	600	700
Retained earnings	400	500	600	700
Working capital	600	600	600	600

3. If-Not, Inc.'s credit manager studied the bill-paying habits of its customers and found that 90 percent of them were prompt. She also discovered that 22 percent of the slow payers and 5 percent of the prompt ones subsequently defaulted. The company has 2,000 accounts on its books, none of which has yet defaulted. Calculate the total number of expected defaults, assuming no repeat business is on the horizon.

4. Given the data in problem 3, revenues from sales of $1,300, and the cost of sales of $1,100, what is the expected profit or loss from extending credit to slow payers?

5. Estimate the average level of revenues that makes it just worthwhile to extend credit to slow payers in problem 4.

6. Is it worthwhile for the credit manager of If-Not, Inc., to engage in a credit search to determine whether customers are slow or prompt payers if the cost of each search is $11, the

probability of identifying slow payers is 0.06, and the expected cost of a slow payer is $55? Show all calculations.

7. At what sales level would the credit manager in problem 6 be indifferent? Show all calculations.

8. Say there is a 0.92 probability that a repeat customer of If-Not, Inc., will not default. How should the credit manager evaluate the original extension of credit to a customer who has been identified as a slow payer but also as certain to place a repeat order? The required return on an investment of this risk is 12 percent.

Essay Questions

1. Discuss the statement: "A firm may extend trade credit to a customer who may not be credit worthy by the standards of a typical bank loan officer."

2. What role does financial ratio analysis play in credit evaluation? Explain both the advantages and disadvantages of financial ratio analysis.

3. What should be the primary goal of credit policy?

4. What are Z scores, and how are they used in credit analysis?

5. "I don't know about other financial managers, but as the credit manager of RamWay Corp., I consider maximization of profits, concentration on dangerous accounts, and repeat orders to be the most influential on my credit decisions." Evaluate this statement.

ANSWERS TO EXERCISES

Fill-in Questions

1. Cash discounts
2. Trade acceptance
3. Commercial draft
4. Sight draft, time draft
5. Promissory note

6. Does not; large
7. Factor
8. Multiple-discriminant analysis
9. Open account
10. Aging receivables

Problems

1. 3/10, n/30: Per-period cost = dollar cash discount/dollar amount of loan
$$= \$3/\$97$$
$$= 3.093 \text{ percent}$$

Number of periods = 365/20 = 18.25

$$\text{Effective annual cost} = [(1 + 0.0309)^{18.25} - 1] \times 100$$
$$= 74.26 \text{ percent}$$

3/10, n/45: $\text{Effective annual cost} = [(1 + 0.309)^{10.43} - 1] \times 100$
$$= 37.36 \text{ percent}$$

3/10, n/60: $\text{Effective annual cost} = [(1.0309)^{7.30} - 1] \times 100$
$$= 24.88 \text{ percent}$$

4/10, n/30: $\text{Effective annual cost} = [(1.0417)^{18.25} - 1] \times 100$
$$= 110.77 \text{ percent}$$

5/10, n/30: $\text{Effective annual cost} = [(1.05263)^{18.25} - 1] \times 100$
$$= 155.00 \text{ percent}$$

6/10, n/30: $\text{Effective annual cost} = [(1.0638)^{18.25} - 1] \times 100$
$$= 209.17 \text{ percent}$$

2. $Z_1 = 3.3\left(\dfrac{\text{EBIT}}{\text{total assets}}\right) + 1.0\left(\dfrac{\text{sales}}{\text{total assets}}\right) + 0.6\left(\dfrac{\text{market value of equity}}{\text{book value of debt}}\right)$

$\qquad + 1.4\left(\dfrac{\text{retained earnings}}{\text{total assets}}\right) + 1.2\left(\dfrac{\text{working capital}}{\text{total assets}}\right)$

$Z_1 = 3.3\left(\dfrac{200}{1{,}000}\right) + 1.0\left(\dfrac{2{,}000}{1{,}000}\right) + 0.6\left(\dfrac{50 \times 40}{400}\right) + 1.4\left(\dfrac{400}{1{,}000}\right) + 1.2\left(\dfrac{600}{1{,}000}\right)$

$Z_1 = 3.3(0.20) + 1.00(2.00) + 0.60(5.00) + 1.40(0.40) + 1.20(0.60) = 6.94$
$Z_2 = 1.10 + 2.00 + 5.76 + 0.58 + 0.60 = 10.04$
$Z_3 = 1.41 + 2.00 + 8.40 + 0.60 + 0.51 = 12.92$
$Z_4 = 1.65 + 2.00 + 10.97 + 0.61 + 0.45 = 15.68$

3. Prompt payers $= 2{,}000 \times 0.9 = 1{,}800$
    Slow payers $= 2{,}000 \times 0.1 = 200$

$(\text{Prompt} \times \text{probability}) + (\text{slow} \times \text{probability}) = (1{,}800 \times 0.05) + (200 \times 0.22)$
$$= 90 + 44$$
$$= 134$$

A total of 134 accounts--6.7 percent of the total--is expected to default.

4. Expected profit $= 0.78(\$1{,}300 - \$1{,}100) - 0.22(\$1{,}100) = -\$86$

5. $0.78(\text{REV} - \$1,100) - 0 = \$242$
    $$\text{REV} = \$1,410$$

6. Expected payoff $= (0.06 \times \$55) - \$11 = -\$7.70$

7. $0.06x - \$11 = 0$; $x = \$183.33$

8. Step 1: Expected profit on initial order $= p_1 \times \text{PV(revenues - cost)} - (1 - P_1) \times \text{PV(cost)}$
    $$= (0.78 \times \$200) - (0.22 \times \$1,100)$$
    $$= -\$86$$

    Step 2: Next year's expected profit on repeat order $= p_2 \times \text{PV(revenues - cost)} - (1 - P_2) \times \text{PV(cost)}$
    $$= (0.90 \times \$200) - (0.10 \times \$1,100)$$
    $$= \$180 - \$110$$
    $$= \$70$$

    Step 3 Total expected profit = expected profit on initial order + probability of payment and repeat order $\times$ PV of next year's expected profit on repeat order
    $$= -\$86 + \frac{0.78 \times \$70}{1.12}$$

    $$= -\$86 + \$49 = -\$37$$

31

Cash Management

INTRODUCTION

This chapter deals with cash management. Efficient management of a firm's resources tends to maximize the value of the enterprise. Cash is as important to the value and survival of the firm as the management of any of the firm's assets and liabilities. The object of efficient cash management, as always, is to ensure the solvency of the enterprise and to add to the value of the firm. Financial managers knowingly forego the interest return on invested money in exchange for liquidity. The object of cash management is to ensure the proper balance between too little and too much cash (liquidity) and to implement an efficient collection and disbursement system. Cash management also includes systems for efficient flow and collection of cash flowing into and out of the firm.

KEY CONCEPTS IN THE CHAPTER

Cash as Inventory: Firms hold cash because cash provides liquidity. Liquid balances are needed to meet the daily transaction needs. This liquidity comes at the cost of lost interest. What is the optimal balance that a firm should hold? Economists and management scientists have tried to model the trade-off of holding cash against the lost interest. Several inventory models have been developed to solve the problem of how much cash or cash substitutes to keep on hand. In the Baumol model, the three variables of concern are the interest forgone from holding cash, the fixed administrative expenses of buying and selling highly marketable securities, and the rate of cash disbursement.

At the margin, *order costs* are reduced when larger and larger orders are placed, but *carrying costs* rise. The object is to order the needed cash such that the *marginal reduction in order cost* equals the *marginal carrying cost*. The optimal order quantity of cash Q, (the amount of securities to be sold each time to replenish the cash), is given by:

$$Q = \sqrt{\frac{2 \text{ X annual cash disbursement X cost per sale of treasury bills}}{\text{interest rate}}}$$

The Baumol model assumes that cash is depleted and replenished at a fixed rate. The model gives both the optimal amounts of cash to replenish and the frequency and implies that high interest rates imply a low Q.

The assumption of steady depletion is unrealistic. Firms typically face lump sum demands very often. As the transaction cost of converting securities into cash comes down, the level of cash held becomes less and less. Firms hold cash at least partly to compensate banks for the services rendered by them. Decentralized management of operations also results in the need for a higher level of cash than if the system were to be totally centralized. Efficient cash management does imply centralization and most corporations have centralized systems for collections and disbursement.

Cash Collection and Disbursement Systems: Managing collection and disbursement is a very important part of the cash management function. Managing collection and disbursement means managing the flow of cash, which leads to managing the float. Float arises because of the difference in the dates when checks are received for payment of goods and services and when they are cleared. Financial managers estimate the net float between checks written and checks received and adjust cash balances accordingly. Managing float means speeding up collections and optimizing (not to say slowing down) disbursement. Corporations use different systems for speeding up collections. These include:

- *Concentration banking* with centralized accounts and bank accounts close to customers so that checks are likely to clear faster.
- *Lock-box systems* which have optimized collection locations and speedy processing of incoming checks. The system is often used with concentration banking so that collected checks are deposited into one account for optimal disbursement and control.
- Controlled and optimal disbursement.
- Use of information technology, which reduces transaction costs, speeds up transfers, and automates record keeping.

International Cash Management: Efficient cash management across the borders is complicated by the differences in currency, banking systems, and legal structures. Regional systems are typical with local concentration accounts with a bank in each country, surplus cash is then swept into multi-currency accounts in a single center, from which marketable securities can be bought and sold. A company may have several accounts with the same bank in different countries, in different currencies, or both. The bank may agree to take all the accounts together when it calculates the interest it pays or charges. Electronic transfers and computer-based cash management systems are especially valuable in international business.

Electronic Funds Transfer: An instantaneous way of transferring large sums of money is through wire transfers by Fedwire. The international electronic transfers use the CHIPS. Fedwire, operated by the Federal Reserve operates by the gross system (i. e. each transaction is paid off separately) and CHIPS operates as a net system (cross payments are netted out). Fedwire and CHIPS are efficient means of transferring very large sums of money. The Automated Clearinghouse (ACH) system can be used for routine transfers of bulk transactions like wages, dividends, regular payments to suppliers, etc. ACH can transfer funds in two to three days.

Bank Relations: Banks play a major role in cash management. Most of the transactions and cash flows go through the banking system. Thus, relationships with banks are important.

Compensating balances go a long way toward cultivating "friendly" bankers. Good banking relations are essential to efficient cash management.

WORKED EXAMPLES

1. As the financial manager of NUTS Corp., you want to use the Baumol model to determine how frequently you should sell your U.S. Treasury bills in order to cover day-to-day cash outflows, which average $100,000 a month, or $1.2 million a year. If the annual rate of return on your bills is 8.5 percent and it costs $50 each time you sell bills, what is the optimum number of times per year that you should sell the bills?

SOLUTION

To solve this problem, determine the optimum amount of money that will be needed. Using Baumol's formula, the results are as follows:

$$Q = \sqrt{\frac{2 \times \text{annual cash disburement} \times \text{cost of sale of T bills}}{\text{interest rate}}}$$

$$= \sqrt{\frac{2 X \$1,200,000 X 50}{0.085}}$$

$$= \sqrt{\frac{\$120,000,000}{0.085}}$$

$$= \sqrt{\$1,411,764,706}$$

$$= \$37,573.46$$

The optimal amount of bills to be sold is $37,573, rounded to the nearest dollar. Because $100,000 per month is needed, you should sell Treasury bills 2.66 times ($100,000/$37,573) a month, or about 32 times a year (2.66 X 12).

2. As the financial manager of Brady Bunch Company, you forecast that you will need new cash at the rate of $5 million per year. You estimate the cost of money at 9 percent and temporary excess cash balances may be invested at 5 percent. The cost of raising money is $3,000 regardless of the amount raised. How often should you go to the market for capital?

SOLUTION

To solve this problem, you may use the Baumol cash management model, with a twist. First solve for Q, the optimal quantity of cash raised each time:

$$Q = \sqrt{\frac{2 X 5{,}000{,}000 X 3{,}000}{(0.09 - 0.05)}}$$
$$= \$866{,}025$$

This means that you need to make $5,000,000/$866,025 = 5.8 trips.
The best solution is to raise about $900,000 about every 66 days (365 X 0.9/5).

3. Brady Bunch Company has a disbursement float of 2 days and on average sends out $50,000 worth of checks a day. The average return obtainable in the year is 8 percent. What is the annual dollar return obtainable from investing the "unused" portion of your checking account?

SOLUTION

The average amount available   = average float X daily flow
$$= 2 X \$50{,}000 = \$100{,}000$$

Interest earned = $100,000 X 0.08/365 = $21.92

4. Your company is offered a lock box system with the following details

Average number of daily payments	300
Average size of payments	$1,200
Daily interest rate	0.02%
Saving in mailing time	1.3
Saving in processing time	0.7
Bank's charge per check processed	$0.30

Assume 250 processing days per year.

SOLUTION

Daily estimated net profit = [(items per day X size of payment X number of days
saved) X daily interest rate] – bank charges
$$= (300 X \$1{,}200 X 2 X 0.0002) - 300 X 0.28$$
$$= \$144 - \$84 = \$60/day$$
Annual benefit = $60 X 250 = $15,000

SUMMARY

Cash management is an important part of the financial management function. Cash provides liquidity, but does not pay any interest. The balance held by the firm should be optimized. Innovatory type models give optimal "order" quantity. This is a starting point to decide the

382

optimal level of cash holding. Companies, of course, often hold more cash than needed for purely transaction needs and suggested by models like the Baumol model.

The other part of cash management is managing the flow of cash. This deals with collection and disbursement systems. Collection and disbursement systems are designed for managing float, both the collection float and disbursement float. Centralized collection systems using concentration banking, lock boxes, and electronic transfers of excess cash is the key to efficient flow management.

LIST OF TERMS

Automated Clearinghouse system (ACH)	Float
Carrying costs	Lock-box system
CHIPS	Marginal carrying costs
Concentration banking	Payment float
Electronic funds transfer	

EXERCISES

Fill-in Questions

1. The two costs of holding inventory are _____ cost and _____ cost.

2. The _____ is used for transfer of routine and regular payments such as wages and dividends.

3. The _____ and the _____ are two means of electronic funds transfer.

4. The main cost of holding cash is _____.

5. The (higher, lower) _____ the interest rate, the higher the optimum amount of Treasury bills sold.

6. The time lag in the checks that have been written but have not yet cleared is called _____.

7. _____ banking requires customers to make payments to a local bank rather than directly to the company.

8. Renting a post office box to which customers make payments and from which the bank collects the payments is known as the _____ system of cash management.

Problems

1. Burgers & Burgers, Inc., has $2 million invested in Treasury bills yielding 8 percent per annum; this will satisfy the firm's need for funds during the coming year, in addition to the cash it has on deposit, of course. If it costs $50 to sell these bills, regardless of the amount, how much should be withdrawn at a time?

2. If Burgers & Burgers, Inc., needs $167,000 a month, under the conditions of problem 1, how frequently should the financial manager sell off Treasury bills?

3. The financial manager of Burgers & Burgers is explaining why it does not pay to hold more cash than is needed. The company currently has a total of $5 million in cash but estimates that it will need only $1.5 million during the next 3 months. If the cost of transacting in each is the same, what daily dollar return may the financial manager expect if the annual returns on marketable securities are as follows?

U.S. Treasury bills	9.55 percent
Federal agencies	9.75
Negotiable time CDs	10.00
Commercial paper	9.90
Bankers' acceptances	9.80

4. Your banker has offered to set up and operate a lock box system for your company. Details are given below. Estimate the savings.

Average number of daily payments	325
Average size of payments	$1250
Daily interest rate	0.021%
Saving in mailing time	1.3
Saving in processing time	0.9
Bank charges	$0.30

Assume 250 processing days per year.

Essay Questions

1. What rationale can you give for holding cash, especially when it is considered that no interest is earned? Explain fully.

2. In Baumol's model, the higher the interest rate one uses, the lower the quantity Q of cash that is optimal. Explain why this is so.

3. Describe the importance of float management clearly explaining how float may work either for or against a business.

4. Describe how companies manage collection and disbursement systems

ANSWERS TO EXERCISES

Fill-in Questions

1. Carrying; ordering
2. Automated Clearinghouse (ACH)
3. CHIPS; Fedwire
4. The interest foregone

5. Lower
6. Float
7. Concentration
8. Lock-box

Problems

1. $Q = \sqrt{\dfrac{2 \times \$2,000,000 \times \$50}{0.08}}$
   = \$50,000

2. \$167,000/\$50,000 = 3.34 times per month; once every 9 days (30/3.34)

3. Treasury bills = (0.0955/360) X \$3.5 million = \$928.47
   Federal agencies = 947.92
   Negotiable time CDs = 972.22
   Commercial paper = 962.50
   Banker's acceptances = 952.78

4. Estimated profit = [(items per day X size of payment X number of days saved) X daily
        interest rate] - (number of transactions X cost per transaction)
      = (325 X \$1,250 X 2.2 X 0.00021) - (325 X \$0.30)
      = \$188 - \$98 = \$90 a day

   Annual profit = \$90 X 250 = \$22,500

32

Short-Term Lending and Borrowing

INTRODUCTION

This chapter lists the various sources of short-term loans and the typical short-term investments used by corporations to park their short-term surplus cash. Financial managers invest temporary excess cash balances in short-term securities and have to borrow when they have a shortfall of cash. This chapter tells you where to go for either lending or borrowing. Efficient financial management therefore requires a working knowledge of the short-term securities in which financial managers may invest and the major aspects of borrowing short-term funds.

This chapter brings together both the major instruments of short-term lending and borrowing and the ways in which financial managers use them. Some of their major characteristics are:

-   The marketplace in which the instruments of lending and borrowing are traded is known as the *money market*.
-   Short-term debt is usually a less risky investment than corporate bonds.
-   The method of calculating yields on most money-market investments is different from that on other types of investment. Because they are sold at a discount from their face value, the difference between the purchase price and the discount is the interest earned.

KEY CONCEPTS IN THE CHAPTER

The chapter is essentially a listing of different short-term investment assets and sources of short-term borrowing.

Government Instruments: The dominant money-market instrument is U.S. Treasury bills, which have maturities of 90, 180, 270, or 360 days and are sold at auction either competitively or at the average price of successful competitive bids. Next in importance are United States government agency securities. Although they are not backed by the full faith and credit of the United States government, their quality is impeccable. Next in order of quality are short-term securities of states and other municipalities. Because interest income is exempt from federal income taxation, municipals are very desirable for investors in a high marginal income tax bracket.

Deposits: Although they are insured up to $100,000 by the Federal Deposit Insurance Corporation and similar agencies for non-bank financial institutions, regular commercial time deposits are not typically thought of as money-market investments. They are not sold at a discount from face value and are not negotiable. Negotiable deposits at commercial banks are called certificates of deposit and have denominations of $100,000 or more, minimum maturity of 30 days, and a maximum maturity of 270 days. Time deposits of dollars with foreign banks or foreign branches of United States banks are called eurodollar investments.

Commercial Paper: Commercial paper is unsecured short-term debt issued directly by only the best-known, largest, and safest companies. Commercial paper is a notch down in quality from the money-market investments already discussed. Considerable cost savings are obtainable by issuing commercial paper as a source of financing. The firm has to be of very high financial standing and low risk.

Bankers' Acceptances: Bankers' acceptances are demands written on a bank which, when accepted, become negotiable money-market instruments. When the bank accepts them, they become high quality and the returns on them are slightly more than those available on Treasury bills.

Repurchase Agreements: Repurchase agreements are frequently used for investing very short-term cash (overnight money). They are loans secured by a government security dealer and are highly liquid.

Floating-Rate Preferred Stock: A recent innovation, these securities take advantage of the preferentially low tax to corporations of dividend income (70 percent). The rates are typically tied to the prime lending rate. Since most of the investors are corporations eligible for tax-exempt dividends, the rate on these is typically lower than that available on other short-term investments.

Short-Term Borrowing: When companies are short of cash, often they go to banks where they borrow on either an unsecured or a secured basis. Some unsecured loans are self-liquidating, for the sale of goods and services for which the loan was made provides the cash to repay the loan; others are used for interim financing, being replaced when long-term financing is arranged. Frequently a line of credit, which specifies the limit of monies to be borrowed, is arranged.

Secured bank loans usually require collateral, either receivables or inventory. Although almost all trade accounts receivables are acceptable collateral for loans, not all kinds of inventory are. The more one borrows, the more one is charged for loans, until a point is reached at which no more borrowing is possible and the company faces credit rationing.

Bank loans can come in many forms. Often banks can give *commitment* (and charge a commitment fee) for a line of credit. These are in the form of a revolving line of credit. The line of credit may be *evergreen (*without maturity*)* or for a specified term. Banks may offer a short-term *bridging* loan for the purchase of equipment or other needs as an interim financing until longer term financing is tied up. Interest on bank loans may be fixed or tied to benchmarks like the prime rate or LIBOR (London Inter-Bank Offer Rate). It is possible to get an international loan in a foreign currency. Large money-center banks sell some of their loans to other institutions through loan *participations* or *assignments*.

Term Loans: Term loans are another way in which firms finance their short-term needs, even though their duration is as long as 8 years. Often term loan interest rates vary with the prime rate. A revolving credit enables the firm to borrow up to an assured amount over a period of as much as 3 years.

Those firms, which qualify for direct borrowing in the capital market, can raise funding through issue of commercial paper. This would be the cheapest form of financing. Typically, firms which issue commercial paper have a back-up line of credit from banks, just in case.

WORKED EXAMPLES

1. Grand Mack Corporation (GMC) needs $5 million, and the company's bank has offered to make a loan at 10 percent annually, provided the company maintains a 15 percent compensating balance. The manager of a competing bank, indicated that he would lend the company the needed funds for 12 percent with no compensating balance. Which bank is making the better offer? Explain fully. Would your answer be different if (GMC) normally maintained a $50,000 cash balance?

SOLUTION

The compensating balance is $750,000 ($5,000,000 X 0.15). The amount of interest charged is $500,000 ($5,000,000 X 0.1). The amount of funds actually available for use is $4,250,000. Thus, the cost of the loan is the interest cost of $500,000 divided by the effective amount of money available for use is:

$$\text{Effective cost} = \frac{\$500,000}{\$4,250,000} = 0.1176 = 11.76 \text{ percent}$$

This is cheaper than the offer from the second bank.

If the financial manager normally kept an average of $50,000 on deposit, the amount normally available for use increases to $4,300,000 and the cost per annum is only 11.63 percent.

2. GMC decides to take out a 5-year term loan for $5 million at a cost of 1 percent above the prime rate of interest. If the prime rate is 11, 12, 8, 6, and 5 percent per year in each of the years during which the loan is outstanding, what is the dollar interest cost of the loan? Assume the entire loan is paid off at the end of the term.

SOLUTION

$5 million X 0.12 = $ 600,000
$5 million X 0.13 = 650,000

$$\begin{array}{ll} \$5 \text{ million X } 0.09 = & 450,000 \\ \$5 \text{ million X } 0.07 = & 350,000 \\ \$5 \text{ million X } 0.06 = & \underline{300,000} \\ & \$2,350,000 \end{array}$$

3. Compare the loan in problem 2 with a loan which has a fixed 10 percent per year interest cost but which is payable in equal annual installments.

SOLUTION

Using the calculator, solve for PMT, given:

PV = $5,000,000, FV = 0, N = 5, I = 10
PMT = $1,318,987

Total payment = $1,318,987 X 5 = $6,594,935
Interest paid = $1,594,935

4. If a 180-day Treasury bill is quoted at a discount of 5.5 percent, at what price must it be selling? Show calculations.

SOLUTION

The general formula is:

Discount = [(100 - price)/100] X (360/180)

In as much as we wish to find price, we make that our unknown, x, and solve for it. Thus, we have:

0.055 = [(100 - x)/100] X 2

Solving for x, we obtain 97.25, which means that a $10,000 Treasury bill sells for $9,725. The dollar amount of the discount, $275, is the interest earned. It is taxed as ordinary income, not as a capital gain.

5. What is the annual simple interest return on the Treasury bills discussed in problem 4? What is the effective compound rate of return?

SOLUTION

The relative wealth earned over the 180-day period is given by:

100/97.25 = 1.0283

390

or a return of 2.83 percent. When this result is multiplied by 365/180, the annual simple interest return is determined. Thus,

$$\text{Simple annual return} = 2.83 \text{ percent} \times (365/180)$$
$$= 5.74 \text{ percent}$$

The effective compound annual return is 10.24 percent and was found from:

$$(1.0283)^{365/180} - 1 = 5.82 \text{ percent}$$

It is the convention in finance to use 360 days to determine the number of periods over which interest is paid and 365 days to determine the number of periods over which interest is received. This has the effect of raising the effective rate. For example, savings account banks typically compound interest daily. For a rate of 5.5 percent a year, compounded values are as follows:

Number of Days to Discount	Effective Return
360/365	5.734350
e^x	5.654061
365	5.653624
360	5.653617

SUMMARY

This is the last of the chapters dealing with short-term financial management. The chapter gave an account of the different short-term investments and sources of short-term borrowing. There are a number of investments possible with money market instruments of varying degrees of risk and return. The U.S. Treasury bills have the lowest risk, high liquidity, and the lowest return. You can do better in terms of return with the agency securities, commercial paper, negotiable CDs, and so on. Of course, the risk increases, too.

There are also a number of possible short-term sources of funding. Commercial banks are the main source of much of the unsecured borrowing by corporations. Bank loans come in many flavors with different maturities, different ways of charging interest, and other fees. When computing costs of any financing, all costs, including the opportunity cost of compensating balances, should be considered. Corporations with excellent credit record may be able to borrow directly from the market by issuing commercial paper.

LIST OF TERMS

Bankers' acceptances
Bridging loan
Certificate of Deposit (CD)
Commercial paper

Field warehouse
Floor planning
Interim financing
Line of credit

Evergreen credit   Loan assignment
Loan participation   Revolving credit
Money market   Self-liquidating loans
Medium-term notes (MTNs)   Term loan
Repurchase agreement   Warehouse receipt

EXERCISES

Fill-in Questions

1. In general, the default risk for money-market securities is (greater, less) _____ than it is for long-term debt.

2. Money-market investments are _____ securities.

3. When Treasury bills are selling at a discount, their yield (is, is not) _____ the same as the discount.

4. Noncompetitive bids for Treasury bills are filled at the (lowest, average) _____ price of the successful competitive bids.

5   The income from securities of states and other municipalities is (exempt, nonexempt) _____ from federal income taxes.

6. Time deposits are invariably insured by the Federal Deposit Insurance Corporation up to _____.

7. Negotiable certificates of deposit come in denominations of _____ or more.

8. Commercial paper rates usually are (below, equal to, greater than) _____ the prime rate charged by banks.

9. A bank loan, which enables a financial manager to borrow up to a pre-established limit, is known as _____.

10. A loan which is collateralized by receivables but gives the bank the right to require the firm to meet any deficiencies in collection of the receivables to repay the loan is said to be a loan (with, without) _____ recourse.

11. The major difference between a factor loan and the typical receivables loan of commercial banks is that the former (does, does not) _____ buy the receivables, whereas the latter (does, does not) _____.

12. An automobile dealer usually employs _____ in order to finance inventory. As evidence of this arrangement, the automobile dealer signs a trust receipt, which is redeemed when the automobiles are sold.

13. The principal form of medium-term debt financing is called _____.

14. A certificate providing evidence of a bank time deposit is called a
    _____.

15. Unsecured notes issued by companies and maturing within nine months are called
    _____.

16. A written demand that has been accepted by a bank to pay a given sum at a future date is called a _____.

17. A purchase of Treasury securities from a securities dealer with an agreement that the dealer will repurchase them at a later date at a specified price is a _____.

18. An unsecured loan is called a _____ when the sale of goods will provide the cash to repay the loan.

19. A _____ provides evidence that your company owns goods placed in a public warehouse.

20. If you arrange for a warehouse company to lease your warehouse, and to be responsible for storing your pledged goods, only releasing them on the instructions of the holder of the warehouse receipt, the warehouse is called a _____.

21. A legally assured line of credit with a bank, which provides a put option to borrow on fixed terms for up to three years, is known as _____.

22. Large money center banks often sell their loans to other banks through _____ or _____.

23. A _____ is an interim loan given for a specific purpose till other financing is arranged.

Problems

1. Burgers & Burgers 's bank has offered to lend the firm $5 million at an annual rate of 12 percent, provided the company maintains a compensating balance of 25 percent. Because the financial manager does not think this is the best deal he can obtain, he approached a competitor bank and it offered him a $5 million loan at 15 percent annually with a 10 percent compensating balance. Which is the better deal, expressed on an annual basis?

393

2. What would be the better deal if the company in problem 1 usually kept on deposit an average of $100,000?

3. Whoppers Corp. decided to take out a 5-year $10 million term loan whose rate of interest is 2 percent above the prime rate. If the prime rate is 10, 11, 12, 13, and 9 percent in each of the years the loan is outstanding, what is the dollar amount of interest paid?

4. How does the loan in problem 3 compare with a 16 percent loan, payable in equal annual installments? What is the dollar difference in interest paid?

5. If 91-day Treasury bills were selling at a discount of 8.53 percent, at what price must the bills have been selling?

6. What is the annual simple interest of the bills discussed in problem 5? What is the annual compound rate of return?

Essay Questions

1. Briefly describe the money market and the investments that are traded there.

2. What does it mean when we say, "Money-market investments are pure discount securities"?

3. Discuss the following statement: "Because the middle man is eliminated, or at least most of his functions are eliminated, when commercial paper is issued, there is a significant reduction in the cost of funds when commercial paper is used."

4. What is meant by a self-liquidating loan? Interim financing? Line of credit?

5. What provisions are typically found in a line of credit? Explain why you think they are there.

6. What characteristics should be possessed by assets that are used as collateral for inventory loans?

ANSWERS TO EXERCISES

Fill-in Questions

1. Less
2. Discount
3. Is not
4. Average
5. Exempt

8. Below
9   A line of credit
10. With
11. Does; does not
12. Floor planning

6. $100,000
7. $100,000
15. Commercial paper
16. Banker's acceptance
17. Repurchase agreement (or repo)
18. Self-liquidating loan
19. Warehouse receipt

13. Term loans
14. Certificate of deposit (CD)
20. Field warehouse
21. Revolving credit
22. Loan assignments; loan participation
23. Bridging loan

Problems

1. Bank 1: $5,000,000 X 0.25 = $1,250,000 (compensating balance)
   $5,000,000 X 0.12 = $600,000   (dollar cost)
          Cost = $600,000/$3,750,000 = 16 percent

   Bank 2: $5,000,000 X 0.10 = $500,000   (compensating balance)
   $5,000,000 X 0.15 = $750,000   (dollar cost)
          Cost = $750,000/$4,500,000 = 16.7 percent

2. Bank 1: $600,000/$3,875,000 = 15.5 percent
   Bank2: $750,000/$4,600,000 = 16.3 percent

3. $10 million X 0.10 = $1.0 million
   $10 million X 0.11 =   1.1 million
   $10 million X 0.12 =   1.2 million
   $10 million X 0.13 =   1.3 million
   $10 million X 0.09 =   0.9 million
                          $5.5 million

4. Using the BA II-Plus calculator:
   Solve for PMT given: PV = $10,000,000, FV = 0, N = 5, I = 16
   PMT = $3,054,094 (Annual payment)
   Total payment = $3,054,094 X 5 = $15,270,470
   Interest payment = $15,270,470 - $10,000,000 = $5,270,470

5. $8.53 = \dfrac{100 - x}{100} \times \dfrac{360}{91}$
   x = 97.8438 or $9,784.38

6. 100/97.8438 = 1.022
   Annual simple interest = 2.2 X 4 = 8.8 = 8.8%
   Annual compound rate of return = $1.022^{365/91} - 1 = 9.12\%$

395

33

Mergers

INTRODUCTION

The last two decades have seen a number of corporate mergers or unions. Mergers can be evaluated in the same way as any other investment. As long as the merged firms are worth more combined than when alone, the net present value of the fusion is profitable and shareholders are better off. Financial managers need to know under what conditions it is worthwhile to merge with another firm.

The chapter starts with reasons why companies merge. The motives for mergers include both those, which make sense, and those, which do not. This is followed by coverage of the benefits and costs of mergers and how these are evaluated. The chapter also provides summary coverage of the legal, tax, and accounting issues. A number of examples of recent merger activities are described with a discussion of defensive tactics adopted by companies opposed to being taken over. The last section discusses the benefits and costs of mergers to the economy in general and the effect of the threat of a takeover on corporate management.

Mergers can be the result of a hostile takeover or a friendly union. In either case, mergers typically result in a change of *ownership* and *control*. Even in the so-called mergers of equals, one can see that one company's management dominates the post-merger firm. Thus, merger activities are part of a broader market for corporate control. This market includes not only mergers, but also spin-offs and other restructuring activities, which change the structure of the corporation and provide the right incentives for managers. These and related issues are discussed in greater detail in the next chapter.

KEY CONCEPTS IN THE CHAPTER

Sensible Motives for Mergers: Most mergers are of one three categories: i) horizontal integration, in which two firms in the same line of business are merged, ii) vertical integration, in which firms which have supplier-customer linkage are combined, and iii) conglomerates, in which companies in unrelated businesses are combined. These are possible reasons why two firms may be worth more together than apart. An acquisition adds value only if it generates additional economic rents - providing a further competitive edge that is not easily reproduced. Motives, which make sense, include the following:

- Economies of scale, most common with horizontal mergers,
- Economies of vertical integration, including costs savings through better coordination and administration, technological advantages, and synergy,

397

-   Ability to swap unused tax shields and use of surplus funds, and
-   Combining complementary sources.

These motives can make sense and can add value when the companies are combined. There may be difficulty in realizing many of the cost savings or other benefits because of the problems of coordinating activities across two different organizational "cultures" who are not used to working together.

Dubious Motives: While the above reasons for mergers can make sense, there are other professed motives, which do not. These include the following:

Diversification: It is often argued that by merging across different industries (conglomerate merger), the shareholders can enjoy the benefit of reduced risk. The shareholders get all the diversification they want at a much lower cost and more efficiently than by buying shares in the two companies separately.

Bootstrapping: When a company with a high price-earnings ratio (P/E) merges with a low P/E company, the combined firm can enjoy higher earnings per share. This looks like a neat trick, if you can pull it off. The problem is that the company with the lower P/E probably has a lower P/E because it has lower growth or less reliable earnings. The market will value the combined firm at a P/E lower than that of the high P/E firm, because the combined firm has lower growth or less reliable earnings. Bootstrappers assume inefficient markets and investors, who can't see beyond their nose!

Lower financing costs: The argument is that the combined firm can borrow at a lower rate. It is possible that the larger firm can enjoy economies of scale in terms of issue costs. It is also possible that the merging firms, by effectively guaranteeing each other's debt are lowering the risk of the lenders and thus, are transferring wealth from their stockholders to the bondholders. This is good for the bondholders, but not for the stockholders.

Benefits and Costs of Mergers: A merger adds value if the value of the combined firm is greater than the sum of the values of the individual firms. This will happen if the gain from the merger is more than the cost. We can write the gain from a merger of firms A and B as follows:

$$\text{Gain} = PV_{AB} - (PV_A + PV_B) = \Delta PV_{AB}$$

where PV represents the value of each firm and the combined firm. The cost of the merger is the price paid less the value of the firm. Assume that firm B is being bought by firm A and the price for B is paid in cash. Then the cost is:

$$\text{Cost} = \text{cash paid} - PV_B$$

If the markets for publicly held stocks are efficient, companies selling below their intrinsic value are not likely to be found. The costs of cash deals are straightforward and the cost of a merger is the premium that the buying firm pays for the selling firm over the value of a selling firm's value as a separate entity.

The NPV of the merger will be:

$$NPV = Gain - Cost = \Delta PV_{AB} - (\text{cash paid} - PV_B)$$

This formulation of the NPV of the merger focuses attention on the gain and cost separately. The gain is given by the increase in value by the combination of the two firms. The cost represents the apportionment of the gain between the shareholders of the two companies. When the market anticipates the merger, the target firm's share price might have risen in anticipation. This overstates the true value of the firm. In other words, PV_B would be less than the market value. In such cases, you have to look at the intrinsic, or stand-alone, value of B. The actual cost to firm A will be higher and B's shareholders get more of the gains from the merger.

Cost of a Merger When Financed by Stock: When a merger is financed by stock, the cost of the merger depends on the value of the shares in the new company received by the stockholders of the target firm. If the sellers get N shares and each share is worth P_{AB} after the merger, then the cost is:

$$Cost = \text{Number of shares paid X share price} - PV_B = N \ X \ P_{AB} - PV_B$$

To get the true cost, you have to use the price after the merger.

The presence of a*symmetric information* between the acquiring firm's managers and the outside investors, including firm B's shareholders, may explain when the managers would choose stock or cash methods of payment. If the managers think that their stock is overvalued, then they are likely to use stock as the mode of payment for the merger. This explains why share prices fall when stock-financed mergers are announced.

The Mechanics of a Merger: Mergers are complicated affairs and involve complex legal, tax, and accounting issues. These are briefly discussed below.

Legal Aspects: Federal anti-trust laws can block well-laid plans for mergers. Recent examples of blocked mergers include the planned union of Staples and Office Depot, and Northrop Grumman and Lockheed. There are three principal statutes, which govern legal requirements of mergers and corporate combinations. The Justice Department oversees the observance of the laws. The Sherman Act (1890) made every combination or contract restraining trade illegal. The Federal Trade Commission Act (1914) forbids unfair methods of competition. The Clayton Act (1914), with later amendments and legislation, has the most important implications to merger activities. The law prohibits acquisition of any kind, which may lessen competition or tend to create a monopoly. The Act forbids even potential constraints and the Justice Department has used the Clayton Act as its main weapon to prevent corporate combinations, which, in its opinion, created a threat to competition in any industry or business.

The Form of Acquisition: There are forms of acquisition normally used by corporations in the U.S. The first is to merge the two companies totally combining all assets and liabilities. The acquiring company assumes all the assets and all the liabilities of the seller. The second approach involves buying out the shares of the target firm in exchange for cash, shares, or other securities. In this approach, the buyer can deal directly with the shareholders and by-pass the managers of the seller firm. The last method involves buying some or all of the assets of the seller and the ownership of the assets are transferred to the buyer.

Accounting Issues: The main accounting issue is to decide the accounting treatment of the merger. Two alternatives are used. In the first approach is called the *purchase of assets*. This method shows any premium over the book value paid to the seller as goodwill and amortized over forty years. The alternative is to use the *pooling of interests*. The balance sheets of the two firms are simply added together; no goodwill is shown. In efficient capital markets, accounting treatments should make no difference, as there are no differences in the cash flows.

Tax Issues: Mergers can be *taxable* acquisitions, where the target firm's shareholders are viewed as having sold shares and taxed accordingly. The acquiring firm revalues the assets and starts with new depreciation schedules. In the alternative approach, the transaction is *tax-free* and selling shareholders are seen as exchanging shares for new ones of like kind and quality; the firm is taxed as if two firms had always been together.

Merger Tactics: Many mergers are friendly transactions where the management of the two firms negotiates a mutually acceptable deal. But some acquisitions are *hostile takeovers,* where the target firm, or the management of the firm, is not keen on the merger. This leads to defensive tactics aimed at stopping the merger. What follows is often a battle of legal wits and firepower between the two firms. A colorful language has sprung up around takeover battles. Typically, the acquiring firm can go over the head of the unwilling target firm's management using *tender offers* inviting shareholders to sell shares directly to the acquiring firm. Once they have enough shares or shareholder support, the acquiring firm can start a *proxy* fight to get the needed support from the board of the target firm. Here are some other terms commonly used in the takeover jargon:

Arbitrageurs (or arbs): Speculators who buy the target firm's stocks in the expectation that it will rise quickly.

Golden parachutes: This describes a very liberal compensation package for managers who lose their jobs because of a takeover. The availability of the golden parachute will ensure that the managers will not have an incentive to fight any takeover of the company at the cost of the shareholders.

Greenmail: Buying out the raider's shares at an attractive price, without offering the same price to other stockholders.

Pacman defense: The target firm attempts the takeover of the raider and thus, hopes to takeover before being taken over.

Poison pill: Existing shareholders get rights, which are triggered when there is a significant purchase of the firm' shares, to buy the company's shares at a bargain price. This will make the raider's shares lose value.

Poison put: Bondholders get rights to sell the bonds back to the company, when there is a change of control as a result of a takeover.

Shark-repellent: Amendments to the corporate charter, which will make the firm very unattractive or difficult as a target. The amendments can include: restricted voting rights to new shareholders, requiring super-majority approvals for certain resolutions to be approved by the shareholders, and staggered change of the board of directors.

Many such tactics are challenged in the courts, and states tend to legislate in favor of the incumbent management. It is unclear whether an incumbent management wishes merely to perpetuate itself or act in the best long-run interest of shareholders when it fights a potential acquisition. Managers of target firms could be contesting takeover for protecting shareholders interests and get as high a price as possible for the shareholders. It is also possible that they may be doing it because of the fear of losing their jobs.

Some companies do restructuring of the company's assets and liabilities to ward off the raiders. The restructuring often includes selling non-profitable businesses and increasing leverage, the kind of restructuring typically done by raiders. Firms become targets precisely because they are under-performing and their assets are worth less than they could be. Restructuring improves value and can act as the best long-term defense.

Mergers and the Economy: Mergers seem to come in waves, with the major merger activity occurring during periods of stock market buoyancy. Why then? We do not know. The economic rationale for it is lacking. The 1980s saw the confluence of several major events: large cash flows that did not have a "home," the development of the LBO and MBO concepts, the development of the junk bond market, and the ability of institutional investors to invest heavily in junk bonds. It is still not clear that these factors explain the occasional merger waves we have seen in the past.

A more interesting and important question relates to the impact of mergers on the economy and society. Are mergers good for the economy? There are arguments, which suggest that they are. These include: mergers and acquisitions make firms more efficient; they get rid of inefficient management; and the fear of takeovers makes managers perform better. Others argue that:

401

raiders take a short-term view, often use excessive leverage, and cut R&D and other expenses, which give long-term benefits. Economists cannot seem to agree.

WORKED EXAMPLES

1. Sink, Inc., plans to merge with Swim Corp. The capital market places a value on Sink of $7.875 million and Swim is valued at $500,000, when they are evaluated separately. After the merger, economies of scale will result in additional cash flows, the present value of which is $250,000. Sink will buy Swim for $600,000 in cash. Sink has 150,000 shares outstanding. What are the costs, gain, and NPV of the merger?

SOLUTION

$$\text{Cost} = \text{cash paid} - PV_{\text{Swim}}$$
$$= \$600,000 - \$500,000$$
$$= \$100,000$$

$$\text{Gain} = (\$7,875,000 + \$500,000 + \$250,000) - (\$7,875,000 + \$500,000)$$
$$= \$250,000$$

$$\text{NPV} = \text{gain} - \text{cost}$$
$$= \$250,000 - \$100,000$$
$$= \$150,000$$

2. How did the shareholders of Sink and of Swim make out on the merger?

SOLUTION

To determine how shareholders make out from a merger, begin by recognizing that the cost of the merger is a gain to Swim's shareholders; they capture $100,000 of the $250,000 gain. The NPV calculated above is the gain to Sink's shareholders. It works out this way:

Net gain to acquiring firm's shareholders = overall gain to combination – gain captured by
acquired firm's shareholders
$$= \$250,000 - \$100,000$$
$$= \$150,000$$

3. Here is a Bootstrapping merger. Now say that Sink, Inc., is considering the acquisition of Float Company. The data for this deal are set forth in the table below. Assuming there are no economic gains from the merger, complete the final column of the table and comment on the merger.

The final column is completed as follows. The share price of Sink, Inc., is twice that of Float Company. Sink, Inc., can, therefore, offer 1 share for every 2 of Float Company. The final number of shares in the combined companies will be 225,000 (line 4). The share price (line 2) remains $52.50 and the total market value (line 6) is the product of these ($11,812,500) and also the sum of the two individual market values, since there are no economic gains from the merger. Since the total earnings (line 5) become $1,050,000, earnings per share (line 1) increase to $4.67 and the price-earnings ratio (line 3) becomes 11.25. Sink had been selling at a higher multiple of earnings per share than Float, and as a result, its earnings per share increase. The benefits of such "bootstrapping" is a myth and does not create value.

Impact of a merger on the market value and earnings per share of Sink, Inc.:

	Sink, Inc. (Pre-merger)	Float Company	Sink, Inc. (Post-merger)
1. Earnings per share	$3.50	$3.50	$4.67
2. Price per share	$52.50	$26.25	$52.50
3. Price-earnings ratio	15.00	7.50	11.25
4. Number of shares	150,000	150,000	225,000
5. Total earnings	$525,000	$525,000	$1,050,00
6. Total market value	$7,875,000	$3,937,500	$1,182,500
7. Current earnings per dollar invested in stock (line 1 divided by line 2)	$0.067	$0. 133	$0.089

*Because of rounding, not all the numbers are exact.

4. Now let's say Sink, Inc., wishes to estimate the cost of a merger that entails an exchange of 11,429 (rounded to nearest full share) instead of $600,000 in cash. What are the apparent and true costs of the merger?

SOLUTION

The apparent cost is straightforward:

$$\text{Apparent cost} = (\text{number of shares X market price per share}) - PV_{\text{Swim}}$$
$$= (11,429 \times \$52.50) - \$500,000$$
$$= \$600,023 - \$500,000$$
$$= \$100,023$$

This is the same as before. The true cost is determined by the amount of the new value the Swim shareholders obtain in the deal. Begin by solving for x in this equation:

$$x = \frac{\underline{\text{new shares issued to acquired firm's shareholders}}}{\text{(outstanding shares of acquiring firm + new shares issued to acquired firm's shareholders)}}$$

$$= \frac{11,429}{150,000 + 11,429} = \frac{11,429}{161,429}$$

$$= 0.0708 = 7.08 \text{ percent}$$

Sink, Inc., gives up slightly more than 7 percent of its claim on the total value of the merged firm. Now, we proceed to determine the true cost of the merger in this way:

$$\begin{aligned}
\text{True cost} &= x\text{PV}_{\text{Sink + Swim}} - \text{PV}_{\text{Swim}} \\
&= 0.0708(\$7,875,000 + \$500,000 + \$250,000) - \$500,000 \\
&= 0.0708(\$8,625,000) - \$500,000 \\
&= \$610,650 - \$500,000 \\
&= \$110,650
\end{aligned}$$

SUMMARY

The chapter describes corporate mergers and the various issues involved. These include the benefits, motives, the mechanics, the tax and accounting issues and the defense tactics of firms which do not want to merge or be taken over. Mergers have become quite common in the last two decades. A merger is a positive NPV activity if the value of the combined firm is more than the sum of the values of the combining firms. This gain can come from economies of scale, benefits of vertical integration, improved efficiency, use of tax shields and combination of complimentary resources. At least in some cases, companies merge for dubious reasons. Corporate diversification, for example, gives little benefit to shareholders, as the shareholders do it themselves far more efficiently and cheaply.

The chapter gave several examples of recent takeover "battles." There are some companies, or at least their management, which do not want to be taken over. These management use tough defense tactics and often succeed in preventing takeovers.

Whether mergers benefit the economy and the society is still being debated. Acquisitions and the fear of the same appear to make corporate management more efficient and responsive to shareholders. On the other hand, some people argue that corporate mergers result in leveraging of companies and trade-off long-term gains for short-term profits. These charges, while not quite proven, have a strong appeal. Courts and legislatures in many states appear to side with the incumbent management fighting to retain control over their firms.

LIST OF TERMS

Arbitrageur
Bootstrapping
Clayton Act (1914)
Federal Trade Commission Act (1914)
Golden parachute
Pooling of interest accounting
Purchase of asset accounting
Shark repellent
Sherman Act (1890)
Staggered board

Greenmail
Horizontal mergers
Pac-man defense
Poison pills
Poison put
Super majority
Tender offer
Two tier offer
Vertical mergers
White knight

EXERCISES

Fill-in Questions

1. A(n) _____ is a friendly company, which steps in to prevent a hostile takeover.

2. Investors who speculate on the likely success of takeover bids are called _____.

3. When a firm, which is the target of a hostile takeover bid, mounts a takeover bid for the hostile raider, it is called the _____ defense.

4. The _____ Act of 1890 declared that "every contract, combination . . . or conspiracy, in restraint of trade" is illegal.

5. The _____ Act focuses primarily on unfair competition, and the _____ focuses primarily on acts that tend to lessen competition substantially or create a monopoly.

6. _____ defense tactics include poison pills, super-majority requirements, and staggered board.

7. A(n) _____ merger is one that takes place between two firms in the same line of business; and a(n) _____ merger is one in which the buyer expands forward or backward to the ultimate consumer or the supplier of raw materials.

8. _____ mergers do not create any economic gains and involves two companies with different P/E ratios but similar earnings numbers.

9. _____ gives bondholders the right to sell the bonds back to the company if the management control changes on account of a takeover.

10. A(n) _____ is a general offer made directly to a firm's shareholders to buy their stock at a specified price.

11. When a merger takes place and two firms' separate balance sheets are added, this is called a(n) _____ from an accounting standpoint.

12. When the accounting technique used to give evidence to a merger gives rise to goodwill, it is safe to assume that a(n) _____ method of accounting was used.

13. A (an) _____ is a tender offer which gives a higher price for shareholders who tender their shares earlier.

14. A _____ is a compensation arrangement, which gives a generous package for managers who have to leave the company because of a takeover.

15. _____ is the term used to describe various contractual and financial arrangements that make a firm a less attractive merger target.

16. When shares held by a raider are bought back by the company at a negotiated price above the current market price, it is called _____.

Problem

Use the data for the three separate firms in the table below to answer the following questions. Answer each question independently of all other questions.

a. What are the costs and net present value of the combination of What-Not, Inc., and If-Not, Inc., if, as a result of the merger, the economies expected are $400,000 and What-Not, Inc., plans to pay $3 million in cash for If-not?

b. If What-Not acquires If-Not for $3 million in cash, how will the shareholders of each make out on the deal?

c. What-Not, Inc., merges with Why-Not, Inc. There are no economic gains from the merger and $1.2 million in stock is paid for Why-Not. Show the bootstrapping effect of the merger.

	WHAT-NOT, INC.	IF-NOT, INC.	WHY-NOT, INC.
Earnings per share	$4	$2	$2
Price per share	$64	$28	$12
Price-earnings ratio	16	14	6
Number of shares	200,000	100,000	200,000
Total earnings	$800,000	$200,000	$200,000
Total market value	$12,800,000	$2,800,000	$2,400,000

Book values:

NWC	$1.1	$0.4	$0.3
FA	2.8	1.0	0.8
D	2.0	0.7	0.3
E	1.9	0.7	0.8

d. Calculate the apparent and true costs of the merger between What-Not, Inc., and If-Not, Inc., assuming expected economies of $400,000 and the shareholders of If-Not receive one share of What-Not for every two shares they hold.

e. Show the results of accounting for the merger between What-Not, Inc., and If-Not, Inc., using both pooling of assets and purchase of assets methods, where If-Not is acquired for $3 million.

Essay Questions

1. Explain why buying another company is just like any other investment decision that financial managers make.

2. What are some the motives for mergers and acquisitions, which make sense?

3. What are the dubious reasons given for mergers?

4. Who gains more from a merger, the selling company or the acquiring one? Explain the reasons why you think one gains more than the other does. Is it possible that neither gains? Explain.

5. Many financial management contest takeovers. Why do you think this is the case, and what techniques do they employ?

6. Describe some of the defense tactics used by the management of target firms fighting takeovers.

ANSWERS TO EXERCISES

Fill-in Questions

1. White knight
2. Arbitrageurs
3. Pac-man
4. Sherman Act
5. Federal Trade Commission; Clayton Act
6. Shark repellent

9. Poison put
10. Tender offer
11. Pooling of interests
12. Purchase of assets
13. Two-tier offer
14. Golden parachute
15. Poison pill

7. Horizontal; vertical; conglomerate   16. Greenmail
8. Bootstrapping

Problem

a. Cost $= \text{cost} - PV_{\text{If-Not}}$
    $= \$3,000,000 - \$2,800,000$
    $= \$200,000$

   NPV = gain - cost
    $= [PV_{W+I} - (PV_W + PV_I)] - (\text{cash} - PV_I)$
    $= [(12.8 + 2.8 + 0.4) - (12.8 + 2.8)] - (3.0 - 2.8)$
    $= 16 - 15.6 - 0.2$
    $= 0.4 - 0.2$
    $= 0.200 = \$200,000$

b. Net gain to acquiring firm= average gain to combination - gain captured by acquired firm
    What's gain = \$400,000 - \$200,000 (If's gain) = \$200,000

   What's gain:

   NPV = wealth with merger - wealth without merger
    $= (PV_{W+I} - \text{cash outlay}) - PV_W$
    $= [(12.8 + 2.8 + 0.4) - 3)] - 12.8$
    $= 16 - 3 - 12.8 = 13 - 12.8$
    $= \$200,000$

c. Number of shares used to buy Why-Not= value of Why-Not/market price per share of
    What-Not
    $= \$2,400,000/\$64$
    $= 37,500 \text{ shares}$

   Total shares outstanding after merger $= 200,000 + 37,500$
    $= 237,500$

Bootstrapping effects of the merger between What-Not, Inc., and Why-Not, Inc.:

	What-Not, Inc. (Pre-merger)	Why-Not, Inc.	What-Not, Inc. (Post-merger)
1. Earnings per share	$4.00	$2.00	$4.21
2. Price per share	$64	$12	$64
3. Price-earnings ratio	16	6	15.20

4. Number of shares	200,000	200,000	237,500
5. Total earnings	$800,000	$200,000	$1,000,000
6. Total market value	$12,800,000	$2,400,000	$15,200,000
7. Current earnings per dollar invested in stock	$0.0625	$0.1667	$0.0658

d. Apparent cost = (number of shares X market price per share) – PV_I

$$= (50,000 \text{ X } \$64) - 2.8$$
$$= 3.2 - 2.8$$
$$= \$400,000$$

True cost:

x = new shares issued to acquired firm's stockholders/outstanding shares of acquiring firm + new shares

$$= 50,000/(200,000 + 50,000)$$
$$= 50,000/250,000$$
$$= 0.2$$

True cost = $(x)(PV_{W+I}) - PV_I$
$$= 0.2 \text{ X } 16.0 - 2.8$$
$$= 0.4 = \$400,000$$

e. Purchase of assets vs. Pooling of interest of What-Not, Inc., and If-Not, Inc.:

Initial Balance Sheets:

What-Not, Inc

NWC	$1.1	D	$2.0
FA	2.8	E	1.9
	$3.9		$3.9

If-Not, Inc.

NWC	$0.4	D	$0.7
FA	1.0	E	0.7
	$1.4		$1.4

Pooling Of Interest
What-Not. Inc.

NWC	$1.5	D	$2.7
FA	3.8	E	2.6
	$5.3		$5.3

Purchase Of Assets
What-Not. Inc.

NWC	$1.5	D	$2.7
FA	3.8		
Goodwill	2.3	E	4.9
	$7.6		$7.6

34

Control, Governance, and Financial Architecture

INTRODUCTION

This chapter takes off from the last chapter and looks at issues broader than mergers. Mergers can be considered part of a broader market for corporate control and governance as mergers and acquisitions cause change in corporate control. In the U.S., corporate control and governance take on special meaning as professional managers who are not dominant shareholders of the company manage most large corporations. In other words, there is separation between ownership and control. What makes managers work in the best interest of the shareholders? What are the mechanisms, which will ensure that shareholder interests are heeded by the managers when they decide on important investment and financing decisions? How does the U.S. system differ from its counterparts in other industrialized countries? These are some of the questions raised and answered in this chapter.

The chapter starts with simple definitions of some common terms used in the discussion; *corporate control* denotes the power to make investment and financing decisions. *Corporate governance* stands for the broader oversight structure of a corporation including the role of board of directors and shareholders' actions to influence corporate decisions through the management. In essence, control is the day to day management and governance structure, which ensure that shareholders' interests are kept in mind by the management when it makes important decisions. *Financial architecture* is the financial organization of the whole business; it is partly corporate control and partly corporate governance.

The chapter has three sections. The first section discusses leveraged buyouts (LBO), spin-offs, and other restructuring of corporations as attempts to change corporate control. The well-known RJR-Nabisco buyout of the eighties is described at length in all the gory details, but focussing on the lessons from the tale. The following section takes on conglomerates and the pros and cons for this corporate phenomenon, which appears to have differing degrees of success in different countries. While they are *not* considered particularly successful and appear headed for extinction in the U.S., they are alive and well in many other countries. The next section compares the governance structures in the U.S., Japan, and Germany and points out the striking differences across these three highly successful industrialized countries. It appears that the governance systems and financial architecture of large industrialized companies have evolved in somewhat different ways in these countries. History and ownership structure may be part of the explanation.

KEY CONCEPTS IN THE CHAPTER

LBOs, Spin-offs, and Restructuring: An LBO is the acquisition of a company financed by large amounts of debt. Typically, the company is taken private after the LBO. The group, which takes over the company, will usually be a partnership of investors. When the management of the company leads this group it is termed a management buyout (MBO). The chapter describes the RJR-Nabisco story in great detail. This was the largest LBO to date. The company was taken private by the partnership firm, Kohlberg, Kravis, and Roberts (KKR), after an initial bid by a group of managers led by the company's CEO. The RJR-Nabisco LBO is typical in some ways. Leverage was used to the hilt to finance the takeover. The shareholders of the pre-LBO company made huge gains in the market as their stock shot up from about $56 to $109 in just over a month. The new management cut back on waste and inefficiency and the company became lean and mean.

Was the LBO beneficial to all the stakeholders of RJR-Nabisco? The answer is no. Bondholders, in particular, lost as the value of their bonds declined sharply on account of the leveraging of the company. Thus part of the gain for the stockholders came from the loss of the bondholders. However, there were still gains of about $8 billion for the stockholders and most of this could have only come from improved operations and the value created by the LBO.

Leverage and Value: The prime driver of value in LBOs is the leverage. How does leverage create value? Part of the value comes from the tax deductions (see chapter 18). However, this appears to be a fairly small part. The main motive force is the incentives created by leverage. An LBO appears to make a company much more efficient and the managers and employees work harder, as they have to generate cash to service the debt. Typically, managers are also given incentives through ownership of the company. Empirical evidence supports the view that LBOs and MBOs make the companies more efficient and create value and not just transfer wealth from one group of stakeholders to another.

Leveraged Restructurings: The primary source of value in the LBO is leverage. Therefore, it is possible for companies to take on leverage without going through the buyout. The increased debt servicing requirements can make the company's managers strive harder. There are a couple of examples given in the text (Phillips Petroleum and Sealed Air). The restructuring with leverage appears to work for some companies.

Financial Architecture of LBOs and Leveraged restructuring: As stated before, LBOs, MBOs, and leveraged restructurings are similar. The key components found in all LBOs (and MBOs) are:

- High leverage,
- Incentives for managers, and
- Private ownership.

Leveraged restructurings have the first two but they remain as public corporations.

Spin-offs: A spin-off is a new company created out of the assets and operations of an existing company and the shares in the new company are distributed to the parent company's stockholders. A spin-off allows shareholders to invest in part of the business. Spin-offs can be tax-free to the shareholders of the parent company and are given at least 80 percent of the shares in the new company. Spin-offs can improve incentives for managers and allow them to focus better. If the businesses are independent, the investors can also value them better.

A *carve-out* is similar to a spin-off, but the shares are sold to the public. *Tracking stocks* are stocks tied to the performance of specific divisions. Tracking stocks appear to be gaining popularity as the Internet boom has prompted quite a few companies to start their own Internet companies and tracking stocks tied to internet divisions.

Privatization: There are many government owned companies engaged in all kinds of businesses around the world. This is true not just in the former socialist block countries, but even in the industrialized countries. Airlines and railroads have been government owned in many countries. It is generally accepted now that private corporations do the job better and therefore, privatization has become the rage around the world. Essentially, privatization is the sale of a government owned company to private investors. The main benefits expected from privatization are:

- Increased efficiency,
- Share ownership and participation by employees and small investors, and
- Revenue for the government.

The type of privatization varies from country to country. In some cases, the government owned companies are auctioned off to the highest bidders, and in other cases, only a part of the company is sold to investors in a public offering.

Conglomerates: Conglomerates are companies with many diversified businesses. They were very popular and were the rage in the sixties. This was the time when many American corporations rushed to acquire businesses to diversify and become larger and larger. Some companies had operations in 30 or more different industries. The eighties started seeing the decline and fall of the conglomerates and very few of them remain in the U.S.

The main benefits claimed for this form of corporate expansion are:

- Diversification and reduced risk,
- Better management, and
- Internal capital markets, which will enable channeling, funds to the ones with best growth opportunities.

None of these benefits were of real value. Diversification is of dubious benefit to the shareholder, who can get this at a lower cost directly in the market by buying shares of the

413

companies in different industries. Better management is not the virtue of conglomerates only; in other words, a company can get better management without being part of a conglomerate. Also, internal capital markets are not better than the real (external) capital market. Thus, in a country like the U.S. with well functioning capital markets and a mobile pool of managers, the benefits of conglomerates were far less than the costs. The costs were large bureaucracy, inefficiency, and internal politics. Most conglomerate shares were selling at a discount compared to the value of their assets. The eighties and nineties saw the break up of many conglomerates and most of them have disappeared.

The financial architecture of conglomerates used two managerial tasks:

- Ensure superior divisional performance and
- Operate efficient internal capital market, which is better than the external capital market.

Very few conglomerates succeeded in getting this done straight. The exceptions appear to be the *temporary conglomerates* such as KKR. They are private *limited partnerships*. The general partners manage the business and the limited partners invest most of the funds needed. The general partners look for companies to invest in and give incentives to the managers of individual businesses.

The partnership agreement runs for a limited term, typically ten years or less. The portfolio of companies must be sold and proceeds distributed. The fee structure of the partnership gives the general partners tremendous incentives to produce the best results. In terms of the businesses they buy, the general motto of the successful partnerships is *buy, fix, and sell*. They buy companies, which are poorly managed, fix them, and then sell them. On the other hand, the permanent conglomerates' policy appears to be *buy, manage, and keep*.

While conglomerates are a dying breed in the U.S., they appear to be prospering in some other countries such as Korea, India, and some Latin American countries. There are factors in these countries which probably help in their success in these countries. These include:

- Small markets allowing little economies of scale or other advantages of size if the company is focussed in one industry,
- Undeveloped capital markets imply that internal capital markets can be better, and
- History and tradition.

Overall, it appears that conglomerates can succeed only in markets that are less developed or small. In industrialized countries with well developed capital markets, they are not likely to have any significant advantage.

Governance Structure in Industrialized Countries: The broad governance structure in the U.S. appears capable of taking agency problems and other conflicts of interests created by the separation of ownership and control. This governance structure of U.S. companies have evolved around the following key components:

- Right incentives for managers, such as compensation tied to stock price and performance,
- The legal, accounting, and other institutional structure, and
- The threat of takeover.

The structures in Germany and Japan are very different, probably because of the very different ownership and institutional structures. Again, history and tradition might also be playing a major part. The Brealey and Myers text gives details of the structures in these two countries. Both countries have governance structures, which have significant internal control through corporate cross-holding. The ownership structure is very complex and so is the governance structure. The outside investor does not appear to have a voice. None of the three components which are key to corporate performance in the U.S. (listed above) appears to be very important in either country. The Keiretsu structure in Japan, built around a major bank, internalizes all problems. While this may be good for companies, which are financially distressed, this can also keep inefficient operations going on forever.

The structure may be changing in Germany faster than it is in Japan. More and more German corporations are engaging in cross-border acquisitions and mergers and this will bring in changes in the corporate control and governance structures.

SUMMARY

This chapter provided an overview of some of the issues relating to corporate control and governance. The LBOs and restructuring, along with mergers and acquisitions, are parts of the market for corporate control. The LBOs and leveraged restructuring often make the corporations more efficient and add value. While some LBOs may fail (and have failed) as part of the corporate process of governance and control, they add strength to the system. Shareholders get better value and the management heeds their interests.

The chapter also described the workings of conglomerates and why they have faded out of the American corporate scene. Conglomerates are being broken up by spin-offs, carve-outs, and restructurings with more incentives for managers. The notion of internal capital markets does not appear to work well for most conglomerates. While the American conglomerate is an endangered specie, there are successful conglomerates operating in many countries. The stage of the economy and the capital markets in these countries appear to support the conglomerates better in these countries.

The financial architecture and governance structures in Germany and Japan differ significantly from that of the U.S. and most English speaking countries. The latter have systems based on well functioning financial markets with power to the stockholder, whereas in other countries, the system centers on banks and financial institutions. The international comparisons show different approaches to solving the problem of ensuring that shareholders' interests are taken care of. As cross-border mergers increase, the systems could change rapidly.

LIST OF TERMS

Carve-out

Conglomerate

Corporate control

Corporate governance

Financial architecture

Hostile takeover

Internal capital market

Keiretsu

Leveraged buyout

Leveraged restructuring

Management buyout

Privatization

Spin-off

Temporary conglomerate

Tracking stock

EXERCISES

Fill-in Questions

1. _____ means the power to make investment and financing decisions of the firm.

2. The _____ of a firm is partly corporate control and partly corporate governance.

3. While many acquisitions are friendly mergers, there are also _____ where the target firm is unwilling to merge with the acquiring company.

4. In a _____, part of a company is separated into a new corporation and the shareholders of the parent company receive shares in the new company.

5. When the shares of a new company, created from an existing corporation, are sold to the public, it is usually referred to as a _____.

6. In a(n) _____, a company is acquired by a small group, taken private, and a large part of the acquisition price is debt financed. If this small group includes company's managers, then it is called a(n) _____.

7. _____ is a corporation with many businesses in different, unrelated industries.

8. In a typical conglomerate, the policy is buy, manage, and keep; _____ is characterized by the approach – buy, fix, and sell.

9. _____ is the Japanese network of companies loosely linked by cross holding of stock and usually organized around a major bank.

10. A _____ anticipates a takeover attempt and responds to that by restructuring the company with increased leverage.

11. Many countries around the world are attempting large scale _____ in the hope of improving efficiency of former government owned companies.

12. Conglomerates often have _____, which seek to enforce the discipline of capital markets on their divisions.

13. Many companies issue a separate class of stock known as _____, which are entitled to earnings from only certain parts of their business.

14. _____ refers to the broad oversight of the corporate management, which ensures that the interests of the shareholders are heeded when important decisions are made.

ESSAY QUESTIONS

1. Explain the main differences in the governance and control structures among the U.S., Japanese, and German corporations. What would you expect to happen to the financial architecture of corporations in these countries over the next decade or so?

2. Are conglomerates successful in the U.S.? Why or Why not?

3. What are the differences between temporary conglomerates and conglomerates? Why are temporary conglomerates more successful?

4. Explain the following terms: i) leveraged restructuring, ii) leverage incentives, and iii) leveraged buyout.

5. Discuss the following statements:

   a. LBOs can work very well in certain cases, but there is no way you can attempt an LBO of a company like Hewlett-Packard or IBM.
   b. Good managers do not need leverage incentives or LBOs to make them do an excellent job.
   c. The Japanese Keiretsu is a better way of organizing large businesses. They reduce risk and allow managers to work without fear of being taken over by unscrupulous raiders.
   d. The main benefits from leverage in an LBO are the huge tax gains from interest deductions.

ANSWERS TO EXERCISES

Fill-in Questions

1. Corporate control
2. Financial architecture
3. Hostile takeovers
7. Conglomerate
8. Temporary conglomerate
9. Keiretsu
10. Leveraged restructuring

4. Spin-off
5. Carve-out
6. Leveraged buyout; management buyout
11. Privatizations
12. Internal capital markets
13. Tracking stock
14. Corporate governance

35

Conclusion: What We Do and Do Not Know about Finance

INTRODUCTION

This is it! The end – something you probably have been looking forward to! The thirty-four chapters of this covered the entire landscape of corporate financial management. The concluding chapter does two things: i) it highlights what we can claim with some certainty as things we know – the most important ideas and concepts of corporate finance; and ii) it also points out the areas where we still are a long way from complete understanding.

We dispense with the format used so far in this guide and simply provide a brief annotated list of what we know and what we don't.

What We Know: The Seven Most Important Ideas in Finance

1. *Net Present Value* (NPV) is the most basic and valuable concept in finance and is only proper way by which to evaluate assets. The NPV allows thousands of disparate shareholders to have a common corporate goal. This allows the managers to focus the maximizing the net present value without having to worry about individual stcokholders' risk preferences or wealth levels.

2. The *Capital Asset Pricing Model* (CAPM) gives a simple, almost elegant way of thinking about risk and return. It tells us that assets have two kinds of risk: risks that you can diversify away and those that you cannot. Only the non-diversifiable or market risks count. Thus, an asset's return is a function of the market risk and the risk premiums are calculate as a direct function of the market risk measure, beta. The CAPM should not be judged by the strong assumptions, but by the results it produces and the ease of application. We are probably going to see better theories in the future, but they will almost certainly separate risk into diversifiable and non-diversifiable risk. It is also unlikely that we will see a theory with a simpler intuition.

3. *Efficient Capital Markets* imply that security prices reflect information accurately. The three forms of market efficiency (the *weak form, the semi-strong form and the strong form)* give you degrees of efficiency. You will hear a lot of arguments and debates about how well the theory does or does not hold up. One can find any number of stories of investors making millions (or billions, if they are Warren Buffett or George Soros) by exploiting market inefficiencies, but it is good to remember that capital markets are, by and large, efficient.

Inefficiencies (as different from market imperfections, such as taxes and government controls) are the exception, not the rule. There are no money machines, no easy way of becoming the next Soros or Buffett. Competition in capital markets is very tough and financial managers will do well to remember the lessons of market efficiency.

4. *Value Additivity and The Law of Conservation of Value* states the value of the whole is given by the sum of the parts. The implications are mergers and acquisitions do not add value unless the combined firm produces greater cash flows than either firm produced when it was independent of the other.

5. *Capital Structure Theory* tells us (courtesy Modigliani and Miller) that in perfect markets, changes in capital structure do not affect value. This also comes from the value additivity principle. It is good to remember that the relevance and value of capital structure comes from deviations from the perfect market assumptions of MM. So, look for reasons why you think your firm has an optimal capital structure.

6. *Option Theory* provides us with a whole new way of thinking about many managerial situations and valuation problems. Remember that in finance, *option* refers narrowly to the opportunity to trade (or not to trade) in the future on *terms that are fixed today.* This is quite different from the everyday meaning of options as simply alternatives. Even where we can't justify using the Black-Scholes option valuation formula, the risk-neutral valuation approach may be applied.

7. *Agency Theory* helps us explain why complex contracts and arrangements are needed in many corporate transactions. A business corporation works because there are many men and women working for or with the corporation as managers, employees, lenders, shareholders, customers. Agency theory gives you the framework to optimize contractual and working arrangements with minimal conflicts of interest among the individuals involved. The conflicts can never be eliminated, but an understanding of the conflicts can help us get the best working results.

These seven ideas are basic and fundamental to corporate finance. A financial manager, who understands these, can do her (his) job better. Of course, you do not get cook book solutions to every problem you are likely to face. Remember, that real life problems can be complex and difficult and solutions, which are simplistic are unlikely to work. The above ideas will certainly steer you in the right direction.

Now that we have listed things we know, we come to the list of things we don't. The list is longer, even though the list in the book does not include everything that belongs in this category.

What We Do Not Know: The 10 Unsolved Problems in Finance

1. *How Are Major Financial Decisions Made?* We know very little about the financial decision making process. This is especially true for the major strategic decisions. We know how they

should make them but the process they actually use eludes us, and we understand the "bottom-up" approach to capital budgeting better than the "top-down" part.

2. *What Determines Project Risk and Net Present Value?* We know that NPV is the way to evaluate projects and that the cash flows should be discounted using risk adjusted discount rates. However, we do not know what makes some assets safer than others. We do not know why some companies earn economic rents and many others do not. We do not have a satisfactory general procedure for estimating project betas.

3. *Risk and Return - What Have We Missed?* CAPM, notwithstanding, the risk-return picture is far from clear. CAPM is very hard to prove or disapprove, but it cannot explain many of the observed facts on risk and return. Firm size and book-to-market ratios, just to name two, appear to affect returns. Why? There are many other questions which cannot be answered by CAPM or, for that matter, any other theories we have at present.

4. *How Important Are the Exceptions to Efficient Market Theory?* The evidence is fairly convincing that the markets for financial assets, at the minimum, are fairly efficient, but a disquieting set of evidence has emerged in recent years that suggests that they may not be nearly as efficient as we once thought.

5. *Is Management an Off-Balance-Sheet Liability?* If the value added by the management team is less than the cost of maintaining them, then the answer to the question is yes! Many closed-end mutual funds, real estate companies, and even oil companies often sell at prices below what is justified by the assets they have. Also, a change of management often seems to be the tonic needed by some companies.

6. *How Can We Explain the Success of New Securities and New Markets?* An enormous number of new kinds of securities have been created in the last 20 years or so. What is the reason that some fail and some succeed? We do not have a clear idea what kind of financial innovations can succeed in the market.

7. *The Controversy About Dividend Policy*: The theory and empirical research on dividends provide lots of insights and explanations for almost any position you like to adopt but no resolution of the controversy. More research is needed. But, we can't be very optimistic that it will suddenly provide a single all-encompassing answer.

8. *What Risks Should A Firm Take?* We know much more about how to hedge than we do about which risks should be hedged and which should not. Hedging makes sense when it adds to the value of the firm - but when is that?

9. *What Is the Value of Liquidity?* Corporate managers seem to prefer liquidity well above what can be reasonably explained by the current finance theories. We do not have a good theory of liquidity and can not answer questions like: how much cash should a firm hold?

10. *How Can We Explain Merger Waves?* It is always possible to find reasons why a particular merger occurred, but we cannot explain the aggregate level of mergers or predict specific ones in advance.

The End

Well, that is it! We are finished with covering corporate finance fairly exhaustively. But, to paraphrase an old cliché – end is beginning, your beginning. Now, go out there and practice what you learned, keeping in mind the ifs and buts. This chapter summarized the limitations of finance theory, as we know. It also reminded you that we do know a lot and hopefully you learned quite a bit of that.

Complete List of Terms

425

NOTES

NOTES

NOTES

NOTES

NOTES

NOTES